Diversity of Capitalisms in Latin America

"Is there a unique mode of development in Latin America, or a great diversity, each country being different from others? Between these two extreme scientific positions, Ilán Bizberg explores another perspective, and builds and uses a typology distinguishing various modes of development, i.e. various capitalisms.

An inspiring and innovative demonstration, based on a very solid knowledge both of Latin America, and of economical and sociological theories, including the French Regulation School."

—Michel Wieviorka, *Président of FMSH and Directeur d'études à l'EHESS*

"This is a groundbreaking book in three aspects. Between the extremes of too global and too narrow studies it analyses the trajectories of four different types of capitalisms in Latin America. Second, it presents a rich body of empirical data and historical perspective integrating a political economy with a sociological view (accumulation regime, global connectedness, labor markets, political regime, socio-political power groups and coalitions, labor regulation) always considering long-term historical factors. Finally, it critically integrates carefully different theoretical concepts on comparative social science.

Although not explicitly building on the classic Latin-American theory of dependence Bizberg presents a highly stimulating analysis that is worth to be considered as a new landmark in the long tradition of theory-driven and empirically grounded comparative studies. It should be on the syllabus of any Master or Ph.D. course related to Latin-American studies and to comparative studies of capitalisms."

—Ludger Pries, *Ruhr-University Bochum, Germany*

"Latin America is a maze; Ilán Bizberg searches to make sense of it, using as a tool the diversity of capitalisms, but he is wise enough to leave the solution of the puzzle to the reader. Several are rentier countries exporting commodities; most are outward-looking, liberal and deeply dependent countries; all are falling behind, including Brazil, which searched to be a developmental and social exception but failed."

—Luiz Carlos Bresser-Pereira, *Emeritus Professor of Getúlio Vargas Foundation*

Ilán Bizberg

Diversity of Capitalisms in Latin America

palgrave
macmillan

Ilán Bizberg
El Colegio de México
Mexico City, Mexico

ISBN 978-3-319-95536-0 ISBN 978-3-319-95537-7 (eBook)
https://doi.org/10.1007/978-3-319-95537-7

Library of Congress Control Number: 2018957444

Cover credit: GettyImages/pichitstocker

This Palgrave Macmillan imprint is published by the registered company Springer Nature Switzerland AG
The registered company address is: Gewerbestrasse 11, 6330 Cham, Switzerland

Para Leticia,
para Andrea,
para Iván,
por todo.

Acknowledgements

I am extremely grateful to a number of people and institutions without whom this book would have never seen the light. In the first place to the very generous institution where I have been able to work with total liberty and support for so many years: El Colegio de Mexico, and to all my colleagues of the Center for International Studies. I would like to recognize the CONACYT for its very generous financial support, under the program SEP-Conacyt (project 220018), which has allowed me to travel to most of the countries of Latin America that I analyze in this book, as well as to a number of international conferences where I have been able to present my ideas and get very useful feedback, and learn about other countries outside the continent from other researchers. I want to thank the Humboldt Foundation for the renewal of a research stay that allowed me to spend three very profitable months at the Lateinamerika Institut of the Freie Universität in Berlin. I am especially grateful to my colleagues and friends of the research group we have formed in order to study the diversity of capitalisms in Latin America: many of the ideas that are here exposed are actually the result of our discussions and in no way mine alone. In this respect, I want to thank Alberto Aziz, Graciela Bensusán, Robert Boyer, Jaime Marques Pereira, Bruno Théret, Enrique Valencia; all members of the research group. Robert Boyer was especially generous to take the time to read the manuscript and write an excellent preface.

I am also indebted to academics with whom either in Mexico or some other country in Latin America, Europe and Asia, have contributed with ideas for this book: Carlos Alba, Kaori Baba, Luiz Carlos Bresser-Pereira, Renato Boschi, Taeko Hoshino, Barbara Fritz, Pascal Labazée (deceased), Bruno Lautier(deceased), Yvon Le Bot, Geoffrey Pleyers, Daniela Prates, Ludger Pries, Jean Rivelois, Hélène Rivière d'Arc, Rubén Lo Vuolo, Isik Ozel, Pierre Salama, Brasilio Sallum, Merve Sançak, Marie-France Shapira, Christian Suter, Alain Touraine, Hiroyashi Uemura, Michel Wieviorka, among many others.

I also would like to acknowledge the research assistants that have helped me out throughout these years in collecting the data and bibliography for this book: Ana-Inés Fernández Ayala, Luis Alfonso Gómez Arciniega, Daniela Medina, Adalberto Castañeda, Santiago Álvarez Campero, Daniel Reyes Tinajero. A special mention goes for Daniel Cerdas Sandí who assisted me in the last very busy and complicated months in order to finish the book.

I am equally thankful to my students at El Colegio de México and at Sciences Po, Poitiers, that reacted to my presentations in class with questions and comments that have helped to configure a more coherent work.

I would have not been able to write this book without the support of my wonderful family, I dedicate it to them.

Contents

Acronyms and Abbreviations

ABDI	Agência Brasileira de Desenvolvimento Industrial (Brazilian Industrial Development Agency)
AFJP	Administradoras de Fondos de Jubilaciones y Pensiones (Argentina)
AFP	Administrado de Fondos de Pensiones (Chile)
AGROBANCO	Banco Agropecuario (Peru)
ANDI	Asociación Nacional de Industriales (Colombia)
ANPCyT	Agencia Nacional de Promoción Científica y Tecnológica (Argentina)
APRA	Alianza Popular Revolucionaria Americana (Peru)
APS	Aporte Previsional Solidario (Chile, in English: Solidarity Pension Contribution)
ASSE	Administración de Servicios de Salud (Uruguay)
AUGE	Acceso Universal de Garantías Explícitas (Chile)
BANADE	Banco Nacional de Desarrollo (Argentina)
BANCÓLDEX	Banco de Comercio Exterior de Colombia
BANCOMEXT	Banco Nacional de Comercio Exterior (Mexico)
BNDES or BNDS	Banco Nacional de Desenvolvimento Econômico e Social (Brazil)
BPC	Beneficio de Prestação Continuada (Brazil)
CADEB	Compañía Administradora De Empresas Bolivia
CANACINTRA	Cámara Nacional de la Industria de la Transformación (Mexico)
CCE	Consejo Coordinador Empresarial (Mexico)

CEPAL	Comisión Económica para América Latina y el Caribe, in English ECLAC: Economic Commission for Latin America and the Caribbean
CGE	Confederación General Económica (Argentina)
CGT	Confederación General del Trabajo de la República Argentina
CGTP	Confederación General de Trabajadores del Peru
CME	Coordinated Market Economy
CMHN	Consejo Mexicano de Hombres de Negocios
CMS	Coordinadora de Movimiento Sociales
CNDI	Council for National Industrial Development
CNI	Confederação Nacional da Indústria (Brazil)
CNTE	Coordinadora Nacional de Trabajadores de la Educación (Mexico)
COB	Confederación Obrera Boliviana
COFIDE	Corporación Financiera de Desarrollo (Peru)
COLDECO	Corporación Nacional del Cobre de Chile
CONAI	Consejo Nacional Indígena (Bolivia)
CONAIE	Confederación de Nacionalidades Indígenas del Ecuador
CONCAMIN	Confederación de Cámaras Industriales (Mexico)
CONFENIAE	Confederación de Nacionalidades Indígenas de la Amazonía Ecuatoriana (Ecuador)
CONFIEP	Confederación Nacional de Instituciones Empresariales Privadas (Peru)
COPARMEX	Confederación Patronal de la República Mexicana
CPC	Confederación de la Producción y del Comercio (Chile)
CSUTCB	Confederación Sindical Única de Trabajadores Campesinos de Bolivia
CTC	Confederación de Trabajadores Colombianos
CTM	Confederación de Trabajadores de México
CTP	Confederación de Trabajadores del Peru
CUT (Brazil)	Central Única dos Trabalhadores
CUT (Chile)	Central Unitaria de Trabajadores
ECOPETROL	Empresa Colombiana de Petróleos (Colombia)
ECUARUNARI	Ecuador Runakunapak Rikcharimuy, "Movement of the indigenous people of Ecuador", also known as Confederation of Peoples of Kichwa Nationality
EDESER	Empresa de servicios (Corporation Service Company, Bolivia)
ELECTROPAZ	Electricidad de La Paz (Bolivia)
ELFEO S.A.	Empresa de Luz y Fuerza Eléctrica Oruro (Bolivia, in English: Light and Power Corporation of Oruro)

EMLC	External Market Led Capitalism
ENA	École nationale d'administration (France)
ENDE	Empresa Nacional de Electricidad (Bolivia)
EPS	Entidades Promotoras de Salud (Mexico)
EU	European Union
FDI	Foreign Direct Investment
FEBRABAN	Federação Brasileira de Bancos (Brazil)
FEDECAMARAS	Federación de Cámaras y Asociaciones de Comercio y Producción (Venezuela)
FEDERACAFE	Federación Nacional de Cafeteros de Colombia
FONASA	Fondo Nacional de Salud (Chile, in English: Fund National Health Service)
FREDEMO	Frente Democrático (Peru)
FUT	Frente Unitario de Trabajadores (Bolivia)
GDP	Gross Domestic Product
GEPM	Garantía Estatal de Pensión Mínima (Chile, in English: State Guarantee of Minimum Pension)
GVC	Global Value Chains
IAMC	Instituciones de Asistencia Médica Colectiva (Uruguay)
IDB	Inter-American Development Bank
IEDI	Instituto de Estudos para o Desenvolvimento Industrial (Brazil)
IMF	International Monetary Fund
IMLC	Internal Market Led Capitalism
IMSS	Instituto Mexicano del Seguro Social (Mexico)
INEGI	Instituto Nacional de Estadística y Geografía (Mexico)
IOC	International Outsourcing Capitalism
IOF	Imposto sobre Operações financeiras (Brazil)
IPS	Instituciones prestadores de servicios de salud (Mexico)
ISAPRE	Instituciones de Salud Previsional (Chile)
ISI	Import Substitution Industrialization
ISSSTE	Instituto de Seguridad y Servicios Sociales de los Trabajadores del Estado (Mexico)
ITAM	Instituto Tecnológico Autónomo de México
KBC	Knowledge-based Capital
LME	Liberal Market Economy
LPP	Law of Popular Participation
MAS	Movimiento al Socialismo (Bolivia)
MINSA	Ministerio de Salud (Peru, in English: Ministry of Health)
MIP	Movimiento Indigenista Pachakuti (Ecuador, in English: Indigenous Movement Pachakuti)
MITI	Ministry of International Trade and Industry (Japan)

MNC	Multinational Corporation
MNR	Movimiento Nacional Revolucionario (Bolivia)
MORENA	Movimiento Regeneración Nacional (Mexico)
MPJD	Movimiento por la Paz con Justicia y Dignidad (Mexico)
MST	Movimento dos Trabalhadores Rurais Sem Terra (Brazil)
NAFIN	Nacional Financiera (Mexico)
NAFTA	North American Free Trade Agreement
NHS	National Health Service of United Kingdom
OC	Oversight Committees (Bolivia)
OECD	Organization for Economic Co-operation and Development
OIT or ILO	International Labor Organization
OTB	Organizaciones Territoriales de Base (Bolivia, in English: Territorial Base Organizations)
PAC	Programa de Aceleração do Crescimento (Brazil)
PAN	Partido Acción Nacional (Mexico)
PBM	Plano Brasil Maior
PBS	Pensión Básica Solidaria (Chile)
PDP	Policy of Progressive Development
PDP	Política de Desenvolvimento Produtivo (Brazil, in English: Productive Development Policy)
PEMEX	Petróleos Mexicanos
PETROBRAS	Petróleo Brasileiro
PITCE	Política Industrial, Tecnológica e de Comércio Exterior (Brazil, in English: Industrial, Technological and Foreign Trade Policy)
PJ	Partido Justicialista (Argentina)
Plan PNDII	Second National Development Plan (Brazil)
PMAS	Maximum Pension with Solidarity Contribution
PMDB	Partido del Movimiento Democrático Brasileño
POS	Plan Obligatorio de Salud (Mexico)
PRD	Partido de la Revolución Democrática (Mexico)
PRI	Partido Revolucionario Institucional
Profarma	Financial program for the pharmaceutical industry
Prosoft	Program for the Software
PSDB	Partido de la Social Democracia Brasileña
PT	Partido dos Trabalhadores (Brazil)
RT	Regulation Theory
SABSA	Servicios de Aeropuertos de Bolivia Sociedad Anónima (Bolivian Airport Services)
SEPyME	Secretaría de Emprendedores y Pequeña y Mediana Empresa (Argentina)
SINAMOS	Sistema Nacional de Apoyo a la Movilización Social (Peru)

SMEs	Small and Medium-Sized Enterprises
SNSS	Sistema Nacional de Servicios de Salud (Chile)
SOFOFA	Sociedad de Fomento Fabril (Chile)
SPS	Sistema de Pensiones Solidario (Chile, in English: Solidarity Pension System)
SRA	Sociedad Rural Argentina
SSP	Social Production System
SUMI	Seguro Universal Materno Infantil (Bolivia)
SUS	Sistema Único de Salud (Brazil, in English: Unified Health System)
TIPNIS	Territorio indígena y parque nacional Isiboro-Sécure (Bolivia)
TNCs	Transnational Corporations
UBE	União Brasileira de Empresarios. UCD and another group called the Frepaso (Frente País Solidario)
UCR	Radical Civic Union
UDI	Independent Democratic Union
UDP	Democratic and Popular Union
UIA	Union Industrial Argentina
UK	United Kingdom
UNCTAD	United Nations Conference on Trade and Development
UNDP	United Nations Development Programme
UNT	National Union of Workers (UNT)
US	United States
UTA	Automotive Tramway Union
VoC	Varieties of Capitalism
WTC or OMC	World Trade Organization
YPF	Yacimientos Petrolíferos Fiscales

List of Figures

List of Tables

Prologue

Understanding Latin American Trajectories

How geopolitical factors, economic regimes, social actors, and political systems interact

Within rapidly evolving and uncertain international relations, the place and role of Latin America is especially difficult to assess. Why has the continent been unable to follow the Asian trajectory of successful integration into the world economy associated with a rapid technological catching up? Why have the better pupils of the past Washington consensus, such as Mexico, failed in engineering a self-sustained fast and inclusive growth? Is there a common form of capitalism, quite imperfect indeed, that would explain the crises observed in so many contemporary Latin American economies?

This book proposes a fresh analysis of these issues via the elaboration of a genuine political economy approach that stresses the role of social actors in the transformation of the institutions that shape contrasted socioeconomic regimes. One of the definite merits of Ilán Bizberg is to cleverly mix a theoretical breakthrough with a meticulous historical and empirical account of the transformations of some key Latin American countries. Let us explain first that this book is at the frontier of a research agenda initiated back to the end of the 1970s, second how it clearly distinguishes between an ideal-type approach and the complexity of any specific national configuration and its transformation in history.

Furthermore, the author provides decisive arguments against a pure economic determinism too frequently supposed to govern institutions building and reforms. Last but not least, the book culminates by an impressive analysis of the crises that almost any Latin America society experiences at the end the 2010s. The present preface cursively develops these three ideas.

A New Step in the Generalization of the Régulation Approach

This book is published at an epoch when various theorizing are competing and trying to capture the specificities of modern economies and their recurring crises.

- Mainstream economics continues in considering that all market economies can be analyzed within a single and *general equilibrium model.* The relative performance of any given economy is correlated with its proximity to a configuration where perfect competition prevails on all markets. Within this paradigm, the poor performance of most Latin American countries originates in the inhibition of competition by populist governments and inadequate economic institutions and firms' organizations. Unfortunately, empirical evidence does not confirm this vision: the wide diffusion of the Washington Consensus may have reduced macroeconomic unbalances but not stimulated long-term growth of the continent (*Revue de la régulation* 2012).
- A lively current of research investigates precisely *the institutions that favor development* and for instance traces back how the type of colonialism still shapes the distribution of power among social actors (Kay 2002). This brings more realism into the analysis of Latin America in contrast with Asia but the implicit hypothesis is that the same general mechanism could explain all development trajectories. Nevertheless this is a dramatic simplification of the interrelated social, political and not only economic processes that discriminate between development and underdevelopment traps.
- Another branch of *new institutional economics* explores, on the contrary, the variety of mature capitalisms (Hall and Soskice 2001). The liberal market economies, frequently exemplified by the USA, do not define the only viable configuration. Clearly, coordinated

market economies can also prosper via the effectiveness of the socially elaborated routines at the firm level and basic institutions at the economy-wide level, Germany being an emblematic figure of this alternative configuration. This dualism has been quite useful for the understanding of the coexistence of two contrasted forms of capitalism within OECD. Unfortunately, Latin America does not belong to any of these models: empirical investigations have detected a third one labeled as a hierarchical capitalism (Schneider and Soskice 2009; Schneider 2013). This shows how previous theorizing was dependent over the restriction of the investigation to mature industrial economies. The emerging economies exhibit quite different configurations that overcome the temptation of binary distinction between markets and institutions (Combarnous and Rougier 2017). Furthermore is the existence of a hierarchy among firms and actors and is it specific to Latin America? Do all these economies belong to the same model of capitalism, whatever the mix between natural resources rent and inscription into the manufacturing global chain?

- *The Régulation Approach* is another institutionalist research program that emerged out of the crisis of Golden Age capitalisms (Aglietta 1979). It is part of an historical variant of institutionalism that stresses the need to deliver an integrated interpretation both of seemingly stable socioeconomic regimes and their structural crises. These crises manifest the arrival at the limits of a mode of *régulation* and its capacity to stabilize the dynamic and quite contradictory process of capital accumulation. This stabilization relies upon the coherence of the *institutional forms* typical of any capitalism: the monetary regime, the codification of the wage-labor nexus, the nature of competition, the integration into international relations and finally the nature of State intervention on the economy (Boyer and Saillard 2002). Given the relative contingency of the *social alliances* that entitle the emergence and legitimacy these institutional forms, the number of viable configurations is up to empirical observations and not only all a matter of pure logical deduction. Consequently, the idea of a canonical form of capitalism has been abandoned and replaced by the search for a *variety of capitalisms* that coexist within the same international regime. Within OECD countries, at least five types of capitalisms prosper: market-led, State intermediated, meso-corporatist, social democratic, not to forget family type capitalism (Amable 2003). This taxonomy is limited to a given sample of countries thus it is not fix, because new brands of capitalism emerge, for instance in Asia (Harada and Tohyama 2011; Alary and Michaux 2015). Clearly, China being a striking example of a surprising mix of political control and primacy of market competition (*Revue de la regulation* 2017).

Prolonging a long series of previous researches (Bizberg 2011; Bizberg and Théret 2012, 2015), this book provides an equivalent analysis for Latin America and it makes a clear step in the detection and explanation of the originality of some capitalism brands which were not observed elsewhere. The international outsourcing capitalism of Mexico is at odds with the State led capitalism observed in Brazil. Similarly, rentier regimes have to be distinguished according to two types: some are redistributive within a quasi-closed economy (Ecuador and Bolivia), others are liberal and largely open (Peru, Colombia, and Chile). At its founding epoch, *régulation* approach used to focus upon industrial and financial capitalisms and this had limited its relevance but this flaw is now overcome (Boyer 2015, 2018b). The reintroduction of natural resources rentier regimes into this research agenda is one of the key contributions of Ilán Bizberg. This is an updating of a seminal analysis of the typical rentier regime of Venezuela (Hausmann 1981; Hausmann and Marquez 1986). Nevertheless, this enlargement of socioeconomic regimes it is not the only one merit of this book.

From Ideal Types to Contrasted National Configurations and Trajectories

A second feature is more methodological but quite important: the author articulates *various levels of analysis* that are frequently confused in institutional economics. Many international comparative studies converge towards a single taxonomy of capitalisms, perceived as static ideal-types, and it is directly applied to the characterization of each national case without further investigation. Quite on the contrary, this is only the first step of Ilán Bizberg's analysis that deploys three successive and complementary phases.

- *Ideal-types of socioeconomic regimes* are built according to the nature of the prevailing production/accumulation regime. In the Latin

American case, four regimes emerge from the crossing of two criteria. First issue: is the country relying on capital accumulation based on the production of goods and services or does it dominantly exploits the rent generated by the extraction of natural or agricultural resources? A second question is whether the regime operates via the reliance mainly on markets for organizing value creation and income distribution or does it operate via the mediating role of sociopolitical compromises, embedded into a series of institutional forms. These criteria are sufficient to generate the four brands of socioeconomic regimes already presented: State-led (Brazil) versus Market-led capitalism (Mexico), redistributive (Ecuador) versus liberal rentier regimes (Chile).

- An *empirical analysis of the clustering* of indexes that try to capture the variability of the five institutional forms that sustain each socioeconomic regime, basically confirms the relevance of this taxonomy that had been suggested by a more qualitative approach. Nevertheless, the fit between the two approaches is not perfect and this is a crucial finding: each national configuration is more than its belonging to a given production/accumulation regime. In order to understand the historical trajectory of any Latin American society, the investigation has to explore how social movements and the nature of political intermediation impact upon institutional forms creation and maturation. Thus to quote Ilán Bizberg, it is necessary to take into account *the relation between social actors, their capacity to build a coalition that pursues certain economic mode, and especially the force and capacity of the popular classes to impose their interests and projects.*
- *A complementary sociopolitical analysis* has then to map out how the conflicts and interactions between entrepreneurs, wage earners, workers of the informal sector, and civil society associations influence the action of the State in terms of taxation, public spending, welfare and the strategic choice of an exchange rate regime and the control of Foreign Direct Investment and financial flows entering the country. The observed trajectory is the joint outcome the structural impact of the production/accumulation regime and the deployment of social and political movements in response to the ups and downs of growth, employment, inflation, and income distribution. For instance, within the same liberal rentier regime,

the evolution of Peru is not at all the replication of Chile dramatic transformations of the 1970s because political intermediations drastically differ. Similarly, Argentina and Brazil have recurrently explored the potentiality of a state-led capitalism but the polarization of social actors has generated quite different hegemonic bloc and finally political and economic outcomes.

The book thus displays a rich qualitative and statistical analysis of each of the national economy that embeds all their idiosyncracies, without neglecting the constraints and opportunities implied by its production/accumulation regime revealed by the initial international comparison. Ilán Bizberg is successful in overcoming the perils encountered by most comparative analyses: either a mere description juxtaposes a series of case studies and concludes that there exist as many capitalisms as countries or a structuralist straitjacket that misrepresent some key national patterns and makes problematic the understanding of their transformations and crises.

Against Economic Determinism: Multi-factor Adjustments to Geopolitical Evolutions

This subtle synergy between the rigor of a *structuralist* approach of socio-economic regimes and the dynamic principle brought by *an actionist* point of view delivers a precious antidote to the economic or/and technological determinism that prevail in so many researches by mainstream economists. A brief survey of the various conceptions concerning the relations between the economic sphere, civil society, and political systems points out the originality and relevance of this actionist—structuralist paradigm.

- The *neoclassical economists* continue to consider that General Equilibrium Theory is the only rigorous foundation for macroeconomic analysis (Boyer 2017b). This implies a *complete autonomy of economic activity* with respect to the other domains such as society and any political interference is analyzed as a distortion to the spontaneous market equilibrium that delivers a Pareto efficient allocation of resources. Nevertheless really existing economies suffer from inflationary episodes, long-term unemployment and, financial crises. The interpretation is then that the perverse government's interventions which have created these problems should be forbidden, possibly by a constitutional law. Paradoxically, the politicians should the enforcers of the "economic laws" postulated by theoreticians that actually are ideals but not observed regularities. Thus in practice, the objective of the political system becomes to be servant of economic rationality. Pure economic theory is turned into ***a normative political principle*** concerning the organization of societies. Surprisingly enough such a contradictory and irrelevant paradigm still informs the economic policy of many contemporary governments.

- The legacy of *Marxist theory* stresses that the capitalist mode of production sets into motion a relentless process of capital accumulation featuring the succession of booms and bursts. The related crises are more and more severe as capitalism conquer all domains of society and is extended to new territories. Marx assumed that the contradictions would become so acute that the complete and irreversible collapse of this regime was inevitable. This means that a *complete economic determinism* is assumed to govern the evolution of societies submitted to this mode of production. Class struggle is a key feature and Marx, as an analyst and activist, has written suggestive accounts of contemporary class struggles in England and France but it is not the crucial mover of the collapse of this mode of production (Boyer 2018a). By contrast for Marx, social struggles are central in the emergence of a new mode of production, especially during the decomposition of feudalism and the emergence and implementation of merchant capitalism. The last 150 years history have shown that political forces could significantly alter the inner tendency of capitalism, via labor laws, welfare system building, implementation of progressive taxation, the rise of public expenditure for education and health in response to the political rights conquered by workers and wage earners.
- This was the starting point of *régulation theory*: historical evidence suggests that in the long run *social relations, political systems and accumulation regimes co-evolve*. The central difference with Marx's construction comes from the observation, one century later, that the core social relations of capitalism—the capital/labor relation and the competition among firms—can be embedded into a whole spectrum of configurations (Boyer 2017a). These social relations are converted into *institutional forms* that are the outcome of social struggles, political recognition, and legal enforcement. They can delineate different *accumulation* regimes, contrary to the existence of a canonical accumulation scheme as implicitly postulated in

Das Kapital (Boyer 2004, 2011). The issue of the viability of any accumulation regime is up to the complementarity or at least compatibility of the institutional forms: there is no invisible hand able to warrant such a configuration (Boyer 2005). This property may emerge out a search and error process whereby collective actors mutually adjust their organizational and institutional demands and finally find, by pure hazard or design, a structurally stable socioeconomic regime. The analysis of the post-WWII fordist regime in the USA and France shows that explicit institutionalized compromises have been the main stabilizers of the economy along with Keynesian countercyclical monetary and public spending policies. Conversely when through the succession of business cycles the *accumulation* regime loses its structural stability, the sociopolitical coalition that had agreed upon a series of compromises may enter into crisis: the deterioration of economic performance goes along with renewed conflicts in order redesign the regime according the economic and ideological interests of each social group. This has been observed in many economies since the 1970s with the end of Fordism, since the 1990s with the repetition of financial crises and after the 2008 American and the world crisis. The Italian 2000 crisis is a remarkable example of *the co-occurrence of an economic crisis and collapse of the party system* and corresponding alliance (Palombarini 2001).

This shows that the *co-evolution of economy and polity is all but mechanical.* The redundancy of mechanisms stabilizing accumulation, the innovation capacity of civil society, the specificities of the political system and the open nature of potential new compromises and arrangements, these are the many features that challenge a pure economic determinism (Amable et al. 2017). That is the core message of Ilán Bizberg concerning Latin America and it is a milestone in the research agenda launched at the end of the 1970s for OECD economies. Let us give an example for each of the processes involved.

- The Euro crisis of the 2010s has meant an increase of unemployment all over member-States and austerity policies have put under popular pressure most governments...except in *Germany.* Why? Simply because the labor contract in the exporting manufacturing sector allows an adjustment to activity by hours worked and not via redundancies because firms intent to keep the competencies of skilled workers in anticipation of the next recovery. Public subsidies have complemented this built-in device. Consequently, resilient modes of *régulation* have to display some *room for maneuver*. Firms and economies are not the equivalent of a mechanical system governed by strict determinism.

- The same Euro crisis has generated a surge in unemployment that reached dramatic levels in *Spain* but the exiting political coalition has not burst out under the demands of the population. New parties have gained audience without being in position to build an alternative social bloc. Actually intergenerational solidarity within families—from parents to children, from grandparents to grandchildren—has played the role of shock absorber, mobilizing a feature of Spanish civil society. This is less important in other societies, for instance social democratic where solidarity is organized at the State level. Between the economic and political systems, many *social processes* can mediate—or not—the impact of some adverse macroeconomic events.
- The *sociology of elections* recurrently shows that the citizens who bear the cost of reforms and/or austerity policies do not necessarily vote against the politicians that took responsibility in State decisions. For instance the American citizens, working in the des-industrialized region have transferred their votes from the Democrat to the Republican Party that in fact has been at the origin of deregulation and anti-labor measures (Frank 2005). Generally poor people vote less than richer ones and they tend to exert fewer, if any, influence over economic policies, independently from the role of donation to parties by the richer. If so the *link between economic and political crises is significantly mitigated*. The vote on Brexit shows that a booming economy does not imply the adhesion to government proposals, the more so the more likely the primacy of identity and national sovereignty over personal economic interests: explosion of the party system in a period of economic prosperity (Boyer 2018c). Not clear and invariant determinism runs *from social polarization and the expression of political preferences*.
- The intended or de facto *relative isolation of the political systems* from the social agora is of course another source of relaxation of the links between economic outcomes for the citizens and political resilience. Many electoral systems have been designed in order to favor the formation of a political majority even if such a majority is not present in divided societies. In some cases, the Constitution can be used in order to circumvent the result of a referendum that contradicts the plan of politicians. It has been the case in France in 2005 concerning the approval of a European Constitution. A majoritarian opposition is

> converted into an implicit acceptance: the process of regional integration can unfold, but this has a cost: the rise of anti-European Parties that are a potential threat for the future or regional integration. In any case a comparison of the reaction of the USA, the European Union and China to the 2008 American financial melting down confirms the unfolding of three distinct trajectories that do not derive only from economic specialization divergence but from contrasted political systems: they explain the different objectives and timing of anti-crisis policies (Boyer 2017a). *Political institutions matter* and they are the necessary intermediaries in the transmission of international crises.

This book pushes a step forward the analysis, systematizes these advances, and gives the reader a rich interpretation of the most recent evolutions of Latin America.

Resilience or Crisis: The Present State of Latin American Capitalisms

Seen from world perspective, Latin American countries share many common features: a dependent status in the international division of labor, a specialization in natural or agricultural resources, largely heterogeneous productive structures opposing a modern sector to traditional low productivity firms and the persistence of a very large informal sector in the context of weak State capabilities and a quite problematic implementation of democratic principles. The diagnosis is the quite correct and it has been made very early by Latin American scholars (Cardoso and Faletto 1969). This framework has constantly been enlarged and updated by recent reports elaborated by CEPAL, that allow to characterize the nature of economic and political crises that recurrently strike quite all Latin American countries (CEPAL 2015). Clearly, both their modes of development and structural crises are quite apart compared with the dynamics of East Asian capitalisms (Amsden 2001; Bresser-Pereira 2009, 2017).

Ilán Bizberg goes one step further and states that this common ideal type form of capitalism is not sufficient to understand the contemporary transformations in Latin America. More precisely the divide between rather resilient national configurations and other ones struck by major economic/political crises. Let us mention some important teachings from this approach.

- *The contrasted trajectories of Mexico and Brazil* are one striking counter example concerning the existence of a common form of Latin American capitalism. The first one is fully integrated into the global value chains of modern manufacturing whereas the second has recurrently explored an industrialization based on the extension of a potentially large domestic market. In Mexico social movements have few impacts upon State policies by the very design of a more formal than effective democracy. By contrast, workers and citizens' demands have been part of a sociopolitical coalition built to sustain an inward looking development. Consequently, the interweaving of economic and political crises is different. In Mexico, the threat upon free trade exerted by the American Government puts at risk the political alliance that has promoted the economic integration of Mexican and American economies. This reversal allows the irruption of a new party representing formerly neglected interests of the majority of the Mexican population. In Brazil, the end of the boom of primary products export exacerbates the contradictory interests within the developmentalist alliance since it has failed to build a productive basis that would sustain in the long run an inclusive growth. *Two different dialectics between economy and polity* are at work.
- Within the same mode of development, *Argentina and Brazil* exhibit quite distinct long run trajectories. In Argentina, the recurring incapacity to build a stable compromise between agro exporters, domestic industrial capitalists, workers, and citizens manifests itself via the barrier of a growing external balance deficit (Miotti et al. 2012). In a sense, the 2018 economic situation is not without similarity with the early 1976 crisis but of course the electoral democracy changes the determinants of economic policies. In Brazil, the transition to democracy allows to take into account the voice of the poorest citizens and this is the catalytic ingredient for the constitution of a sociopolitical bloc in position to develop a modest but significant redistribution of national income. This genuine model delivers satisfactory macroeconomic results during nearly two decades, but the financialization and reprimarization finally destabilize both the social bloc and the accumulation regime. The lesson of this comparison is that *political intermediation matters.*
- Rentier regimes can be *liberal or redistributive* and again the dividing line lies in the way social movements interact with the political system in tentatively shaping the design of State interventions.

This opposes for instance *Chile to Ecuador*. In the first case, the social movements have been destroyed and then disciplined by a drastic neoliberal agenda, except for the property of natural resources. In Ecuador, popular movements not only successfully oppose to neoliberal policies but they are also strong enough to impose another policy based upon the concept of "good life." This feature explains the rapid transmission of economic crisis to the political system but also possibly the better legitimacy of anti-crisis programs. Within the same closed redistributive rentier regime, one observes quite different trajectories for *Venezuela and Bolivia*. On one side the absence of a compromise with economic elites triggers an economic war that ends up by the collapse of the economy, while an authoritarian government continues to rule the country. On the other side, the government is sustained by social movements and this entitles to find acceptable relations with the agro business. Of course, geopolitical events have repercussions over all rentier regimes but the national outcomes may significantly differ given the past history, the distribution of economic and political power as embedded into in the production system and the institutional forms. Finally, *the legitimacy of the government* with respect to demands of people is a central determinant of anti-crisis programs.

This brief preface intends to convince a large audience to read this well documented and original analysis that delivers a fresh understanding of the perils that quite all Latin America face. It is also an invitation to socioeconomic scholars to pursue the endeavor of Ilán Bizberg and to contribute to a research agenda launched nearly four decades ago.

Paris, France

Robert Boyer
Institut des Amériques

References

Aglietta, M. (1979). *Régulation et crises du capitalisme*. Paris: Calmann-Lévy.

Alary P., & Lafaye de Micheaux, E. (2015). *Capitalismes asiatiques et puissance chinoise: Diversité des modèles, hégémonie de la Chine. Paris, Presses de Sciences-Po.*

Amable, B. (2003). *The diversity of modern capitalism*. Oxford: Oxford University Press.

Amable, B., Palombarini, S., & Alary, P. (2017). Le néoréalisme, ou comment alliances sociales et politiques publiques se déterminent mutuellement. *Revue de la régulation 2nd semestre/Automn 2017*. http://journals.openedition.org/regulation/12491.

Amsden, A. H. (2001). *The rise of "the rest". Challenges to the west from late-industrializing economies*. New York: Oxford University Press.

Bizberg, I. (2011). The global economic crisis as disclosure of different types of capitalism. *Swiss Journal of Sociology/World Society Studies*, *37*(2), 321–329.

Bizberg, I., & Théret, B. (2012). La diversité des capitalismes latino-américains: les cas de l'Argentine, du Brésil et du Mexique. *La Revue de la Régulation*, Paris, No. 11.

Bizberg, I., & Théret, B. (2015). Las coaliciones sociopolíticas y las trayectorias de los capitalismos latinoamericanos. In I. Bizberg (Coord.), *Las variedades del capitalismo en América Latina: los casos de México, Brasil, Argentina y Chile* (pp. 95–146). Mexico: El Colegio de México.

Boyer, R. (2004). New growth regimes, but still institutional diversity. *Socio-Economic Review*, *2*(1), 1–32.

Boyer, R. (2005). How and why capitalisms differ. *Economy and Society*, *34*(4), 509–557.

Boyer, R. (2011). A new epoch but still diversity within and between capitalism: China in comparative perspective. In C. Lane & G. T. Wood (Eds.), *Capitalist diversity and diversity within capitalism* (pp. 32–68), Abingdon: Routledge.

Boyer, R. (2015). *Économie politique des capitalismes. Théorie de la régulation et des crises*. Paris. La Découverte.

Boyer, R. (2017a). *What does the growing communality of contemporary capitalisms mean for economic theory?* (Unpublished manuscript prepared for the International Conference on Economic Theory and Policy). Tokyo: Meiji University.

Boyer, R. (2017b). Orthodoxie, hétérodoxies et capitalismes contemporains. *Revue de la régulation*. http://journals.openedition.org/regulation/12626.

Boyer, R. (2018a). Marx's legacy, régulation theory and contemporary capitalism. *Review of Political Economy*.

Boyer, R. (2018b). Comparative political economy in the light of régulation theory. In I. Cardinale & R. Scazzeri (Eds.), *The Palgrave handbook of political economy*. London: Palgrave.

Boyer, R. (2018c). Brexit: souveraineté nationale contre internationalization de l'économie. In J. Christ & G. Salmon (Eds.). *La dette souveraine* (pp. 133–172). Paris: Editions de l'EHESS.

Boyer, R., & Saillard, Y., (Eds.), (2002). *Régulation theory: The state of the Art*. London: Routledge.

Bresser-Pereira, L. C. (2009). *Mondialisation et compétition: Pourquoi certains pays émergents réussissent et d'autres non*. Paris: La Découverte.
Bresser-Pereira, L. C. (2017). The two forms of capitalism: Developmentalism and economic liberalism. *Brazilian Journal of Political Economy, 37*(4), 680–703.
Cardoso, F. H., & Faletto, E. (1969). *Dependencia y desarrollo en América Latina*. México: Siglo XXI.
CEPAL. (2015). *Neoestructuralismo y corrientes heterodoxas en America Latina y el Caraibes a los inicios del siglo XXI*. In A. Barcena & A. Prado (Eds.). Libros de la CEPAL (132) (LC/G.2633-P). Santiago de Chile: Comision Economica para America Latina y el Caribe.
Combarnous, F., & Rougier, E. (Eds.), (2017, March). *The diversity of emerging capitalisms. Globalization, institutional convergence and experimentation*. London: Palgrave Macmillan.
Frank, T. (2005). *What's the matter with Kansas?: How conservatives won the heart of America*. New York: Holt McDouglas.
Hall, P. A., & Soskice, D., (Ed.). (2001). *Varieties of capitalism: The institutional foundations of comparative advantage*. Oxford: Oxford University Press.
Harada, Y., & Tohyama, H. (2011). Asian capitalisms: Institutional configurations and firm heterogeneity. In R. Boyer, H. Uemura, & A. Isogai (Eds.), *Diversity and transformations of Asian capitalisms* (pp. 243–263). London and New York: Routledge.
Hausmann, R. (1981). *State landed property, oil rent and accumulation in Venezuelan economy*. PhD Thesis, Cornell University, Ithaca.
Hausmann, R., & Marquez, G. (1986). Venezuela: du bon côté du choc pétrolier. In R. Boyer (Dir.), *Capitalismes fin de siècle* (pp. 141–163). Paris: PUF, Économie en liberté.
Kay, C. (2002). Why East Asia overtook Latin America: Agrarian reform, industrialization and development. *Third World Quarterly, 23*(6), 1073–1102.
Miotti, E., Quenan, C., & Torija, Z. E. (2012). Continuités et ruptures dans l'accumulation et la régulation en Amérique Latine dans lea années 2000; le cas de l'Argentine, du Brésilet du Chili. *Revue de le Régulation*, n11, Premier semestre.
Palombarini, S. (2001). *La rupture du compromis social italien*. Paris: CNRS Éditions.
Revue de la régulation. (2012). Les capitalismes en Amérique latine. De l'économique au politique, n11, 1er semestre, Spring. http://journals.openedition.org/regulation/9602.
Revue de la régulation. (2017). Lectures institutionalistes de la Chine, n21, Spring. https://journals.openedition.org/regulation/12228.
Schneider, B. R. (2013). *Hierarchical capitalism in Latin America: Business, labor, and the challenges of equitable development*. New York: Cambridge University Press.
Schneider, B. R., & Soskice, D. (2009). Inequality in developed countries and Latin America: Coordinated, liberal and hierarchical systems. *Economy and Society, 38*(1), 17–52.

CHAPTER 1

The Theoretical Perspective of This Book

1.1 Neo-Institutionalism

While we may have accepted the idea that there was one mode of development in Latin America during the import substitution industrialization era, between the 1930s and the 1970s, it is now impossible to uphold a single model of development on this continent. In fact, the idea that there was one single model of development was already questioned during the 1970s by the structuralist studies of Cardoso and Faletto, that were the founding works of the dependence school. At the present time, the main perspectives of analysis on the societies of continent, the CEPAL and the neo-institutionalist schools, consider that Latin America can be analyzed as a unity, that the countries within this continent share more or less the same problems, which may be approached with the same instruments of public and economic policies. This is true although of course, both the CEPAL and the neo-institutionalist school also distinguish particularities between the different countries. While the viewpoint of the CEPAL is extremely valuable in order to define the main deficits of the development of the continent and delivers the most significant core of data on Latin America, the matrix of the analysis is taken to be that of the totality. The analysis fluctuates from this general perspective of the continent as a whole, to the particularities of each country. The neo-institutionalist perspective, upon which we will continue the discussion, cannot escape this duality as it focuses on institutions rather than on structures and actors.

I. Bizberg, *Diversity of Capitalisms in Latin America*,
https://doi.org/10.1007/978-3-319-95537-7_1

In this book, we consider that the way to escape this duality is to analyze the economies of the continent from a perspective informed by the differences, based on a typology that outlines different modes of development or capitalism, rather than between each particular country. We defend the idea, of the school of VoC and of the French regulation school because, just as there exist different types of capitalism in the developed world, in our continent we are also confronted with diverse types of capitalism, although they may not be as consolidated and coherent as those of the central economies; in some countries important fluctuations may occur that may make them shift from one type to other. But, it is also true that some countries have shown a very significant stability that strengthens the hypothesis we are defending in this book.

In this chapter, we will concentrate on the criticism of neo-institutionalism because it has elaborated the most detailed and coherent argument of why Latin American countries can be considered as a unique capitalist type. Before discussing the way the VoC school (which epitomizes this perspective) analyses the continent we want to examine its theoretical foundations. While neoclassical economics argues that economic success depends on the extent to which a particular country allows the market to act as efficiently as possible without State intervention and takes advantage of comparative advantages in their relationship with the world economy, neo-institutionalism analyzes the institutions that shape the economy, basically the market, that allow it to function most efficiently or blocks it. While neoclassical economics produces the recipes that all countries should follow in order to develop their economies, based on a general theory of a perfect market and a rational individual, neo-institutionalism analyses the institutions that allow some countries to effectively develop and the institutions that inhibit development. While neoclassical economy proposes a theory based on the myth of the self-regulated market, as Polanyi (1944) has shown, neo-institutionalism discusses the obstacles that a self-regulated market encounters, which are basically the absence of order, democracy, property rights, and in contrast, the excess of the importance of politics, the weight and intervention of the State.

The path-breaking studies of Cardoso and Faletto as well as those of Wallerstein, that offered a very rich political and long-term historical perspective, in which the countries of Latin America were analyzed according to both their internal and external economic, social and political relations. During the 1970s, these analyses were vulgarized by authors that situated themselves within the dependence school and held that the economic situation of the countries depended exclusively on their position in the world economy. In reaction, in the 1980s, mainstream economists simply dismissed the *dependence theory*, rejected any concern with history or politics, and proposed an ahistorical analysis. Riding the liberal wave that was being implemented in the real economy by Reagan and Thatcher, they disinterested themselves in anything other than the definition of universal recipes to reach development. After a short impasse, in the late 1980s, liberal economists rediscovered politics and history to give birth to neo-institutionalism. And in fact, the new institutional economy became the spearhead of neoclassical economics in the study of development. These neo-institutionalist perspectives did not break with the neoclassical hypotheses of the unity and universality of the liberal model of development they formalized. The founders of neo-institutionalism (North and Weingast 1989; North et al. 2002) argue that institutional differences between countries explain development and underdevelopment, that the legal/constitutional framework of societies is the variable that explains economic development. For this current of thought (followed through by De Soto 2005; Acemoglu et al. 2002; Acemoglu and Robinson 2012), what distinguishes developed from underdeveloped countries is the lack, in the latter, of a legal/political framework that assures order in society; in the economic sphere, order is basically ensured by the institutions that guarantee property rights. They discuss the fact that the market requires order, which in turn needs institutions that establish a stable juridical system that imposes rules on the market that everybody accepts and that are effectively implemented by the government. According to North et al. (2002), the absence of such a legal framework imposes high transaction costs on entrepreneurs, obliging them to look for sizeable short-term benefits that maximize performance and accelerate return on investment. Hence the extent of speculation and processes of overexploitation of natural resources and labor force in the underdeveloped countries. De Soto (2005) adds that unless such an order exists, the majority of the population is not able to participate in the economy, or invest; although the poor accumulate significant amounts of wealth, they can neither invest it, nor use it as capital for lack of property rights. Acemoglu and Johnson add that both disorder and extreme power inequality lead to extractive institutions that impede economic development.

North and Weingast put forward the theoretical foundations for justifying the retreat of the State from the economy. They offer the paradox that a self-regulated market requires rules in order to function, that only a strong State can impose. Nonetheless, a strong State can be oppressive, abusive, arbitrary, or as Acemoglu et al. (2002) have analyzed, extractive; which has the contrary effect, that of repressing investment, for the fear of being expropriated. That is why these authors consider that only a strong (but very restricted) State can induce development, something that leads to an un-politicized State, and thus a society where politics has low significance; because where politics has a great weight it overrules economy, and individuals tend to involve in politics in order to acquire privileges, rather than turn their interest toward economics. The State has to be limited by counter-powers, and by its own interest, politics has to be restricted and rules have to be internalized by the population, rather than imposed continuously by government (North et al. 2002).

The ideal model of such a situation is the USA, a political system that has checks and balances, a strong division of powers, and a federal state, where power is decentralized. On the other hand, it is a stable democracy with rule of law, where individuals respect the law not only because they are afraid of the consequences of breaking it, but because they have internalized it. In this situation, there is little need for a strong State, as society, in a great manner, rules itself. Furthermore, the State has little leeway to act because the political system and civil society sets strong limits to its action.

Thus, *in fine*, we can conclude that a limited State is the most effective requisite to pursue economic development a political order founded on consensus of most of the population regarding the rules of the game, and cooperation rather than coercion, where values are both internalized and imposed by a government that does not intervene excessively, that does not depend much on its own intervention. Democracy, in this perspective, is the equivalent of the market in the political sphere, it is the most effective regime for economic development due to the fact that it is best suited to restrict the predatory instincts of the State and/or entrepreneurs (North 1990, quoted by Maravall 1997: 30; Weingast 1995). This is clear when Weingast (1995) considers that thriving markets "… require not only an appropriate system of property rights and contract law, but also a secure political base that limits the state's ability to confiscate wealth" (Weingast 1995: 1).

One of the manners by which the political system can limit the power of the State is the division of power, the other one is the organization of the civil society; both ideas that neo-institutionalism rescues from Locke,

Montesquieu, and Tocqueville. Another manner of limiting the action of the State is through federalism, which is, as Tocqueville wrote, a manner of decentering power. Weingast inverts this conception with his notion of "market preserving federalism," which through its support of the market leads to economic development. He considers federalism as a way of preserving the market from politics, from governmental intervention; as a manner of drastically limiting State interference with the functioning of markets. In addition, he considers that market-preserving federalism incorporates competitive institutions and mechanisms that make the governments have incentives—positive and negative—to respect the rules, which help the system to self-regulate. Nonetheless, according to this author, not all federalisms are effective in pursuing this goal. He states that, for example, "…it is unlikely that federal systems diverging from market-preserving federalism can stimulate its development…" or that they can develop even in the context of democratic rule of law as in the case of India (Parikh and Weingast 1997: 1612).

More significantly, federalism can be a functional substitute for democracy. Weingast deems that the best examples of market-preserving federalism—after England of the Glorious Revolution (late seventeenth and early eighteenth centuries) and the USA ("from its constitution and until the mid-1930s")—is current China, since the beginning of the transition to capitalism, as it undertook extreme decentralization (Montinola et al. 1996). All of this infers something that was implicit in the writings of North, that democracy is less important in itself, as a specific political regime that entails a certain type of political culture and a specific type of political system, but that it is more significant for its capacity to limit the State; this is the only way we can understand that these authors can consider China in this context, which is evidently far from being a democracy. Market-preserving federalism is a functional substitute for democracy and rule of law, only if one considers that its principal function is to limit State power. Rodrik poses an even more utilitarian relation between democracy and development. He considers, on the one hand, that democracy allows for the peaceful transfer of political power from a leading group that has implemented failed economic policies toward another one that can attempt new policies. On the other hand, institutional mechanisms that allow "loser" social groups to make their voices heard reduce the utility of violent protests and manifestations that affect the accumulation and investment capacity of a society (Rodrik 2001: 27).

Thus, the rule of law need not be democratic or, in other words, to ensure the political freedom of the individual, since it is committed to defending property rights and the "free" functioning of markets. In a sense, the profound link between democracy and development, that seemed to emerge in the first works of the neo-institutionalists, is evidently broken: thus, in a sense, free markets replace free individuals. Both, the rule of law and democracy (and/or federalism) induce the economic development of a country due to their capacity to limit the scope of the State, *in fine* of politics as they exist in the developed countries. In contrast, in the underdeveloped countries, in Latin America for example, politics, government and the State have all an ample capacity to modify the status quo. In these countries, the concern of individuals is set upon controlling politics, the State, in order to obtain the privileges that it can distribute, rather than invest in economics. On the contrary, more stable political regimes, where politics enjoy a smaller scope, because of the division of power, civic culture, a stable constitution, an/or federalism, and in general, a consensus regarding the rules of the game both on the part of the citizens and the politicians, like the USA, have thrived economically (North et al. 2002; Haber 1997).

1.2 The Limits of Neo-Institutionalism

The studies of Haber and Rodrik, and partly those of Haggard (when he addresses the situation of Mexico and Brazil), are an extension of these ideas. However, an innovation of both Haber and Haggard, which goes beyond the legal approach and the character of the political regime, is the analysis of the impact of the sociopolitical coalitions on economic development. According to Haber, the reason why Latin American countries failed to take off as the developed countries of North America (Canada and USA) did is essentially that development was limited to a small coalition that coalesced over the defense of the import substitution model. For Haber, while the developmentalist coalition, that brought together businessmen, State officials and workers of the most advanced economic sectors, and prevailed during the 1950s and 1970s, effectively achieved the industrialization of certain countries of the continent, its benefits were monopolized by this coalition, which did all to block the entry of new groups. This coalition demanded and received protection from the government, that rigged the rules of the game, deterred the market, and eventually prevented further development; this was clearly observable in all Latin America, excepting Brazil for a certain period, and was especially true concerning the financial markets, that limited their resources by narrow oligopolies and by special privileges allocated by the State (Haber 1991; Maurer and Haber 2004). In sum, the emergence of a developmentalist coalition—based on ISI and with the State as the main actor—prevented the expansion and deepening of economic development.

In his 1990 book, Haggard has a similar point of view regarding Mexico and Brazil. He considers that neither country was able to transit from an import substitution model to an export-led one, as Taiwan and Korea, because the coalition that benefited from ISI did not give the State sufficient autonomy to gradually eliminate the protection of the national industry (Haggard 1990: 40). Nonetheless, he deepens considerably in his analysis of Korea and Taiwan, as we will see below.

The most recent neo-institutional analyzes, of which Rodrik's is the most innovative, pose that the universal orthodox prescriptions for promoting development do not work because basic conditions differ from country to country. This author considers that, although the principles of the "Washington Consensus" are simple common sense and in this way they are probably correct, they are too abstract for their application to concrete situations. He argues that there is a weak relationship between the principles of neoclassical economics and the specific recommendations that can be made to "put into practice" these principles. There are, thus, a plurality of applications of such principles and, therefore, of ways to develop. In order to put into practice the general principles of development of capitalism, these must be set in their institutional context in order to design appropriate measures for the specific realities of each country, with the possibility that their application differs or even opposes that of particular countries. In order to define the measures to be taken, a diagnosis must first be made of the specific problems that a certain type of development poses for each country (Rodrik 2007).

In order to advance these ideas, he examines cases that deviate from the general rules, especially the one according to which the State should not intervene in the economy. Rodrik notes that in China, the authorities have been orienting economic development, creating a dual economy, led by both the State and the market. For example, China did not proceed to totally liberalize agriculture, but did so marginally, while retaining the central planning structure. In this way, it allowed peasants to freely sell their surplus in the market after they fulfilled their obligations according to the national economic plan. This dual system was gradually extended to other sectors such as steel, coal and the labor market. In this way, China was able to increase its economic efficiency without generating resistance. Another example is that of Mauritius, where a highly protected internal market sector was combined with a free export zone until the 1980s. In this way, there was no general liberalization of the economy, but a *maquiladora* free zone was created, that on the one hand opened new investment opportunities and, on the other sheltered the coalition that benefited from protection and opposed opening (Rodrik 2007: 22–29). In the case of Latin America, Rodrik argues that most countries of the continent have failed to achieve development because they have been unable to cope with the deterioration of the terms of trade and the interest rate shocks; their institutions have not allowed them to simultaneously face macroeconomic adjustments and distributional problems.

These examples show, according to Rodrik, that we must dismiss the idea that it is possible to provide general recipes to countries on how they should modify their institutions. On the contrary, we must proceed by analyzing the institutions in order to identify the causes of their inability to initiate or sustain economic development. Nonetheless, the positive economic results obtained in the cases we mentioned above do not represent the success of economic heterodoxy, but orthodox results achieved through heterodox methods and institutions. They are, thus, heterodox methods that lead to one unique result: stimulate the market, impose property rights and contribute to macroeconomic stability (Rodrik 2007: 23–24). The title of his book, *One economics many recipes*, is indicative of this. Although the recipes diverge, the ultimate goal is the same: a liberal capitalist economy determined by the international division of labor. In other words, Rodrik recuperates the idea of State intervention to save the Ricardian liberal model (Bizberg and Théret 2012).

For all these authors sharing the neo-institutionalist perspective, development is impossible out of a normative framework dictated by neoclassical precepts, which consists in a system of self-regulated markets. Even Rodrik's view that countries are different and that this invalidates the possibility of applying single recipes, and hence the strategies recommended by the IMF and the World Bank for decades, is within the framework of mainstream economy. While in some cases the State may be a central actor of economic development and political institutions and social organizations are key to deal with distributive conflicts in times of crisis, they are a mere functional substitute of a self-regulated market.

All these viewpoints posit a model of capitalism considered ideal (that of the USA—a self-regulated market) while the rest of the economies are considered imperfect forms of this model.

In contrast to these perspectives, economists and sociologists who have studied the trajectories of the development of Asian countries (Haggard, Amsden, Evans, Aglietta, Arrighi, Boyer, among others), the path followed by these countries does not fit the theory which defends the efficiency of self-regulated markets. They describe how the Asian countries that developed in the past (Taiwan, Korea, and Japan), as well as those that are currently developing (China, India), have not implemented liberal market policies, but base their economic growth on a developmentalist State. This State and the policies it pursues are not an unorthodox way to achieve orthodox goals, nor a residue of the past (as Rodrik would have it), but a fundamental characteristic of these economies, that define them as a different type of capitalism. They are all economies where markets are coordinated by the State (China, India), or where the State promotes large private conglomerates (in many cases with strong links to the State) (Korea, Japan). Although all these cases could be thought of as an Asian exception, the fact is that the majority of countries that developed after the first industrializing wave of the eighteenth and nineteenth centuries have based their economies on a strong intervention of the State (Germany, France, Japan), which stimulates some sectors of its economy that seem not to be competitive according to the theory of comparative advantages, that establishes limits to the market, that opens their economies selectively, etc. (Bresser-Pereira 2018).

In contrast to the neo-institutionalist presupposition and ideological support of the imposition of a "one best way," of a benchmark that all countries have to pursue if they want to develop, and contrary to the idea that the market can regulate itself, when it is sufficiently developed, and that State intervention is detrimental, the VoC school made a first step to a more complex conception of development. VoC proposes that there are two, radically different but equally effective, permanent VoC, that have led to developed economies. One of them is the formalization of the economy of the USA, the liberal market economy (LME), the other the ideal type of the German economy, based on the coordination of the market by the social actors and the State, the coordinated market economy (CME), which, according to the authors, is generalizable to all continental European countries as well as the Asian ones; an affirmation we will absolutely contest below (Hall and Soskice 2001).

Although they are both market economies, they differ in the manner in which the State and the organized social and economic actors relate to the market. While the liberal market economies (LMEs) are governed by the market, the coordinated market economies (CMEs) are governed by the interaction (both conflict and cooperation) of social actors, basically the unions, the entrepreneurial organizations, and the State. The analysis of the VoC focuses on the firm, on the logic of action of the firms, on the manner in which they interact with their environment in each of these types of economy. The firms react differently to each of the environments because they are confronted to different institutions in five distinct spheres: industrial relations, relations between the enterprises, internal governance of the firms, the coordination of the firms with their employees, and the educational and formation systems. In all of these spheres, there are radical differences in both types of capitalism defined by the way in which sociopolitical institutions organize the market. One can synthesize the differences by saying that while in the LMEs the relations between the businesses and the workers, their suppliers, the banks, are defined by civil contracts and the judicial system, in the CMEs all these relations are continuously negotiated between social actors and the State. This is so because in the coordinated economies the social actors, the unions and the entrepreneurs, as well as the State are strongly organized and are omnipresent when defining salaries, working conditions, in the internal governance of the enterprises (unions are seated in the administrative councils of the plants), in the configuration of the skill formation institutions (Hall and Soskice 2001).

While in the liberal economies, industrial relations are either weak or strongly oppositional, in the coordinated economies, because both unions and entrepreneurial organizations are strong, negotiations prevail in almost all aspects of the relations between unions and employers: salaries, work conditions, investment projects, restructuring of companies. While in the LMEs enterprise governance is defined within each particular company, which defines its strategy in its own interest without consultation with its suppliers, in the CMEs governance of each firm is closely related to its relation with the suppliers, the banks that allocate the financial resources (usually on a very long term), the unions, and even the consumers. In the LMEs, the relationship between workers and employees with their enterprises is very often set by an individual contract and particular conditions (especially in the case of the employees), on very flexible and short or medium terms, in the CMEs the relationship is defined collectively, through union-employers negotiations (mostly branch level), for a long term (in many cases a lifetime relationship). Finally, all of this has very significant effects on the educational and skill system, because while in LMEs the relation is more individual, less durable and more flexible, the educational system tends to orient itself to allocating individuals with general knowledge and skills, in the case of the CMEs it is oriented toward specific knowledge and skills, that prolong themselves during the entire professional career; the German dual education system epitomizes this latter model, as it combines both theoretical formation and apprenticeship in plants, where most students end up working (Hall and Soskice 2001).

In the case of Latin America, the VoC school loses its flexibility and considers that Latin America can be classified as a single type, a hybrid between the liberal and coordinated economies. The Latin American type is in part coordinated by large family groups, that include businesses from very different sectors, and transnational groups pertaining to a global conglomerate, and liberal in what concerns the relationship between the firms and the workers (Schneider and Soskice 2009). The characteristics of these economies are: (1) Firstly, the existence of large economic groups that are basically family owned, very diversified in different sectors of the economy, exert an oligopolistic situation in the economies of the Latin American countries, and, more importantly, entertain hierarchical but not productive or technological relations between the different enterprises that comprise them (in contrast, e.g., to the Japanese firms that, although they are also family owned and diversified, are organized around a vertically integrated core production, and are thus able to generate a dynamic that leads them to innovate and upgrade); (2) Secondly, the Latin American economies are likewise dominated by another group of firms, the transnational, which function according to an international logic that primes over the national, and does not contribute to a dynamic interrelation with the national companies; (3) Partly as a consequence of the dominance of these two types of companies, the labor market is segmented between a formal and informal labor market, where large firms have formal workers, and medium and small firms have informal workers and extensive labor turnover. This is also the consequence of the existence of a formal regulatory scheme, with a low level of compliance. All of this leads to, and is in part the result of, weak, or politically subordinated unions, badly represented inside the enterprises; and (4) Fourthly, all of this combines and results in a low level of schooling, and of skill education and formation (Schneider and Soskice 2009; Schneider 2013).

This type of capitalism is defined as hierarchical, not only because the dominant enterprises are thus organized, because the family groups are not connected productively as the particular businesses that constitute them are so diverse, and are controlled by the head of the family, while the subsidiaries of the transnational firms are subordinate to the decisions of the conglomerate headquarters, and also due to the inequality that characterizes all of the countries of the continent. In addition, they are characterized by hierarchical relations between the transnational and the large national oligopolistic groups and the other medium and small enterprises, an unrepresentative political party system, and industrial relations, where workers are rarely defended by well-organized unions and are thus submitted to the company administration (Schneider and Soskice 2009). In several articles by Schneider and Soskice as well as in the book of the first, they consider that this type of capitalism evolves in a vicious cycle of non-development, as it does not promote capital or human upgrading, as it does not encourage a process of innovation and creation of a domestic technological core, which are its prerequisites.

The perspective of these authors is interesting for various reasons. In the first place, it includes Latin America in a discussion that had been limited to advanced capitalisms. It is also relevant that it conceives a type of capitalism that is considered as a type in itself, rather than a derivative, an incomplete, or an unfinished version of a developed type; although it is inefficient, it endures. It is also significant as it points to some of the main characteristics of the situation of the Latin American countries that explain their inability to upgrade and because it tries to build an explanation integrating all these characteristics rather than doing what most of the studies on this continent do, signal one or a couple of features: corruption, low education levels, transnational companies, inequality. Finally, it is also interesting that the characteristics that define this type of capitalism are specific to the Latin American cases, rather than a transposition of the ones that define the types that exist in the advanced economies.

Nonetheless, even if we identify the VoC as an innovation with respect to the first neo-institutionalist explanations of development, we reject many of their presuppositions, some of them shared with neo-institutionalism. In the first place, similarly to this latter perspective, to which in fact they pertain, although they recognize more than one type of capitalism, more than one economics, they limit their analysis to the "standard" economy and the rest. That means that they in fact remain prisoner of the one type that they consider as the benchmark, while the other one is envisaged as an exception. As Théret has written, comparisons can only be made considering more than two cases (Théret 2004). More fundamentally, the positing of only two capitalisms, especially in what concerns the merger of all the rest of the economies into one type, does not do justice to the differences of, for example, France and Germany, where while the social actors play a distinctive role in coordinating the market in the latter, in France it is the State that has this role, as unions and entrepreneurial organizations are weak. The same for the difference between Germany and Japan and other Asian economies where, in the latter the coordination of the market is defined by the large private conglomerates, that concentrate banks, parent companies, suppliers, including commercial centers, and that define internally, paternalistically, salaries, labor standards, working conditions, etc., a model that has been called "companyist" or meso-corporatist (Lechevalier 2011). Finally, the economies of the northern European countries, although they share many of the characteristics of the German model, are nevertheless much more coordinated by the social actors themselves, they are more flexible, more open to the world market, depend on the export of certain products oriented toward production niches, but what characterizes them especially is that great part of their economy is oriented toward social services and products demanded by their extensive social protection system, toward "solving social problems" (Boyer 2005). The criticism of the French regulation school to the VoC is that it is not open enough to differences in the modes of capitalism that co-exist, a position that derives, in fine, of its closeness to the neoclassical, neo-institutionalist economy. The regulation school commends a more pluralistic position toward the modes of capitalism, for example, when studying the Asian types of capitalism after a profound investigation on the economies of the continent, the researchers found 5 types of distinct forms, although they had started with one type (Boyer et al. 2012).

Although we consider that proposing the existence of a hierarchical capitalism is a step toward a more pluralistic conception of the modes of capitalism, as it is defined as a hybrid of both cases that does not coincide with either one of the two ideal types, the LME or its opposite the CME, and is considered as a faulty one, involved in a vicious cycle, we are in fact left with the other two. On the other hand, the concept of hierarchical capitalism for all the countries in Latin America does not recognize the differences between specific countries, nor with certain groups of countries that share similarities, and distinguish themselves from other countries that constitute other groups or clusters, which is the main argument of this book.

Another criticism of the VoC perspective (including Hall and Soskice and Schneider) is that it analyzes the economies from the outlook of **the firm**, considered as the central actor of the capitalist economy. The institutions, the sociopolitical regime, are considered to be the environment in which the action of the firms takes place, the situation they are obliged to confront and learn to adapt to. The analysis is oriented to study the relations established by the firms, both internally with its workers, and externally with other companies, clients, unions, banks and the State (Schneider and Soskice 2009). This means that to define its typology, the VoC school considers a single axis that goes from the internal to the external relations of the company. Boyer argues that when a single axis is taken to construct a typology, one can always construct a totally different one. Thus, within the logic of this perspective, taking into account the rationality of the firms, their aptitude to face the challenges of their environment, it is possible to build a completely different typology that the one constructed by Hall and Soskice, in which companies in Japan and Germany follow the logic of alliance, those of Korea and France a "voluntarist" rationale and finally those of Taiwan and Italy follow a family logic (Boyer 2002–2003). The same can be said with the four principles that Schneider offers to define four ideal types of capitalism: markets, negotiation, trust, and hierarchy, that define, respectively, the capitalism of the USA, Germany, Japan, and Chile/Latin America (Schneider 2013: 23). One could consider that under the principle of negotiation we could include Japan rather than Germany, and in the one of Trust, Germany rather than Japan. Under hierarchy, we could set Japan, or other Asian capitalisms like Korea, rather than Latin America. Then, while these three principles are effectively principles, the one that defines the USA is rather an institution. Finally, where does a country like France fit in? There does not seem to be a place for its type of capitalism, in which the State is central. In fact, VoC not only leaves out cases that do not fit certain definite principles, but it "...excludes other truly hybrid cases, which are combinations of several characteristics of two ideal types, such as France" (Théret 2011).

On the other hand, the VoC school analyses the economies from the viewpoint of the ***firm*** and considers all the institutions that affect it (industrial relations system, governance within and outside of the enterprises, the educational system) as given, and constant. Institutions are assumed, there is no discussion on how they arise, how they are modified, but the argument ponders only on the manner in which the firms have to adapt to them. The basis of its discussion is a static image of capitalisms. Nonetheless, the book of Hall and Soskice was written when the German and the other European economies were already undergoing very significant transformations, that are not envisaged. In addition, other actors, such as the unions, employers' organizations, and the State are merely considered as institutions, and not as actors that modify institutions by their conflict, negotiations, and provisional settlements. They are taken as the context in which the enterprises have to evolve; different institutions constitute different environments and demand different conducts on the part of the firms. In the case of Latin America, the existing institutions lead to an inefficient type of capitalism that perpetuates the main characteristics of third world countries: inequality, poverty, low technological development, etc. (Schneider 2013). Nevertheless, institutions are the result of social conflict, they change owing to different results of this struggle: the defeat of one actor, an agreement between actors, etc. They are in continuous transformation.

More specifically, regarding the application of Schneider of the VoC perspective to Latin America, there is a notable absence, which was included in the VoC, although in a very restrictive function: the State. Actually, neo-institutionalism (North et al. 2002) limits the State as a guarantee of the market, which perfectly coincides with their conception of capitalism as a LME, as an auto-regulated market. The State only serves as the instrument to impose sanctions if rights and obligations are not respected, especially property rights. But the State never has an economic role; a position that completely ignores other types of capitalism where the State does have this role. On the other hand, the State is considered as a neutral agent, it represents society as a whole, it preserves order. But the State is never neutral, it is an arena where different social actors and sectors contest each other's projects and interests, and it acts according to the result of these struggles.

In the case of the VoC, it considers only two hierarchical principles of capitalism: the market and the coordination by the social actors, while relegating the State to an adjunct to the coordination between actors.

Although this may be, in effect, the situation of Germany and of some of the socio-democratic northern European countries, where the action of the social actors is more significant than of the State, the fact that countries such as France, Japan, and Korea are included in the CMEs is puzzling. Moreover, Schneider decides to ignore this actor, arguing that he considers the action of the State as an obstacle to the development of enterprises especially in the case of the peripheral capitalisms (Schneider 2013: 21). This is what allows him to conclude that in Latin America there is only one variety of capitalism, because as we will discuss all along this book, the role of State is crucial to distinguish the diversity of capitalisms in Latin America. In reality, the State is a crucial actor of capitalism as has been shown in numerous studies and historical accounts of the development of certain countries like France, Japan, Germany, Korea, Taiwan, and presently China. It was also a central actor in Latin America during import substitution industrialization, and in some countries in the present: Brazil, Argentina, Uruguay, Bolivia. Actually, the role of the State distinguishes diversities of capitalism in this continent.

1.3 Toward an Actionalist-Structuralist Political Economy

We agree with the neo-institutionalist idea that an economic mode depends on the institutions that act upon it, but we attempt to avoid the many pitfalls of institutionalism and of VoC that we have discussed above. The first is its focus on the enterprise, and the consideration of the institutions merely as the environment where the enterprises evolve. In contrast, the school of regulation takes into account "... the interdependencies and forces that ensure the cohesion of a set of institutions, organizations, norms and behaviors. The notion of a business system [of the institutionalist perspective] allows to incorporate all the institutions that govern the organizational choices of companies and to question their degree of complementarity [...] The concept of social production system (SSP) [of the regulation school] has the same objective as that of the business system, only that while the problematic in terms of the first considers that the imitation and the creation of institutions belong essentially to the companies, the SSP offers a determining role to politics, to constitutionalism and to law in the genesis of institutions with respect to which firms must quickly determine their organizational choices and strategies" (Boyer 2002–2003: 145).

The other main pitfall of VoC is "putting into parenthesis" the fact institutions do not explain themselves, that they are created, implemented and preserved by social actors, among them very significantly the State, by different coalitions of social actors, by external geopolitical configurations, and by even more structural conditions as what a country produces and how it consumes what it produces. Institutions are "… a codification of fundamental social relations" (Boyer 2002–2003: 136). And because we consider that institutions are the concretion of more or less lasting agreements of social conflict, we give a decisive importance to social conflicts and their political translation in the public space (ibid.). In fact, what interests us about institutions is not themselves and the way in which they counteract or permit change, the main objective of institutionalist path dependence analysis, but rather the way in which conflicts lead to a compromise that results in an institution, which can be both formal or informal; for example, the labor-management conflict gives rise to both collective bargaining and informal ways of regulating factory work; in the electoral sphere, both electoral rules and clientelistic relations, etc.

This also means that, unlike the perspective of the neo-institutionalist school, we do not consider institutions or the State as neutral. Just as the State may favor one or another sector of society, so industrial relations may tilt the balance for workers or employers, faulty institutions and higher transaction costs, are not equal for society in its totality. These costs, as Amable says, are not "paid" by society in abstract, but by a specific sector of society. This explains why situations that seem totally dysfunctional may perpetuate, or as Amable says, institutions do not change even in societies where transaction costs are very high. This is because the status quo benefits someone (Amable 2005).

On the other hand, for neo-institutionalism, the domestic institutions are autonomous from the mode of insertion of a country in the world economy. This is the basis of their rejection of the dependence theory, which they argue gave too much weight to this factor. Nonetheless, as we have already discussed, the most serious studies of dependency theory balances between the external and the internal factors. In fact, external relations are absent in most neo-institutional analyses, although in the more recent and significant ones, like that of Thelen (2014), they are present.

Our main argument is then that we have to pass from a purely institutional analysis to a political economic one, or even a structural one like those of the dependence theory. We adopt an intermediary position between an institutionalism that forgets the origins of institutions and reifies them into sort of structures, ignoring that they are originated historically, through social conflict, and on the other hand the impact of structures: economic, social, and domination structures, that likewise define the shape of institutions. A methodology that Restrepo Botero defines in more ambiguous terms as "open structuralism," that he defines as a perspective that accepts that "…necessarily, the economy and politics affect the institutional arrangements, in the same manner that the modes of organization of the State have a significant impact on the economy and on politics" (Restrepo Botero 2015: 480–481). We will attempt to understand both the impact of structures on institutions, as well as the manner in which institutions affect structures. In addition, as we assign a fundamental role to the action of civil society, unions and social movements, we also define the methodological perspective of this book as actionalist. As we have already stated, we consider that it is the actions of the social organizations and movements that define the shape of institutions. But we are institutionalist, because we consider institutions as the central intermediaries between structures and actions. And finally structuralists, because we take very seriously the impact of certain structures on the capacity of action of social actors, and thus on their capacity to change the institutions.

Central to this *demarche*, which for its structuralist dimension is inspired by a long tradition exemplified by the works of Barrington Moore, Sckocpol, Rueschemeyer, Esping Andersen, Colin Crouch, Cardoso and Falleto, Haggard, and the French regulation school, is the idea that institutions by themselves cannot determine a specific capitalistic mode, because institutions are the result of the conflict between social actors or agents, and the State. Moreover, the capitalist mode a country pursues is not only the result of an internal sociopolitical dynamic, which results in a dominant social coalition (although this is central), but it also depends on the manner in which the country inserts itself in the world economy, something that partly depends on the dominant coalition and partly on the main production of the country, whether it is commodities, manufactures, or financial products. Each of these products and their weight on the economy has a definite impact on the economy of a country (Boyer 2017). This perspective is what we call structuralism, in contrast to institutionalism.

Structuralism considers institutions as the result of the conflictual relationship between social actors: social classes (workers, entrepreneurs, social movements) and the State (which is not only an institution, or an arena where social actors confront each other, but a proper ***actor***, and a very significant one in some capitalisms). Institutions, or better still, institutional forms or regimes, that are constituted by a series of institutions that interact, are the temporary result of social interactions and are modified by the relationship between these actors. While neo-institutionalism and VoC are focused on institutions, the structuralist perspective centers its view on how the social actors shape institutions through their conflicting interactions and temporary agreements. Structuralism analyzes the social and political dynamics of a society in order to understand the capacity of social actors and coalitions of social actors to shape and modify institutions. The focus of this perspective is not a single actor performing in an institutional environment, be it the firm or any other actor, but a series of social actors that build coalitions in a conflictual environment that are capable to consolidate a certain economic mode. While the perspective that focuses on institutions tends to analyze their interaction synchronically, the structuralist schools favor a diachronic analysis.

In their classical book written at the beginning of the 1970s, Cardoso and Faletto signaled how an enquiry of capitalism in Latin America should be approached historically and combining the analysis of what a country produces, its international insertion and of the internal sociopolitical configuration, especially the building up of developmentalist coalitions. They began from the colonial times, affirming that what and how the countries produced during this period was crucial to, first, define the way they responded to the shock of independence. They identified two radically different situations: on the one hand the colonies of population (where massive migration from the metropole occurred, because there were opportunities and conditions to establish themselves) that produced food (grains, meat) or products necessary for the production of food in the central countries (nitrates), expanded their production to large regions of the territory and developed a national oligarchy; on the other hand, the countries that produced minerals for the metropolis, where production was concentrated in enclaves, isolated from the rest of the country, and were owned by foreign capitals, concentrated production of tradables geographically and were incapable of generating a domestic oligarchy, or at best engendered one that was dependent on the metropolitan interests; this type of productive structure also maintained most of the local population under traditional social relations. These contrasting conditions led to radically different situations after the shock of independence, because while the production of the colonies that were food supplies for the metropoles was for them essential and continued stimulating production and domestic entrepreneurs, the countries with productive enclaves went into a deep depression and did not succeed in developing a local entrepreneurship (Cardoso and Faletto 1969). This had a significant impact after the 1929–1932 economic crisis, when the capacity of the Latin American countries to industrialize depended on the force of the industrializing coalition: both on the strength of the alliance between industrialists, urban middle classes and workers, and the capacity of the State (as an actor within the alliance) to lead the country in a path toward industrialization. In some countries, the coalition led by the State was successful, Brazil, Mexico, Argentina, while in others, where the coalition was weaker, it was incapable to succeed (Cardoso and Faletto 1969).

Comparing the countries of Latin America with those of East Asia, Haggard also emphasizes the impact on the specific countries of the international system, both politically and economically. In the case of Taiwan and Korea, it was very significant that until after the Second World War they were colonies of Japan that produced agricultural goods for the metropole, and the fact that during the Cold War the USA strongly supported them with financial aid and opening its internal market for their products. He also highlights the internal coalitions that incite industrialization and puts a great emphasis on the role of the State in this coalition. He signals the role of the State in Korea and Taiwan as very significant, not only because it was the main promoter of a national project of development, crucial for the survival of these countries as independent countries in the context of the Cold War and in their specific neighborhood. Although he highlights the strength, coherence, and strategic vision, he specially emphasizes the embeddedness of the State with the entrepreneurs, which meant that although they were not capable of imposing their interests on the State, the government worked closely with them and implemented policies that helped them develop and upgrade. While in Asia there was an embedded State with close relation to business, but where the State was dominant, in Latin America the State was captured or had little autonomy from employers (Haggard 1990).

Other authors have also emphasized the role of coalitions and of the State. Esping Andersen highlights the significance of coalitions in shaping distinct welfare regimes: while the Bismarkian welfare regimes are State led, to advance in order to build a State-organized labor relationship, the social-democratic welfare States of the north European countries are based upon a coalition of land proprietaries and workers, to which the middle classes adhere. In contrast, liberal welfare State emerge where the force of organized civil society is lacking, while the Beveridgian welfare State is imposed by the State, under pressure of the labor movement, but lacks the support of the middle classes in order to become more generous (Esping-Andersen 1990). Crouch explains the cooperative, contentious or radical character of worker's unions by the trajectory of the relation between the State, the church and the international context (Crouch 1993). Amable and Boyer put emphasis on the character of the dominant coalition, and the crucial participation of the salaried class in determining the diversity of capitalisms. Fordism was a compromise between the interests of the entrepreneurs and the workers in order to redistribute the wealth generated by industrialization between profits and wages (Amable 2005; Boyer 2015). The international context, the world economy is also present in this perspective, because Fordism was only possible by the fact that the economies were closed, that they allowed for the intervention of the State, and that the international economy cooperated with this scheme by way of the Bretton Woods consensus; which in contrast to the Washington Consensus did not impose the opening of the national economies, the retreat of the State, and strong competition replaced cooperation (Boyer 2015).

In contrast to most of the criticism against of the school of dependency, their best representatives (among them Cardoso and Falleto) never envisaged that what a country produces or the external relation of the countries determined the economies of the underdeveloped countries, in that case Latin America, but that it was through a dialectical relation between the insertion of the countries in the world economy and the internal sociopolitical dynamics that these economies developed. What a country produces and its international insertion define the existence of certain social sectors, which then evolve with their own dynamics. In this sense, their analysis is much less heteronomous and deterministic than the institutional analysis of Acemoglu and Johnson, who consider that underdevelopment depends on whether the colonizers imposed themselves on a preexisting extractive sociopolitical structure in the countries they arrived at or whether they migrated in great numbers, did not meet an established civilization they could occupy, and were thus forced to establish a more inclusive and democratic society that stimulated economic development (Acemoglu and Robinson 2012). And less determinant than a position like that of Engerman and Sokoloff who propose that factor endowments define the evolution of a country. They consider that the highly profitable products from colonial times (coffee, sugar) led to slavery, and that the countries that were rich in minerals and had a large population led to great wealth concentration that, in turn led to ample land concentration, both of which could only be maintained by extractive sociopolitical configurations. On the other hand, less populated regions that produced less valuable products attracted a larger number of colons who produced grains in smaller properties, something which headed to a more equitable sociopolitical formation, to a more equal and democratic society, more prone to industrialize (Engerman and Sokoloff 2000).

While analyses like those of most neo-institutionalist only envision institutions, independent of the social relations that generate them, in this book we will concentrate on the relation between social actors, their capacity to build a coalition that pursues a certain economic mode, and especially the force and capacity of the popular classes to impose their interests and projects. This was crucial in the implementation of a Fordist regime in Europe and in the USA between the end of the Second World War and the mid-1970s, as it was in Latin America during import substitution industrialization, and again in the first decade of the years 2000 in a number of countries in this continent. Our main argument is that it is possible to build an alternative typology on the basis of the relationship between social actors (entrepreneurs and civil society), the action of the State, and the insertion in the international market. This perspective allows for a more open perspective regarding the types of capitalism that exist in Latin America. Already in the developed countries, the regulation school rejects the idea that there exist only two types of capitalism. While, in effect, as Hall and Soskice write, some capitalist regimes are more liberal and based on the market (US), others are more coordinated by social actors (Germany, North Europe), in others that do not fit in this typology, it is the State which has a crucial role (France), and still in others, the conglomerates of banks and industries play the main role (Japan and Korea) (Amable 2005; Boyer 2005). Thus, although I agree with the consideration that inequality and hierarchy are central features of Latin American countries, I reject the idea that in Latin America there exists a unique hierarchical type: one where that the main actors of the economy (multinationals and domestic family groups), the industrial relations, the welfare and educational system, combine into a unique variety that is a faulty variant of the LME (Schneider and Soskice 2009). In this book, I will defend the idea that in Latin America there are different types of capitalism.

Finally, a few methodological notes. The VoC and Schneider's interpretation of Latin America have a functional conception of the relationship between the different institutions that conform a type of capitalism. Institutions, according to the VoC, define the ways in which firms in each type of capitalism solve the problems of coordination with the various agents with which they interact and in the different societal spheres (Schneider and Soskice 2009). The existence of two ideal types means that the existing institutions are complementary, that is, they are mutually reinforcing to solve coordination problems of each type. In the case of the hierarchical capitalism, the different institutions reinforce the faulty type of capitalism that exists in the continent. For this school, complementarity is defined simply as increasing the efficiency of one institution by the existence and action of the other. Nonetheless, complementarity should not be considered functionally, not all institutions "cooperate" in order to constitute pure or stable forms of capitalism. In fact, most capitalisms are hybrids of pure types, and especially in Latin America, they configure forms that are not stable. Thus, we must be open to accept and consider different capitalistic modes rather than try to include a certain group of countries within one single form in order to simplify the analysis or because they are part of the same geographic area.

There is effectively a question of coherence. Both the VoC school and the regulation theory (RT) consider that in some cases the dialectic between the mode of integration to the world economy, the mode of accumulation and the relation between actors and the State define a sociopolitical configuration where the different institutions are complementary and configure a coherent capitalist form. In the less developed countries, non-complementarity between the institutional forms shape a non-coherent or disarticulated form of capitalism. In the case of Latin America, capitalistic types are still less coherent, and institutions are less complementary. Additionally, in this continent, more radical changes occur regarding State intervention, the insertion of the country in world economy, industrial relations, and political instability. That means that while some institutions may be complementary and point to a specific type of capitalism, they are contradicted by other ones that point in other directions. Nonetheless, while in the past the developed economies have had institutions that were more complementary and established more coherent types than the ones of the developing countries, since the end of *Fordism*, this assumption is being questioned. The more articulated and coherent forms of the more advanced countries are increasingly subject to increasing pressures that tend to disarticulate them (Lechevalier 2011; Thelen 2014; Boyer et al. 2012).

A more general remark. Most neo-institutionalist analyses pretend to find a general law that explains development and underdevelopment. In the case of North, Summerhill and Weingast it is the manner in which countries impose order, whether consensual or authoritarian, that determines their capacity to develop or fail to do so. In the case of Acemoglu, Johnson, and Robinson, this latter capacity is defined by the institutions that colonists imposed on the different countries. But social dynamics is too complex to be defined by any single law, or by focusing exclusively on one of the societal dimensions, in this case institutions. Institutions play a very significant role, but they cannot determine if a country develops or doesn't. A nation's dynamics is a dialectical relation between the economic, societal, political and ideational dimensions, to focus on only one of them is too restrictive and simplistic.

References

Acemoglu, D., & Robinson, J. A. (2012). *Why Nations Fail: The Origins of Power, Prosperity and Poverty*. New York: Crown Business.

Acemoglu, D., Johnson, S., & Robinson, J. A. (2002). Reversal of fortune: Geography and institutions in the making of the modern world income distribution. *The Quarterly Journal of Economics, 117*(4), 1231–1294.

Amable, B. (2005). *Les cinq capitalismes*. Paris: Editions du Seuil.

Bizberg, I., & Théret, B. (2012). La diversité des capitalismes latino-américains: les cas de l'Argentine, du Brésil et du Mexique. *La Revue de la Régulation* (11). Paris.

Boyer, R. (2002). Varieté du Capitalisme et Théorie de la Regulation. In Association recherche et régulation, *L'année de la Régulation, n° 6 (2002–2003): Économie, institutions, pouvoirs* (pp. 125–194). Paris: Presses de Sciences Po (P.F.N.S.P.).

Boyer, R. (2005). How and why capitalisms differ. *Economy and Society, 34*(4), 509–557.

Boyer, R. (2015). *Économie politique des capitalismes, Théorie de la régulation et des crises*. Paris: La Découverte.

Boyer, R. (2017). *What does the growing communality of contemporary capitalisms mean for economic theory?* (Unpublished manuscript prepared for the International Conference on Economic Theory and Policy). Tokyo: Meiji University.

Boyer, R., Uemura, H., & Isogai, A. (2012). *Diversity and Transformations of Asian Capitalisms*. London and New York: Routledge.

Bresser-Pereira, L. C. (2018). *Rentier-financier capitalism* (Unpublished manuscript to be published in the *Revue de la Régulation*).

Cardoso, F. H., & Faletto, E. (1969). *Dependencia y Desarrollo en América latina*. México: Siglo XXI.

Crouch, C. (1993). *Industrial relations and European State traditions*. Oxford: Oxford University Press.

De Soto, H. (2005). *Le mystère du capital: Pourquoi le capitalisme triomphe en Occident et échoue partout ailleurs*. Paris: Flammarion.

Engerman, S., & Sokoloff, K. (2000). History lessons. Institutions, factor endowments, and paths of development in the new world. *Journal of Economic Perspectives, 14*(3), 217–232.

Esping-Andersen, G. (1990). *The three worlds of welfare capitalism*. Princeton, NJ: Princeton University Press.

Haber, S. (1991). Industrial concentration and the capital markets: A comparative study of Brazil, Mexico and the United States, 1830–1930. *Journal of Economic History, 51*(3), 559–580.

Haber, S. (Ed.). (1997). *How Latin America fell behind. Essays on the economic history of Brazil and Mexico*. Stanford: Stanford University Press.

Haggard, S. (1990). *Pathways from the periphery. The politics of growth in the newly industrializing countries*. New York: Cornell University Press.

Hall, P. A., & Soskice, D. (Eds.). (2001). *Varieties of capitalism: The institutional foundations of comparative advantage*. Oxford: Oxford University Press.

Lechevalier, S. (2011). *La grande transformation du capitalisme japonais*. Paris: Presses de Sciences Po.

Maravall, J. M. (1997). *Regimes, politics and markets: Democratization and economic change in Southern and Eastern Europe*. Oxford: Oxford University Press.

Maurer, N., & Haber, S. (2004). *Related lending and economic performance. Manuscript*. Monterrey: Instituto Tecnológico Autónomo de Monterrey and Stanford University.

Montinola, G., Qian, Y., & Weingast, B. R. (1996). Federalism, Chinese style: The political basis for economic success in China. *World Politics, 48*(1), 50–81.

North, D. C., & Weingast, B. R. (1989). Constitutions and commitment: The evolution of institutional governing public choice in seventeenth century England. *Journal of Economic History, 49*(4), 803–832.

North, D. C., Summerhill, W., & Weingast, B. R. (2002). Orden y desorden y cambio económico: Latinoamérica vs. Norte América. *Revista Instituciones y Desarrollo*, (12–13), 9–59.

Parikh, S., & Weingast, B. R. (1997). A comparative theory of federalism: India. *Virginia Law Review, 83*(7), 1593–1615.

Polanyi, K. (1944). *The great transformation*. New York: Farrar & Rinehart.

Restrepo Botero, D. (2015). *Procesos de descentralización en Bolivia y Colombia, 1980–2005: Una propuesta de economía espacial comparada*. Bogotá: Universidad Nacional de Colombia.

Rodrik, D. (2001). ¿Por qué hay tanta inseguridad económica en América Latina? *Revista de la CEPAL*, (73), 7–31. https://repositorio.cepal.org/bitstream/handle/11362/37886/RVE73_es.pdf?sequence=1&isAllowed=y.

Rodrik, D. (2007). *One economics, many recipes. Globalization, institutions and economic growth*. Princeton and Oxford: Princeton University Press.

Schneider, B. R. (2013). *Hierarchical capitalism in Latin America: Business, labor, and the challenges of equitable development*. New York: Cambridge University Press.

Schneider, B. R., & Soskice, D. (2009). Inequality in developed countries and Latin America: Coordinated, liberal and hierarchical systems. *Economy and Society, 38*(1), 17–52.

Thelen, K. (2014). *Varieties of liberalization and the new politics of social solidarity*. New York: Cambridge University Press.

Théret, B. (2004). Del principio federal a una tipología de las federaciones: algunas propuestas. *Foro Internacional, 44*(1), 29–65.

Théret, B. (2011). The place of national systems of social protection and political representation in socio-economic regulation: A morphogenetic structuralist view on institutional change in comparative perspective with special references to Japan and France. *Evolutionary Institutional Economic Review, 7*(2), 177–208.

Weingast, B. (1995). The economic role of political institutions: Market-preserving federalism and economic development. *The Journal of Law, Economics, and Organisations, 11*(1), 1–31.

CHAPTER 2

Four Types of Capitalism in Latin America

2.1 Dimensions of the Analysis and Definitions

From what we have discussed in the first chapter of this book, it is clear that we consider that it is possible and useful to construct a typology of the countries of Latin America that transcends a general theory for development, a unique type of capitalism for the whole of Latin America, as well as a particularistic view that considers the uniqueness of each case. In order to construct our typology, we discuss the cases of nine countries of the continent on the basis of six analytical dimensions:

1. **The accumulation regime** is probably the most important concept of the regulation approach. It is defined as the totality of regularities through which the accumulation of capital assures its progression (Boyer 2015: 61). In the first place, every type or form of capitalism is characterized by a specific **mode of accumulation**. This mode includes the productive structure of the country: what the country produces (in the Latin American case commodities or manufactured products), how it produces, and the manner in which it redistributes wealth between profits and wages.

   The manner in which a country's economy grows can be either extensive or intensive: when growth is obtained through the extension of production without a significant change in production techniques, accumulation is extensive. When a permanent transformation of the organization of production and an increase in

I. Bizberg, *Diversity of Capitalisms in Latin America*,
https://doi.org/10.1007/978-3-319-95537-7_2

productivity attained, we are in face of an intensive mode of accumulation. The second feature of the accumulation regime is the mode of consumption; it can be strongly or weakly related to production. It is loosely related when consumption is basically assured by an agricultural sector, characterized by a small mercantile production and rentier relations. It is strongly related to Fordism, when it includes the workers themselves: as the salaried sector grows, the way of life of workers is transformed and is increasingly dependent on the production of the capitalist sector (Boyer 2015: 61–62).

2. **The form of integration to the world economy** is fundamental in order to analyze the peripheral or dependent economies, as they are in one way or another dependent on the international market. Nonetheless, there are differences: they can be very dependent when most of the tradable products that a country produces and exports are determined by international demand, such as commodities, like Peru, Chile, Bolivia, and Venezuela. They can also be radically dependent when it is an economy that produces manufactures that depend on the activity of international companies that use the country as an outsourcing platform, like Mexico (but also of some countries of Central and Eastern Europe; Drahokoupil and Myant 2015; Nölke and Vliegenthart 2009). Finally, they can be dependent on external financial resources and partially on the export of commodities, but have a significant internal market, like Brazil. On the other hand, their relation to the world economy can be more or less passive, defensive, or proactive.
3. **The State** In the institutionalist perspective, the State is not considered to be an actor, or in any case, it is a subsidiary one. It is merely another institution or the arena where the conflict between different social actors occurs. A perspective derived from a conception of an economy that functions based upon a self-regulating market: the State and politics, in general, are contrary to the efficient operation of the market if they intervene decidedly; they are efficient when they deal only with the imperfections of the market. In this perspective, the State is considered as an institution: a more or less solid and coherent one that allows for the correct functioning of the market, ensuring the rule of law: property rights, the enforcing of the contracts, the penalties for non-compliance, etc. (North et al. 2002).

On the other hand, the neo-institutionalist school thinks the State as neutral, when the State is an actor that responds to certain interests. The State is not a pure Weberian bureaucratic institution that responds to formal rules and represents the interests of the society as a whole. The State responds partly to its own interests, and because it is also an arena where social conflicts between the interest of distinct social sectors and classes are represented, it responds to the interest and projects of certain social coalitions that have gained more power inside or upon the State. According to Evans, the State should be defined by its strength (its internal cohesion, its capacity to impose its interests and projects on other actors), its autonomy (both of which define its Weberian character as a rational bureaucracy), and its capacity to act as an embedded State (Evans 1995).

The RT considers the State as an actor, and its role goes far beyond the mere regulatory function and the imposition of the rule of law. In addition, it is not a neutral actor, and it represents certain interests and acts in their favor (Amable 2005). It may be a central actor in a coalition, which can lead a country to develop in one or another direction. It can be a significant actor to insure the development of capitalism as it happened in all the countries that developed after the Second World War (Bresser-Pereira 2017; Evans 1995; Haggard 1990). In addition, these interests are not static, and they can be modified by the pressure of the popular classes or by other entrepreneurial sectors that are not being benefited by its action.

It can, to be sure, renounce to be an actor and become a mere agent of the international forces (Beck 2002); it can be the agent of a specific sector of society, or of a dominant coalition (Poulantzas, Amable, and Boyer); or it can try to compromise between two or more sectors of society and be an incoherent actor (Théret 1995).

4. **Actors and coalitions of actors** give rise to a dominant coalition that lies behind one or another mode of accumulation. After the first wave of industrialization of Great Britain, most countries achieved industrialization by means of a developmentalist alliance between the State and the urban bourgeoisie, in alliance with the middle classes and the workers. At the present time, only if the State is able to build an ample social coalition, consisting of

financial capital, industrialists, middle classes, and workers, it can become a significant actor for the development of capitalism (as in Bismarckian Germany, Japan, Korea, Taiwan, and present-day China) (Bresser-Pereira 2017).

In Latin America, Cardoso and Faletto signaled the importance of this alliance during the period of import substitution. Hall and Soskice, Amable, and Boyer have indicated the prominence of this alliance in all but liberal capitalisms. They all emphasize the relationship between the entrepreneurs, labor and the State, and the position of the traditional agrarian interests, and more recently, the financial sector, as crucial to define the type of capitalism. In the case of peripheral or dependent capitalisms, the presence of foreign capital and multinationals is crucial (Bizberg and Théret 2015; Marques Pereira and Bruno 2015; Schneider 2013).

5. The effect of the action of civil society on the economic regime is mediated by **the political system**. According to Tilly, the political system can be more or less responsive to social pressures. Similarly, for Théret, from the perspective of more or less decentered and more or less federal states, we can infer that some forms of the State are more open to the civil society than others. On the other hand, we can typify different political regimes (in this case, we only take democracies into consideration) whether they are more or less institutionalized, more or less representative, more important for our purpose, if they are more or less determined by the action of civil society.
6. The interaction of the social actors that gives rise to the emergence of a dominant social coalition together with the form of the State and the type of political regime gave rise to different social compromises and to distinct social contracts which express themselves as a **wage relation** (Lechevalier 2011; Valencia Lomelí 2018). The latter is the manner in which the social actors have concurred to organize production and distribute wealth. There may be a social pact that excludes the workers and concentrates wealth—another where wealth is redistributed through salary hikes and social protection system. Fordism is a special compromise, in which the increase in wealth achieved through productivity gains is distributed in order to increase internal demand for the products manufactured by industry.

The wage relation constitutes a **socioeconomic regime** that is constituted by different relations between the labor market and the social protection systems. The wage relation does not refer exclusively to wages, but also to social protection (health, pensions, unemployment insurance, parental leave, etc.). It includes the action of the State, which intervenes actively in all types of economies (even in the most liberal ones, such as that of the USA) with Medicare, national security pensions. Labor markets can be more or less regulated, they may tend to more or less formalization of workers, with stronger or looser requirements for formalization. Wage policy can be expansive or restrictive (Brazil and Argentina versus Mexico), or strictly related to productivity gains. Finally, the social protection system may tend toward universalization (Brazil, Argentina, and Uruguay) or toward assistance (Mexico, Peru, and Chile).

In our previous analyses (Bizberg and Théret 2012; Bizberg 2015) as well as those of Boyer (2014), Théret (2015), Marques Pereira and Murillo (2015), and Fritz and Lavinas (2015), we found significant differences between Mexico and Brazil in their economic and monetary policies, social protection systems, and socioeconomic performance. On this basis, we formalized/stylized two economic types (Bizberg 2015):

1. The first one, a stylization of Mexico, is an ***international outsourcing capitalism*** that shares characteristics with the Central American countries and the Dominican Republic. It is a disarticulated form of capitalism that assembles imported spare parts that come from parent companies situated in the USA or other central countries. The production chain is disconnected from the rest of the national productive structure; there are few, if any, backward national linkages. It produces manufactures, which can be of relatively high technological content; however, as the process is mainly the assembly of spare parts, the aggregate value added is very low. The mode of accumulation is extensive, as productivity gains are low. The country is a platform for the last stage of the production process. It thus depends on low labor costs and high flexibility of the labor market, and the repression of internal demand. The mode of consumption is profit led. The model is totally dependent on the external market and on foreign investment.

The State is weak, and it is an agent of the market, having been more or less dismantled after having adopted the orthodox recipes of neoliberalism. The State has no intent in inducing a developmentalist industrial policy in order to upgrade the industry on the basis of national suppliers to the exporting enterprises; it considers that the market will do the job.

The sociopolitical conformation that favors this type of capitalism is one of the weak social actors, of a dominant coalition made up of financial capital, large domestic and international companies. The State structure is centralized and the political system has very low representativity, is a particracy.

The wage relation is based upon the repression of wages and labor costs, a flexible labor market, and large informal sector. The social protection system, mainly State financed, is basically assistentialist: a safety net that helps out the population that is unable to enter the labor market. In the specific case of Mexico, while the economy suffers from very low productivity growth, some of the exporting industries such as automobile, steel, electronics profit from an ample differential between productivity (at international standards) and wages (high by domestic standard but low by international ones) (Palma 2005). This model has resulted in an increase in poverty and inequality.

2. A second capitalist variety, a stylization of the mode of development that was followed by Brazil from the beginning of the years 2000 up to 2014,[1] is a **neo- or *socio-developmentalist*.** This capitalistic form produces both commodities for the external market and manufactures for the internal one. It is a mode of accumulation that is based both on extensive and intensive production of commodities and on the intensive production of some manufactured products, steel, arms, planes, biofuels, among others. It is a capitalist form that depends on the external demand for commodities and the income of financial capital as well as internal market growth (Fig. 2.1).

   The State tries to equilibrate the external dependence of peripheral commodities producing economy, financial capital, and industrial production destined to both the external and the internal

[1] A mode that has its roots in past economic trajectories as we tried to show in an article (Bizberg and Théret 2012).

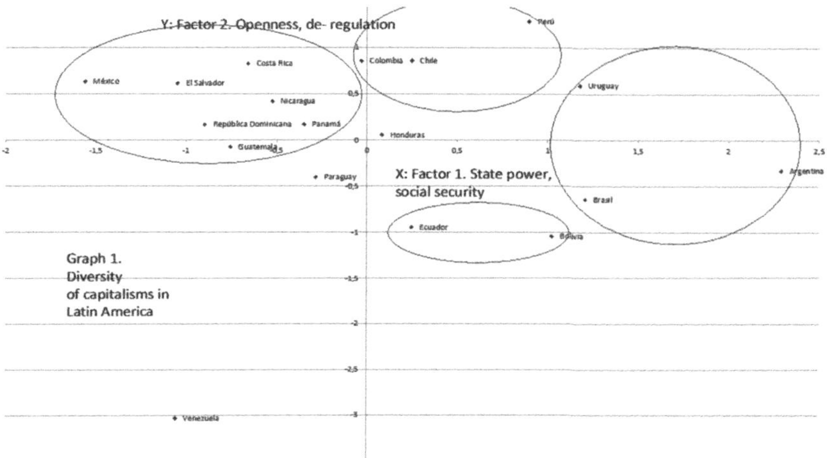

Fig. 2.1 Diversity of capitalisms in Latin America, cluster analysis (*Source* Own elaboration, with the collaboration of Jaime Ramirez Muñoz)

markets. The mode of consumption is also a mediation between capital and popular interests: attraction of foreign investment, support of industry, and increasing wages and a generous social protection system that serves both to popular consumption, the decrease in poverty and the growth of internal demand—a balance between a wage growth and a profit-led model.

The sociopolitical conformation upon which this type of capitalism is based is a strong, dense civil society that exerts pressure on the State to redistribute. The dominant social coalition includes the State arbitrating between the international and national capitals, financial interests, and the popular classes: the poor, the workers, and the low middle classes.

The social pact or the wage relation is characterized by expansive wage policies, incentives for collective negotiations and formalization, and an expanding social protection system oriented to universality. The result is the reduction in poverty, the growth of the vulnerable and middle sectors, and a reduction in inequality.

These two types do not comprise all the countries of Latin America, most notably those that depend almost totally on the production and export of commodities that are rentier economies, like most Andean countries. We thus knew that if we added other countries to the analysis, we would find new types of capitalism. As an auxiliary method to find these other types, we made use of a factorial analysis.[2] Based on the contrast between these two cases, I collected series of data (from the year 2000 to 2014) for all the countries of Latin America. I then chose those series of data that showed a clear difference between these two contrasting cases upon which I developed the first two modes of capitalism and excluded the rest. With these variables, I launched a factor analysis, with which I pretended to define the clusters of countries that were most similar to Brazil and Mexico, and find out if there were other ones that differed from these two. The first two variables (the most significant) of the factorial analysis defined the degree of openness of the economy and the degree of regulation (y-axis), and State intervention and social policies (x-axis).

This analysis resulted in Fig. 2.1, with four distinct clusters that helped me to define two additional types of capitalism for Latin America.

[2] Based on the qualitative information of two cases from a previous project, and inspired on the method of Harada and Tohyama, 2011, I collected a series of quantitative data on all the countries of Latin America (excluding Cuba and Haiti from the factorial analysis, because of lack of most of the data) and launched a factorial analysis with the information that I considered most significant because it distinguished more clearly my two contrasting cases: Brazil and Mexico. The factorial analysis that I present here does not pretend to be, as, for example, the one done by Combarnous, F. et Rougier, E. (eds.), an ex-ante method to find possible similarities between countries that then have to be explained post-facto, but rather as an auxiliary post-facto method. In this sense, it is an "informed" factorial analysis that emerges from a previous qualitative study where we have already defined the very deep differences that exist between two countries of Latin America: Brazil and Mexico. In fact, the factor analysis serves us to situate the other countries of Latin America with respect to these two countries. From a previous research (Bizberg 2015), I concluded that Brazil and Mexico were two extreme opposite types of capitalism in Latin America. With this qualitative assertion, of the totality of variables I had collected, I chose those where these differences were clearer, excluding the variables where very small differences between these two countries appeared. It is with these variables that I proceeded to elaborate a factorial analysis, with which I pretended to define the clusters of countries that were most similar to Brazil and Mexico, and find out if there were other ones that differed from these two. I used the factorial analysis as a manner of concentrating into two variables (opening/closing

Table 2.1 Matrix of rotated components

	Component			
	1	*2*	*3*	*4*
Exports of goods and services (% of GDP)*				0.831
Total exports (% of GDP)*	0.422	−0.467		0.414
Index of economic freedom**		0.884		
Ease of doing business*		0.869		
Health expenditure, public (% of GDP)*		0.504	0.487	
Total government revenue (w/social contributions (general government)***	0.788		0.482	
Regulation+		0.872		
Labor market regulation+		0.885		
Public expenditure on social security and prevention (% of GDP)***	0.648		0.494	
% Real minimum wage increase (1981–2000)***				0.833
% Real minimum wage increase (2001–2010)***	0.900			
Unionization rate (%)++	0.811			
% Non-formal employment rate*			−0.894	
% Pension coverage rate++			0.898	
% Collective bargaining coverage rate++	0.679		0.504	
Poverty reduction 2006–2012*	0.877			

Source Own elaboration, with the collaboration of Jaime Ramirez Muñoz
Extraction method: Principal Components Analysis
Rotation method: Varimax normalization with Kaiser
*World Bank Databank (2013); **Heritage Foundation (2012); ***CEPALSTAT (2013); +WEF. The Global Competitiveness Report 2013–14; ++ILO, ILOSTAT (2013) and Hayter and Stoevska, 2011, for Argentina and Brazil

of the economy and regulation/deregulation (y-axis); State capacity and social policies (x-axis)) a series of other variables which constitute the factorial that are listed in the table that accompanies the clusters, where the weight of each of the different variables is defined. It is thus an auxiliary method, informed by my previous research. It is auxiliary that supports my previous qualitative analysis of the other countries I consider in the paper and in my present research. It is not a parting point, but an intermediary one that permits me to reinforce my idea that, in addition to the clusters of countries that are similar to Brazil and Mexico, there are two other types of capitalism that we will then define as two rentier types: one more closed and redistributive and another more open and non-redistributive, liberal, that I then describe in the rest of the article. The rotation converged into six interactions. We present the data of the matrix of rotated components of the four components that resulted from the factorial analysis. Of the four components created, we decided to maintain the first two that show the strongest relation between the largest number of variables. In this manner, we had the first factor that explains 27.2% of the correlations and the second one 22.4%, adding to a total of 49.6% (see Table 2.1).

In the first place, we can see a cluster with Mexico and the other Central American economies that also base their economies on outsourcing, although they are much smaller, and thus may be more performative, like Costa Rica. On the other side, as a mirror image, we have the cluster formed by Brazil, Argentina, and Uruguay; although the latter is much more open and dependent on exports and finance.

The factorial analysis (Fig. 2.1), where the y-axis measures openness and deregulation of the economy, while the x-axis measures the intervention of the State in labor and social policies, allows us to distinguish four distinct clusters that I will use in this article to complement the qualitative analysis and to include two additional types of capitalism for Latin America. In the first place, we can see a cluster with Mexico and the other Central American economies that also base their economies on subcontracting, although they are much smaller, and thus may be more successful, like Costa Rica. As a mirror image of this first type, we have the cluster formed by Brazil, Argentina, and Uruguay; although this latter is much more open and dependent on exports and finance, that explains why it is nearer to Peru on the y-axis, but closer to Brazil on the x-axis, a tendency we give preference to from what we know of this country in terms of its State intervention and its social policies. Two other clusters appear: that of Chile, Colombia, and Peru versus Ecuador and Bolivia. They help us confirm the existence of other two types of capitalism that share the characteristic that they depend on both commodities and rentier capitalisms, although one is a liberal type and the other a redistributive type—something that makes sense from what we know from the Peruvian, Colombian, and Chilean economies and societies in contrast to the Ecuadorian and Bolivian. However, some authors consider that rentierism is not capitalistic (Keynes; Boyer 2015), because it does not induce innovation, a more efficient use of resources, productivity growth, but merely a more extensive use of them. Nonetheless, although these countries are very dependent on external markets and their exports are mainly commodities, their economy is not only a primary economy; if one looks at the value added, one sees they are much more diversified (see Table 3.2 in Chapter 3).

Although the mode of accumulation and the dependency on commodities and on the external economy are similar, there are significant differences with respect to the dominant coalition and the wage relation, the manner in which the gains of the rent are distributed.

The two rentier economies are as follows:

3. ***The liberal rentier capitalism*** is a stylization of Peru, Colombia, and Chile. Although these countries have certain specific characteristics, they all depend on the export of commodities, and the percentage of mining, oil and gas extraction, and extensively produced agricultural products (like soy) represented in GDP is very great, more than 15%. They all are very open economies and very dependent on the external demand for their products and on foreign capital that invests in extractive activities with procedures that the countries lack. The mode of consumption is oriented toward profits.

   The State intervenes very little in the economy, it is mainly an agent of mostly foreign capital, and it has no intent of promoting industrialization or of upgrading production, even the production of commodities. While Chile shares most of the characteristics with these two countries, the Chilean State has a capacity that other liberal States such as the Peruvian, Colombian, or even the Mexican State do not have, although it does not intervene in the economy.

   The socioeconomic conformation is defined by weak unions and weak social actors. In all three countries, civil society is almost absent. Thus, the dominant social coalition is formed by large foreign and domestic companies, and a technocratic elite that is responsive to them (Bresser-Pereira 2018). The State structure is very centralized (except for Colombia which is very decentralized). The political system is either totally destructured as the one of Peru and Colombia that are a type of empty democracies or institutionalized as the Chilean, very close to a particracy. In any case, the State and the political system function without much interrelation with civil society.

   Finally, the wage relation is characterized by low salaries, deregulation of the labor market, and an assistance-oriented social security system. Wages grow below productivity gains. Nonetheless, although during the last commodities super cycle these countries achieved reducing poverty, they did not manage to reduce inequality (except Peru).
4. The ***redistributive rentier capitalism*** is equally dependent on the international commodities market and on foreign investment. Nonetheless, the State is interventionist, with projects of, scaling

Table 2.2 Types of capitalism in Latin America

	International outsourcing	*Socio-developmentalist*	*Rentier/liberal*	*Rentier/redistributive*
Mode of accumulation/consumption	Extensive/profit-led growth	Extensive and intensive/profit- and wage-led growth	Extensive/profit-led growth	Extensive/profit- and wage-led growth
International insertion	Subordinated	Defensive	Passive	Passive
State intervention	Agent of the market	Redistributive/interventionist	Weak/subsidiary	Redistributive/clientelist
Civil society	Weak unions and civil society	Social corporatism	Weak unions and civil society	Active social movements
Dominant coalition	MNC/big domestic groups/State/middle classes	State/national entrepreneurs/middle and popular classes	MNC/big domestic groups/State/middle classes	State/popular classes
Political system	Particracy	Participative democracy	Particracy/empty democracy	Movementist/delegative democracy
Wage labor nexus	Labor market deregulation/low minimum salaries/assistance social policy	Collective negotiation/high minimum salaries/universalization of social protection	Labor market deregulation/low minimum salaries/assistance social policy	High minimum salaries/universal assistance social policy
Stylization of country	México; Central America	Brazil; Argentina (2003–2014); Uruguay	Chile; Peru; Colombia	Bolivia; Ecuador

Source Own elaboration

in the value added chain of commodities as well as of developing industry. The consumption mode is wage led, as the State taxes the extractive companies in order to redistribute part of the created wealth.

The sociopolitical conformation is characterized by strong social actors that exert pressure on the State and force it to intervene in the economy and redistribute the rent. The State structure, albeit centered, is quite decentralized, especially in Bolivia. The political system is very open to social actors and movements; it is a movementist democracy, which makes the State to be very sensible to social demands.

Table 2.2 synthesizes the main characteristics of the four types of capitalism in Latin America according to the different dimensions we will analyze in this book.

2.2 The Political Economy of the Four Types of Capitalism in Latin America

2.2.1 The Mode of Accumulation

As we have mentioned above, this dimension includes ***what*** a country produces, ***how*** it produces it, and the manner in which it ***distributes*** its gains between profits and wages. Fordism was an economic form, in the central economies, based on the production of manufactured goods, where production was increased through productivity escalations (intensively) and through a mode of consumption that combined profits and wages. Even though the Latin American countries, or peripheral capitalism in general, have industrialized to a certain degree, a profit-led mode, which depends on the appropriation of rent on the part of an oligarchy has almost always prevailed. During the import substitution industrialization (ISI) period (1945–1980), an intensive mode of accumulation was implemented in the largest countries of the continent that was accompanied by a form of consumption based upon redistribution through wages and social protection. Starting with the "lost decade", when the import substitution was abandoned, a bifurcation of the trajectory of the different countries in the continent began. Some countries abandoned ISI to return to the production of commodities. This situation included countries that had basically never industrialized (Bolivia and Ecuador) or that de-industrialized (Colombia, Peru, and Chile). Other countries became outsourcing platforms assembling manufactures for export: Mexico and smaller countries in Central America. Finally, some countries tried to continue developing industry: Brazil. While the countries that depended on commodities followed an extensive mode of accumulation, the countries that pretended to industrialize imposed a more intensive mode.

A fundamental distinction between the Latin American economies is whether they mainly produce commodities or manufactures, or a combination of both. While the first type of economy, the rentier, bases its increase in production on extension, the other types depend on the intensity of production, on the increase in productivity. To a certain degree, all Latin American economies depend on extension, as they are partly rentier: the case of oil and other mining products' exports in the case of Mexico and agricultural, mining, and oil in the case of Brazil. Finance can also be considered a rentier activity, and this is the case of both Mexico and Brazil (Boyer 2015). On the other hand, international outsourcing depends more on extension of investment than on innovation and productivity hikes; neither the State nor capital intend to modify the organization of production in order to increase productivity. As Palma (2005) has proven, outsourcing in Mexico depends less on productivity increases than on the differential between levels of productivity similar to those of the advanced countries and salaries of the peripheral countries.

We define the types of capitalism depending on whether the mode of accumulation is based on rent or productivity, and whether the mode of consumption is led by profits or wages. Fordism, where wages follow closely and sometimes surpass increases in productivity, is a wage-led growth, based on the increase of demand. The liberal mode of development that has been implemented since the demise of Fordism is a profit-led growth, based on the increase of supply (Boyer 2015; Stockhammer 2011).

The socio-developmentalist model is a wage-led growth mode that, in an open economy, has to balance internal demand with domestic supply, in order to prevent the growth impulse to be transferred to the exterior through imports (Bresser-Pereira 2015). The international outsourcing capitalism is based on profits, on the gap between advanced economies productivity and peripheral economies salaries, where the State's function is to repress salaries and social protection costs. The liberal rentier economy channels rents toward profits, while the redistributive rentier regime reallocates part of them toward wages.

None of these two latter models is a sustainable growth model as it depends wholly on the price of commodities that are determined by the world market, the natural resources are depleted, and there is no effort to develop alternative economic sources. In the case of the redistributive type, redistribution does not lead to a wage growth regime, but basically to demand that is funneled toward imports: resources that are obtained by the export of commodities directly by State enterprises or through taxes and royalties mostly lead to increase in imports as the economy is subject to the "Dutch disease" and there is practically no industrial policy.

The mode of consumption depends on the strength and character of the social pact, between the State and the social actors. While in the countries where civil society is strong and autonomous, the mode of consumption is redistributive (Brazil, Argentina, Uruguay, and Bolivia); in those countries where civil society is weak, they are profit led (Mexico, Chile, Peru, and Colombia). In Mexico and, in general, in the outsourcing economies, both accumulation and consumption are disarticulated. While the mode of accumulation is disarticulated as it is dependent on a productive structure that lies between countries (in the case of Mexico and Central America, mainly between the USA and the home country), the mode of consumption depends heavily on remittances sent by a significant proportion of the population that has migrated, as well as other resources coming from all kinds of illegal activities, including drug smuggling. This is complemented by an offer of cheap consumer products that are distributed by the informal commerce—some of which are smuggled into the country and do not pay taxes, salaries, or rent as they are sold in the street.

2.2.2 The International Insertion

The international outsourcing capitalism and the two types of rentier economies share the external orientation of their economies, and although the socio-developmentalist type may produce and export commodities, it is fundamentally oriented toward the internal market. Data concerning the weight of exports in both groups of countries confirm this: while in Brazil and Argentina the aggregate demand is balanced between the external and the internal markets, in the case of Mexico the external market is much more significant. However, it is also true, as we will discuss further that Brazil became increasingly dependent on both the export of commodities and the entry of foreign currency. All the rentier economies, be they liberal or redistributive, Colombia, Chile, Peru, Bolivia, and Ecuador, export primary and manufactured goods based on commodities at around 90%.

The type of integration of a specific country to the world economy is also dependent on the capacity of its State to be proactive, defensive, or an agent of the economic actors of world market. While the outsourcing model is characterized by being very open, and by a State whose role is to act as an agent of the large foreign, as well as national enterprises; the State only sets the stage for the companies to profit from the economy of the country as an outsourcing platform. The liberal rentier countries are also very open and liberal, and the State is merely an agent of liberalism (Beck 2002). The governments of Chile, Peru, and Colombia are totally open, and they do not impose any restrictions on foreign capital. The distributive rentier countries are in a contradictory situation: on the one hand, they pose an autonomous discursive posture toward foreign capitals; on the other, they greatly depend on foreign investment in mining, oil, and other commodities.

The socio-developmentalist economies are more protectionist, as they project to industrialize the country with safeguards, subsidies, loans, and industrial policies. Their relation to the exterior is much more defensive. The financial sector is not as open as most banks are still in the hands of the State or of national capitals. Brazil has not signed any free trade agreements that would oblige it to be much more liberal, much less with the USA. It has, at some moment or other, imposed customs tariffs or set a prohibition to import certain products. Moreover, most analysts have mentioned the failure to control overvaluation.

2.2.3 *The Intervention of the State*

We can define the types of capitalism on whether the State plays a central role in pursuing capitalist development or the economy is left to the market (Bresser-Pereira 2017). We can identify two types of capitalism where the State has a significant role: in one, it orients capitalism toward the internal market, by applying active industrial policies and increasing internal demand, through a distribution of profits between the entrepreneurs and the workers. The State exerts a strong fiscal pressure on the employers and consumers and tries to achieve an active integration to the world economy. It regulates and defends national capital and internal demand, by implementing countercyclical measures. In general, facing a strong State, there are strong unions and business organizations that, in turn, exert pressure on the government in order to preserve their particular or common interests, forcing redistribution, although there are exceptions where the developmentalist State is authoritarian such as Korea and Taiwan in the 1950s and 1960s, and more recently China, where social actors are absent.

In the case of the redistributive rentier mode, the role of the State does not consist of boosting an economy oriented toward the internal market through industrial policies, investment, or innovation, but it is almost "purely" redistributive. Both the political and social relationships, as well as the economic ones, are defined by the fact that the State owns or extracts taxes and royalties from the private companies that exploit natural resources. In many cases, its abundant financial resources are distributed without any productive goals, and they are expended in a clientelistic or State-corporatist logic. They may either support an authoritarian government or used to foster organizations that would serve the State as a political base in order to attain a delegative regime (Venezuela), or when there are pressures from below, from social organizations or movements autonomous from the State, they may foster a participatory democracy (Bolivia, Ecuador).

The other two forms depend more on the market, where the State has a much weaker role, either subsidiary (Chile) or subordinate (Mexico, Colombia, and Peru). In both cases, not only the State is weak and has little autonomy from the entrepreneurs, but social actors are also weak, and coordination between unions and capital (and the State) is almost nonexistent. The way of incentivizing either productive investments, in the case of the outsourcing model, or investment in commodities in the rentier type is through the safeguarding of high profits, low salaries, low social security costs, a State-financed residual/assistance-oriented welfare system, a flexible industrial relations system, low fiscal pressure, and low environmental regulation.

2.2.4 The Dominant Social Coalition

What the country produces and exports, how it does it, and the character of the international insertion of an economy are, in many respects, determined by the orientation that the State and the dominant social coalition give it. If these were not so, we would be living in a perfect Ricardian world where every country would produce what it is best endowed to produce (Haggard 1990). That is why one of our most fundamental assumptions is that the mode of accumulation and the wage relation are defined *in fine* by the character of the dominant social coalition. Thus, in our four types of Latin American capitalism, the composition of the coalition is also crucial to define its character.

Where social actors are strong enough to form part of the pact, and the State is capable of creating a broad coalition including industrialists, middle classes, in a compromise with agro-exporters and financial sectors, we have either a socio-developmentalist type of capitalism if based on productivity gains or a rentier redistributive regime if based on rents. On the other hand, where social actors are weak and the social pact is basically oligarchic, essentially constituted by the State, multinationals, large national and foreign entrepreneurs, and financial capitals, then gains in either productivity or rent are mostly oriented toward profits.

The four countries that have served to formalize the diversity of capitalisms in Latin America went through a different trajectory in what concerns the relation between the State and the national and international capitalistic groups and the national social sectors. In the 1980s and 1990s, new coalitions arose in almost all the countries in Latin America. Central for determining the character of these coalitions was the response to the debt crisis of the 1980s and the path of democratization they followed. The crisis resulted in a process of economic liberalization and democratization; most countries abandoned ISI, while others continued an industrialization effort. This depended greatly on the participation of civil society in the democratization process and the sequence between liberalization and democratization. In Mexico and Chile, civil society was not crucial to push through democratization, and thus liberalization occurred prior to democratization. This meant both a more orthodox liberalization and undermining of social actors, especially the unions by liberalization. In this case, the dominant sociopolitical coalition that emerged during the 1990s and 2000 did not include organized civil society.

In the international outsourcing capitalism and the liberal rentier capitalism, the dominant bloc is constituted by multinationals, large national entrepreneurs, and financial capital, together with the middle classes that profit from the establishment of the foreign enterprises, and the commerce and service sectors that these enterprises require. The State acts basically as an agent of the foreign and national multinationals. As in the process of democratization civil society was basically absent, the process gave rise to a liberal, purely electoral democracy, with strong particratic tendencies, impervious to the interests of the popular classes and the poor. In some cases, as in Peru and, partially, in Colombia, both civil society and the political system equally destructured, and the State can be defined as "pure" technocratic government, equally impervious to popular interests (Bizberg 2010; Aziz 2015).

Where civil society was a central actor in the process of democratization and this process preceded liberalization, some of the institutions and policies of ISI endured, and civil society strengthened through democratization and by its resistance against the liberalization process. It emerged, reinforced by both processes, and imposed itself as part of the sociopolitical coalition that emerged during the 1990s or 2000. This was the case of Brazil, where unions and civil society were central in the political transition and contributed to the creation of a socio-democratic party, the PT, and of Argentina after the emergence of a myriad of social movements in the wake of the deep sociopolitical crisis of 2001–2002. In Bolivia, a country that did not industrialize in any significant manner, the liberalization process that followed the debt crisis of the 1980s that led to the privatization of State companies and the installation of foreign companies in the water and gas fields and the expansion of agribusiness in the east of the country (the Media Luna) was not reversed but was re-oriented toward redistribution with the upsurge of the social movements against the privatization of water and gas that sustained the government of the Movimiento Al Socialismo (MAS).

Both the socio-developmentalist capitalism and the distributive/rentier capitalism are based on a coalition where the State is an active actor of the economy as it arbitrates between the foreign capital, the large domestic groups that are oriented toward the export markets, and the local economic groups oriented toward the internal market and the domestic social groups. It is a capitalist form where the State has a significant interventionist role. The political regime is a stable democracy, when a coalition can be constructed (Brazil), or a "movementist" democracy (Bolivia), when the demand for redistribution comes from below, from autonomous social movements (Bizberg 2010; Aziz 2015), or from a political regime with a tendency toward a delegative democracy if and when the State uses the resources obtained by the exports of commodities in order to control social organizations in a clientelistic or corporatist manner (Venezuela).

2.2.5 *The Form of the State and the Type of Political System*

The effect of the action of civil society and of the dominant classes on the economic regime is mediated by the structure of the State and by the political system. As Tilly has analyzed in his book on *Democracy*, he considers that a democratic regime depends on the openness of the political system to societal demands and to the capacity of the State to implement them. With regard to the possibility of social demands to reach the State, he only focuses on the openness or closeness of the political system. Here, we will typify different political regimes, in the case we only take into consideration democracies, whether they are more or less institutionalized, more or less representative, and, more important for our purpose, more or less determined by the action of civil society. Following the perspective of federalism of Bruno Théret, according to whom some forms of the State are more open to civil society than others, depending first on whether a State has a federal or centralized structure and then on whether federalism is decentered or centered, we will add this dimension to the analysis in order to define another characteristic that determines the character of the different types of capitalism.

The characteristic of the dominant social pact is very dependent on the existence of a dense, organized, and autonomous civil society. Nonetheless, the capacity of this actor to impose its interests and projects on the economy is mediated by the political system. Where the political system is impervious to pressures from civil society, the State can be dominant by either a technocratic elite or an agent of the international capitals. The same goes for a centralized State structure. On the contrary, an open, representative political system together with a decentralized State structure is conducive to a strong involvement of civil society in orienting the economy. Some State structures are more open, because they are federal and decentralized, while others are more closed, because they are centered and centralized. On the other hand, more responsive political systems are those where political systems are institutionalized and civil society is organized, while particracies, clientelistic, and delegative democracies are less responsive to social demands. Where we find a more decentralized, more responsive political system and an active civil society, we also find a more active role of the State that popular interests are part of the social coalition and in consequence a higher probability of State-/wage-led economy with redistribution. Where a less decentralized structure coincides with a less responsive political system and a less active civil society, we also find less State intervention, popular interests excluded from the social coalition and in consequence a higher probability of a market-/profit-led economy without redistribution.

2.2.6 *The Social Pact/The Wage Relation*

The wage relation does not only comprise wages, but also indirect forms such as the labor market regulations and the social security system (health, pensions, unemployment benefits, etc.). State intervention, as well as the strength and organization of the labor movement and of the employer's organizations, and their relation, is central to define the character of the wage relation that reposes upon a social pact between these three central actors.

We have basically two situations: while in the outsourcing (Mexico) and in the liberal rentier models (Chile, Peru, and Colombia) the industrial relations have been radically deregulated and flexibilized and social protection systems have been transformed into assistantship, although in the socio-developmentalist (Brazil, Argentina, and Uruguay) industrial relations have also been liberalized, the force of the labor movement and the fact that the government has had, at some moments, a close relationship to workers and other social organizations, defines that the labor market continues to be regulated and social protection systems have better endured in their traditional forms.

In the case of Mexico, the corporatist relationship that existed since the 1930s has almost completely disappeared, at least in what concerns the negotiating capacity of the unions and the benefits for the workers. Negotiations in Mexico, Chile, as well as Peru and Colombia occur mostly by enterprise, and unionization rates of the total of salaried earners are very low. Although industrial relations have also been flexibilized in Brazil, unionism has managed to retain an important degree of autonomy and capacity of action. This is partly due to the fact that the labor movement in Brazil was a central actor (together with numerous other social movements) in the democratization process, but also because it never lost its character as an interlocutor of the successive governments, even with the more liberal ones. Although during the 1990s the Argentinian Menem government tried to weaken the unions and partially succeeded, they were re-activated during the Kirchner and Fernandez governments to the extent that Etchemendy and Collier (2007) qualified the relationship between government and labor as socio-corporatist (Palomino and Trajtemberg 2006; Cerdas Sandí 2017).

In Argentina and Brazil, social movements were also been very active: the *piqueteros* and the human rights movements in the first, and in the second a myriad of different social organizations that pushed forward the democratization process and the drafting of the 1988 Constitution have maintained their intervention on social policies through informal and formal (the councils) channels (Izunza Vera and Gurza Lavalle 2012). These movements, more than the unions, were a very significant mobilizing force that have managed to impose a popular alliance on the State in the rentier distributive capitalisms: in the case of Bolivia, the indigenous and coca producers of Chaparé are the basis of the MAS that led Evo Morales to the presidency, while in the case of Ecuador, the CONAIE has been the central social and political actor.

A very direct indicator of the character of the social pact is the data on the rise of wages, especially minimum salaries that have an impact on both active workers and pensioners. They are also a good sign of whether the mode of economic growth is redistributive or liberal, and on the weight that is given to either profits or wages. In the liberal rentier type (Peru, Colombia, and Chile), salaries have grown moderately, while in the outsourcing type (Mexico), they have stagnated; in both, the State represses salaries, especially in the outsourcing model as they constitute its principal competitive advantage. In contrast, in both the socio-developmentalist (Brazil and Argentina) and the redistributive rentier (Bolivia and Ecuador), minimum salaries have grown strongly.

The character of the social protection systems is also very contrasting between the different types of capitalism. Social protection policies have a short-term impact on demand through pensions, unemployment compensations, health investment and expenditure, and a medium- and long-term effect through productivity growth. The expansion of public resources dedicated to social policies and health is very significant in the three countries (Argentina, Brazil, and Uruguay) we have catalogued as socio-developmentalist. The rest of the countries have all lagged well behind. In general, social security (pensions) and health coverage are more extended and more generous than in countries with a strong labor movement or strong social movements and with governments that apply public policies aimed at the formalization of workers. While in the case of Mexico and Peru practically nothing has been done to reduce informality, in Argentina and Brazil, tax incentives and stricter work inspection have resulted in a decrease in informality (Maurizio 2014; Berg 2011).

Since the 1980s, the Mexican social security system has been evolving toward a more universal, albeit minimalist scheme. Since the mid-1990s, social programs have decidedly shifted to assistance (Valencia Lomelí 2008). The main social program *Prospera* focalizes on the poorest. Brazil and Argentina (since 2003) stand in sharp contrast to Mexico: in the first place, the welfare regimes were practically not modified, especially in the case of Brazil. In Argentina, in 2008, the Fernandez government renationalized the pension funds which had been partially privatized during the Menem presidency.

The impact of a socio-developmentalist mode of growth is clear in the case of Argentina and Uruguay, as well as Brazil, in terms of both decreasing inequality and reduction in extreme poverty and expansion of a middle class. This is also the case of a redistributive rentier economy such as Bolivia. The countries near the liberal rentier type have also shown a very positive performance in reducing inequality and extreme poverty, less as a result of the increase in wages, formalization, or social security expenditure, because the wage relation is favorable to profits, but most probably through a "mechanic" effect of economic growth. The outsourcing model, typified by Mexico, is exemplary by its stability in terms of inequality and poverty; in fact, although the relative percentage of poor has decreased slightly, in absolute terms there are more poor in Mexico.

References

Amable, B. (2005). *Les cinq capitalismes*. Paris: Editions du Seuil.

Aziz, A. (2015). ¿Democracias diferentes?: México, Brasil y Argentina. In I. Bizberg (Ed.), *Variedades de Capitalismo en América Latina: los casos de México, Brasil, Argentina y Chile* (pp. 283–380). México: El Colegio de México.

Beck, U. (2002). *Poder y Contrapoder en la Era Global, La nueva economía política global*. México: Paidos.

Berg, J. (2011). Laws or luck? Understanding rising formality in Brazil in the 2000s. In S. Lee & D. McCann (Eds.), *Regulating for decent work: New directions in labour market regulations*. Geneva and Basingstoke: ILO and Palgrave Macmillan.

Bizberg, I. (2010). La democracia vacía. In I. Bizberg & F. Zapata (Eds.), *Los Grandes Problemas de México. Los movimientos sociales*. México: El Colegio de México.

Bizberg, I. (Coord.) (2015). *Las variedades del capitalismo en América Latina: los casos de México, Brasil, Argentina y Chile*. Mexico: El Colegio de México.

Bizberg, I., & Théret, B. (2012). La diversité des capitalismes latino-américains: les cas de l'Argentine, du Brésil et du Mexique. *La Revue de la Régulation*, Paris, No. 11.

Bizberg, I., & Théret, B. (2015). Las coaliciones sociopolíticas y las trayectorias de los capitalismos latinoamericanos. In I. Bizberg (Coord.), *Las variedades del capitalismo en América Latina: los casos de México, Brasil, Argentina y Chile* (pp. 95–146). Mexico: El Colegio de México.

Boyer, R. (2014). *Is more equality possible in Latin America? A challenge in a world of contrasted but interdependent inequality regimes* (DesiguALdades.net, Working Paper Series 67). Berlin: Freie Universität Berlin.

Boyer, R. (2015). *Économie politique des capitalismes, Théorie de la régulation et des crises*. Paris: La Découverte.

Bresser-Pereira, L. C. (2015). *Reflecting on new developmentalism and classical developmentalism* (Working Paper No. 395). São Paulo: FGV.

Bresser-Pereira, L. C. (2017). The two forms of capitalism: Developmentalism and economic liberalism. *Brazilian Journal of Political Economy, 37*(4), 680–703.

Bresser-Pereira, L. C. (2018). *Rentier-financier capitalism* (Unpublished manuscript to be published in the *Revue de la Régulation*).

Cerdas Sandí, D. (2017). *La Disputa por el Poder de Asociación de los Trabajadores: Veto Empresarial y Democracia Restringida en América Latina*. Tesis doctoral del Programa de Doctorado en Investigación en Ciencias Sociales, con mención en Ciencia Política. México: Facultad Latinoamérica de Ciencia Sociales.

Drahokoupil, J., & Myant M. (2015). Putting comparative capitalism research in its place: Varieties of capitalism in transition economies. In M. Ebenau, I. Bruff, & C. May (Ed.), *New directions in critical comparative capitalisms research*. London: Palgrave Macmillan.

Etchemendy, S., & Collier, R. B. (2007). Down but not out: Union resurgence and segmented neocorporatism in Argentina (2003–2007). *Politics & Society, 7*(3), 363–401.

Evans, P. (1995). *Embedded autonomy: States and industrial transformation*. Princeton, NJ: Princeton University Press.

Fritz, B., & Lavinas, L. (Eds.). (2015). *A moment of equality for Latin America? Challenges for redistribution*. Surrey and Burlington: Ashgate.

Haggard, S. (1990). *Pathways from the periphery: The politics of growth in the newly industrializing countries*. New York: Cornell University Press.

Izunza Vera, E., & Gurza Lavalle, A. (2012). Arquitetura da participacao e controles democráticos no Brasil e no México. *Novos Estudos, 92*, 105–121.

Lechevalier, S. (2011). *La grande transformation du capitalism japonais*. Paris: Presses de Sciences Po.

Marques Pereira, J., & Bruno, M. (2015). *Path dependence blocking the emergence of a new type of capitalism favoring redistribution in Brazil: A new view on the possibility of a developmental coalition* (Unpublished manuscript). Université d'amiens, France.

Marques Pereira, J., & Murillo, V. S. (2015). El problema del tipo de cambio y la posibilidad de revertir la desindustrialización. Una comparación entre Argentina, Brasil y México a la luz de una concepción alternativa de la moneda como institución social. In I. Bizberg (Coord.), *Las variedades del capitalismo en América Latina: los casos de México, Brasil, Argentina y Chile* (pp. 381–472). México: El Colegio de México.

Maurizio, R. (2014). *Labour formalization and declining inequality in Argentina and Brazil in the 2000s: A dynamic approach* (ILO Research Paper No. 9). Geneva: ILO.

Nölke, A., & Vliegenthart, A. (2009). Enlarging the varieties of capitalism: The emergence of dependent market economies in East Central Europe. *World Politics, 61*(4), 670–702.

North, D. C., Summerhill, W., & Weingast, B. R. (2002). Orden y desorden y cambio económico: Latinoamérica vs. Norte América. *Revista Instituciones y Desarrollo, 12–13*, 9–59.

Palma, J. G. (2005). The seven main 'stylized facts' of the Mexican economy since trade liberalization and NAFTA. *Industrial and Corporate Change, 14*(6), 941-991.

Palomino, H., & Trajtemberg, D. (2006). Una nueva dinámica de las relaciones laborales y la negociación colectiva en la Argentina. *Revista de Trabajo, 2*(3), 47–68.

Schneider, B. R. (2013). *Hierarchical capitalism in Latin America: Business, labor, and the challenges of equitable development*. New York: Cambridge University Press.

Stockhammer, E. (2011). Crecimiento basado en los salarios: introducción. *Boletín Internacional de Investigación Sindical, 3*(2), 183–208.

Théret, B. (1995). *L'État, la finance et le social. Souveraineté nationale et construction européenne*. Paris: La Découverte.

Théret, B. (2015). La diversidad de los federalismos en América Latina: Argentina, Brasil y México. In I. Bizberg (Coord.), *Las variedades del capitalismo en América Latina: los casos de México, Brasil, Argentina y Chile* (pp. 147–282). México: El Colegio de México.

Valencia Lomelí, E. (2008). Las transferencias monetarias condicionadas como política social en América latina. Un balance: Aportes, límites y debates. *Annual Review of Sociology, 34*, 499–524.

Valencia Lomelí, E. (2018). *¿Hacia nuevos compromisos sociales en las trayectorias de los regímenes de bienestar? Los casos de Brasil, Corea del Sur y México*, (Unpublished article). Universidad de Guadalajara.

CHAPTER 3

The Accumulation Regime

The accumulation regime is one of the most important concepts of the regulation perspective, together with the mode of regulation. The accumulation regime is defined as "The totality of the regularities that insure a general and relatively coherent progression of capital accumulation which lessen or spread out in time the distortions and disequilibria that permanently emerge from the process itself" (Boyer 2015: 61; own translation).

Every type or form of capitalism is characterized by a specific mode of accumulation. This mode includes the productive structure of a country: what it produces, how it produces it, and the manner in which it redistributes its gains between profits and wages. A country may orient its economy fundamentally toward manufactures or commodities; both have been discussed in the literature as having significant impacts on social organization. The other aspects of the mode of accumulation are **the manner in which** production is achieved and **how the benefits of production are distributed** between the different sectors of society. The manner in which production is achieved can be either extensive or intensive; when growth is obtained through the mere extension of production, without a significantly changing the technology, the techniques, or the organization of labor, accumulation is extensive; in contrast, when the organization of production is transformed through innovation, the integration of technology, a different way of organizing work, in sum through an increase in productivity, we talk of an intensive mode of accumulation. The third feature of the accumulation regime is the mode of consumption. It can be

I. Bizberg, *Diversity of Capitalisms in Latin America*,
https://doi.org/10.1007/978-3-319-95537-7_3

Table 3.1 Mode of accumulation

	International outsourcing	*Socio-developmentalist*	*Rentier/liberal*	*Rentier/ redistributive*
Productive structure	Low added value manufactures (assembly)	Commodities and manufactures	Commodities	Commodities
Mode of accumulation	Mainly extensive/ intensive in some specific sectors	Extensive/ intensive	Extensive	Extensive
Mode of consumption	Profit-led growth	Wage-/profit-led growth	Profit-led growth	Wage-/profit-led growth
Character	Disarticulated productive structure	Intent to articulate external and internal markets	Articulated upon the external market	Articulated upon the external market

Source Own elaboration

strongly or weakly related to the production of the capitalist system. It is weakly related when consumption is basically assured by an agricultural sector, characterized by a small mercantile production and rentier relations. It is strongly related in Fordism, a system that distributes productivity gains and extends consumption to the workers themselves; which means that as the salaried sector grows, the way of life of workers is transformed and is increasingly dependent on the production of the capitalist sector (Boyer 2015: 61–62). Fordism is a virtuous circle where what is produced and the manner in which it is produced engages in a process of redistribution that leads to increasing demand of the workers, which in turn stimulates innovation and productivity growth.

Table 3.1 synthesizes the mode of accumulation of the four types of capitalism, making references to the specific countries that have served to formalize them.

3.1 The Productive Structure

The literature analyzing the consequences on its sociopolitical organization of what and how a country produces is considerable: Cardoso and Faletto (1969) point to the relationship between what a country produced during colonial times and the existence of a national bourgeoisie who, eventually, allows the country to industrialize. Engerman and Sokoloff (1997) connect climate and productive structure with socioeconomic organization, as well as with equality and industrialization; Evans (1995), Amsden (2001), Kay (2002) link rentier productive structure with the character of the State, and consider that the wealth of nations in primary products usually leads to a depredatory State that translates this source of economic power into political power, either through authoritarianism or clientelism. Karl (1997) and Hausmann and Rigobon (2003) tie productive structure to democracy, as rentier economies tend to favor authoritarianism or weak democracies. From a macroeconomic perspective, Boyer (2015), Bresser-Pereira (2012), Salama (2012) analyze the negative relation which exists between all types of rentier economies (commodities, agricultural, financial, housing) and development, as rentierism promotes non-productive investments. In addition, exporting commodities is directly related to the incapacity to industrialize, to the Dutch disease, and even to de-industrialization.

The VoC also considers a relation between a particular productive structure and the institutional conformation existing in a specific society, although in this case it is institutions that influence what a country produces, rather than the opposite. Liberal economies tend to produce manufactures that depend on radical innovation, such as information technology, new materials, biotechnology, pharmaceuticals, semiconductors; this is due to their flexibility, risk investments, general education. Coordinated economies tend to specialize on products that depend on incremental innovation, such as machines, vehicles, engines, civil engineering; this is due to their stability, long-term/patient investment, specialized education and training (Hall and Soskice 2001: 42–43). Although we do not preclude the structuralist point of view which considers that, in certain situations and to a certain degree, what a country produces determines its sociopolitical conformation, we are more in line with the VoC school in thinking that it is the institutional (in our case the sociopolitical) configuration that determines specific productive patterns; this idea will be the basis of the rest of the book.

Following the French regulation school, we define the mode of accumulation as what is produced, how it is produced, and the way created wealth is distributed. Thus, the first fundamental division between the Latin American economies is whether what is produced is mainly commodities or manufactures, or a combination of both. The first case is that of the rentier economies, while the other two are more complex economies.

In Table 3.2, we can clearly see that in five countries: Bolivia, Chile, Colombia, Peru, and Ecuador, exports are extremely concentrated in commodities: 57% of the total of Bolivia's exports are natural gas and

Table 3.2 The principal exporting products (2014)

	Argentina (%)	*Bolivia (%)*	*Brazil (%)*	*Chile (%)*	*Colombia (%)*	*Ecuador (%)*	*Mexico (%)*	*Peru (%)*
1	Oilseed cake (18)	Natural gas (52.3)	Iron ore (11.6)	Refined copper (24)	Crude oil (48.4)	Crude oil (52.6)	Crude oil (9.2)	Copper ores (21.1)
2	Lorries and Trucks (5.8)	Zinc ores (8.5)	Soya beans (10.4)	Copper ores (22.3)	Coal (12.1)	Bananas (10.5)	Passenger motor cars (8.2)	Refined copper (5.7)
3	Soya beans (5.7)	Silver ores (6.3)	Crude oil (7.3)	Fish (6.1)	Coffee (4.7)	Crustaceans (10.2)	Motor car parts (5.8)	Meat and fish (4.1)
4	Maize (5.3)	Oilseed cake (6)	Sugar (3.3)	Blister copper (4)	Flowers (2.6)	Prepared fish (5)	Trucks (5.5)	Zinc ores (3.6)
5	Soy bean oils (5.2)	Crude oil (5.1)	Poultry (3.2)	Wood pulp (3.4)	Petroleum derivatives/ polyethylene (2.2)	Flowers (3.7)	Statistical machines (5.3)	Lead ores (3.1)
6	Cars (4.6)	Tin and tin alloys (3)	Oilseed cake (3.1)	Wine, grapes (2.4)	Bananas (1.6)	Cacao (2.4)	Televisions (4.3)	Natural gas (2.8)

Source Own elaboration with data from Cepalstat

oil and 25% minerals; 52% of Ecuador's exports are crude oil and 20% bananas and crustaceans; Chile exports copper ores and refined copper for 48% of the total; Colombia's exports are basically crude oil (48%) and coal (12%); finally, minerals comprise 34% of Peru's exports. In Table 3.3, we can see that these rentier countries depend much more (three times in average) on mining and agricultural products than the other four. In three of the rentier economies (Chile, Peru, and Bolivia), mining (including gas and oil extraction) represents between 11 and 16% of GDP. In contrast, in the other three countries, Argentina, Brazil, and especially Mexico, exports are more diversified.

Nonetheless, when one looks at the productive structure one can see that it is more diversified. While Bolivia's value added is based on 16% on mining, 14% on manufacturing, 12% on financial intermediation, 4% on construction. For Chile, mining represents 14% of its GDP, manufacturing another 11%, construction 6%, and financial intermediation a very high 23%. In Peru, mining represents 14% of its economy, 14% manufacturing, 11% financial intermediation, and 8% construction. In Ecuador, mining is 11%, manufacturing 13%, financial intermediation 16%, and construction 11%. Finally, Colombia seems a more balanced economy as mining represents 8% of GDP, manufacturing 12%, construction 9%, and financial intermediation a very high 23%, like Chile. When one includes agricultural products, commodities represent between 15% in Chile and 30% in Bolivia of total GDP. Thus, although exports are totally dependent on commodities in these countries, the internal economy is more diversified.

Although Argentina, Brazil, and Mexico also export commodities (the first two do so in large proportions, while in Mexico only oil is a very significant export product), these activities represent a much lower proportion of added value: between 4 and 7%. While Argentina produces less mineral products, it has a relatively high production of agro-products, which amounts to a total that comes close to that of the rentier countries. In both Brazil and Mexico, commodities have a lower weight in their economies. In these two countries, value added is more diversified; Mexico has the highest rate of value added in manufactures, together with Argentina, both around 17%. However, there is an evident contrast between the very high percentage of Mexican manufacturing exports and the relatively low value added of manufacturing; this is a clear indicator of an assembly model, with low value added activities. The fact that Brazil has a very high public administration value added has the effect of reducing the proportion of all the other sectors. In fact, if one

Table 3.3 Percentage of value added by sector of activity (2016)

	Argentina	*Bolivia*	*Brazil*	*Chile*	*Colombia*	*Ecuador*	*Mexico*	*Peru*	*Uruguay*
Agriculture	8.0	12.3	5.2	3.8	6.6	10.5	3.3	6.7	8.1
Mining	3.9	16.4	3.5	14.4	8.5	10.7	5.7	13.7	0.3
Manufacture	17.2	14.0	12.1	10.9	12.3	13.0	17.5	14.3	14.6
Electricity	1.6	2.9	2.8	3.8	3.6	1.9	2.2	2.0	3.5
Construction	4.7	3.9	6.7	6.4	9.4	10.8	7.5	6.3	8.0
Commerce	16.9	11.6	11.4	12.1	12.9	12.3	18.8	15.8	15.5
Transportation	7.8	11.4	10.0	10.1	6.7	8.2	10.2	10.1	10.9
Financial intermediation	15.7	12.0	15.6	22.5	22.7	16.4	22.6	11.0	23.8
Public administration	24.1	21.3	32.7	16.1	17.3	16.2	12.3	20.0	19.7

Source Own elaboration with data from Cepalstat

"puts in parenthesis" the value added by public administration in the three countries and re-calculates the proportion added by all the other activities, the value of the manufacturing industry in Brazil attains 18%, while that of Argentina reaches 23% and that of Mexico 20%. Part of the explanation of the large public administration of these countries is that they have a very extensive and relatively high (compared to the other Latin American countries) national social protection system (pensions, education, health, housing); we will discuss this issue at greater length in the last chapter of this book.

The countries with the smallest public administration are Mexico, Chile, and Colombia, with around half of value added of Brazil; Mexico is the lowest, with a mere 12%. In Chile, Colombia, Mexico, and Uruguay, financial intermediation occupies a significant proportion of the economy, around 23% of GDP. In this manner, we can characterize the more liberal countries, irrespective of whether they are rentier or not, as having a weak public administration and depending on high financial intermediation. By contrast, redistributive countries have low financial intermediation and high public administration (in this respect, Peru's productive structure looks more like a redistributive country).

When one now looks at the population employed in each sector of activity regardless of the value added, as expected, the proportion of people occupied in the industrial branch is higher in Argentina, Brazil, Chile, and Mexico and lower in the rentier countries. When one focuses on more specific data, this situation is even clearer; in Argentina, Brazil, and Mexico, the percentage of workers in the manufacturing branches is similar: 12% for Brazil, 13% for Argentina, and 16% for Mexico. As we have already mentioned, although the fact that Mexico is such a large manufactures exporting country is not well reflected by the amount of added value manufacturing represents due to the special characteristics of the *maquiladora* (assembly) industry, but it shows relatively more in the number of people working in this activity. However, in a more global comparison, the numbers for all the countries of Latin America pale with respect to those of the BRIC countries; in 2008, Russia had 32% of its population occupied in industry (including construction), while in China it was 27% (Goldstein and Lemoine 2013: 41) (Figs. 3.1 and 3.2).

The specialization of the different countries is much clearer when one looks at the structure of their exports. Above, in Table 3.2, unsurprisingly, we can see that the six most important export products of the rentier countries are as expected all commodities, they comprise more

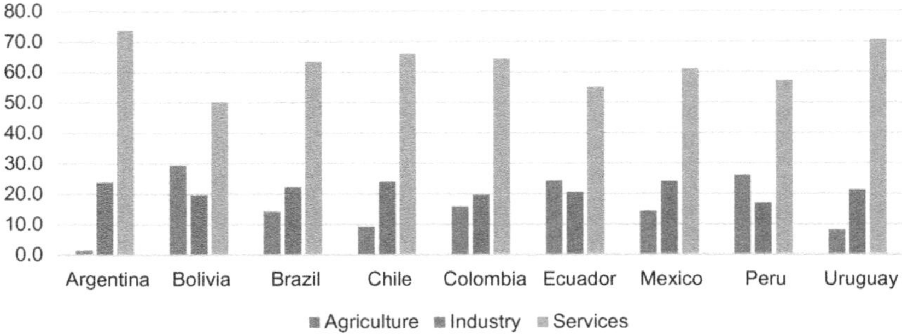

Fig. 3.1 Structure of total occupied population, by main sector of economic activity (2014) (*Source* Own elaboration based on Cepalstat)

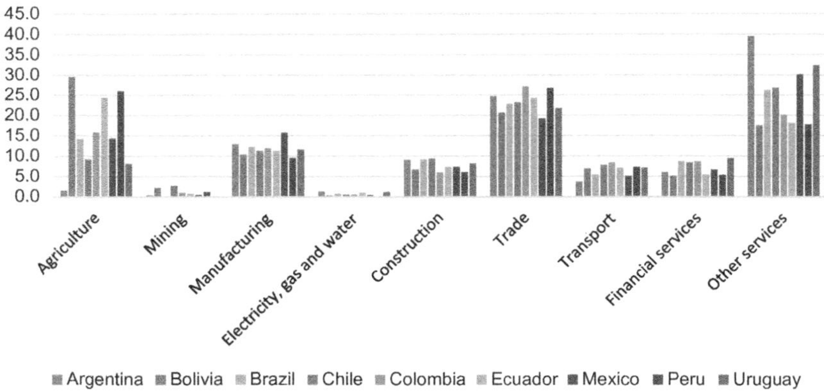

Fig. 3.2 Structure of total employed population, by main sector of economic activity (2014) (*Source* Own elaboration based on Cepalstat)

than 50% of the total. When we look at the countries that we consider as developmentalist, Brazil and Argentina, although commodities amount to less than 50%, they are thus still considerably high, however these countries are more diversified: in fact, in the case of Argentina, the second exporting product is trucks and the sixth cars, with 5.8 and 4.6% of the total exports, respectively. Unexpectedly, in the case of Brazil, no manufacturing product is in the six principal exporting products, which may be a result of what the critics of developmentalism in this country (Bresser-Pereira, Salama, Marques Pereira and Bruno) have called premature de-industrialization. These data can lead us to affirm that all the countries of Latin America are to a lesser or higher degree rentier. This with the exception of Mexico that exports mainly manufactured products; after its first exporting product, oil at around 9% of the total, the rest are cars, car parts, and electronic devices. However, the Mexican State, which until 2015 had the monopoly of oil exploitation, is definitely rentier as it depends heavily on the resources of oil exports.

On the other hand, Mexico's conversion into a manufacturing power and the continuous growth of this sector of the economy is due to the arrival of an increasing amount of subsidiaries that supply with spare parts the main foreign enterprises installed in the country, especially in the automobile and electronics industries. While most Mexican analysts have signaled low salaries and low social protection costs as the main pull factor for FDI, according to the UNCTAD, **nearshoring** is a very significant element due to the advantage of "…bringing products into the United States market more quickly." This factor is "… boosted by the rapid growth of labor costs in China and the volatility of rising fuel costs, which have made the shipment of goods across the Pacific less attractive" (UNCTAD 2013: 61). The UNCTAD considers that the exchange rate is … "an additional factor, with the yuan's appreciation against the dollar and euro in the past several years." Significantly, the Mexican growth is heteronomous; it is mainly due to the interests of the MNC to complete their supply chains and can thus be shaken up by external factors over which the Mexican government has no control. On the other hand, as manufacturing in Mexico is merely the last link of a global supply chain which is specialized in adding labor and low added value activities, "Mexico still lags behind China in terms of location choice for manufacturing. China offers the important advantage of deeper supply chains than Mexico, where international companies have trouble finding local suppliers for parts and even for packaging. Unlike in China, where the Government identifies 'pillar industries' and supports them, smaller companies in Mexico that are eager to start or grow businesses and establish linkages with foreign companies, suffer from a lack of affordable access to financing" (UNCTAD 2013: 62).

If we now look at the composition of the exports (Fig. 3.3), we have a similar image. The rentier countries, represented here by Colombia, export mostly raw materials, up to 60%, some intermediary goods, and finally consumer goods, almost no capital goods are exported. On the other side of the spectrum, Mexico exports mostly capital goods (around 50% of the total), as we have seen cars, car parts, and electronic

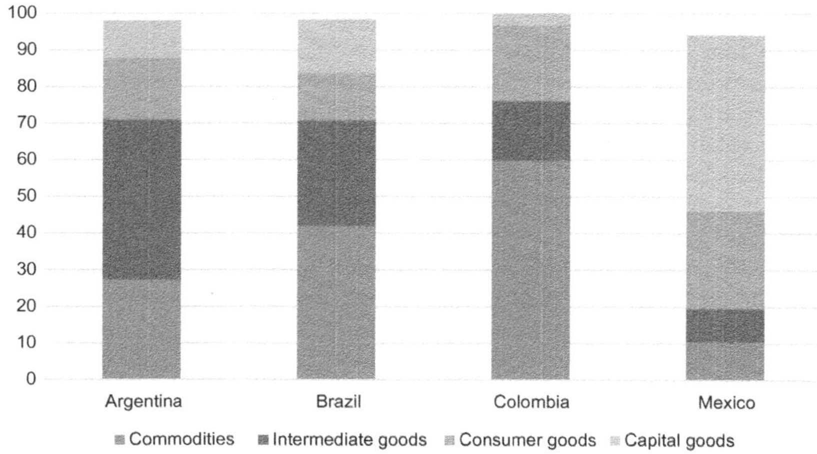

Fig. 3.3 Structural composition of exports (*Source* Own elaboration based on the Atlas of economic complexity/Harvard University)

equipment, consumer goods, as well as a low proportion of intermediary goods and raw materials. The other two countries that we have called developmentalist, have a different composition of their exports—a very large amount of raw materials for both Brazil and Argentina, intermediary goods that are the majority of what Argentina exports, and a lesser amount of consumer and capital goods that are the most valuable in terms of value added. This graph gives a fairly clear difference between these three types of economies.

Other data, founded on whether exports and imports are based on natural resources, labor intensive, scale intensive, engineering-science based, constructed according to the criteria of Nassif et al. (2015), regarding the composition of exports and imports, give us a similar picture. While the rentier countries (that are not included) mainly export products based on natural resources, and some that are labor intensive, in Fig. 3.4, where we have the case of Mexico and Brazil, we can see that only Mexico exports a significant proportion of products that are scale intensive and engineering-science based. This figure also allows us to discover a very significant characteristic of the Mexican productive structure which is that the country simultaneously exports scale intensive and engineering science-based products and imports these kind of products in an even larger proportion. This can be interpreted as the proof that what the Mexican

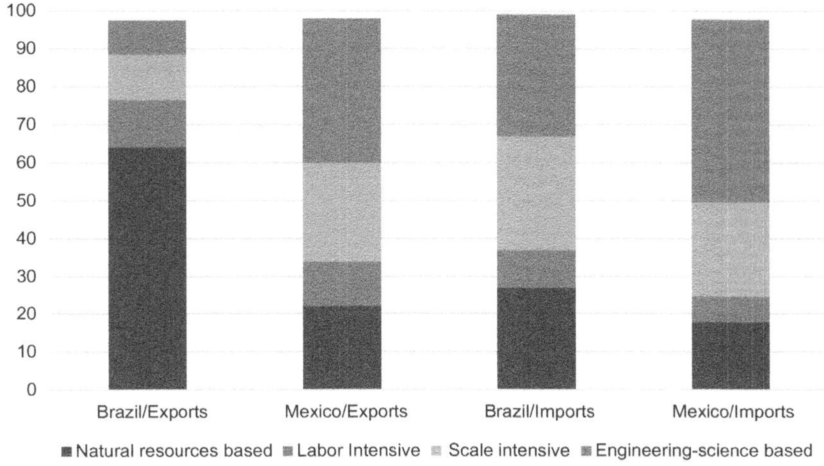

Fig. 3.4 Proportion of exports and imports by type of product (*Source* Own elaboration based on the Atlas of economic complexity/Harvard University)

industry does is import most of the more sophisticated products, assembles and re-exports them. In the case of Brazil, analysts that have discussed the mode of development this country implemented during the beginning of the 2000s have concluded that the end result has been an ever-growing dependence of this country on natural resource-based exports, larger than that of the 1980s and 1990s, something that seems evident in this same graph (Table 3.4).

In fact, the next tables show how until 1980 (Table 3.5) and even until the mid-1990s (Table 3.6), Brazil was more advanced than Mexico both in terms of the proportion of value added in manufacture and of the type of value added. And in fact, manufacturing industry was quite stronger in Brazil than in Mexico at the end of the 1970s, before the crisis that hit all of Latin America. The Brazilian manufacturing sector had increased its share from 1947 to 1980 from 19.3 to 31.3%. In the 1970s, it grew considerably, by 5% (Nassif et al. 2015: 1313). This in contrast to what happened in both Mexico and Argentina. In Mexico, during the 1970s, not only manufacturing did not grow, but it slightly reduced its weight, going from 26.1 to 25.1%. Another indicator of the strength that the Brazilian manufacturing sector had achieved in the wake of the crisis is that while in 1964 the percentage of manufactures in exports

Table 3.4 Value added composition, year 1994

	Argentina	*Brazil*	*Chile*	*Colombia*	*Mexico*	*Peru*
Value added composition	%	%	%	%	%	%
Intensive in engineering (metal mechanics / electro-electronics)	17.6	23.8	8.6	10.6	12.6	5.2
Transportation equipment	13.4	8.7	2.0	6.7	11.1	3.6
Subtotal	**31.0**	**32.5**	**10.6**	**16.3**	**23.7**	**8.8**
Intensive in labor	22.3	20.7	19.7	25.5	20.7	31.0
Intensive in natural resources	46.7	46.8	69.7	57.2	55.6	60.2
Total	**100**	**100**	**100**	**100**	**100**	**100**
Structural change index	0.31	0.31	0.65	0.36	0.31	0.68

Source PADI Industrial Dynamics Analysis Program from Cepal [https://www.cepal.org/software/padi/padinuevo.ppt]

Table 3.5 Value added of manufacture (%GDP)

Country	*1960*	*1970*	*1980*	*1990*	*2000*	*2010*
Mexico[a]	20.2	26.1	25.1	23.4	22.9	20.4
Brazil[b]	25.6	27.4	31.3	20.7	17.2	14.6

Sources
[a]Romero Tellaeche (2014: 89)
[b]Nassif et al. (2015: 1314)

in Brazil was 14%, it had reached 57% by 1980 (Nassif et al. 1316). In contrast, Mexico's manufacturing exports amounted to around 25% of the total in the 1980s (Romero Tellaeche 2014: 30) and began booming in the 1990s with NAFTA. Another indicator of the advance of the Brazilian manufacturing industry with regard to the Mexican, up

Table 3.6 Value added composition (1970–1994)

	Argentina			*Brazil*			*Mexico*		
	1970	*1990*	*1994*	*1970*	*1990*	*1994*	*1970*	*1990*	*1994*
Value added composition	%	%	%	%	%	%	%	%	%
Intensive in engineering (metal mechanics/ electro-electronics)	15.6	14.3	17.6	18.8	22.9	23.8	13.3	12.3	12.6
Transportation equipment	9.9	8.5	13.4	9.9	7.0	8.7	5.5	9.5	11.1
Subtotal	**25.5**	**22.8**	**31.0**	**28.7**	**29.9**	**32.5**	**18.8**	**21.8**	**23.7**
Intensive in labor	30.6	24.1	22.3	26.5	24.2	20.7	26.5	22.5	20.7
Intensive in natural resources	43.9	53.1	46.7	44.8	45.9	46.8	54.7	55.7	55.6
Total	**100**	**100**	**100**	**100**	**100**	**100**	**100**	**100**	**100**

Source PADI Industrial Dynamics Analysis Program from CEPAL (https://www.cepal.org/software/padi/padinuevo.ppt)

until the middle of the 1990s, is the comparison between the composition of value added among manufactures with respect to their composition regarding engineering, labor, or natural resource components (Table 3.6). While until 1995 the proportion of Brazilian manufactures in engineering components was 32%, in the case of Mexico it was only 23.7%. All this to say that at the wake of the crisis that began with the Mexican default on its debt in 1982, Brazil's manufacturing industry was much stronger, diversified and competitive than the Mexican one, as can be seen comparing both tables.

++

The divergence of the trajectory of Mexico, Brazil, and Argentina in the 1970s and 1980s. If we go back to the period of import substitution industrialization, we can see that although the three main countries that industrialized the most followed similar trajectories, there were already significant differences between them before the 1990s, when ISI was abandoned. Since the mid-1980s, there was a bifurcation of the trajectories of Mexico that abandoned completely ISI; Brazil that continued with ups and downs; and Argentina that oscillated between an open economy and a developmentalist one (Bizberg and Théret 2012).

In effect, when in the 1970s, Latin America faced one of its recurrent balance of payments crises, Brazil and Mexico started to diverge. While Brazil continued to industrialize up to the mid-1980s and has de-industrialized since the 1990s, as it turned to commodities, Mexico de-industrialized in the 1970s and 1980s, and then reversed trajectory under an outsourcing model during the last three decades. Brazil, then governed by the military, who based their legitimacy on continuous economic growth, adopted import substitution of intermediary and capital goods in order to reduce its external dependence. Mexico's fate was to find vast oil reserves and become an important exporter. Although during the 70s the Mexican State also tried to deepen import substitution, investing in steel and heavy industry, such as railcars and machinery, it discovered huge reserves of oil that made it possible to opt the "easy way." This fact, together with the huge amounts of external credit the Mexican government acquired, allowed the governments of the PRI to delay the transformation of its import substitution scheme (Pereira and Théret 2004).

There was also a political rationale for this decision. Mexico arrived to the 1970s under the PRI regime, a civilian-authoritarian regime that depended on its control of the popular organizations and its revolutionary legitimacy. It was an inclusionary-authoritarian-corporatist regime in contrast to the military-exclusionary regimes of the Southern Cone. Due to the challenge posed by the student movement in the late 1960s and the labor movement in the early 1970s, the regime was more concerned with political stability than with the viability of the economic system (Bizberg 2004). The discovery of oil reserves and the possibility of acquiring debt seemed to be a perfect solution to the dilemma of how to deepen the import substitution model, while continuing to redistribute and give concessions to its protected entrepreneurs. Although the Mexican State tried to do both, it basically ended up doing the latter while expanding its oil exporting platform and its debt. Because the Mexican State set distribution rather than economic growth as its priority during the 1970s, its economic structure and its dependence on oil and debt became stronger, leading to a very fragile situation in 1982 that obliged it to abandon its role as an actor of development much more radically than the Brazilian State did.

The 1982 crisis put the industrial bases of the Latin American countries again at stake. In the case of Mexico, it disclosed the weakness of its industrial base and the fragility of a redistributive mode based on oil exports and debt. When in 1981 oil prices plunged and interest rates soared, Mexico suspended payments on its debt and recurred to the IMF that imposed draconian measures. The financial catastrophe and the recipes of the international financial institution convinced many of the Mexican leaders that the country had to abandon import substitution and orient its economy toward the external market. In the span of one *sexenio*, Mexico radically opened its economy and abandoned industrial policy with practically no social or political opposition. The new export-led growth model led to an exceptional expansion of the *maquiladora* industry and the assimilation of other exporting industries to outsourcing, once the government abandoned the idea of enhancing the integration of local production to sectors dominated by foreign capital, thinking that this would happen automatically under the pressure of the market forces.

This model directed Mexico to a process of increasing its proportion of manufacturing exports, although with a rationale that did not integrate productive chains but on the contrary destroyed them (Dussel Peters 2006). A process some have named export substitution, where products that were exported beforehand are now imported, such as textiles, toys, while other products that were imported, such as cars, electronic devices, are now exported, but where the components of these products are imported.

Brazil followed the contrary path. The economic scheme implemented by the military was accelerated growth with no wealth distribution (Hermann 2005a). This mode of growth reached its limits at the beginning of the 1980s when the financial international context reversed (Hermann 2005b). At that moment, Brazil had to depend on its own resources in order to confront the disequilibrium created by economic growth under extremely unequal wealth distribution. This situation eventually led to rampant hyperinflation as the redistributive conflict could not be controlled in the context of a democratization process where social forces were very active and had no intention of accepting to pay for the adjustment (Pereira and Théret 2004). The divergence between both countries reversed in the 1990s and 2000, in part due to the re-primarization of the Brazilian economy, but also because, with NAFTA, Mexico became an exporter of manufactured products, with an ever higher content of technology.

In contrast to both of these countries, Argentina abandoned import substitution in 1978 (Canelo 2009), a situation that endured until the beginning of the years 2000. The military that ruled Argentina from 1976 to 1983 had as their main purpose to extricate popular pressure from politics in order to "depoliticize" the State. The fact that the labor movement in both countries was deeply entrenched in the political system explains in part the virulence of the military as well as the predominance of political over economic rationale. The Argentinean military opened the economy, reduced the weight of the State, and limited redistribution. Argentina responded to the balance of payments crisis of the 1970s with the imposition of a new economic model (for Argentina: Rapoport and Collaborators 2005: 600–701).

****

We will talk further ahead on the reasons of this evolution, suffice it for now to mention the fact that many countries in Latin America suffered a re-primarization process, provoked by the increased demand of raw materials by China. Something that had a significant impact on the rentier countries who deepened their dependence on these products, while in the case of the more industrialized countries, they reversed course: most notably Brazil and Argentina.

Nonetheless, we have to tone down what we have been saying up to now. In the first place, exports do not express what happens to the whole internal production, especially in a country the size of Brazil. Although its exports and to a certain extent its economy in general have been increasingly dominated by commodities, only 8.8% of the value added of the Brazilian economy is dependent on agriculture, mining, and oil extraction. Thus, in contrast to the rentier countries, most notably Bolivia, Chile, Ecuador, and Peru, exports do not define what happens with the entire economy of this country, it is more differentiated. The same can be said of Argentina and to a certain extent of Colombia. This is the reason why we can see that, although moderate, there has been a growth of manufacturing in all these countries. Nonetheless, Mexican and Brazilian manufacturing growth has been very slow, and in the case of the latter, it has been slowly descending from 2010 onward. In the case of the rentier countries, growth of the manufacturing production is an effect of the surge of commodities, its consequence on the growth of internal demand, and the fact of the low industrial base of these countries, more than a catch-up effect of industrialization. The country that saw the highest increase in manufacturing production was Argentina, due to the very great devaluation of its currency resulting from the end of convertibility and the boost of internal demand, together with the under-utilized installed industrial capacity due to the deep economic crisis of the beginning of the years 2000, but also as a result of industrial policies that oriented manufacturing toward new *niches* (Santarcángelo et al. 2017) (Fig. 3.5).

In the case of Mexico, it is necessary to make it clear that the boom of exports has not been accompanied by a significant increase in GDP growth, as the export platform is disconnected from the rest of the economy; it is in many respects an enclave. In fact, exports have grown continuously faster than the rest of the economy. This is evident if we consider that the rate of investment in Mexico is low, less than 20% of GDP annually (Ibarra 2008; Puyana and Romero Tellaeche 2009;

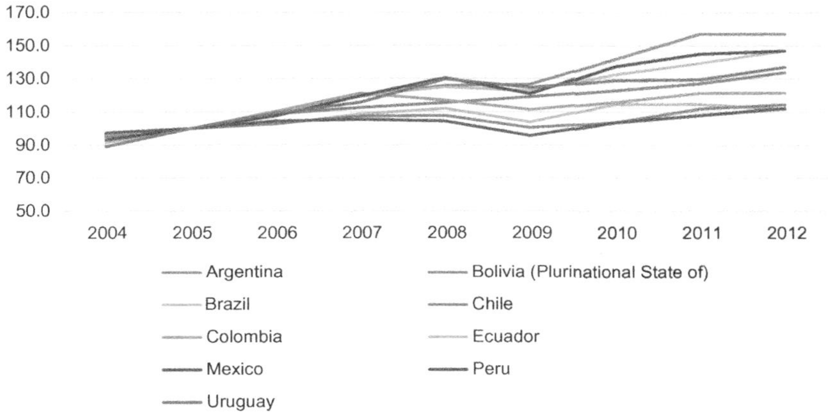

Fig. 3.5 Manufacturing production index (*Source* Own elaboration based on Cepalstat)

Guillen Romo 2012). If we look again at Fig. 3.4, although Brazil also has a low investment rate, similar to the one of Mexico, it imports 30% of engineering science-based products that include machinery and other capital equipment. While the differential between capital exports and imports in Mexico is 10%, in Brazil it is 20%, meaning either a higher amount of acquisition of equipment in the latter or imports of higher value added. In the case of Mexico, due to the advantages of NAFTA and its regional content rules, many companies that assemble in Mexico have recently set up plants of their suppliers in the country.

Figure 3.8, further down, is very clear in this respect. We can notice how, in the case of Mexico, the backward linkages are very dependent on imports, up to 32%, the highest in Latin America, similar to other outsourcing countries of Asia: Malaysia, Thailand, Vietnam, and China. Although the indicators for China and Mexico are similar, they just say a small part of the story, because while in Mexico this integration to the international chain has had no impact on upgrading the economy, the way in which the Chinese State has imposed its rules to international companies has led to a very successful and rapid upgrading process. China is partly an outsourcing platform like Mexico or the other countries of Asia we have mentioned, however it is fast becoming a very successful manufacturing country producing high technological products like planes, trains, satellites, and robots. In fact, even Brazil, which in this same graph looks like an economy that has a very low integration to international value chains, has a number of high-tech sectors like aeronautics (it is home of the third largest exporter of commercial airplanes: Embraer), oil drilling (it is one of the specialists in the exploitation of deep water oil wells), and biotechnology (one of the first producers, with India, of generic medicines and an innovator in the use of sugarcane to produce fuel) (Schneider 2013).

3.2 Mode of Production

In Fig. 3.6, we see that productivity in Latin America has grown, in general terms, very slowly. As a consequence, the gap (Fig. 3.7) between these countries and the developed economies and certain developing countries like India and China continues to be very large. According to the regulation theory, while a rentier economy bases its growth on extension, as it does not depend on innovation and modification of the techniques of production, other capitalistic forms depend on the intensity of production, on the increase of productivity and innovation (Boyer 2015: 63).

This may be explained by the fact that, to a certain degree, all Latin American economies are either principally or partly rentier: the case of oil and other mining products in the case of Mexico; of agricultural, mining, and oil in the case of Brazil; of agriculture in the case of Argentina.

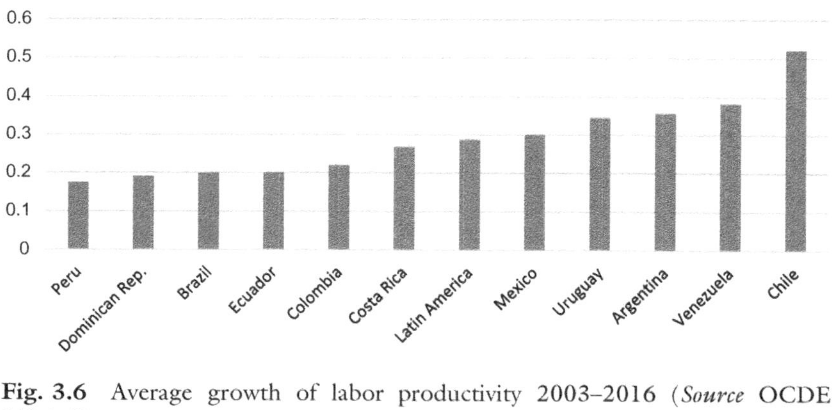

Fig. 3.6 Average growth of labor productivity 2003–2016 (*Source* OCDE 2016: 2)

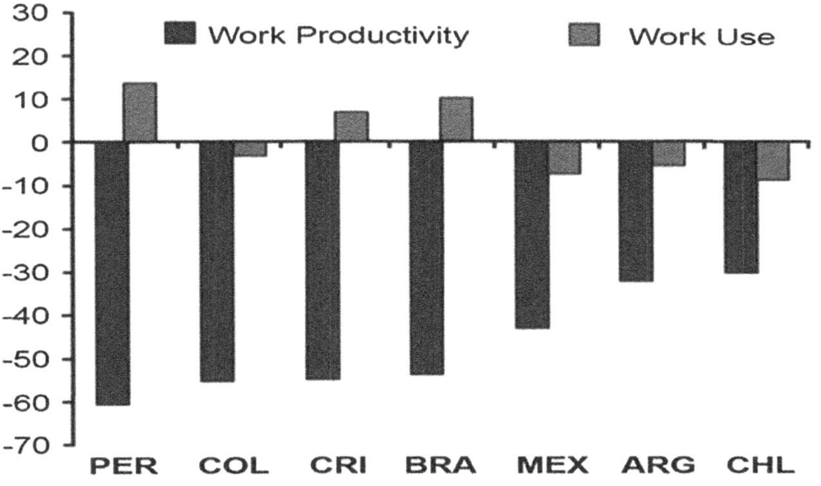

Fig. 3.7 Percentage difference of productivity with the OECD average, 2013 (*Source* OCDE 2016: 2)

Finance can also be considered a rentier activity, and this is the case in Mexico, Brazil, Argentina, and Chile; all of them have a very high proportion of value added due to financial intermediation (Boyer 2015). On the other hand, because the international outsourcing capitalism is a manufacturing model that is highly dependent on imports of the most sophisticated and higher value added parts, productivity growth is low; Mexico has had the lowest productivity growth of all Latin America. It thus also depends more on extension of investment than on innovation and productivity increases. The difference between these three countries and the fully rentier economies is that in Mexico, Brazil, and Argentina there exist "islands" of highly productive sectors, like the automobile in Mexico, airplane, biotechnology, and oil drilling in Brazil, automobile and agrochemicals in Argentina; while the rentier economies are almost totally dependent on an extensive mode of production.

In addition to productivity, the manner in which each productive structure is linked to the global value chains is another very significant indicator of the productive structure, of the mode of production. While a country like Mexico is closely integrated to the global value chains, because it is very open, it is nonetheless integrated with very low internal added value. Other countries, we have considered as developmentalist, are less integrated, because their productive structure is more oriented toward their internal markets, such as Brazil and Argentina in Latin America, and India and Turkey in Asia. It is also true that the rentier countries are less integrated to the global value chains because they only export commodities. "These countries may have lower upstream participation levels, both because of the nature of their exports (natural resources and services exports tend to have less need for imported content or foreign value added) and because larger economies display a greater degree of self-sufficiency in production for exports. They may also have lower downstream participation levels because of a focus on exports of so-called final-demand goods and services, i.e., those not used as intermediates in exports to third countries" (UNCTAD 2013: 134).

In the case of Mexico, in the same way as Costa Rica and other outsourcing economies, the foreign value added is very high because they must import essential inputs of the manufactures that they export, which they do not produce. "While developing countries (25 per cent) have a lower share of foreign value added than the world average (28 per cent), their foreign value added share is significantly higher than in the United States and Japan – or than in the EU, if only external trade is taken into account. Among developing economies, the highest shares of foreign value added in trade are found in East and South-East Asia and in Central America (including Mexico), where processing industries account for a significant part of exports. Foreign value added in exports is much lower in Africa, West Asia, South America and in the transition economies, where natural resources and commodities exports with little foreign inputs tend to play an important role. The lowest share of foreign value added in exports is found in South Asia, mainly due to the weight of services exports, which also use relatively fewer foreign inputs" (UNCTAD 2013: 126).

Another study done by the OECD, that also goes beyond a simple index of integration of a country in the global value chains in order to characterize the specificities of this integration, considers two forms of value chain integration: backward and forward participation in GVC. While a high backward participation index means a high level of integration of imported products and thus less national added value, high forward integration means high integration of domestic products into exports and thus a higher domestic added value (see Fig. 3.8).

This study mentions that Mexico and Costa Rica, as well as other Central American countries, which we have considered within the

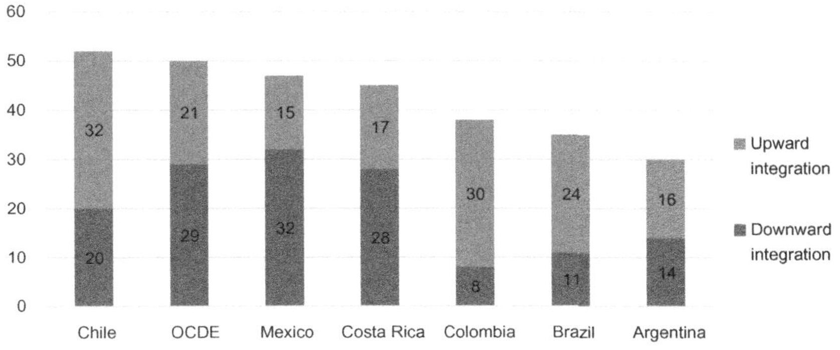

Fig. 3.8 Upward and downward integration into global value chains of some Latin American countries. In percentages of national exports, 2011. *Note* The downward integration corresponds to the foreign value-added incorporated in a country's exports; the upward integration, to the domestic value-added that is used in the exports of other countries (*Source* OCDE 2016: 4)

outsourcing model, are countries that have a strong backward, but weak forward participation; this is because they are specialized in exporting manufactures constituted of intermediate parts that are assembled in the country (Cadestin et al. 2016: 15). For Mexico, "...foreign content is particularly high in exports of computer, electronic, electrical and optical equipment, vehicles and transport machinery and other manufacturing sectors; foreign content accounts for more than 50% of gross exports and exceeds the rest-of-the world averages" (ibid.: 17). This is an average figure, but in some cases, such as the *maquiladora* industry, that constitute around 60% of all Mexican exports, foreign content is even higher, of more than 95% (Ibarra 2008). Even in the automotive industry, although the suppliers have relocated their production in Mexico as inter-industrial integration is very high (Mendoza Cota 2011) and they can take advantage of NAFTA, imports of intermediate parts are significant and the integration of domestic production is very low, between 10 and 25%, according to Manuel Montoya Ortega, director of Automobile cluster of Nuevo León,[1] although other authors consider it to be around 50%. One of the reasons of this situation is that "...very few, if any, of

[1] http://www.elfinanciero.com.mx/empresas/necesaria-mayor-integracion-nacional-en-industria-automotriz.html.

the SMEs in the second and third tiers have been able to leverage their links to GVCs as springboards for their own internationalization. Market pressures and the introduction of international standards do encourage suppliers to improve both product and processes when they first join GVCs, but the use of modularization (driving suppliers to produce standardized components) limits access for the lower-tier suppliers to the new information, knowledge and activities of assemblers and top-tier suppliers" (UNCTAD 2013: 161).

In fact, what happens in the case of Mexico is that "the value added of indirect exports – or supplier firms contributing domestic value added to exporters – remains predominantly with other TNCs located in host economies. For instance, the automotive industry, where lead firms develop close and complex relationships with suppliers, is characterized by mega-suppliers that can co-locate and co-produce with their customers on a global scale, taking prime responsibility for selecting and coordinating lower-tier suppliers. As a result, domestic value added may occur predominantly among TNCs. Evidence of TNC dominance in specific industry segments was found mostly among first-tier suppliers in the automotive industry, e.g., in the Czech Republic and in Colombia," and in this same industry and most others that dominate the productive structure of Mexico (UNCTAD 2013: 153).

In contrast to this outsourcing model, Brazil and Argentina "…record lower than average backward GVC participation across the majority of the sectors examined" (ibid.: 17). While backward linkages for Mexico and Costa Rica amount to 32% and 28% of foreign value added, respectively, for Brazil and Argentina backward linkages amount to 11% and 14% value added, respectively. Whereas the exports of China have a similar value added content than those of Mexico, however, as many studies have mentioned, this country is undergoing a fast upgrading process, while Mexico is not. Developed countries exports contain a similar value added content than that of Brazil or Argentina: USA-CAN (13%) and Japan (15%). The case of the European countries is interesting as the foreign content of their exports is much higher, similar to the Mexican, around 25%, which is explained by the effect of the European integration, as the countries of Europe incorporate spare parts from a great number of countries. Airbus airplanes are a good example: they are assembled in Toulouse with components coming principally from France, Germany, Spain, Italy and Great Britain.

While the domestic value added of the consumer products being expended internaly or exported by Mexico is known to be very low in most sectors, especially in household appliances, as they are mainly imported from China, in Brazil, the domestic value added of this sector is higher: the total share of domestic value added in the Brazilian household appliances is 61%. This is explained by the UNCTAD study: "... the Brazilian household appliances originates from within the industry—i.e., within the producing firm itself or from suppliers within the same industry—... In this industry, suppliers produce a variety of steel (semi-fabricates, laminates, bars and tubes), plastic or paper products, and the services sector accounts for 14 per cent of value added (providing business services, finance and insurance, information services and freight transport)" (UNCTAD 2013: 153). Another explanation of Brazil's relatively low downward integration rates in GVC is that, like other larger economies, such as India, Argentina, and Turkey, as well as the rentier countries, it exports high quantities of commodities which are used as intermediaries by third countries.

Finally, the rentier Latin American countries, but probably those of other continents too, have a rather low foreign content and a high forward participation: Chile (20% and 32%, respectively) and Colombia (8% and 30%, respectively) (see Fig. 3.8). This situation is due to the fact that they export few finished products, and they merely export raw materials. Thus, their integration in the world market results in little added value coming from the exterior, but on the contrary a high added value that is integrated by the exports of other countries.

Although in terms of productivity growth we were not able to find a clear relation between rentier, outsourcing, and developmentalist capitalisms, the relation between added value and these different types seems quite clear. While the outsourcing model has a high upward and low downward value added, the rentier economies have a low downward and high upward value added. What is common to both is their dependence on foreign value added, in the case of the first, foreign value that is added to its exports, and in the second, national value that is added by third countries. One may extrapolate both of these situations as extensive growth, because they depend on the expansion of investment rather than on innovation. The developmentalist mode is more internally oriented, less added value by foreign investment, thus more dependent on domestic investment, and possibly with more innovation and an intensive character of the growth regime, although this may not be necessarily so.

3.3 Mode of Consumption

Where the disparities between the different modes are definitely clear is in their mode of consumption. In the Latin American countries, and in peripheral capitalism in general, the mode of consumption previous to industrialization was definitely profit led, as it hinged on the appropriation of rent on the part of an oligarchy (in general an agricultural one). During ISI, a different mode of accumulation was intended; on the one hand, with industrialization, a more intensive mode of production was implemented in the largest countries of the continent. Concordantly, a different form of consumption was set up, based on redistribution through wages and social protection, a mode of consumption that led various authors to portray this mode of development as a peripheral or incomplete Fordism, as it only concerned a sector of workers of the economy and not their totality; nevertheless, the totality of workers was contemplated as its temporal horizon. Beginning with the lost decade, when import substitution was abandoned, a bifurcation of the trajectory of the different countries in the continent began that hinged on whether the proto-fordist model was totally abandoned or in partially preserved.

Some countries abandoned ISI to become producers of commodities, as they had been before industrialization. This situation included countries that had only faintly industrialized (Bolivia and Ecuador) or that had industrialized to a certain degree, but then deeply de-industrialized (Colombia and Peru). They specialized even more decidedly in the extraction of raw materials with the commodities super cycle led by the demand of China and India, in the first decade of the twenty-first century. Other countries became outsourcing platforms: mostly in Central America and one large country, Mexico. Finally, some countries tried to continue developing their industry: Brazil and Argentina, with mixed results. More related to the consumption mode, the countries that abandoned ISI completely also instituted a profit-led consumption mode, because they opted for an external market growth that required them to attract foreign investment. The countries that did not dismantle ISI completely (Brazil), or those that tried to retrieve this mode of development after the meltdown of their export-led economy (Argentina), tested a mixed model, combining internal and external market growth, and a wage (or redistributive)-led growth; or more exactly a compromise between wages and profits. The countries that abandoned ISI and became commodities exporting economies, imposed either a profit-led (Chile,

Peru, and Colombia) or a partial wage-led consumption mode (Bolivia and Ecuador). In the case of the developmentalist economies, the choice of wages vs profits was due to both an economic project based on the growth of the domestic market and the existence of an autonomous and active civil society, while in the case of the rentier economies a redistributive policy was the result of the upsurge of civil society, as we will discuss in Chapters 6 and 7.

The data on the wage share of GDP (Fig. 3.9) allows us to clearly distinguish between a mode of consumption based on profits and one based on wages. While the countries upon which we have based our formalization of socio-developmentalism (Argentina, Brazil, Uruguay) and Ecuador, among the rentier redistributive capitalisms, have seen this share grow, on the contrary Mexico, as well as the rest of the Central American countries that we have considered as outsourcing, and the rentier liberal Peru and Colombia, have seen how the wage share has practically plummeted. The case of Chile is interesting because although it is definitely a profit-led economy, it has managed to maintain stable the proportion between wages and profits; this is probably due to the fact that its economy has grown almost continuously and with little

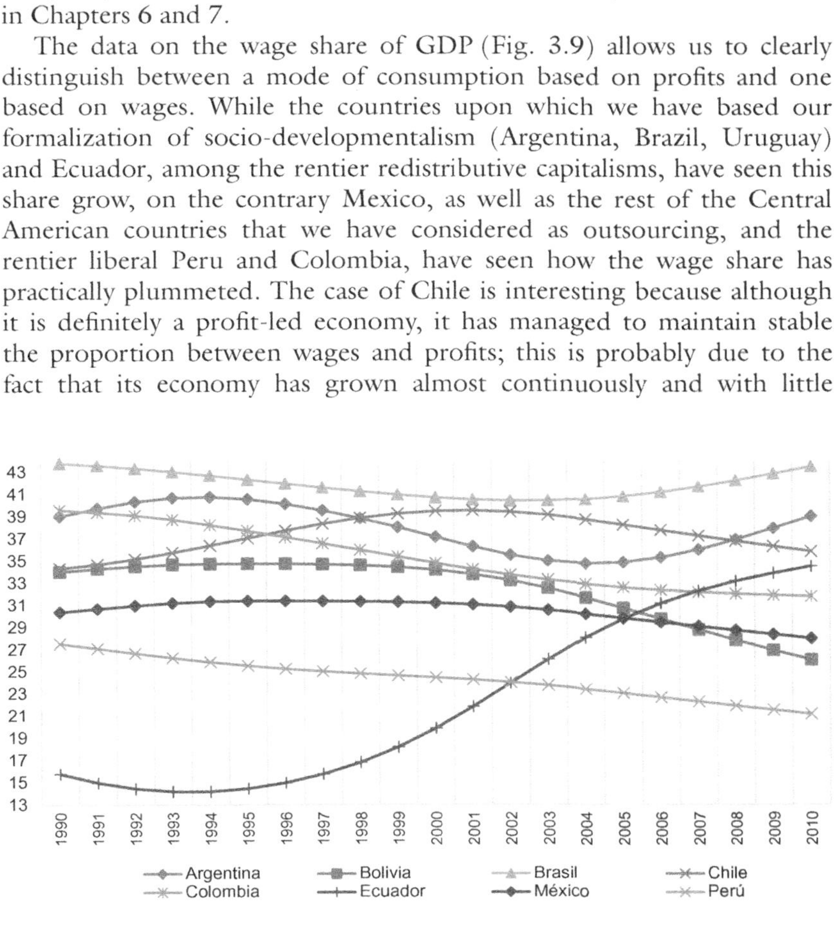

Fig. 3.9 Share of wages in GDP, 1990–2010 (*Source* Elaborated by Daniel Cerdas Sandí on the basis of the original data base of Alarco Tosoni, Germán, 2014)

inflation during the last 30 years; they have also reduced poverty and informality from 15% to 2%, and from 37% to 28%, respectively, since the 1990s (Amitrano 2017). It is a profit-led model that has even achieved to reduce inequality, although it continues to be very high. The case of Bolivia is paradoxical; it is a redistributive rentier capitalism but the wage share has been dropping drastically, as in the liberal rentier countries. This may be explained by the fact that it is a country that is divided into a region that depends on rents distributed by the government, while in the eastern part of the country (the *media luna*) there exists a very successful agribusiness sector that concentrates wealth. On the other hand, in this country, as we will see more in detail in the next chapters of this book, social policies have greatly expanded, but are still assistentialist; they are mainly focalized monetary transfers, similar to those of Peru and Mexico. The countries that have implemented minimum pensions, expanded non-contributory pensions, and implemented universal health systems, like Brazil, Argentina and Chile have seen and increase in the share of wages in GDP.

A study done on the relation between redistribution and growth in Latin America between 1990 and 2010 comes to the same conclusions with respect to the countries that we have typified as wage and profit led. Amitrano considers that Brazil, Argentina, and Uruguay can be considered as wage-led, while Peru and Chile are profit-led economies. His study is less conclusive in the case of Colombia and Venezuela, that are borderlines (Amitrano 2017: 164).

Typically, a mode of accumulation such as Fordism which existed in the developed countries between the end of the world war and the mid-1970s, where wages followed closely increases in productivity, is a wage-led growth, a capitalist model based on the increase of domestic demand, while a liberal mode of development, such as the one that has been implemented since the demise of Fordism is a mode based on offer, a profit-led growth (as defined by Stockhammer 2011). Both Brazil and Argentina, in the first decade of the 2000s intended a wage-led growth that faltered because demand grew faster than domestic offer, and the multiplicator was transferred to the external market by way of imports. On the other hand, an international outsourcing capitalism, such as the one implemented in Mexico, is based on profits, as it is a mode that depends on the gap between productivity and salaries (Palma 2005), where government maintains a downward pressure on salaries and social

Fig. 3.10 Mode of accumulation/consumption (*Source* Own elaboration)

protection (as the are considered as costs), as they are the basis of its competitive advantage.

On the other hand, the rentier model can either promote the concentration of profits or redistribute them, through wages and social transfers, what we have called a liberal rentier capitalism versus a redistributive rentier capitalism. Both of these rentier types are fragile and heteronomous, as they depend wholly on the price and the demand of commodities, which are determined by the international market. On the other hand, because there isn't a coherent or proactive industrial policy, as we have seen in Bolivia and Ecuador, redistribution does not lead to a growth regime, but basically to demand that is channeled toward imports; the resources that are acquired through the export of commodities, directly by State enterprises or through taxes and royalties, lead to an increase in demand, which is met through imports. In the case of the rentier liberal model there is no redistribution, as the emphasis is on profits, which may or may not be invested in the country, depending on the decisions of capital; the government merely sets the conditions for this investment which may or may not have a positive result. Figure 3.10 illustrates the relation between the mode of accumulation and that of consumption for our four types of capitalism.

The relation between socio-developmentalism and a consumer mode oriented toward wages is clearly seen in the cases of Brazil, Argentina, and Uruguay, where minimum salaries increase well above productivity and mean salaries, as we will see in more detail in Chapter 8.

The promotion of wage growth by the State is evident as the minimum salaries (that the State controls, and that have an impact not only on wages, but also on pensions and monetary transfer programs that are based on minimum salaries) increase more rapidly than those which are defined through collective conventions. In fact, the intention to elevate minimum salaries over average salaries responded to a will to reduce inequality and to limit the impact of increasing demand on inflation. The only country where both minimum salaries and the mean salaries went up is Argentina, which is most probably explained by the force of the unions in this country, something we will be discussing in Chapter 6 (Figs. 3.11, 3.12 and 3.13).

The case of Bolivia is an example of a rentier distributive capitalism where real minimum salaries increase at a rate similar to those of the socio-developmentalist mode, although their effects on the economy are not significant in terms of increasing the production of higher added value goods, as one can see by the fact that productivity barely grows. The next four cases go in the direction we have mentioned above, three liberal rentier modes that, except for the case of Chile, are consistent with the idea that liberal types are profit oriented. The case of Peru is the clearest, with salaries (both mean and minimum) well below productivity, something that is coherent with what we saw above in the case of

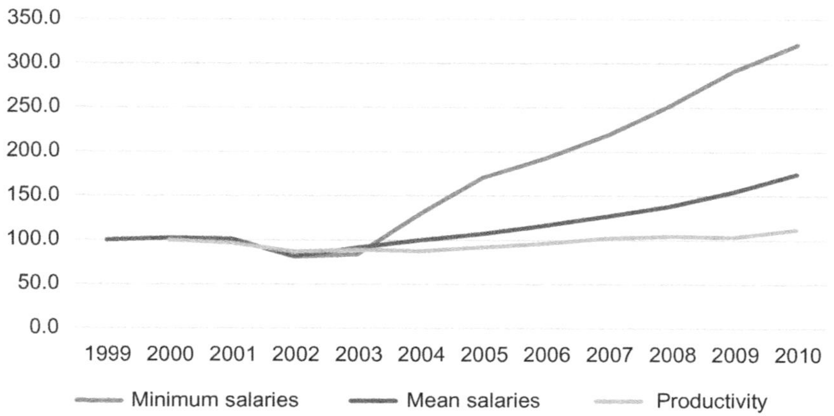

Fig. 3.11 Minimum salaries, mean salaries, and productivity. Argentina (*Source* Own elaboration on the basis of CEPALSTAT (salaries) and ILO (productivity))

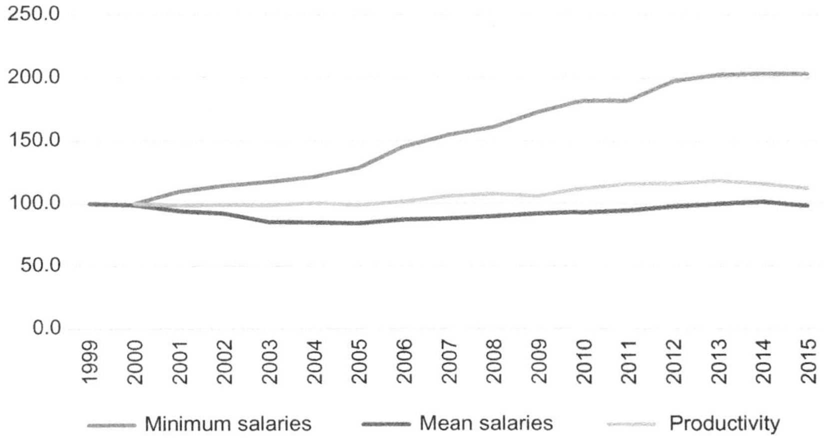

Fig. 3.12 Minimum salaries, mean salaries, and productivity. Brazil (*Source* Own elaboration on the basis of CEPALSTAT (salaries) and ILO (productivity))

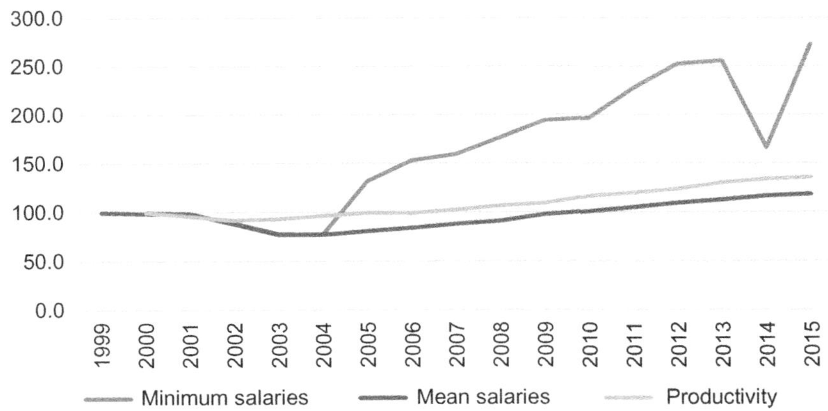

Fig. 3.13 Minimum salaries, mean salaries, and productivity. Uruguay (*Source* Own elaboration on the basis of CEPALSTAT (salaries) and ILO (productivity))

the participation of wages in GDP, that has been descending sharply in the last years, irrespective of the economic boom. Then, in Colombia, although productivity is not higher than salaries, they are very close to each other (Figs. 3.14, 3.15 and 3.16).

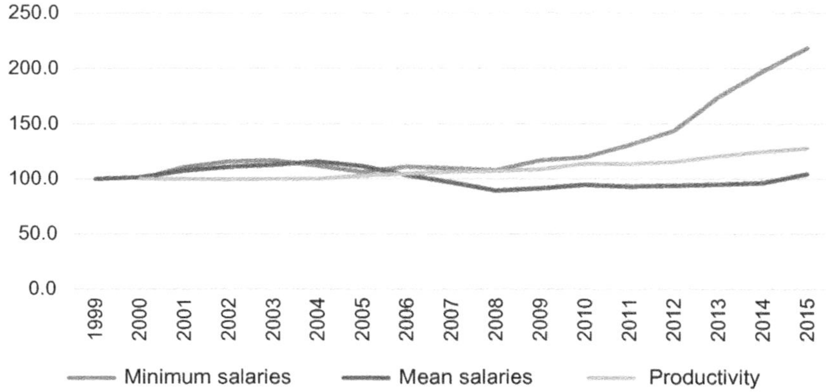

Fig. 3.14 Minimum salaries, mean salaries, and productivity. Bolivia (*Source* Own elaboration on the basis of CEPALSTAT (salaries) and ILO (productivity))

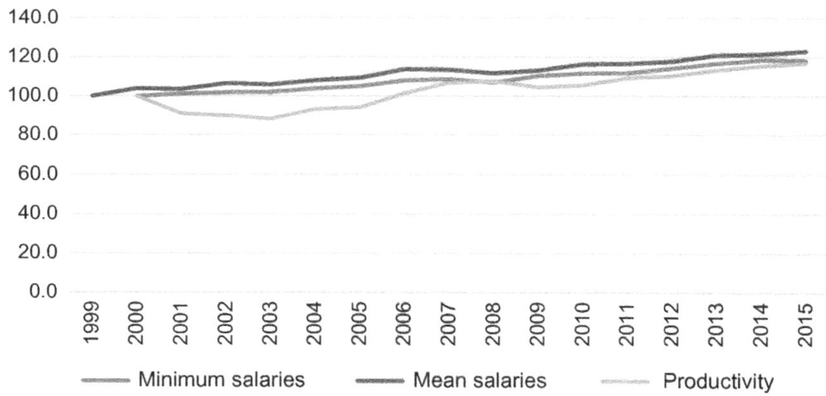

Fig. 3.15 Minimum salaries, mean salaries, and productivity. Colombia (*Source* Own elaboration on the basis of CEPALSTAT (salaries) and ILO (productivity))

The case of Mexico, an international outsourcing model, is based on what Palma has shown: although the general productivity is low, in some sectors it is very high. In fact, the gap between high productivity (to similar levels as those of the advanced economies) in certain exporting sectors (auto, auto parts, steel, petrochemicals) and relatively high (for the country) salaries in these same sectors, but low salaries with respect to

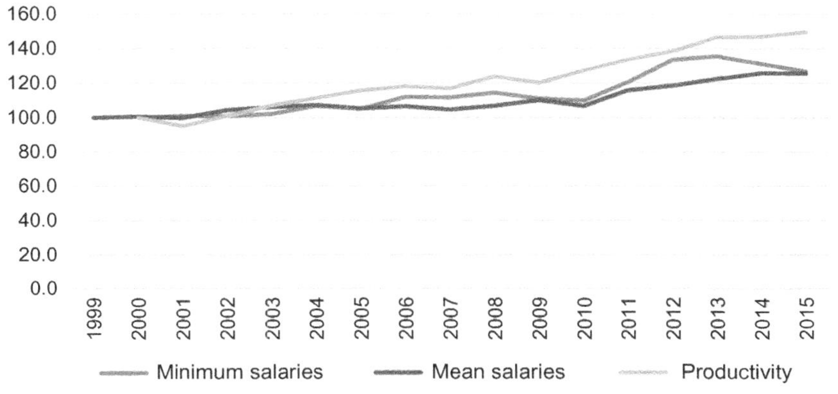

Fig. 3.16 Minimum salaries, mean salaries, and productivity. Peru (*Source* Own elaboration on the basis of CEPALSTAT (salaries) and ILO (productivity))

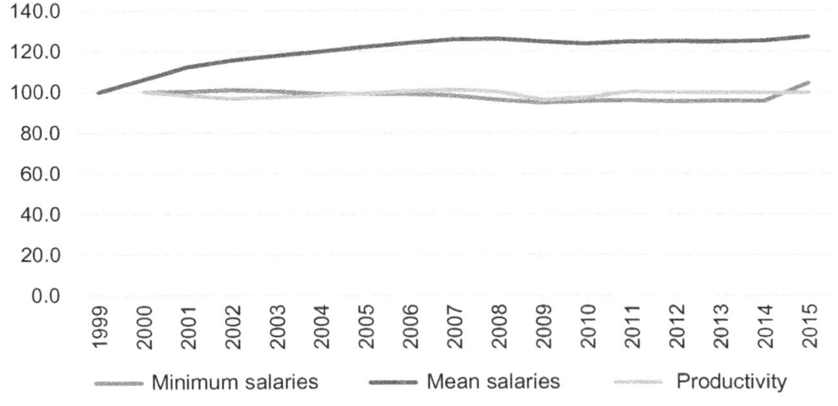

Fig. 3.17 Minimum salaries, mean salaries, and productivity. Mexico (*Source* Own elaboration on the basis of CEPALSTAT (salaries) and ILO (productivity))

the advanced economies where similar products are manufactured, gives the enterprises an exceptional competitive advantage (Palma 2005). The low minimum salaries are a way in which the State assures that the general wage levels remain low and that mean salaries are anchored although they rise faster (Fig. 3.17).

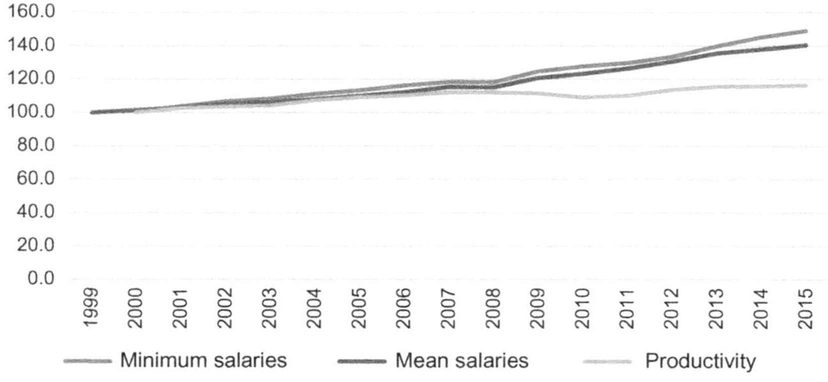

Fig. 3.18 Minimum salaries, mean salaries, and productivity. Chile (*Source* Own elaboration on the basis of CEPALSTAT (salaries) and ILO (productivity))

Finally, in Chile, growth of salaries is probably a direct effect of economic growth. Chile has been growing continuously for the last 30 years, and it has experienced a low of informal labor and of unemployment; salaries are thus a mechanic result of this process (Fig. 3.18).

As we will discuss in Chapter 6, the mode of consumption depends on the strength of the social actors (unions and social movements) and in their alliance with the State, on the embeddedness of the State and civil society, irrespective of what the countries produce and of their mode of production. Nonetheless, in the developmentalist economic model, redistribution is fundamental to increase the internal demand, so the pressure of the social actors coincides with a State-led project. While in those countries where civil society is strongly mobilized and/or organized, the mode of consumption is redistributive (Brazil, Argentina, Uruguay, Bolivia), in those countries where civil society is weak, they are profit led (Mexico, Chile, Peru, Colombia).

In Mexico, and in general in the outsourcing economies, not only the mode of accumulation is disarticulated between the parent companies and the subsidiaries, between the production of the parts and their assembly, but the consumption mode is equally disarticulated. In the case of Mexico, its economy depends heavily on the remittances sent by around the equivalent of 10% of the population that has migrated and of other resources coming from all kinds of illegal activities, including drug smuggling to the USA, It also depends on cheap imported consumer products that are sold by the informal economy which are able to maintain low prices because they do not pay taxes, nor salaries (most enterprises are familiar firms), a rent for the local as they sell in the street; an economy that is complementary to the formal one.

References

Alarco Tosoni, G. (2014). Participación salarial y crecimiento económico en América Latina, 1950–2011. *Revista CEPAL* (113), 43–60.

Amitrano, R. C. (2017). Income distribution, productive structure and growth in South America. *Panoeconomicus, 64*(2), 139–168.

Amsden, A. H. (2001). *The rise of "the rest" challenges to the West from late-industrializing economies*. New York: Oxford University Press.

Bizberg, I. (2004). Trayectorias políticas e institucionales de México y Brasil: el caso de las relaciones entre el Estado y el sindicalismo. In C. Alba Vega & I. Bizberg (Coord.), *Democracia y globalización en México y Brasil*. Mexico: El Colegio de México.

Bizberg, I., & Théret, B. (2012). La diversité des capitalismes latino-américains: les cas de l'Argentine, du Brésil et du Mexique. *La Revue de la Régulation* (11). Paris. http://journals.openedition.org/regulation/9658; https://doi.org/10.4000/regulation.9658.

Boyer, R. (2015). *Économie politique des capitalismes, Théorie de la régulation et des crises*. Paris: La Découverte Editions.

Bresser-Pereira, L. C. (2012). Os trés ciclos da sociedade e do estado. *Perspectivas, 41*, 13–51.

Canelo, P. (2009). La política contra la economía: los elencos militares frente al plan económico de Martinez Hoz durante el Proceso de Reorganización Nacional (1976–1981). In A. Pucciarelli (Ed.), *Empresarios, tecnócratas y militares. La trama corporativa de la última Dictadura*. Buenos Aires: Siglo XXI.

Cardoso, F. H., & Faletto, E. (1969). *Dependencia y Desarrollo en América latina*. México: Siglo XXI.

Cadestin, C., Gourdon, J., & Kowalski, P. (2016). *Participation in global value chains in Latin America: Implications for trade and trade-related policy* (OECD Trade Policy Papers, No. 192). Paris: OECD Publishing.

Dussel Peters, E. (2006). Hacia una política de competitividad en México. *ECONOMÍA unam, 3*(9), 65–81.

Engerman, S., & Sokoloff, K. (1997). Factor endowments, institutions, and differential paths of growth among new world economies. A view from economic historians of the United States. In S. Haber (Ed.), *How Latin America fell behind. Essays on the economic histories of Brazil and Mexico* (pp. 261–304). Stanford: Stanford University Press.

Evans, P. (1995). *Embedded autonomy. States and industrial transformation*. Princeton, NJ: Princeton University Press.

Goldstein, A., & Lemoine, F. (2013). *L'économie des BRIC: Brésil, Russie, Inde, Chine*. Paris: La Découverte Editions.

Guillen Romo, H. (2012). México: del desarrollo "hacia adentro" al desarrollo "hacia fuera". In J. L. Calva (Coord.), *Análisis Estratégico para el Desarrollo* (Vol. 3, pp. 245–283). México: Juan Pablos Editor.

Hall, P. A., & Soskice, D. (Eds.). (2001). *Varieties of capitalism: The institutional foundations of comparative advantage*. Oxford: Oxford University Press.

Hausmann, R., & Rigobon, R. (2003). An alternative interpretation of the 'resource curse': Theory and policy implications. In J. M. Davis, R. Ossowski, & A. Fedelino (Eds.), *Fiscal policy formulation and implementation in oil-producing countries*. Washington, DC: IMF.

Hermann, J. (2005a). Reformas, endividamento externo e o 'milagre' económico. In F. Giambiagi, A. Villela, L. Barros de Castro, & J. Hermann (Eds.), *Economia brasileira contemporânea (1945–2004)* (pp. 69–92). Rio de Janeiro: Elsevier.

Hermann, J. (2005b). Auge e Declínio do Modelo de Crescimento com Endividamento: O II PND e a Crise da Dívida Externa (1974–1984). In F. Giambiagi, A. Villela, L. Barros de Castro, & J. Hermann (Eds.),*Economia brasileira contemporânea (1945–2004)* (pp. 93–115). Rio de Janeiro: Elsevier.

Ibarra, C. (2008). La paradoja del crecimiento lento de México. *Revista de la CEPAL* (95), 83–102.

Karl, T. L. (1997). *The paradox of plenty: Oil booms and petro-states*. Berkeley and Los Angeles, CA: University of California Press.

Kay, C. (2002). Why East Asia overtook Latin America: Agrarian reform, industrialization and development. *Third World Quarterly, 23*(6), 1073–1102.

Mendoza Cota, J. E. (2011). La crisis de la industria automotriz en México en el marco de la integración económica con Estados Unidos. *Economía UNAM, 8*(22), 55–73.

Nassif, A., Feijó, C., & Araújo, E. (2015). Structural change and economic development: Is Brazil catching up or falling behind? *Cambridge Journal of Economics, 39*(5), 1307–1332.

OCDE. (2016). *Fomentando un Crecimiento Inclusivo de la Productividad en América Latina. Serie Mejores Políticas*. Paris: OECD Publishing. Available at: https://www.oecd.org/latin-america/fomentando-un-crecimiento-inclusivo-de-la-productividad-en-america-latina.pdf.

Palma, J. G. (2005). The seven main 'stylized facts' of the Mexican economy since trade liberalization and NAFTA. *Industrial and Corporate Change, 14*(6), 941–991.

Pereira, M., & Théret, B. (2004). Mediaciones institucionales de regulación social y dinámicas macroeconómicas: los casos de Brasil y México. In C. Alba & I. Bizberg (Eds.), *Democracia y Globalización en México y Brasil*. México: El Colegio de México.

Puyana, A., & Romero Tellaeche, J. (2009). *México. De la crisis de la deuda al estancamiento económico*. México: El Colegio de México.

Rapoport, M., & Collaborators. (2005). *Historia económica, política y social de la Argentina*. Córdoba: Ediciones Macchi.

Romero Tellaeche, J. (2014). *Grandes Problemas. Los límites al crecimiento económico de México*. El Colegio de México-UNAM.

Salama, P. (2012). China-Brasil: industrialización y 'desindustrialización temprana'. *Cuadernos de Economía, 31*(56), 223–252.

Santarcángelo, J. E., & Schteingart, D., & Porta, F. (2017). Industrial policy in Argentina, Brazil, Chile and Mexico: A comparative approach. *Revue Interventions économiques* (59). http://journals.openedition.org/interventionseconomiques/3852. Accessed 13 June 2018.

Schneider, B. R. (2013). *Hierarchical capitalism in Latin America: Business, labor, and the challenges of equitable development*. New York: Cambridge University Press.

Stockhammer, E. (2011). Crecimiento basado en los salarios: introducción. *Boletín Internacional de Investigación Sindical, 3*(2), 183–208.

UNCTAD. (2013). *World investment report, global value chains: Investment and trade for development*. New York and Geneva: United Nations Publication.

CHAPTER 4

The Mode of Integration to the World Economy

The manner in which a country inserts itself in the world economy is fundamental to characterize any economy, but even more definitely the peripheral as they are much more dependent of the international market, even if nowadays all countries are dependent on each other to a certain degree (Boyer 2015). For one thing, what a country produces is crucial, as countries that produce and export raw materials are extremely dependent on the developed countries because the demand and the prices of these materials are contingent on the needs of the countries that industrialize these products. On the other hand, these countries, as the dependency school and the CEPAL argued, based on the **Prebisch–Singer hypothesis**, are based on primary products that lose their value in relation to the industrialized products, something they called the deterioration of the terms of exchange between raw materials and industrialized products. Their argument was that: (1) there was a transfer of the gains of productivity to the central countries due to the oligopolistic structure of the production of the manufactured products in the developed countries, against the competitive structure of the producers of primary products; (2) the increasing returns of industry resulting from the use of technology and of mass production; and (3) the low elasticity of demand of the

I. Bizberg, *Diversity of Capitalisms in Latin America*,
https://doi.org/10.1007/978-3-319-95537-7_4

industrial products in contrast to the high elasticity of demand of the primary products (Barros de Castro: 144). This latter factor can be interpreted in two different ways: in the first one, a small reduction in the prices of commodities strongly diminishes revenues in the peripheral countries; in the second, due to either the power relation of the world center against the world periphery as Wallerstein has it, or the highly dissimilar power of the working class in the central economies against peasants or miners with no bargaining power in the peripheral countries, it drives the prices of manufactures to a higher level than those of the primary products.[1] Although this idea has been contested by the periodic booms of the prices of commodities, such as the one during the first decade since the years 2000, and the concurrent reduction in the prices of manufactures coming from the central countries, it seems that at some moments there is some sense to this theory. But, more importantly still, this idea was the theoretical justification of the strategy of import substitution industrialization, of the impulse to escape from the dependence on commodities of the Latin American countries, their determination to industrialize and their aspiration to protect the nascent industrial firms in the peripheral countries. Although the idea of the deterioration of the terms of exchange has lost significance, they were absolutely right in pointing out the fact that as exports of commodities depend on the demand of the central countries founding an economy on them; this implies a heightened fragility and dependence of the countries that produce them in relation to the countries that demand them, as we have seen lately in most Latin American countries that have been suffering from the reduction in the price of commodities due to the decline of growth of China and other countries beginning in 2014.

A synthesis of the international insertion of the four types of capitalism we will discuss is in this Table 4.1.

[1] https://en.wikipedia.org/wiki/Prebisch%E2%80%93Singer_hypothesis.

Table 4.1 International Insertion

	International outsourcing	*Socio-developmentalist*	*Rentier/liberal*	*Rentier/redistributive*
Type of production	Assembly platform/ manufacturing enclave	International and national	Oil/mineral enclave/MNC	Oil/mineral exports/ partly State owned
Orientation	External led	Internal led	External led	Internal (consumption)/ external led (exports of commodities)
Openness/ protectionism	Open	Protectionist	Open/Chile (1990s)	Open/defensive (Bolivia)
Defensive measures	None	Temporary	None (Colombia defensive)	None
Capital controls	None	Temporary	None	None
Transfer of technology	None	Intention	None	None
Character	Passive/subordinated	Active/proactive	Passive/oriented toward the external market	Active/proactive oriented toward preservation

Source Own elaboration

4.1 Degree of Openness

Looking at the countries that have adopted an international outsourcing mode, we can see that they are dependent although they produce industrial goods, in a very similar way as the countries that have been defined as a dependent type of capitalism by Drahokoupil and Myant (2015), and Nölke and Vliegenthart (2009). This is because they depend, like the countries that produce commodities, on the external market, in this case on the demand of the products they assemble. The *maquila* industry in Mexico (but also in other countries, such as Dominican Republic and Central America) is dependent on the demand of their parent companies, which are situated in the central countries. The elasticity impact of a lower demand, as in the case of commodities, is very high, especially in terms of labor. The assembly model concentrates the sectors that are most labor demanding, and thus a lower demand of the products they assemble has very strong repercussions in the labor markets of the outsourcing countries. They are also very fragile with respect to jobs going to other countries that have low salaries as was the case in Mexico when China entered the OMC in 2001; many *maquiladoras* closed down to transfer their production to the Asian country. Mexico lost around one-third of its jobs in the sector, which eventually came back at the end of the first decade of 2000 (Ibarra 2008, 2011). According to the INEGI, in the years 2000, there were 3590 enterprises with 1,291,000 workers, which was reduced in 2003 to 2860 plants employing 1,062,000 workers. By 2006, the number of firms stayed almost static, but the number of employed increased to 1,200,000 workers. Nevertheless, the model rests fragile, because even though the Chinese salaries have increased, there are always countries with lower salaries, although the vicinity of Mexico with the USA continues to be a significant advantage.

While the international outsourcing capitalism and the two types of rentier economies share the external orientation of their economies, and although the socio-developmentalist capitalism also produces and exports commodities, it has a significant orientation toward the internal market. Data concerning the weight of exports in both groups of countries confirm this: while in Brazil and Argentina the aggregate demand is balanced between the external and the internal market, in the case of Mexico the external market has a much higher weight. The impact of exports on the growth of GDP for Mexico was 58% between 2000 and 2008, and 67% in the previous decade (1990–2000); for Chile, the percentages were 48 and 39%, respectively. In contrast, for Brazil and Argentina, the numbers are 27 and 29% respectively between 2000 and 2008 (Bensusán and Moreno-Brid 2012). In terms of the proportion of exports with respect to GDP, Mexico's exports constituted around 19% of GDP in 1990, while in 2016 they constituted almost 38%; Chiles exports were 34% of its GDP in 1990 and 28% in 2016; Bolivia's were 22% in 1990, 47% in 2012, and 25% in 2016. In contrast, the percentage of exports in Brazil's GDP was 8.9% in 1990 and went up to 12.5% in 2016. In Argentina, it has stayed more or less constant: 13.1% in 1990 and 12.7% in 2016, although it went up to 28.3% just after the terrible crisis of 2001 (World Bank; data.worldbank.org).

Nonetheless, although in the socio-developmentalist countries exports account for a smaller proportion with respect to GDP, they have also become increasingly dependent on the export of commodities and the entry of foreign capital. This was the consequence of the enhanced growth of commodity exports of all the Latin American countries in the first decade and a half of 2000, which was in part caused by the impressive growth of China, but also by the financial resources that the USA injected into the world economy, first to fund its trade deficit, and then after the 2007–2008 global crisis to fight the dearth of liquidity caused by this crisis (Boyer 2014). In Brazil, the country that came nearest to the socio-developmentalist model, by 2014 primary or manufactured goods based on commodities constituted 66% of its exports, while in Argentina the proportion was 70%. It is true that in the rentier countries, this percentage was even higher: Colombia, Chile, Peru, Bolivia, and Ecuador primary and manufactured goods based on commodities comprise around 90% of their exports. Although the outsourcing model exports manufactures and not commodities, it is externally led to such a degree that not only have we seen an impressive growth of exports, but also of imports: in the case of Mexico exports grew from 30,691 million dollars in 1988 to 390,000 million in 2014, while imports have increased consequently, to 384,000 millions in 2014 (http://atlas.cid.harvard.edu). This has led the analysts to propose that there is a disconnection between the exporting platform and the internal production, an extremely poor integration of national production to the export sector that results in a recurring and almost permanent commercial deficit (Palma 2005; Dussel Peters 2006; Ibarra 2008; Puyana and Romero Tellaeche 2009).

There are several indexes that reveal the degree of openness of a country to the world economy, most of them are too general, probably not too exact, and maybe even politically biased, but they nevertheless show a certain tendency. The liberal/rentier countries are highest in the index of openness: Mexico is 49th, Chile is 55th, Peru is 58th, and Colombia is 59th. On the other hand, the redistributive rentier countries and the developmentalist ones are way down in the index of openness: Bolivia is 152th, Brazil is 125th, Argentina is 117th, and Ecuador is 118th (WB 2018). Uruguay is an exception because although it shares many of the sociopolitical characteristics of the redistributive countries, it is a very open small economy that shares the characteristics signaled by Katzenstein for the small economies of Northern Europe: economic openness and a continuous dialogue between the social partners (social corporatism), as their dependence on the external context makes them vulnerable to external shocks that force the social actors and the State to be ready to negotiate internally any circumstance in order to find ways to share the costs of the shock and ways to overcome it rapidly (Katzenstein 1985). Uruguay depends much on its exchange with its bigger neighbors, Argentina and Brazil; it is also a financial center for South America; thus, it is 38th in the *Doing Business Index* for 2018.

These types of indexes have been broadly criticized as lacking objectivity, since they are based on a "free market" benchmark that is defined based on a particular perspective. A less questionable measure is the index of participation in global value chains. We consider that open economies are more linked to the global value chains than the more closed or protective ones. And in effect, the OECD mentions Mexico, Costa Rica, Peru, and Chile as the Latin American countries that are more closely related to global supply chains, while the first two countries are integrated in the North American region, Chile and Peru "... specialize in upstream mining and agricultural inputs destined for Asian markets" (Cadestin et al. 2016: 11). "Chile, with more than 52% of its gross exports accounted for by either foreign value added processed in Chile or Chilean value added exported further by its trading partners, is the country with strongest GVC links in the region and the only one where this ratio is higher than the average for the rest of the OECD. In the region, Chile is followed by Mexico (47%), and Costa Rica (45%). In contrast, Brazil and Argentina are further behind: Brazil (35%) and Argentina (30%), with Colombia in a middle position (38%)" (Ibid.: 12). Thus, Chile, Mexico, and Costa Rica are the more open economies, the most linked to global value chains, while Brazil and Argentina, although also linked, are less so.

Thus, one can say that socio-developmentalist economies are less open and, as we will see next, also more protectionist. This is coherent with the idea that this mode of capitalism pretends to industrialize the country with safeguards, subsidies, loans, and industrial policies. Its relationship to the exterior is much more defensive than one of the more liberal countries, both international outsourcing and rentier. However, the redistributive rentier countries are in a contradictory situation: on the one hand, they pose an autonomous and defensive (sometimes even offensive) discursive posture toward foreign capitals while on the other hand, they greatly depend on foreign investment in mining, oil, and other commodities. For example, when Evo Morales won the presidency, the Bolivian government modified the conditions of the concessions of the companies that exploited the gas deposits, but did not expropriate them (although it declared it had done so). In fact, it has recently overruled its own legislation concerning the preservation of an indigenous reserve, the *Territorio Indígena y Parque Nacional Isiboro Sécure* TIPNIS, and has confronted one of its social bases, in order to allow for its exploitation by international enterprises and by its own social base, the coca leaf producers (Achtenberg 2017). The governments of Chile, Peru, and Colombia are totally open; they do not impose any kind of restriction on foreign capital.[2] This is also the case of Ecuador, which though closer to a redistributive/rentier capitalism, the fact that it does not have an autonomous national currency, as it is dollarized, excludes any possibility of exerting control over circulation of international currency (Fritz 2017).

One of the indicators of openness is FDI. We can clearly see in Fig. 4.1 that the highest investment in proportion to GNP is in the more open economies. In the years 2000, Chile was the country that admitted the highest level of FDI with respect to the size of its economy and then Peru and Uruguay. While both Bolivia and Argentina received a great amount of FDI during the 1990s, in their more open phase, before the arrival of Evo Morales in the case of the first country and during the Menem administration in Argentina, in the 2000s the rate has gone down very significantly. Although Brazil is the fourth investment destination worldwide, the proportion of FDI with respect to GDP is lower than that of the rest of the countries we are considering. On the other hand, Brazil is a significant foreign investing country, especially in Africa, where its investments increased significantly in the years 2000, aided by the public investment bank, the BNDS (UNCTAD 2013: 5).

[2] Notwithstanding, the Chilean State implemented a tax mechanism (*encaje*) on foreign portfolio investments that limited its unpredictability during the 1990s that has since been abandoned (Ffrench-Davis 2008).

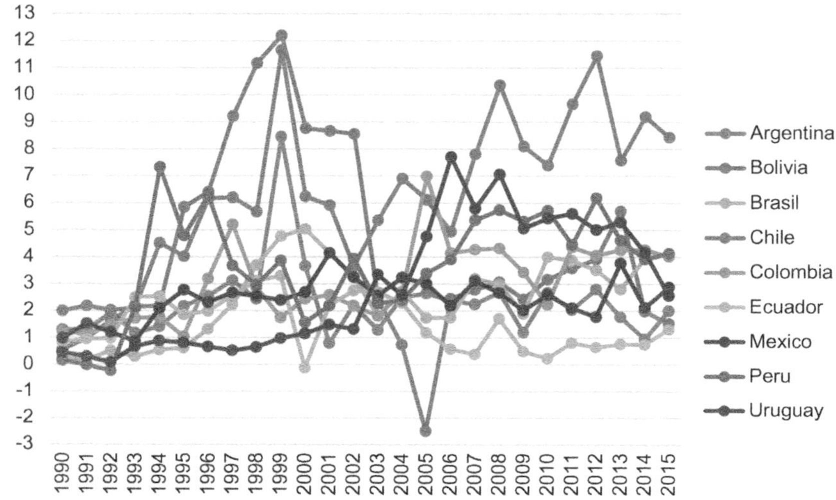

Fig. 4.1 Foreign direct investment 1990–2015 (Net entry of capital as % of GDP) (*Source* Own elaboration based on World Bank database, available in https://datos.bancomundial.org)

We have some other indicators of the attitude of countries toward foreign investment. The liberal rentier countries have depended largely on FDI in order to increase their export capacity of commodities. "The share of the extractive industry in FDI stock in Colombia was 26 per cent in 2002, this industry attracted 53 per cent of total FDI flows between 2003 and 2012. In Chile, its share in FDI stock increased from 27 to 39 per cent between 2006 and 2011, while in Peru, it increased from 14 per cent in 2001 to 27 per cent in 2011." "In Peru, [it] accounted for at least 75 percent of all metal mining investment in 2011–2012, and in Chile, 62 percent of all investment in large-scale copper and gold mining in 2012, while their share in all copper production increased from 48 percent in 1991–2001 to 59 percent in 2002–2012" (UNCTAD 2013: 60).

One indicator of the relationship with the external market is the attitude toward foreign direct investment FDI, and another is the rate of return that FDI gains in each country. According to the UNCTAD, while in 2011 the global rate of return on FDI was 7.2%, and has been decreasing since 2008 in the developed economies, in developing and transition economies, "they are higher [...] for example, in Peru, they are an enormous 27%; in Colombia 16%; in Bolivia 13%, and in Chile 12%" (UNCTAD 2013: 33). In contrast, the study of the UNCTAD highlights that although this is the situation of most of Latin American countries that exploit natural resources (regardless of their mode of capitalism), in Argentina and Brazil, who have a strong national entrepreneurial class, this is not the case. In Brazil, the extractive industry is in the hands of domestic capitals. In the case of Argentina, foreign investment in the industry was actually reduced during the presidencies of Kirchner and Fernández. In fact, due to the fact that Argentina was cut from the external financial circuits from 2001 to 2015, this country "... witnessed a decline in the share of the extractive industry in total FDI stock during the second half of the 2000s, from 40 per cent in 2005 to 31 per cent in 2011. The share of the extractive industry in FDI stock further decreased in 2012 after the nationalization of a 51 per cent stake in YPF" (UNCTAD 2013: 60, 88).

Concerning the financial sector, we have also seen how, in the last years, the banking system of all the countries of the continent has experienced increased intervention of foreign capital. While traditionally the banking sector of the Latin American countries was protected, the economic crisis in the 1990s, as well as the privatization and deregulation measures, led most of the countries to deregulate the sector and open it up to foreign capitals (Jeanneau et al. 2007: 17). This did not have the same effect on all countries; while in some countries, like Peru and Mexico, foreign capital has acquired most of the domestic banking system, and in others, the presence of foreign banks is much more limited. While in these two countries, the banking system is around 95% for the first and 85% for the second, in other countries, like Bolivia and Chile, it is around 40 and 30%, and in Argentina and Brazil, it is under 30%. In fact, in both Argentina and Brazil, the financial sector was not as open until the end of the presidencies of Fernández and Rousseff, but it may change with the new presidencies of Macri and Temer. In the case of Brazil, most banks are still in the hands of the State or of national capitals. The case of Colombia is again contrasting it has a very low proportion of its financial sector in the hand of foreign banks, less than 20% (Fig. 4.2).

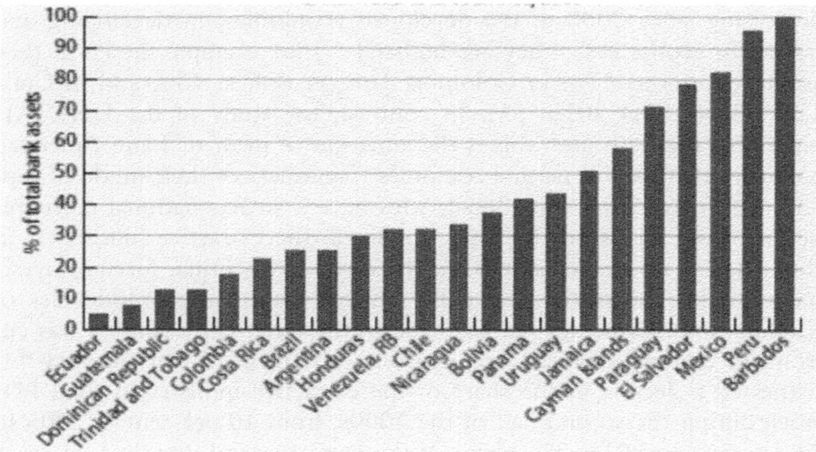

Fig. 4.2 Foreign-owned bank assets as a percentage of total banks assets, individual LAC countries, 2005 (*Source* De la Torre et al. 2012: 75)

While the situation of the financial sector of Peru and Mexico and that of Argentina and Brazil coincide with our hypothesis of more open and more protectionist economies, respectively, the case of Chile and Bolivia does not, for contrasting reasons. While in the case of Chile we would have expected a larger opening to foreign banking, in the case of Bolivia we would have expected a lower one. In the next chapter, where we will analyze State intervention, we will see that Chile, though a very liberal economy, has a much stronger defensive position than one of the other liberal countries. In the case of Bolivia, one can understand the situation by recalling the very liberal policies before the presidency of Evo Morales.

On the other hand, it is not only the proportion of the banking system that is in the hands of foreign capital what signals dependency on external actors, but also the level of dollarization of the economy. The banking systems of most of the countries in Latin America have a high level of their deposits and debt in dollars. In Bolivia, Peru, and Uruguay, as well as Ecuador, more than half of deposits and debts are in dollars. In fact, in the case of Ecuador, due to its formal dollarization, 100% of them are in this currency, while in Bolivia they are 90%, and in Peru they are nearly 60%. In Argentina and Brazil, the percentage of dollarization is very small or null; in Colombia, it is null; in Chile, it is 13%; in Argentina, it is 11%; and in Mexico, it is only 3.4%. In all of these latter countries, deposits and debts in foreign currency are either prohibited or strongly restricted (Jeanneau et al. 2007: 15, 78). Thus, the proportion of dollarization depends in part on the type of economy, as in the case of Argentina and Brazil, but it is clear that small countries such as Bolivia and Ecuador, although they try to reorient their economy away from liberalism, are rentier countries, very dependent on foreign currencies; this is especially true in the case of Ecuador that has a formally dollarized economy (Fritz 2017).

Nonetheless, the idea of openness is too general; we therefore need to analyze the specific arrangements that define a country as more open or closed. In this sense, we can identify two different types of protectionist instruments, a type that is more defensive, which is used in case the country is subject to strong external pressures, or in the event of a crisis. Among these measures, we can reckon elevating import tariffs, implementing qualitative barriers, elevating dumping procedures, among others. Other types of actions, also basically defensive, although more proactive, as they may modify the conditions of the internal economy, are reacting to a crisis by a rise in financial liquidity by the central bank, subsidizing certain sectors, and imposing capital barriers; all of these can increase the competitiveness of a certain sector of the economy independently of the crisis. Finally, there exist proactive measures that do not react to a crisis, but try to shape the insertion of the domestic economy in the world economy, such as the constraints on foreign capital, in terms of its relationship to industries that produce local components, in terms of transfer of technology, among others. We will thus divide the rest of this chapter into two types of instruments: defensive and proactive.

4.2 The Defensive Actions

Brazil and Argentina have at times implemented protectionist measures implemented by. During the global crisis of 2008 "… Mercosur member countries (Argentina, Brazil, Paraguay, and Uruguay) decided to raise their common external tariff by 5 percentage points on numerous items, including wine, peaches, dairy products, textiles, leather goods, and wooden furniture" (Bouët and Laborde 2009: 59). During this same crisis, Brazil chose up to 100 products to impose on them a 35% tax, the maximum authorized by the OMC. It chose these products with regard to the evolution of its imports and their degree of penetration in the internal market, as well as the capacity of the country to cope with their demand. In the list of products were included electrical equipment, resins, plastics, laminated products, tubes, paper bricks, and glass.

Complementary to this rising of duties, the government instituted lowering taxes and financial help for the sectors that had been most hurt by the crisis (El País 2012).

Another manner of measuring protectionism is through the claims that a country initiates in order to claim dumping from another country. "While India initiated the most anti-dumping investigations in 2008, this country was followed by Turkey and Brazil (23 investigations) Argentina (19), the US and the EU (18 each), China (7), Colombia and Australia (6 each), Korea (5), and Canada, Pakistan, and South Africa (3 each). Regarding the application of new final anti-dumping measures, India applied 26 new measures in 2008—two measures less than it applied in 2007—, the US applied 23 new measures in 2008, followed by the EU and Brazil (15 each), Turkey (11), South Korea (8), Argentina and China (4 each)" (Brown 2009: 55–56).

One of the moments where protectionist measures came most to the fore was the global crisis of 2008. Argentina imposed non-tariff measures on auto parts, textiles, TVs, toys, shoes, and leather goods and Ecuador raised tariffs on more than 900 items (Baldwin and Evenett 2009: 4). Although the government of Lula tried to "… impose widespread licensing arrangements and import controls," it had to reverse course because the private sector rejected them (Brown 2009: 52). In the case of Argentina and Brazil, protectionism has sometimes been directed toward their own partners in the common market—a contradictory measure that shows the limits of Mercosur, as this integration process constitutes a manner of protecting an economy at a larger scale than that of the nation-state. One example is a quite recent call by Argentinian entrepreneurs, the Union Industrial Argentina (the UIA), to protect local production against Brazilian exports that had grown 4.4% in 2016 with respect to 2015, while the exports of Argentina to Brazil slumped 10.6%, generating a deficit of 4650 million dollars. The UIA called for non-tariff barriers such as technical norms and quality standards, something they said would in return help the Argentinian entrepreneurs to increase their own competitivity.[3]

Facing the global crisis, the central banks of many countries in the continent implemented anti-cyclical actions; they injected financial resources into the economy, as did the USA and the European Union.

[3] http://www.informeindustrial.com.ar/verNota.aspx?nota=M%C3%A1s%20apoyo%20de%20Brasil%20a%20su%20industria___844.

These actions were defensive, although they implied a somewhat more proactive perspective. Among the countries that were more proactive confronting the crisis were Brazil, Argentina, and even a liberal country like Chile. "... Central banks with large foreign exchange reserves have generally been able to supply foreign currency to local banks and importers generally through repurchase agreements. Since October 2008, Brazil's central bank has provided \$10 billion to the local market. The Korean central bank has pledged \$10 billion of its foreign exchange reserves to do likewise. The central banks of South Africa, India, and Indonesia are also engaged in similar operations" (Auboin 2009: 78).

Another aspect of the anti-cyclical actions was to give subsidies to certain economic branches that were in trouble: "... subsidies proposed for the auto industry have proliferated and total some \$48 billion worldwide, mostly in high-income countries (\$42.7 billion). In addition to the US direct subsidy of \$17.4 billion to its three national companies, Canada, France, Germany, the UK, China, Argentina, Brazil, Sweden and Italy have also provided direct or indirect subsidies ..." (Brown 2009: 50). "Some countries, such as Argentina and Russia, intervened in exchange rate markets, generally to prevent further depreciations" (Gamberoni et al. 2009: 52).

In the case of Mexico, the government of Calderón (2006–2012) did not implement any anti-cyclical action even if the crisis had an enormous effect on the country's economy, one of the strongest impacts in the world. As has been discussed by numerous Mexican analysts, the rules upon which the Mexican State functions always entail a pro-cyclical action when confronted with a crisis. By the Federal Budget Law, Mexican governments are bound to maintain a zero deficit in their accounts; as they are barred from incurring in any fiscal deficit; during a crisis they collect less taxes, have less to spend, and are thus incapable of aiding the economy. On the other hand, the objectives of the Mexican central bank are also pro-cyclical. This institution is also limited in its possibility to inject financial resources into the economy, as the Constitution defines its role basically as taking care of inflation. In contrast, the Fed, as almost all other central banks, have as their function to arbitrate between inflation and growth of the economy (Esquivel 2010). Finally, the Mexican government lacked an instrument such as a stabilization fund; it failed in its aim of creating one though it had tried to constitute such a reserve during the Fox administration (2000–2006), when Mexico was exporting great amounts of crude oil at a very high price; a time when prices exceeded what was programmed in the budget. It is very significant to mention that in contrast to Mexico, the Chilean government used such a reserve fund to expand its expenditure without incurring in a fiscal deficit.

Other types of measures can be taken by any country in order to defend its economy in the face of a crisis, to prevent a run of foreign investments, or to avert or counter the reevaluation of its local currency, which would hurt its own industry and economy by making imports cheaper and exports more expensive. In 2011, the Dilma government introduced measures to limit the circulation of capital in order to counter the reevaluation of the real. It also cut taxes for certain sectors, increased its loans to industry through the BNDS, and implemented a program of governmental purchases destined to favor Brazilian products against importations.[4] Dilma declared the rationale behind these procedures as an action against what she called a "currency war": "We have to protect our economy, our productive forces and our jobs." Many analysts have mentioned that these measures were taken too late, and that they were thus ineffective to control overvaluation, as only in 2014, in the second presidency of Dilma, did the government try to control it by lowering the central bank interest rates; in order for these actions to have been effective, they should have been imposed since the Lula government (Prates et al. 2017).

One of the most important measures against the revaluation of the local currencies and against the sudden exit of financial flows that have deeply hurt the economy of developing countries in the past are capital controls. Although these are rather exceptional measures in the open economies of the present time, some countries have implemented them more frequently in the 1990s than in the 2000s. In fact, the government of Dilma Rousseff implemented capital controls in order to prevent the continuation of the reevaluation of the real and the expansion of a financial bubble that introduced a significant level of uncertainty in the local financial market after the global economic crisis. According to Chamon and Garcia, "Controls may have helped

[4] http://www.lanacion.com.ar/1394530-con-nuevo-plan-brasil-protege-su-industria.

Brazil to avoid a bubble and perhaps worse" (2016: 24). This action also serves as a defensive measure to mitigate the effects of an economic crisis. In fact, "in the wake of the financial crisis, nations such as Brazil, Indonesia, South Korea, Taiwan and Thailand have all used capital controls to stem the massive inflows of speculative investment entering their economies and wreaking havoc on their exchange rates and asset markets" (Gallagher 2011: 2).

From October 2009 to January 2011, Brazil implemented a series of capital control measures which, although they did not have all of the desired effects, exposed the defensive attitude of the Brazilian government toward foreign capital flows. The list and periodicity of these procedures were as follows:

> 10/19/2009 2 percent tax on portfolio equity and fixed income inflows
> 11/18/2009 1.5% tax on the issuance of DRs into local equities
> 10/4/2010 Tax rate raised to 4 percent for fixed income inflows
> 10/18/2010 Tax rate raised to 6 percent for fixed income inflows
> 12/30/2010 2% tax on the cancellation of DRs into local equities
> 1/6/2011 Unremunerated reserve requirement of 60 percent on bank's gross FX positions beyond US$3 billions
> 3/28/2011 6% tax on borrowing abroad with maturity below one year
> 4/6/2011 6% tax on borrowing abroad extended to maturity below two years
> 7/8/2011 Unremunerated reserve requirement of 60 percent on bank's gross FX positions beyond US$1 billion
> 9/16/2011 Tax on notional amount of derivatives takes effect
> 12/1/2011 Tax on portfolio equity inflows eliminated
> 2/29/2012 6% tax on borrowing abroad extended to maturity below three years
> 3/1/2012 Restricts anticipation of payments to exporters to one-year horizon
> 3/9/2012 6% tax on borrowing abroad extended to maturity below five years (Ibid.).[5] (Chamon and Garcia 2016)

[5] "The recent imposition of inflow controls by Brazil, which ignited strong disapproval from investors, who viewed the measures as harmful, a 'blunt instrument,' and reminiscent of the widespread capital controls in Latin America during the period of hyperinflation and weak economic performance in the 1980s." (Ghosh and Qureshi 2016: 33)

Brazil has implemented capital controls in the past: in 1994 and again in 1999. "In 1994, it imposed a 1 percent tax on foreign investment in the stock market, that was eliminated on March 10, 1995. The tax on Brazilian companies issuing bonds overseas was raised from 3 percent to 7 percent of the total. The tax paid by foreigners on fixed interest investments in Brazil was raised from 5 percent to 9 percent. In March 1999, the Government ordered local investment funds to increase their holdings of government bonds. The central bank raised to 80 percent from 60 percent the minimum amount of sovereign debt that must be held in the country foreign investment fund" (Magud et al. 2005).

The case of Argentina is different because it did not introduce capital controls in order to control the flux of financial flows coming into the country and prevent the overvaluation of its local currency or the sudden retreat of portfolio investments, but rather due to a very profound economic crisis that in 2001 led to a bank run and to procedures taken by the government of De la Rua intended to stop its own citizens from suddenly and massively retrieving their savings. Argentina imposed what it called "the *corralito*" when it ended the Convertibility Plan in 2001. "The *corralito* limited bank withdrawals and imposed restrictions on dollar transfers and loans, it 'pesofied' the dollar deposits at a low level of change of 1.4 pesos per dollar," when people had invested in dollars to preserve their buying power. "In December 30th of that year, the country suspended external payments, defaulting on its loans. In September 2002, it required that stocks should be traded in domestic currency. In December 2002 the *corralito* was rescinded" (Magud et al. 2005). Nonetheless, this led to the disconnection of Argentina from the international financial capital markets that lasted until the present-day Macri government entered into negotiations with its debtors.

The Chilean government, against its liberalism, enforced defensive measures on foreign capital in the 1990s. In June 1991, it "... imposed a non-remunerated 20 percent reserve to be deposited at the Central Bank for a period of one year on liabilities in foreign currency for direct borrowing by firms. The stamp tax of 1.2 percent a year (previously paid by domestic currency credits only) was applied to foreign loans as well. This requirement applies to all credits during their first year, with the exception of trade loans" (Magud et al. 2005).

The case of Colombia is interesting because although it is a liberal rentier country like Chile, it has imposed a series of capital control plans since the 1990s and, in contrast to Chile, it has continued applying them in the years 2000. "Colombia has had a long experience with capital controls. It started the liberalization of its capital markets in 1991, but some controls remained in place until 2000, including an unremunerated reserve requirement (URR) that was effective between 1993 and 2000, with the goal of stemming the appreciation of the Colombian Peso" (Gallagher 2011: 3). In 2002 and 2004, it forced foreigners investing in domestic markets to keep their money in the country for at least one year (Magud et al. 2005). Again in 2007, it required "... foreign investors to park a percentage of their investment in the central bank, which helped that nation escape some of the damage from the global financial crisis" (Gallagher 2011: 2). Since the signature, in 2012, of the Trade Promotion Agreement between Colombia and the USA, it has renounced to these types of controls, as they are prohibited under the treaty (Gallagher 2011: 4). The same goes for Mexico, who signed NAFTA with the USA and Canada in 1992. This is one of the reasons why Brazil has not signed a free trade treaty with any country, much less with the USA.

Peru also imposed capital controls in the face of the global crisis. "It extended a 60 percent reserve requirement for new foreign holders of debt with maturity up to three years. Extended the income tax rate of 30 percent to all nonresident gains on financial derivatives transactions" (Ghosh and Qureshi 2016).

In sharp contrast to all these measures, Mexico did nothing to face the 2008 global crisis,[6] and it simply awaited for the crisis to pass and waited for the recovery of the US economy. As we have already mentioned, Mexico has not imposed any kind of controls since the 1970s and 1980s, when it defaulted its debt and nationalized the banking system, because they are prohibited by NAFTA. In fact, as a signal of how the country should react, ex-President Ernesto Zedillo declared that "What we do know with certainty is that protectionism could derail all those efforts applied on the fiscal and monetary fronts. Despite the multitude of statements against protectionism made by leaders and their finance and trade ministers in recent months, it would be irresponsible not to recognize that the mercantilist specter is knocking at everybody's door. Unfortunately, as the recession gets worse,

[6]We will analyze more closely the measures taken by Mexico and the other countries of Latin America to face the global crisis in the next chapter, dealing with the role of the State.

protectionist forces will become even stronger. A perverse cycle of feedback between recession and protectionism is no longer an historical reminiscence of the 1930s but a possible scenario now hopefully still with a low probability in the months and years to come" (Baldwin and Evenett 2009: 1). This is a clear confirmation of Mexico's passivity toward foreign capitals.

4.3 Proactive Measures

One of the main proactive manners in which a country can profit from foreign direct investment is to stimulate the generation of suppliers, to drive them to integrate vertically with the large multinationals. Another manner is by stressing for the transfer of technology. In China, for example, both manners are actively sought by the government, in many cases as a condition for allowing an enterprise to invest in the country.

Most Latin American countries did not allow foreign direct investment during the first part of the import substitution period. Once they had arrived at a phase where they need to deepen industrialization, they began opening up to foreign investment, imposing the condition that they should co-invest with national capitals, and in some cases with State capitals (as in Brazil), as a manner of being able to have access to their technology. At present time, most countries are open to FDI, some of them have tried to either stimulate or support financially national capitals to become suppliers of foreign companies, and in some cases they have tried to impose certain conditions on foreign investment, although most analysts consider that few countries have the leverage of China, where foreign capitals accept the conditions of the government because the country is a huge market for their products.

Nonetheless, we think that some Latin American countries could have such a leverage. In the first place, China is able to impose these conditions not only because it has such a large population, but because it has been able to grow and incorporate a large population as consumers every year. In contrast, although India is also growing rapidly, it has much less power, because its future is less certain. The biggest Latin American countries could have a leverage if they could grow at the high rates and constantly, like China. Smaller countries are more vulnerable in this respect, although countries like Bolivia or Chile, with some of the largest lithium reserves, to mention just one example, could also set their conditions for its exploitation.[7]

Both Argentina and Brazil apply incentives to their exports, in the form of tax exemptions, be them taxes such as VAT, or on imported spare parts. While in Brazil the main mechanism is the exemption or suspension of taxation, in Argentina it is a refund, a drawback mechanism, which is much less effective, because it is slower (Bekermann and Dalmasso 2014: 169). Mexico's main aid to exporters is permitting temporarily import products (raw materials, supplies, components, containers, as well as machinery and equipment) to be utilized in the assembly of their manufactures, without having to pay for the general tax on imports, the VAT, and other compensatory taxes. In order to benefit from these exemptions, the enterprise has to export a minimum of 500,000 dollars or 10% of its total production.[8]

According to Bekermann and Dalmasso, who compare Brazil and Argentina ".... Brazil has shown to have a strategy of international insertion much better defined than the one implemented by Argentina from the mid-nineties to 2008" (2014: 168). Brazil implemented a combination of tariff deductions (which we have mentioned above) and financing for exports, which has resulted in a continuous increase in Brazilian exports. In Argentina, by contrast, the volatility of the macroeconomic context and the institutional weaknesses have been very harmful for the promotion of exports (Ibid.: 169). On the other hand, "while Argentina opened up more intensively to capital goods. TIC's and electronics, trying to increase its productivity incorporating foreign technology, Brazil kept a higher level of protection to its local production in those sectors" (Ibid.: 169). In the years 2000, Brazil has pursued an aggressive strategy of expansion in the world commerce, leaving behind its focus on commercial balance and axing on exports. The BNDS and the *Banco do Brasil* have been crucial, as they allocate financing to strategic sectors.

[7] http://www.eleconomista.es/materias-primas/noticias/8856549/01/18/Bolivia-quiere-ser-la-Arabia-Saudi-del-Litio-y-avisa-Vamos-a-poner-el-precio-para-a-todo-el-mundo.html.

[8] http://www.2006-2012.economia.gob.mx/comunidad-negocios/industria-y-comercio/instrumentos-de-comercio-exterior/fomento-a-la-produccion-y-las-exportaciones.

In Argentina, resources have been more limited, while the BDNS has a program of support for the internationalization of Brazilian companies, conditioned to their contributing to raise exports. As an example, Brazilian companies bought a number of Argentinian companies after 2002 (Ibid.: 170).

One of the main ways of successfully inserting an economy in the world economy is through upgrading and innovation; technology is crucial for both. Technology can either be generated domestically or through the transfer from more advanced economies. We will be analyzing the transfer of technology in this chapter, as it is related to the integration to the world economy, while we will leave the discussion on the internal generation of technology, investment in R&D, and education for the next chapter, which deals with the role of the State in the economy. With regard to transfer of technology, it is well known that Asian capitalism acquired technology by copying (legally or illegally) the fabrication procedures, or the technological content of a product, and then innovating upon it. In fact, as both the economic historian Bairoch and the technology historian Mokyr have written, technological transfer was done in this same way at the beginning of industrialization, with the artisans and engineers going freely from one country to the other, looking at new production methods and bringing them back to their home countries. As the other East Asian countries did in the past, Chinese capitalism has been both imitating as well as obliging foreign firms to enter into co-investments with Chinese firms and in this manner having access to the technology. More recently, the Chinese companies, many of them public–private enterprises, have been acquiring top companies in Europe and the USA, in order to acquire technology directly (Martina 2017) and innovating.

In terms of technological transfer, while China only allows foreign investment if there is a co-investment with a local partner, no Latin American country has imposed such an approach. Nonetheless, the present government of Bolivia has declared that it will put pressure on foreign investors that want to exploit the very great lithium reserves of the country so that they co-invest with private or State national capital. Evo Morales has announced several times during the last years his interest in foreign companies—German, Chinese, Russian, and American to be incorporated with the Bolivian State to install a plant to produce lithium carbonate, to eventually produce batteries and even electric cars in Bolivia.[9]

[9] http://www.lostiempos.com/actualidad/economia/20180123/definiran-este-ano-empresa-planta-litio.

The relation between FDI and transfer of technology has been discussed on three different levels: in the first one, it has been argued that when FDIs acquire existing firms in a country, it does not imply transfer of technology as the company continues at the same technological level. When an FDI installs a new plant on a greenfield, there is a higher probability of a transfer due to the fact that it is usually accompanied by the latest technology. Nonetheless, there is usually no transfer because the company does not share its knowledge with local suppliers (Chiarini 2016). Finally, there is a higher possibility of a transfer of technology when a company co-invests in a country; something that we mentioned is almost always the case in China, but very rare in Latin America.

The conclusion of a study done by the UNCTAD with regard to this possibility for all developing countries is very pessimistic. The study considers that there are several manners in which local enterprises can get access to technology, they mention "... to operate across value chains. Another is linked to strategies to raise local firms' bargaining power (e.g. diversification of buyers, proactive internal technology development to expand their product portfolio). Collective actions by local producers in developing countries can also facilitate knowledge transfer and absorption [...] [which] can take place in industry clusters, where SME's combine knowledge and technical resources to improve their export potential or facilitate adoption of standards." Nonetheless, their conclusions on the automotive industry, one of the most extensively studied, is that "... tier 1 suppliers are typically dominated by a small number of foreign TNCs, particularly so since the emergence of global mega-suppliers that meet the needs of their customers across many countries has undermined the position of mostly domestically oriented local companies. Domestic suppliers tend to be numerous in tier 2 and tier 3. However, the highly-concentrated structure of the industry means there is little room for knowledge transfer to lower-tier suppliers (which operate predominantly through market transactions). In Mexico, very few, if any, of the SMEs in the second and third tiers have been able to leverage their links to GVCs as springboards for their own internationalization" (UNCTAD 2013: 61).

Although we have been discussing the fact that the capacity of the entire Latin American countries to induce technological transfer is low, we have, nonetheless, mentioned other measures implemented by certain countries, most notably Brazil and to a lesser degree Argentina, that seem to have worked to a certain degree, if one takes into consideration the differences between these countries and others like Chile and Mexico in terms of value added. We have already mentioned the study of the OECD, according to which in Mexico, 32% of value added of all exports is accounted for by foreign (backward) value added, while in Costa Rica the proportion was 28%. Argentina, Brazil and Colombia were located toward the lower end of the distribution in terms of backward value added (14, 11, and 8, respectively) and toward the higher end for forward value added participation (16, 24, 30), which means that they incorporate little foreign value in their exports, while they contribute a much higher percentage to the exports of the countries toward which their exports are oriented (Cadestin et al. 2016: 13).

We do not have an indicator of how these data have changed in time for all the countries we have been discussing; we only have information about Mexico and Costa Rica, two outsourcing economies. In both countries, the domestic value added has been reduced since 1990, although their participation in global value chains has increased. Among the countries included in the study, it is the East Asian countries—Malaysia, Philippines, and Thailand—who have increased their domestic value added share. By the studies done by Taeko Hoshino in Mexico and in East Asia, we know that while in Mexico local entrepreneurs have not been able to integrate the Japanese automaker chains, in Asia they have (Hoshino 2018). This proves that higher integration to global value chains does not automatically mean higher value added, but it may be on the contrary a lower one, which also means that foreign investment, even with higher technological content, does not automatically lead to upgrading (Fig. 4.3).

For the UNCTAD, the problem of the transnational companies that supply the exports of certain economies is not the repatriation of earnings, and they affirm that "…although overall domestic value added trade in developing economies in 2010 was more than 20 times higher than total repatriated FDI income from developing countries, the situation for individual countries may be more nuanced" (UNCTAD 2013: 154). Nonetheless, we consider the main problem to be the fact of upgrading, of technology transfer, which is impeded when suppliers are foreign, as is the case of Mexico. The Asian strategy and success in upgrading have been to substitute foreign suppliers by domestic ones and through co-investment and acquisition, to eventually substitute the mother company.

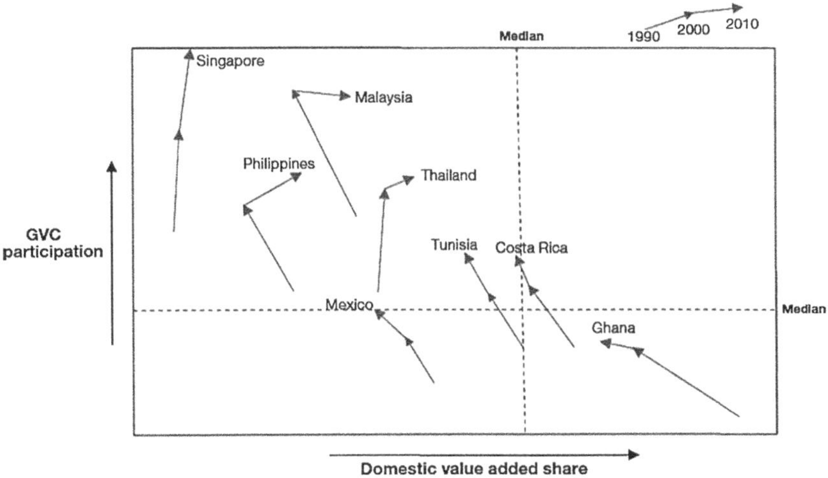

Fig. 4.3 Global value chains development paths (*Source* UNCTAD 2013: 172)

Central American countries display higher levels of backward integration, but tend to source more from North America, the European Union, and Asia. In Mexico and Costa Rica, only 3 and 11% respectively of foreign inputs come from other Latin American countries, while 40% comes from the USA and Canada. In this sense, Central American countries belong more to North American GVCs. Forward linkages with regional partners are most developed in Argentina and Colombia, with Latin America accounting for 17 and 14% respectively of intermediate exports, compared to 8 and 3% for Mexico and Chile (Cadestin et al. 2016: 16).

In Brazil, one could suppose a higher value added if one takes into consideration that this country has developed the technology to build airplanes, to drill in deep waters, to produce ethanol, among others. Nonetheless, it is also true that in the last years, with the intent to develop socio-developmentalism, it became a large exporter of commodities, which have increasingly integrated their exports, it has de-industrialized due to the Dutch disease, and thus has lost value added.

References

Achtenberg, Emily. (2017, August 19). Why is Evo Morales Reviving Bolivia's Controversial TIPNIS Road? *NACLA Reporting on the Americas.* https://nacla.org/blog/2017/08/22/why-evo-morales-reviving-bolivia%E2%80%99s-controversial-tipnis-road. Accessed 18 October 2018.

African Development Bank Secretariat. (2009). What can the G20 do on trade that can benefit Africa? In R. Baldwin & S. Evenett (Eds.), *The collapse of global trade, murky protectionism, and the crisis: Recommendations for the G20.* London: VoxEU.org Publication/Centre for Economic Policy Research (CEPR).

Auboin, M. (2009). Restoring trade finance: What the G20 can do. In R. Baldwin & S. Evenett (Eds.), *The collapse of global trade, murky protectionism, and the crisis: Recommendations for the G20.* London: VoxEU.org Publication/Centre for Economic Policy Research (CEPR).

Baldwin, R., & Evenett, S. (Eds.). (2009). *The collapse of global trade, murky protectionism, and the crisis: Recommendations for the G20.* London: VoxEU.org Publication/Centre for Economic Policy Research (CEPR).

Bekerman, M., & Dalmasso, G. (2014). Políticas productivas y competitividad industrial. El caso de Argentina y Brasil. *Brazilian Journal of Political Economy, 34*(1), 158–180.

Bensusán, G., & Moreno-Brid, J. C. (2012). *El desempeño de las política macroeconómicas y laborales y las respuestas a la crisis internacional (1990–2010).* In M. Puchet Anyul, M. Rojas, R. Salazar, G. Valenti & F. Valdés Ugarte (Eds.), *América Latina en los albores del Siglo XXI: 2. Aspectos sociopolíticos.* México: Flacso.

Bouët, A., & Laborde, D. (2009). The potential cost of a failed Doha round. *SSRN Electronic Journal.* Available at SSRN: https://doi.org/10.2139/ssrn.1396335.

Boyer, R. (2014). Is more equality possible in Latin America? A challenge in a world of contrasted but interdependent inequality regimes. *DesiguALdades.net, Working Paper Series 67.* Berlin: Freie Universität Berlin.

Boyer, R. (2015). *Économie politique des capitalismes, Théorie de la régulation et des crises.* Paris: La Découverte.

Brown, C. P. (2009). Protectionism is on the rise: Antidumping investigations. In R. Baldwin & S. Evenett (Eds.), *The collapse of global trade, murky protectionism, and the crisis: Recommendations for the G20.* London: VoxEU.org Publication/Centre for Economic Policy Research (CEPR).

Cadestin, C., Gourdon, J., & Kowalski, P. (2016). *Participation in Global Value Chains in Latin America: Implications for Trade and Trade-Related Policy* (OECD Trade Policy Papers, No. 192). Paris: OECD Publishing.

Chamon, M., & Garcia, M. (2016). Capital controls in Brazil: effective? *Journal of International Money and Finance,* (61), 163–187.

Chiarini, T. (2016). A inercia estructural da base productiva brasileira: O IDE e a transferencia internacional de tecnologia. *Revista de Economia Política, 36*(2), 286–308.

De la Torre, A., Ize, A., & Schmukler, S. L. (2012). *Financial Development in Latin America and the Caribbean. The Road Ahead.* IBRD, World Bank: Washington, DC.

Drahokoupil, J., & Myant, M. (2015). Putting comparative capitalism research in its place: Varieties of capitalism in transition economies. In M. Ebenau, I. Bruff & C. May (Eds.), *New directions in critical comparative capitalisms research.* London: Palgrave Macmillan.

Dussel Peters, E. (2006). Hacia una política de competitividad en México. *ECONOMÍA unam, 3*(9), 65–81.

Esquivel, G. (2010). De la inestabilidad macroeconómica al estancamiento estabilizador: el papel del diseño y la conducción de la política económica. In N. Lustig, *Los grandes problemas de México. IX Crecimiento Económico y Equidad.* México: El Colegio de México.

Ffrench-Davis, R. (2008). *Chile entre el neoliberalismo y el crecimiento con equidad. Reformas y políticas económicas desde 1973.* Santiago: J. C. Sáez editor.

Fritz, B. (2017). *Conceptos Actuales del desarrollo económico y social: Opciones para Ecuador.* Cámara de Comercio de Guayaquil, Ecuador: Power point.

Gallagher, K. P. (2011). Trading away financial stability in Colombia: Capital controls and the US-Colombia trade agreement. *SerieBrief,* (66), Latin American Trade Network. http://www.ase.tufts.edu/gdae/Pubs/rp/Brief66_TradingAway_Gallagher.pdf. Accessed 15 May 2018.

Gamberoni, E., & Newfarmer, R. (2009). Trade protection: Incipient but worrisome trends. In R. Baldwin & E. Simon (Eds.), *The collapse of global trade, murky protectionism, and the crisis: Recommendations for the G20.* London: VoxEU.org Publication/Centre for Economic Policy Research (CEPR).

Ghosh, A. R., & Qureshi, M. S. (2016). *What's in a name? That which we call capital controls IMF.* Working Paper 16/25. Available at: https://www.imf.org/external/pubs/ft/wp/2016/wp1625.pdf. Accessed 15 May 2018.

Hoshino, T. (2018). *Red de proveeduría de la industria automotriz en México. ¿Es posible la incorporación de las empresas mexicanas?* Guadalajara: Universidad de Guadalajara.

Ibarra, C. (2008). La paradoja del crecimiento lento de México. *Revista de la CEPAL, 95,* 83–102.

Ibarra, C. (2011). México: la maquila, el desajuste monetario y el crecimiento impulsado por las exportaciones. *Revista CEPAL, 104,* 199–215.

Jeanneau, S., Tovar, C. E., & Moreno, R. (2007). Introduction. In S. Jeanneau, & C. E. Tovar. *Evolving banking systems in Latin America and the Caribbean: challenges and implications for monetary policy and financial stability* (BIS Papers No. 33, pp. 1–2). Basel, Switzerland: Monetary and Economic Department, Bank for International Settlements.

Katzenstein, P. J. (1985). *Small states in world markets industrial policy in Europe*. Ithaca and London: Cornell University Press.
Magud, N. E., Reinhart, C. M., & Rogoff, K. S. (2005). *Capital controls: Myth and reality-a portfolio balance approach* (Working paper). Oregon: University of Oregon, Economics Department.
Martina, M. (2017, August 24). Exclusive: In China, the Party's push for influence inside foreign firms stirs fears. *Reuters*. https://www.reuters.com/article/us-china-congress-companies/exclusive-in-china-the-partys-push-for-influence-inside-foreign-firms-stirs-fears-idUSKCN1B40JU. Accessed 15 May 2018.
Nölke, A., & Vliegenthart, A. (2009). Enlarging the varieties of capitalism: The emergence of dependent market economies in East Central Europe. *World Politics, 61*(4), 670–702.
Palma, J. G. (2005). The seven main 'stylized facts' of the Mexican economy since trade liberalization and NAFTA. *Industrial and Corporate Change, 14*(6), 941–991.
Prates, D., Fritz, B., & de Paula, L. F. (2017). *Brazil at crossroads: A critical assessment of developmentalist policies* (Manuscript). Berlin: Freie University of Berlin.
Puyana, A., & Romero Tellaeche, J. (2009). *México. De la crisis de la deuda al estancamiento económico*. México: El Colegio de México.
UNCTAD. (2013). *World investment report, global value chains: Investment and trade for development*. New York and Geneva: United Nations Publication.
World Bank. (2018). *Doing business 2018. Reforming to create jobs*. Washington, DC: World Bank Publications.

CHAPTER 5

The Role of the State

We have already discussed the effects of the influence of the theories of economic institutionalism *à la* North and Weingast on the new institutionalist perspective that pretends to define a political economy excluding the State. This position derives from their conception of a "self-regulated market," in which politics is considered the main obstacle to the efficient working of the market, to democratic order, and to development. This is the reason why neo-institutionalism has tried its best to conceal the significance of the State. It is very revealing that the most valuable texts of the institutionalist school outright overlook the State. For example, Hall and Soskice, Thelen, Steinmo, and even Streeck do not have a definition of the State in their most important works. Steinmo's valuable book about the modern States does not have a section on the State, but it has one on "methodology" (on what he calls an evolutionary narrative) which is divided into subsections such as the "global standard," "what went wrong," "political science," "politics as evolution," "evolutionary theory," and "historical institutionalism." In his general index, the State has no entry—its only mention is when he talks about the Welfare State (Steinmo 2010). The same can be said about the multi-cited book on the varieties of capitalism by Hall and Soskice. The core of the book, as we have discussed in chapter one, is the firm, an actor that evolves in a certain environment that includes the State. But the State is not a central actor, or institution, not even an arena. In fact, when one looks for the entry for State in the index, the reader is referred to: government/State, which has sub-entries such as: business relations,

I. Bizberg, *Diversity of Capitalisms in Latin America*,
https://doi.org/10.1007/978-3-319-95537-7_5

decentralized cooperation, high and low level of intervention (see CMEs and LMEs respectively), labor market policy, power of. The State is taken into consideration as its function, and assimilated to government, to an institution. Nonetheless, the State is implicit in the analysis of the two types of economy: absent for the most part in the liberal type, extremely present in the coordinated economy. The same can be said for Ben Schneider, who explicitly writes that his analysis will not consider the State, due to the fact that the book is focused on the enterprise, and that the State/government is basically an obstacle to its development—it is this a negative element in the analysis. This desire to minimize the action of the State is the reason why the VoC defined only two types of capitalism, the market-/liberal-oriented one, where the State is absent, and the coordinated one, where the social actors are central, and the State occupies a subsidiary position. This is why VoC was incapable of recognizing the existence of other types of capitalism where the State is central, like France, Korea, Taiwan, China, and even Japan. All of these capitalisms were simply included in the coordinated type, although their characteristics are divergent.

Although Evans' book can also be included within the institutionalist perspective, it does focus on the State, because he wants to understand what characteristics it needs to have in order to be capable of to developing an economy. He considers the State as an institution and as an actor. As an institution, it may be a more or less Weberian bureaucracy that follows institutional and legal rules, and is not politicized as to favor some sectors of society rather than others, and orients its action toward the general interest of society as a whole rather than particular interests. It may also be a more or less coherent institution; in his examples, the government officials of the East Asian States go to the same schools, pass the same examinations, and construct a strong *esprit de corps* that assures they represent the State and then the collective interests of the nation, rather than their particular ones. He also considers the State as an actor that can adopt different postures, that of a "demiurge," a direct producer of certain products, steel, oil, etc.; that of a "midwife" that induces entrepreneurs to invest in certain sectors; or a kinf of "husbandry", which promotes or helps entrepreneurs in a new sector of the economy (Evans 1995: 74–85).

Evans considers that qualifying the State as weak or strong is too vague, because a strong State may be either developmentalist, as Korea and Taiwan, or a predatory State that extracts resources from the economy and society and does nothing to further development. He also affirms that the concept of autonomy, although necessary, is not sufficient. While any State that is not autonomous cannot enhance development, since it is captured by a sector of society, i.e. and by a sector of economic interests that hinders the development of other segments of the economy for since they fear of being weakened by competing economic and political interests. In fact, an extractive State is autonomous of society as a whole, and tries to disarticulate and disorganize civil society (Evans 1995: 43–73).

Evans' main argument is that a developmentalist State is not totally autonomous. It is autonomous with respect to any specific group or sector of society as it has to represent the interests of the whole. Nonetheless, it is an embedded State that intervenes in the economy that helps, guides, or even forces entrepreneurs in a certain direction. It is closely linked to the social group of particulars with which it shares a collective project of economic transformation. It also has to be a State with a Weberian, not politicized bureaucracy, a technocratic State, with an internal coherence, a certain *esprit du corps*, like one of Japan's MITI, the State functionaries of Korea and Taiwan, and the French ENA. In Latin America, according to this author, the States have been captured by the group of entrepreneurs that they created; they are clientelistic and fragmented States with an isolated autonomy. Thus, although these States, for example, Brazil, did achieve a certain degree of development, they did not succeed as well as the East Asian ones, which were more autonomous, more coherent, and more embedded (Evans 1995).

Evans defines certain characteristics of the State that are extremely useful for an analysis like the one we are undertaking in this chapter, he defines the State in terms of its strength (determined by its internal cohesion, and its capacity to impose its interests and projects on other actors), its autonomy (which added to its strength defines its Weberian character as a rational bureaucracy), and its capacity to act in a complementary mode with the entrepreneurs. In addition, Evans considers the State not only as an institution that sets the rules of the game, but also as an actor that is involved in the task of developing a country. Nonetheless, he does consider the possibility and desirability that the State be neutral with respect to the social sectors or classes that constitute society (Evans 1995). The predatory State is an actor that benefits itself, the clientelistic or captured State acts for one sector of society, and the embedded-developmental State acts on behalf of the interests of the totality of society (1995).

Whereas in the institutionalist perspective, the State is either merely an institution among others, or a neutral actor, in the structuralist tradition

(Cardoso and Faletto 1969; Haggard 1990; Skockpol 1984; Moore 1969; Bresser-Pereira 2018), it is never a neutral agent; being the central actor of any society, it is connected to a coalition of social actors and acts on behalf of them, pressing for a certain type of economy that benefits certain sectors more than others (Poulantzas, Amable, Boyer). It can orient society in one or another economic direction (Cardoso and Faletto, Haggard, Kay). In addition, it can lead a country toward a democracy or an authoritarian regime (Moore, Skockpol, Rueschemeyer). It can also renounce to be an actor and become a mere agent of the international economic forces (Beck 2002) or try to compromise between two or more sectors of society, and become an "incoherent"[1] actor (Théret 1995).

In this conception, the State is "a field of power struggles between bearers of different powers, an arena where agents and institutions have a certain amount of specific capital (economic or cultural, especially), sufficient to occupy dominant positions within their respective fields" (Bourdieu 2013: 375, cited by Rodriguez Salazar 2015: 14). Théret, on the other hand, recognizes that the State has a certain autonomy from the social conflict and that it thus does not only respond to the temporary compromise between the forces that are in struggle in its midst, but that the "…state structure imposes itself […] as a solution to a certain number of crises that affect both the social structure and that, in some way, are a manner of resolving the contradictions of the previous political constructions. [In this way, the State] is a social relation that is contradictory with the capitalistic relation, a relation that dominates and structures a political order according to an antagonistic logic with that of prevailing capitalism…" (Théret 2002, cited by Rodriguez Salazar 2015: 15).

This means that the State is a field of power (which is different from saying that it is an arena), where the conflict between different social actors takes place, and in this sense, it acts according to the interests that are dominant within it. Nonetheless, as this internal conflict never gives an absolute winner, but always a compromise between forces, and in the other hand, as the State is a specific actor in an economic-social-political structure, it preserves the capacity to act against the dominant actors, against capital, in order to resolve certain contradictions that appear in the economic, social, political, and international spheres.

[1]We are simplifying the argument of Bruno Jobert, who analyzes the ambiguity of the State due to the contradictory exigencies that the political order has to fulfil, presented by Théret in his introduction.

5.1 Two Types of State Action: Agent of Liberalism or Developmentalist State

In this chapter, we will discuss the role of the State in each of the types of capitalism in Latin America—its determination and capacity to become either an actor of development or an agent of the market. We consider that while during ISI, some Latin American States neared the characteristics of the Asian developmentalist States, that is, they displayed a capacity of building an ample social coalition, consisting of financial capital, industrialists, middle classes, and workers that allowed them to become a significant actor for development (as in Bismarckian Germany, Japan, Korea, Taiwan, and present-day China) (Bresser-Pereira 2018), this is not the case in most of them, although there are significant differences.

We begin our analysis by redefining the types of capitalism based on whether the State plays a central role or whether the economy is left to the market (Bresser-Pereira 2018). We can combine this taxonomy with our prior binary classification on the accumulation regime, based on the emphasis given to either profits or wages. Our four types of capitalism in Latin America result accordingly (Fig. 5.1).

In two types of capitalism, the State has a significant role: in one of them, the social-developmentalist, the State drives investment and productivity by way of industrial policies, State investments in infrastructure and science and technology, allocates direct loans at low interest rates

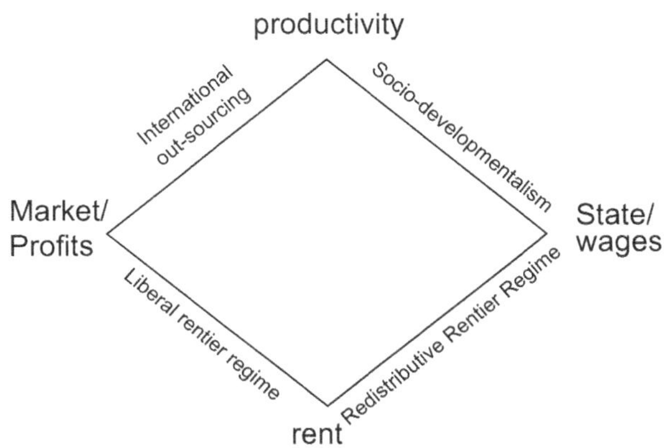

Fig. 5.1 State intervention against market (*Source* Own elaboration)

through its investments banks, and occasionally applies some protection to its economy, be it through taxing imports or devaluating its currency. In addition, It may not only support offer, but also encourage demand through actions that expand the internal market, through the redistribution of profits among the entrepreneurs and the workers, by increasing minimum wages, stimulating collective negotiations, inducing the formalization of labor, and expanding the social protection system. As all these require high State expenditure, it exerts a strong fiscal pressure on society. The State also protects national capital and internal demand by implementing countercyclical measures to respond to external shocks. In general, facing a solid State we find powerful unions and strong business organizations that, in turn, exert pressure on the government in order to preserve their particular or common interests—although there are exceptions where the developmentalist State is authoritarian such as Korea and Taiwan in the 1950s and 1960s, and more recently China where sectorial organizations are prohibited. The countries that approach this type the nearest are Brazil, until the impeachment of Dilma, and Argentina, during the Kirchner–Fernandez presidency (2003–2015).

In the case of the redistributive rentier mode, the role of the State does not orient the economy toward the internal market through industrial policies, investment, innovation, but it is basically "purely" redistributive. Both the political and social relationships, as well as the economic ones are defined by the fact that the State owns the production of commodities or extracts taxes and royalties from the private companies that exploit natural resources. In many cases, The State's abundant financial resources are distributed without any productive goals; they are expended due to the pressure of social organizations and are politically productive in a clientelistic or State-corporatist logic. The fact that the State has very abundant financial resources implies a certain tendency to authoritarianism, or when the regime maintains itself within democratic limits, a tendency to what O'Donnell called a delegative democracy, which we will analyze in Chapter 7. Resources are used to foster social organizations that will serve the State as a political base (Venezuela), or try to coopt autonomous social organizations or movements, in order to control them (Bolivia, Ecuador). Nonetheless, the authoritarian or delegative tendencies are dependent, in the last case, on the power of the social organizations, which may cause the political system to tend toward social corporatism.

The other two forms depend more on the market. As the State has a much weaker role; they are both the exact opposite of what Chalmers, Evans, Amsden, and Bresser-Pereira consider a developmental State.

In the case of the international outsourcing model, which resembles Mexico very closely, the action of the State is simply to establish the best conditions for foreign, but also national, capitals to invest. It is thus subordinate to large foreign and domestic capitals; it is an agent of liberalism or of neoliberalism as Beck has written. In this case, the State does not pursue any industrial policy. As the Minister of Economy in 1994, Jaime Serra Puche said when NAFTA came into effect, "…the best industrial policy is NO industrial policy."[2] The State exerts very low fiscal pressure, applies loose environmental regulation measures, and represses salaries, as ways by which it seeks to attract investments. It does not subsidize through loans or other means, not only because it does not consider they are pertinent, but also because it has restricted resources. This is also the reason why its investment in infrastructure, as well as in research and development, is very limited. The State is not only weak in financial terms, but has little autonomy from the entrepreneurs. Monetary policy is fundamentally oriented toward preserving exchange rate stability, which generally leads to the overvaluation of the local currency, a situation that is favorable for the interests of foreign capital, as it facilitates the import of spare parts to be assembled and a stable return on capital. It is a model oriented to achieve high profits, maintain low salaries and low social security costs that is stabilized by a State-financed residual/assistance-oriented social security system. The main competitive advantage of the assembly platform economy are salaries.

Like the outsourcing and rentier economies, the liberal rentier economies are dependent on the external market, and as liberal economies, they are founded on a weak State, which at most acts as a regulatory instance. It does not intervene in the economy, nor does it try to stimulate the internal market, because it considers that investments in commodities will naturally lead to the growth of the economy. Fiscal pressure is low, there is no industrial policy, and salaries increase according to the forces of the market, although they are pulled down by the wage policies of the government, the low level of the minimum salary, the lack of union representation and collective agreements, and the great proportion of informal workers in countries like Peru and Colombia. Facing a weak State, there is a weak civil society and powerless unions, which are incapable of exerting social and political pressure to increase salaries or reduce the proportion of informal workers that exert a downward pressure on salaries (Tables 5.1 and 5.2).

[2] https://www.forbes.com.mx/el-tabu-de-la-politica-industrial/.

Table 5.1 State intervention 1

	International outsourcing	*Socio-developmentalist*	*Rentier/ liberal*	*Rentier/ redistributive*
Character	Neoliberal State/agent of neoliberalism	Intent of an embedded State	Subsidiary State	Tendency toward a clientelistic/ corporatist State
Fiscal pressure	Weak	Strong	Weak	Relatively strong
Ideology/ discourse	Liberal	Structuralist	Liberal	Structuralist
State financial capacity	Weak	Strong	Weak	Weak
Regulatory capacity	Very low	High	Low	Low
Industrial policy	None	Strong	None	Weak/lack of resources

Source Own elaboration

Table 5.2 State intervention 2

	International outsourcing	*Socio-developmentalist*	*Rentier/liberal*	*Rentier/ redistributive*
Autonomy	Weak	Strong	Weak	Strong
Embeddedness	Weak	Relatively Strong	Weak	Weak
Stateness	Weak	Strong	Weak (Chile—relatively strong)	Strong

Source Own elaboration

5.2 The Ideology, the Discourse, Regarding the Role of the State

Just as autonomy and force, what certain authors call State capacity does not necessarily signify more or less intervention or a tendency to become an actor of development. This is especially true in the case of Chile, for example, where there is broad consensus that in this country the State has the capacity of imposing the rule of law, regulation, and taxes, but that it is more an agent of the market than an actor. While the Chilean and Uruguayan States are considered to have a strong capacity, those of Peru, Bolivia and Ecuador are low capacity States (Quispe 2017).

This is why the discussion of this chapter will analyze their capability of becoming a developmentalist State.

We will begin by examining the ideology of the governmental elites. The ideas expressed by the leadership of a country regarding the economic role of the State are not purely discursive, but also performative, since they guide the action of the State. Performativity is the capacity of speech, or of an inquiry not only to represent the world, but also to provoke, to realize it, to transform it. The concept originates in linguistics and describes a statement that institutes that about which one talks (Muniesa and Callon 2013), performativity exists when communication accomplishes or induces an action.

Ideology, ideas, and thus discourse are then significant because, to a large degree, they define the orientation of an actor, in this case the State. Since the 1980s, the idea of an auto-regulated market that does not require the action of the State and that stems from the appreciation that politics and governmental action always introduce distortions to be avoided has dominated the ideological orientation of most functionaries linked with the economic ministries. This conception has been imposed by economists who have studied in the USA, that have gained high posts in government, and that have replaced traditional Latin American politicians, which were mainly lawyers. They have been supported by the international economic institutions (like the IMF, WB, the OECD). In some countries, heterodox economists have been able to resist and defend the idea that the State has a very significant role to play in the development of a country, and they have been able to influence on the government, but in others they haven't.

During the "lost decade," in the 1980s, most countries in Latin America implemented a liberal model, based on the "Washington consensus." Mexico is interesting because while many of the other countries of the continent have, at one moment or another, adjusted their economic model, Mexico has been astonishingly constant. The liberal ideology was implemented in Mexico during the debt crisis and has survived until the present due to the fact that it was implemented by an authoritarian government and no serious rejection that has yet been organized. In the decade of the 1990s, the orthodox liberal program was anchored by NAFTA, as this treaty made it very difficult for the State to intervene in the economy.

In Mexico, a discourse promoting State intervention, protection, subsidies, or fomenting certain sectors of the economy has been out of the question since the mid-1980s. The dominant conception is that the State just sets the stage for private investment, and that all investment decisions are to be taken by private capital. The totally passive posture of the Mexican government is clearly posited in this quote by Calderón, the former president of Mexico (2006–2012): "I invite you, my friends, to make our country one of the best investment destinations in the world, not to be afraid of investing to generate jobs, to take without prejudices and without complexes the opportunity to make our country an attractive land so that this investment arrives precisely to generate the jobs we need."

President Peña Nieto has the same position when he affirms that "Today what prevails in the world is a huge uncertainty, a great uncertainty. The big investors do not really know where to take their money. Yes, there is liquidity, yes there are resources, big companies have financial capabilities, the big issue is: where do they put it to give profitability and security to their investments."[3] And he synthesizes the economic policy, in fact industrial policy of the country, in as a no-policy: "We must be very clear: the industrial policy of this administration is based on commercial openness, not on protectionism. Mexico's industrial policy is now based on strengthening our competitiveness, not on establishing barriers that inhibit competition. Our policy of industrial development is based on confidence in our abilities to succeed, and not on the fear of being overcome."[4]

Finally, Luis Videgaray, the Minister of Foreign Relations, stated: "With the structural reforms we have opened ourselves to generate innovation, cheaper products and better services. This is not only a business opportunity for the investor but it will allow us to grow more rapidly."[5] Absolutely no mention of any kind of role for the State.

Chile was the first country that implemented an orthodox liberal program after the *coup d'Etat* against Salvador Allende in 1973, in what Ffrench-Davis (2008) has called a "pure neo-liberal experiment," when

[3] https://www.gob.mx/presidencia/prensa/palabras-del-presidente-licenciado-enrique-pena-nieto-durante-el-evento-4-anos-transformando-a-mexico-encuentro-con-servidores-publicos?idiom=es.

[4] https://www.gob.mx/presidencia/prensa/reafirma-el-presidente-enrique-pena-nieto-su-total-compromiso-con-la-transformacion-de-mexico.

[5] https://www.20minutos.com.mx/noticia/100682/0/inversion-extranjera-permitira-crecer-mas-aceleradamente-videgaray/.

the so-called Chicago Boys implemented an orthodox liberal economy in the 1970s. The pure Chilean model was defined by Ffrench-Davis as "…a generalized […] retreat of the action of the State. This implied public property, its developmental role and the orientation of indirect economic policies, that were posited as being absolutely 'neutral'. The conception of the subsidiary State was applied with huge restrictions, as it was assumed that the market could assume numerous functions that in fact it was not able to assume satisfactorily" (Ffrench-Davis 2008: 83). Paradoxically, in the face of the economic crisis of 1981–1982, this radically liberal economic model was modified in the contrary direction, allowing for more State intervention, while in the rest of the continent, liberalization was implemented.

Nevertheless, the situation has changed since the arrival of the first socialist presidents, Lagos and Bachelet, with the same coalition, *Concertación por la Democracia*. A first change was discursive: in her speech to Congress on the State of the nation, Bachelet declared that "We will need more market and we will need more State. A better market and a better State. Because, in the new economy, market and State are not antonyms. The crisis not only made evident the insufficiency of laissez-faire and the need to establish strict rules for the financial markets. It also made clear the regulatory incapacity of some States, out of lack of interest or embedded interests."[6] With this discourse, we seem to have gone a long way from the pure retreat of the State of the 1970s. Nonetheless, Piñera, who won a second presidential term in January 2018 has a more liberal point of view. According to him, "…we will replace the old discussion of more or less State by the new challenge of building a better State, a more modern, more transparent and more efficient one, at the service of the people. A State that not only insures the base of security, but lifts the roof of opportunities." "Our State is weak in the fight against crime, drugs and the eradication of poverty. And, on the other hand, we have too much State in areas such as the bureaucratic paperwork that drowns our entrepreneurs."[7] The theme on the efficiency of the State, of its modernization, has been recurrent in neoliberalism.

Other liberal officials of the Andean countries have a very similar discourse. The first idea is that the State is too big, although it has already endured a very intense liberalization process during the 1990s.

[6] https://www.camara.cl/camara/media/docs/discursos/21mayo_2009.pdf.

[7] https://www.camara.cl/camara/media/docs/discursos/21mayo_2010.pdf.

Uribe, president of Colombia from 2002 to 2010, talking about the reforms that have reduced considerably the weight of the State, asserted: "These reforms do not dismantle the State, they are oriented to put it at the service of the community and not of the alliance between politicking and trade union excesses. These reforms have had to overcome the obstacle of ideological radicalism. We will continue with them as a definitive legacy of security in public finances and legitimization of the social function of the State."[8] He goes on to consider that while the State has a social responsibility, it should restrain its action in the economic areas. We will see in Chapter 8 that the responsibility of the State in the social sphere has been reduced to a minimum. "Our state is a giant bureaucracy, it is ineffective in the face of the corruption that deforms political attitudes and it is dangerously small in social investment. The State must be the promoter of development, guarantor of social equity and distributor of public order. It should not be an obstacle to private initiative, nor be absent from social demands."[9] Uribe went as far as coining the concept of "Communitarian State" which he defined as intermediary between a neoliberal conception that abolishes the State and a bureaucracy that bankrupts the State.[10]

In Peru, like in Argentina (with Menem), liberalism was promoted by Fujimori, with radical privatization programs. He considered that although the State had its main function to encourage private capital investments, it should try to orient the economy toward exports—what the Mexican government has been doing for the last years. In a speech, Fujimori declared: "I have no doubt that industrial activity, in its various branches, requires the promotion of the State, with the aim of orienting it to exports. [...] The State, even when it intervenes outside its scope, will do so only temporarily and with the purpose of guaranteeing the universal dissemination of the market and development."[11] Very clearly, the intervention of the State has to be temporary, and its main objective

[8]Discurso completo del presidente Uribe durante instalación del Congreso, 20 de julio de 2008, https://www.elespectador.com/noticias/politica/articulo-discurso-completo-del-presidente-uribe-durante-instalacion-del-congreso.

[9]Álvaro Uribe, Discurso de toma de posesión, 7 de agosto de 2002, http://www.eltiempo.com/archivo/documento/MAM-1339914.

[10]Discurso ante el Congreso, 20 de julio de 2010, http://www.vanguardia.com/historico/69584-lea-discurso-completo-de-alvaro-uribe-velez-en-instalacion-del-congreso.

[11]Mensaje a la nación ante el Congreso el 28 de julio de 2001, http://www4.congreso.gob.pe/museo/mensajes/Mensaje-2001-2.asp.

is to impose the market, which once imposed will take care of itself without the need of the State.

The impact of liberalism in Peru has been even stronger than in Chile, as we can see from the position of the two presidents that succeeded Fujimori. Alan García, of the center-left party APRA, declared that "We do not believe in the owner state, we do not believe in the bureaucratic State that has failed and continues to fail in the countries where it is prompted. We promote investment and trade, but we must also promote regulation to prevent abuses and monopolies."[12] Even Ollanta Humala, who was looked upon as a leftist leader before he arrived at the presidency of Peru, expressed a similar position to one of Uribe: "We will establish a new relationship between the State and the market, different from the failed extreme recipes of the interventionist State or the minimal and excluding State. In this new relationship, the State will be a promoter of investment and development, guarantor of the exercise of rights and freedoms, promoter of opportunities for all."[13]

In contrast, in the countries in which during the 1980s and 1990s, labor, social organizations, and movements exerted significant resistance to the implementation of neoliberalism, this model could not be imposed in its orthodox form. In the countries where social movements were active, a backlash led to a change in the economic model (Brazil, Argentina, Ecuador, Bolivia), which brought back the State and, based on the resources from the super commodities boom, tried to implement a socio-developmentalist model during the years 2000–2013.

In Uruguay, for example, President Tabaré Vazquez, affirmed that: "[Uruguay is] a country with a strong statist tradition. A tradition that dates back to the beginning of the twentieth century, when the governments of José Batlle and Ordóñez (especially the second, between 1911 and 1915) nationalized the Bank of the Republic, when the Mortgage Bank was founded, the State assured the monopoly of insurance and electricity services, and increased its participation in water services, railways and trams."[14] He defined the role of the State and the market as follows:

[12]Mensaje ante el Congreso, 28 de julio de 10, http://www4.congreso.gob.pe/museo/mensajes/Mensaje-2010-1.asp.

[13]Mensaje ante el Congreso, 28 de julio de 2011, http://www4.congreso.gob.pe/museo/mensajes/Mensaje-2011-1a.asp.

[14]Tabaré Vázquez, Toward a more balanced and sustainable economy: the role of the public sector, http://asip.org.ar/hacia-una-economia-mas-balanced-and-sustainable-sector-of-ector-public/.

> I believe that a country can simultaneously grow held by the hand of the market and by distribution induced by the State. Without ignoring the role of the State in other areas and strategic activities concerning the sovereignty and viability of a nation, the State is irreplaceable in its task of distributing the benefits of growth to the entire population through sound, effective, and efficient public policies. It is the only mechanism by which the population that is least favored by the market may have access to high quality public goods [...] [We are neither in favor of an] omnipresent State nor of an absent State. The State has to do what it is set to, which no one can do better than him, and do it well. [Ibid.]

Another President of Uruguay, José Mugica, denoted the same position in a couple of interviews. He mentioned that Uruguay had carried out a referendum where it was decided that the State should continue being the owner of electric energy, communications, as well as the refinement and distribution of oil. He considered that although "We know that if they were private they would be better administered [...] if they were private, due to the investments they have, [the gains] would leave the country. It is essential that a country like ours keep a strong State that does lots of things, if it were not so we would be like a leaf at the mercy of the wind."[15]

In Ecuador, President Correa expressed a similar viewpoint, which he used to legitimize some of the nationalizations he applied. He placed the role of the State in a broader context and that of a different type of development that "...does not only reflect the perceptions, experiences and interests of dominant groups or countries, that does not oppress society, lives, and people within the entelechy of the market; but where the State, through planned and collective action, retrieves its essential role for progress; where intangible assets like social capital are preserved; where apparent demands of the economy do not exclude, or even worse, antagonize social development."[16]

After the serious crisis of 2001–2002, Néstor Kirchner, president of Argentina, declared: "We want to retrieve the values of solidarity and social justice that will allow us to transform our present reality and move towards the construction of a more balanced, more mature and more

[15] Interview by Jordi Évole with José Mujica, https://www.youtube.com/watch?v=ZlE-9ohXgDI.

[16] Inaugural speech by Rafael Correa, http://democraciasur.com/2007/01/22/ecuador-discurso-de-toma-de-posesion-de-rafael-correa-como-presidente/.

just society. We know that the market organizes economically, but it does not articulate socially, we must have the State seek equality where the market excludes and abandons."[17] The following president of Argentina, Cristina Fernández, facing the crisis of 2008, considered that: "The State must play a much more active role in regulation and control, because this great crisis was caused by the absence of the State, which was not able to control, neither the rating agencies, nor the investment banks, nor financial capital. The financial system ended not only self-destructing, but affecting the functioning of the real economy."[18]

In the same logic, during the global crisis, Lula da Silva considered that "…it was the governments who saved the world from the international economic crisis. At the time, when the tongs tightened, it was the State, who had the confidence of the people, who needed to intervene in the economy; the same State that had been discredited for so long by the Washington Consensus, by the neoliberal policies."[19] During her campaign, Dilma Rousseff, the president of Brazil that was illegitimately (although legally) ousted from the presidency in 2017, defended the intervention of the development bank and the "*política industrial ativa*" of the government in these terms: "There will be no long-term investment in the country if there is no long-term credit, and today the long-term credit is allocated by the BNDES […] it is the State's role to encourage the domestic production of everything that can be produced locally, including the case of pre-salt exploration equipment, a sector in which, according to the critics of the government, Brazil does not have competitiveness […] To ensure industrial policy was considered outdated, [nonetheless] that is the reason why although Brazil did not have a [naval] industry, it is now building ships."[20]

Finally, the president of Bolivia, Evo Morales, proposes an economic model where the State is central for development, as it "…will determine a productive and commercial policy that guarantees an offer of sufficient goods and services to adequately meet the basic domestic needs and

[17] http://www.lanacion.com.ar/498849-el-texto-completo-del-discurso-presidencial.

[18] Discurso ante la OIT, http://staging.ilo.org/public/libdoc/ilo/2009/109B09_327_span.pdf.

[19] https://www.terra.com.br/noticias/brasil/lula-volta-defender-maior-presenca-do-estado-na-economia-e-na-promocao-social,d03b4999eed4b310VgnCLD200000bbcceb0aRCRD.html.

[20] https://exame.abril.com.br/brasil/as-propostas-de-dilma-para-a-economia.

strengthens the export capacity. The State will strengthen the productive infrastructure and the manufacturing, industrial and basic services for the productive sector [...] and promote and support the export of value-added goods and services."[21]

5.3 Financial Strength of the State

Although some of these speeches are ambiguous, especially those of the Andean liberal countries, and although political discourses do not always determine real action, nonetheless they are performative, which means they orient actions that increase either State intervention or, on the contrary, the retreat of the State. This is why we must now analyze the instruments that the State has in hand, especially its financial resources. The first such indicator, and probably the most crucial, is the fiscal pressure of the State. And we can see that the more interventionist discourses coincide with a higher financial capacity.

In Fig. 5.2, we can clearly see the difference between three groups of countries: Brazil, Argentina, Uruguay and, to a certain extent, Bolivia[22] (a country where the fiscal pressure is lower than in the other three, but which has been increasing very rapidly and constantly from a very low level), where the pressure is high. The next group is that of Chile, Colombia, and Peru, where we see a relative and slight increase in the fiscal pressure, which coincides with the more ambivalent discourse where the State is considered to be neutral with respect to the economy, although it is announced to have a social function, especially regarding assistance to the poor. We finally have the case of Mexico, which is certainly that of the other international outsourcing economies of Central America, an extremely low fiscal pressure which, together with wage repression, constitute the main ways these countries conceive inducing private investment.

We can clearly see how Brazil has experienced a continuous increase in State revenue since the mid-1990s, departing from a rather high level, and approaching the European standard, although still far from it, as the latter is around 50% of GDP. Uruguay also has a high level

[21] http://anterior.gacetaoficialdebolivia.gob.bo/normas/verGratis_gob2/154210.

[22] In Ecuador, there has also been a constant and fast increase of fiscal pressure, although it has not reached the level of Bolivia.

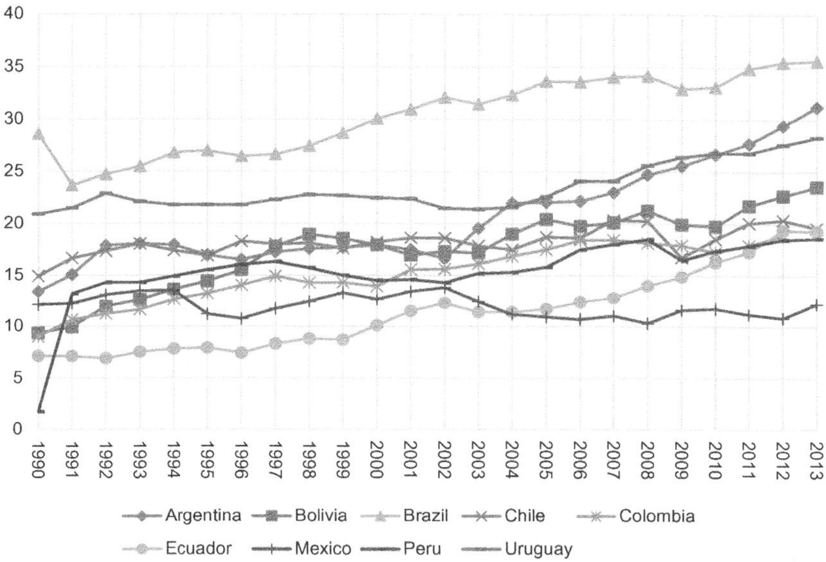

Fig. 5.2 Total tax income (including social contributions), as a percentage of GDP (*Source* Own elaboration based on Cepalstat)

of tax revenue concentrated by the State. Argentina, after the Menem presidency, when taxes were at the low level of the other Latin American countries we are considering, and after the deep economic crisis resulting from the convertibility scheme that this presidency adopted, began to increase its taxes and contributions to a similar level to Brazil's. Since the arrival of the MAS, Bolivia also began to increase considerably its tax pressure. The government of Correa also expanded public expenditure considerably, around 50%, surpassing Mexico and Peru, and catching up with Chile. Finally, although the other more liberal countries, such as Peru, Colombia, and Chile, have increased their tax collection by about 5%, they are still at a low level, under 20%. Mexico has merely maintained its total tax collection at about 10% of GDP; we should mention the fact that we have to add the resources that the State gains through its oil company, Pemex, which represents around 30% of the total (depending on the price of oil) and amounts between 6 and 8% of GDP, which raises the resources of the Mexican State to about 18%, an amount equivalent to that of the other three liberal countries, although its taxing capacity is much lower.[23]

State capacity has also to be defined by the financial power of the State, through the existence or not of a development bank and by its characteristics. A first approach is to consider the weight of the development banks in the different countries in Latin America, which we can see in the next table (Fig. 5.3).

In this table, we can see that Brazil has the largest development banks, concentrating more than 20% of the total financial resources in the country. This country is followed by Mexico, Chile, Ecuador, and Argentina. It is interesting to notice that the Chilean and Ecuadorian development banks are larger than those of Argentina and Colombia, although they are much smaller countries. Nonetheless, purely quantitative consideration can be misleading, as we have to consider the characteristics of the development banks in the different countries.

The Brazilian federal government has a financial instrument to promote development unparalleled in Latin America and, in fact, in most of the world, the BNDES. This development bank modified its role during the two governments of Lula, because while in the previous administrations it had acted as the main agents of State reform and privatization, between 2003 and 2013, it operated in the context of a developmentalist strategy. It became the coordinator of growth policies rather than of macroeconomic adjustments and transformed into the main source of the government's investment policy (Bachiller 2012: 231). Before the present crisis, the BNDS allocated 20% of the total credit to the private sector, 18% of GDP, which added to what the other public banks, *Banco do Brasil* and *Caixa Econômica*, lend, amounts to around 38% of the total (Boschi and Gaitan 2017). In the 2000s, the BNDS became the first source of long-term financing (Santana 2011; Hochstetler and Montero 2012). It played a very significant role in making credit available during the global crisis as part of an aggressive anti-cyclical policy. From 1999 to 2009, the disbursements of this bank grew from 3% to 8.5% as percentage of GDP. (Hochstetler and Montero 2012). However, although the bank's increased action was intended to transform it into the main actor of a renewed industrial policy of the Brazilian government (about half of its investments are committed to industry), most of

[23] Calculated on the basis of Puyana (2008) and Torres Gutierrez (2014).

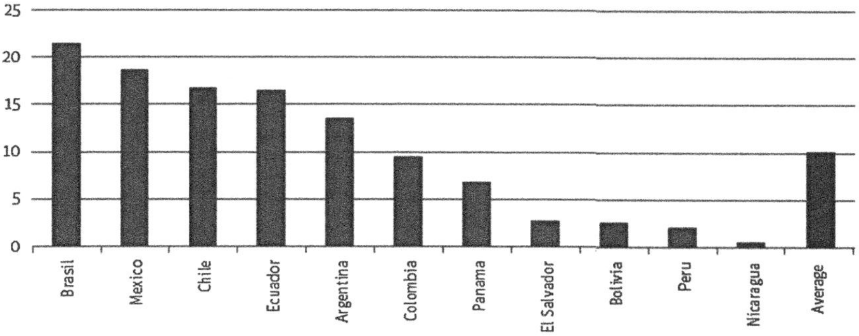

Fig. 5.3 Participation of the pure public banks for development (PBD) within the financial system, 2010 (investment of Pure PBD on total investment in each country, in percentage) (*Source* De Olloqui and Palma (2013: 4). *Note* The Inter-American Development Bank holds the copyright on the above graphic, which appears in the book "Bancos Públicos de Desarrollo ¿Hacia un nuevo paradigma?", available in the following link: https://publications.iadb.org. The book and its content may be freely reproduced with attribution to the Inter-American Development Bank and for any non-commercial purpose)

its loans were concentrated in a few large companies that dominate the Brazilian economy: Petrobras, Vale, Eletrobras, etc. (Hochstetler and Montero 2012).

In contrast, the Argentinian BANADE was dissolved by a presidential decree of Menem on May 1993, and the obligations and the passives of this bank were transferred to the *Banco de la Nación*, a State bank, the largest in the country. In the same decade, Argentina's other development bank, the *Banco de Desarrollo Industrial*, was also shut down (Golonbek 2008). Starting with the reform of the central bank of 2012, quite late with respect to the arrival of the Kirchner and Fernandez government that overturned the economic policy of Menem, the central bank was given the possibility of regulating the conditions of the loans, establishing interest rates, extending deadlines, or using bank reserves in order to assign credit (Lavarello and Sarabia 2015: 79). In addition, banks were obliged to orient 5% of their deposits to a credit line with fixed interest rate (15%), destined to finance investment projects that would have acquiring capital goods and new plants as their main objective (Goldstein, 2013, cited by Lavarello and Sarabia 2015: 79). In the case of Argentina, there are other institutions that implemented programs for the access to credit for medium and small enterprises like the SEPyME y la ANPCyT, and gave credits for investment. While Argentina did not create any new financial institution dedicated to financing productive investments, it modified the existing financial institutions in order to give them more leeway for them to solve some of the problems of a country with high macroeconomic instability (Lavarello and Sarabia 2015: 79).

Mexico advanced in the opposite direction. Although it underwent a very extensive privatization process in the 1980s and 1990s, the Mexican State has maintained under its control six development banks, the most important being *Nacional Financiera (Nafin)* and *Bancomext*. The former was created in 1934 and was the most important Mexican bank during ISI. Measured in terms of assets, these two count among the largest banks in Latin America; nonetheless, they cannot be considered as development banks due to the fact that they "… are regulated and supervised on par with commercial banks and are required by law to preserve the real value of their capital" (De la Torre et al. 2012: 157). In fact, their functions were radically restricted. *Nafin* reduced its role since the 1982 crisis and intensified its withdrawal with the trade and financial opening of the 1990s. Credit operations for productive investment of *Nafin* were reduced by 70% between 1996 and 2004; its main function became to serve as warranty for loans offered by commercial banks to small and medium enterprises. *Nafin* has also focused on "*factoring*": paying in advance the bills owed by suppliers or clients to small and medium enterprises in advance. Finally, it serves as an intermediary for the funds received by the Mexican government from international organizations for different economic and social programs (Manrique 2007: 111–113).

Like in the case of Mexico, in Colombia the State-owned banks do not finance investments directly, due to the conception that giving out loans directly to enterprises politicizes credit allocation (Eslava et al. 2014: 16). Thus, "…much of the public provision of credit is in the hands of *Bancóldex*, which provides loans under the second-floor model: *Bancóldex* grants credit to a [private] financial institution, which in turn uses the resources to fund loans for the productive sector. Bancoldex's lines of credit are not subsidized, and many are not directed at specific sectors of activity, or at specific types of firms" (Eslava et al. 2014: 15). In the case of Peru, the development bank COFIDE is a public–private law entity, and also a second-floor development bank that does not approve operations directly, but functions exclusively as an intermediary.[24] It was founded in the 1970s as a development bank, but since 1992 it was restricted to a second-floor bank. Agrobanco is a more recent real development bank oriented to finance agribusiness, but it is rather insignificant, with gross placements representing only 0.2% of local financial system placements (Castillo Torres 2005: 15).

The development banks of all the liberal countries like Mexico, Colombia, Peru, and Chile, among others, were reformed in the late 1990s, in order to "… create second-tier institutions or to transform first-floor banks into second-tier banks […] Almost 45% of the institutions conduct second-floor operations (22.2% on the first and second floors, while another 22.2% on the second floor alone). 55.6% only carry out first-floor operations" (De Olloqui and Palma 2013: 11). In all these countries, the function of development banks is to foster "pro-market activism," which includes "…the creation of infrastructures to promote participation and to help financial intermediaries achieve economies of scale and reduce the costs of financial services; investment bank–type activities centered on coordinating various stakeholders around structured finance schemes, and on enhancing such structures with State guarantees; and partial credit guarantee schemes to promote private sector lending to priority sectors" (De la Torre et al. 2012: 151). In the case of both Mexico and Chile, a dominant "residual" activity of these second-level banks is factoring. As a matter of fact, factoring in both Mexico and Chile has become one of the "…largest among emerging economies, with an accumulated volume of 12 billion euros in 2009 (10.7 percent of GDP) and about 14,000 users. Factoring in Mexico also represents an important market, with total industry turnover estimated at almost 11 billion euros in 2007 (almost 2 percent of GDP)" (De la Torre et al. 2012: 49)

We can graphically see the differences we have signaled between the different countries in the next table. The action of the public banks stands out between the liberal and the developmentalist group of countries. In this table, we can see the evolution of the lending of the public banks. We can clearly see how in the developmentalist economies they have increased significantly their lending activity, while basically in Mexico they have been very low. An interesting case is Chile, where the development banks are much more active than in other liberal countries. This is what has led us to define this country as a hybrid when talking

[24] http://www.timov.la/article/cofide-el-banco-de-de-development-of-per-perhaps-approval-for-innovation-private-part.

Table 5.3 Evolution of the assets and investments of the Public Development Banks (in percentage)

Country	*Assets of the Public Development Banks*		*Investments of the Public Banks of Development*		*Total investments of the Financial System*	
	Annual average change, period 2000–2005	*Annual average change, period 2005–2010*	*Annual average change, period 2000–2005*	*Annual average change, period 2005–2010*	*Annual average change, period 2000–2005*	*Annual average change, period 2005–2010*
Argentina	−8.4	13.1	−15.1	18.7	−14.0	17.4
Bolivia	9.1	−8.2	10.6	−8.3	−7.1	16.7
Brazil	5.9	27.6	1.8	34.9	11.1	30.7
Chile	2.9	22.1	6.2	13.3	10.8	12.3
Colombia	12.8	16.1	15.5	17.8	6.1	17.9
Ecuador	7.0	26.5	13.8	33.9	21.5	16.2
Mexico	−2.6	4.0	−3.7	−3.3	−0.1	9.7
Peru	−5.3	18.6	−20.1	28.1	1.7	25.1
Uruguay	−5.8	12.6	−7.3	15.2	−17.1	16.0
Simple average	3	13.0	2.6	16.2	8.7	15.0

Source De Olloqui and Palma (2013: 3). Modified by the author. *Note* The Inter-American Development Bank holds the copyright on the above graphic, which appears in the book "Bancos Públicos de Desarrollo ¿Hacia un nuevo paradigma?", available in the following link: https://publications.iadb.org. The book and its content may be freely reproduced with attribution to the Inter-American Development Bank and for any non-commercial purpose

about the action of the State; a liberal country with a strong State capacity, here shown in terms of its development banking system: liberal, but strong. On the contrary, in the case of Peru, Colombia, and Mexico, State capacity is weak (Table 5.3).

5.4 State Ownership

The privatization undertaken by most of the governments of Latin America in the 90s was very ample; in some countries it was radical, privatizing the most fundamental governmental services: oil companies, electricity, postal services, and even water distribution. Without any doubt, it was the Argentinian and Bolivian governments who proceeded to liberalize more radically during the 1990s. The Menem government achieved this with the complicity of part of the *peronist* unions, as the

CGT divided upon the question of accepting the measures of Menem in exchange of keeping the control of the *obras sociales* (the health services). Thus, in this country where the withdrawal of the State from the economy went the furthest (Boschi and Gaitan 2017). Nonetheless, as we will discuss, in both countries, the governments of Cristina Fernández and Evo Morales renationalized some of the companies.

While in Brazil the privatization surge was also very strong, especially during the Collor and Cardoso governments, nonetheless "Unlike other liberalizing governments of the 1990s, the Brazilian State devised several means to retain control or influence in State enterprises it privatized. In some companies (especially Embraer and Vale), the government retained a 'golden share' allowing it to veto major changes in ownership structure and location" (Schneider 2013: 172). On the other hand, "...the BNDS and the pension funds of the State-owned enterprises that had not been privatized (basically public banks and Petrobras) became major shareholders in many of the privatized companies and the merged firms the bank promoted in order to concentrate ownership in key sectors. By the late 2000, BNDS had a significant share in many merged companies. These shareholders did not adopt a passive attitude in the enterprises they invested in. For example, in 2011 they managed to defenestrate Rogel Agnelli from the presidency of Vale" (Schneider 2013: 172).

In the case of Brazil, gradualism and relatively delayed reforms allowed it to preserve the core of technical and bureaucratic expertise, which was considerable, especially in the economic ministries and in the development bank, the BNDES (Evans 1995: 61; Sikkink 1988). Even when these government officials were converted into agents of privatization, they succeeded in protecting some of the institutions because they had a totalizing vision of State action. They either promoted less radical reforms and privatizations, or advanced with a more integrated perspective of what remained in the hands of the State and its complementarity with the country's economic structure (Boschi and Gaitán 2017).

In the case of Argentina, the government of Cristina Fernández implemented ample nationalizations that reversed some of the most significant privatizations of the Menem government, in some of the most crucial sectors: oil, air travel, water, postal service, shipbuilding, and pensions. First, in June 2006, the government acquired 20% of *Aeropuertos Argentinos*, which control 32 terminals in all the country, as well as the shipbuilders *Astilleros Tardanor*. In October 2008, her government announced the nationalization of the airline company *Aerolíneas*

Argentinas, which had been privatized in 2001 to a Spanish tourist company. Also in 2008, in the wake of the global crisis, the government renationalized the pension funds that had been privatized in the 1990s. On May 2012, the State expropriated 51% of the shares of the oil company *Yacimientos Petrolíferos Fiscales* (YPF), a State company that had been created in 1922 and had the monopoly of the exploration, extraction, and commercialization of oil, and had been sold by the Menem government to the Spanish company Repsol in 1999. The administration of the postal service and water, which had also been privatized by Menem was also renationalized during the Fernández administration (Maradona 2012; Diario La Información 2012; Niemetz 2009).

The pluri-national State of Bolivia issued a decree that provided for the transfer of all the shares of the electricity distribution companies of La Paz (Electropaz) and Light and Power Corporation of Oruro (ELFEO SA), as well as all the shares of the management and investment service companies Business Bolivia SA (Cadeb) and Corporation Service Company (Edeser), all of which were held by *Iberbolivia* Investment Corporation, belonging to the Spanish firm Iberdrola, to the State-owned Empresa Nacional de Electricidad (ENDE). It also nationalized the Bolivian Airport Services (SABSA), a subsidiary of the Spanish firms Abertis and Aena, which operated the Bolivian airports of El Alto, Cochabamba, and Santa Cruz (UNCTAD 2013: 95). In 2007, Bolivia nationalized the *Empresa Nacional de Telecomunicaciones*. In 2008, it transformed the State oil enterprise YPFB into a corporation in order to lead the nationalization of the oil sector and began a shared administration with the Spanish Repsol in order to administer YPFB Andina. In 2009, it expropriated 36,000 hectares of land from large landowners in order to distribute them to indigenous communities. After his reelection in 2009, the government expropriated four electric enterprises, among them the Spanish-owned *Red Eléctrica* and a Swiss metallurgical company (Maradona 2012).

Nonetheless, in contrast to Venezuela, all these actions did not build up a statist economic model, nor did they alienate national and foreign capital, but they were mainly oriented to renegotiate the terms of the concessions that had been given to private capital in the 1990s, which were extremely favorable to its interests, in order to try to recompose the relation between the State and private capital in more advantageous terms for the State. The purpose was to give the State more resources to invest in its social policies and to regulate private capital, without alienating it. The nationalization policy also served to maintain the popular support of the social movements in favor of the government. In fact, the decree nationalizing the hydrocarbons sector was a manner of renegotiating the contracts with the companies operating in the oil and gas industries (Lehoucq 2008: 117, cited by Kennemore and Weeks 2011). "In practice, Morales' economic reforms have not signaled a dramatic shift towards socialism but rather a pragmatic way for a centre-left government to better capture the capitalist surplus necessary for state spending" (Stefanoni 2005, cited by Kennemore and Weeks 2011). Nationalization of, for example, the main exporting sector, oil and gas, was actually "… transforming contracts for operating into contracts of shared production and allowing oil companies to carry out exploration and exploitation activities independently in the name of the State company, Yacimientos Petrolíferos Fiscales Bolivianos (YPFB)" (Leiva 2008: 231, cited by Kennemore and Weeks 2011). All of this explains why the foreign companies accepted the policies of the MAS government.

The government of Ecuador did not proceed to an expropriation of its natural resources or crucial economic sectors, but it did raise taxes and royalties, and in the case of oil (the main export product), it modified the principle of ownership of the product without a formal nationalization procedure. In fact, in a speech, Correa himself declared that there "…was no need to nationalize anything in Ecuador."[25] Nevertheless, in 2009, after the country experienced several months of power cuts due to limited outputs from the country's largest hydroelectric plant, which caused a significant fall in Correa's approval rating, he did re-nationalize the dam. His attitude toward oil companies was different; in 2007, Correa increased taxes on the enterprises of this sector, raising the royalty tax on profits from 50 to 90% (Conaghan 2008: 209, cited by Kennemore and Weeks 2011). With the new hydrocarbon law that came into effect in 2010, the rules of the game changed for the foreign oil companies, although there was no nationalization. The new model signifies that the previous participation contracts change to service contracts, which means that instead of the oil companies keeping part of the oil and

[25] "Correa afirmó que no hay que nacionalizar nada en Ecuador", El Comercio, 20 de octubre de 2007 [en línea], disponible en, http://www.elcomercio.com/noticiaEC.asp?id_noticia=144738&id_seccion=3.

paying taxes to the State, the State becomes the owner of 100% of the oil and pays the companies a tariff. The law included the threat of expropriation to the companies that did not accept the new conditions, but all complied.[26] A year before, with the new mining law that the National Assembly had approved, foreign companies were allowed to continue exploration and extractive practices, but included new provisions that entitled the State to more than half of a company's profits (Hoffman 2009, cited in Kennemore and Weeks 2011: 275).

In the case of Chile, Mexico, Peru, and Colombia, privatizations that were undertaken in the 1990s were not reversed; in fact, they were even expanded, as was the case of the Mexican pension system, which was privatized in 1997 and then in 2007, and the energy sector, which was opened to private capital in 2013. In Chile, while the State did not privatize the State copper company *Codelco*, which had concentrated the totality of the copper industry expropriated by President Allende at the end of the 1960s and thus preserved part of the ownership of copper, it has expanded the concessions to private capital in copper extraction, with the consequence that the State enterprise has been continuously reducing its share of the industry. Colombia has also continued the privatization process in the years 2000, transferring important electric companies to the private sector.[27] Nonetheless, the State still has around 90% of the capital of *Ecopetrol*, the largest oil company of Colombia, which functions as an anonymous society and is the largest exporting firm of the country.

The fact that the State in Mexico, Brazil, Chile, and Colombia, have retained control of strategic sectors, and that Argentina and Bolivia, have recuperated partial control of the oil companies is not only important in terms of their ability to regulate the economy, but also in order to fund State investments, especially because they are the most significant sources of foreign currency.[28] There are nevertheless important differences regarding how each of these countries deals with these

[26] Mena Erazo, Paul. 27 de julio de 2010. Nuevas reglas de juego para petroleras en Ecuador. *Diario BBC*. Consultado el 201 de octubre de 2017 en, http://www.bbc.com/mundo/america_latina/2010/07/100727_0504_ecuador_entra_vigencia_reforma_petrolera_lf.

[27] http://www.elcolombiano.com/negocios/empresas/isagen-segunda-privatizacion-mas-alta-de-colombia-BD3432245.

[28] This is one of the main reasons why the government of Cristina Kirchner re-nationalized the oil company in 2012.

resources. In the case of Mexico, PEMEX is mainly used as a source of revenue for the State budget, something that partly explains its low capacity to raise taxes and the rentier character of the Mexican State. The resources of copper in the case of Chile are partly saved in a stabilization fund. Brazil found oil reserves much later and in much more complex extracting conditions, forcing *Petrobras* to become a very dynamic State-owned (with private participation) company, with administrative "autarky."

5.5 Regulatory and Industrial Policies

Brazil was the only Latin American country that implemented a significant industrial (vertical) policy since the beginning of the years 2000 (actually, since the arrival of Lula in 2003); it was the only country where a more oriented, targeted industrial policy was applied. In contrast to Argentina and Chile, where a horizontal, more generalized, industrial policy was employed. Argentina only began implementing a mixed (vertical and horizontal) industrial policy as a reaction to the global crisis in 2008 (Santarcángelo et al. 2017). Nonetheless, judging from the results, de-industrialization, and economic crisis, we can conclude that the results of these policies were not successful; we will address this question in our conclusions.

Apart from the resources allocated by the BNDS, which were directed to selected sectors, the new development strategy of the Lula government was composed of various policies. The most important were: the Industrial, Technological and Foreign Trade Policy (PITCE), the Policy of Progressive Development (PDP), the *Plan Maior*, and the Policy of Acceleration of Growth (PAC). According to Bachiller, while none of these three programs, separately, can be considered developmentalist if one compares it to the policies of the 1950s, 1960s, and 1970s, as they are much more restrained, and oriented to only some areas, they "...are included in a broader development agenda to which they give coherence reciprocally, which recovers the importance of the State as an promoter of economic growth" (Bachiller 2012: 240).

These industrial policies built upon what had been implemented in the 1960s and 1970s, in sectors such as ethanol production, which was launched at the wake of the oil crisis of the 1970s, and petroleum exploration since the discovery of the huge reserves in the pre-salt deposits. These "... are the best examples of legacy benefits – long-term policies that involved decades of subsidy, investment, training and policy experimentation, and that started reaping major returns in the 2000." Enterprises like *Embraer*, the steel industry, agricultural research, and petrochemicals were also created by governmental programs in the 1960s and 1970s, and some of them were State-owned enterprises (Schneider 2013: 169). The development of ethanol was a State enterprise that "was driven by technological advances all along the productive chain, from cane production, to fuel for automobiles, to fuel engines, to diversification in electricity, biodiesel, and ethanol-based petrochemicals." By 2004, Brazil produced one-third of the world's sugarcane, and sugarcane produced 16% of total energy consumption in Brazil in 2007. On the other hand, Petrobras has more lately developed the technology necessary for deep drilling due to the fact that the oil it had discovered was located offshore, in deep-sea deposits (Schneider 2013: 169).

Although during the presidency of Cardoso, the *câmaras sectoriais* implied a very innovative vertical industrial policy model that stimulated certain branches of the economy, especially automobile, textile, and electronics, by way of a reduction in taxes and an increase in wages to stimulate productivity gains (De Souza Keller 1994), both in this administration and even more clearly in one of Collor de Melo, vertical industrial policy was practically absent (Santarcángelo et al. 2017). Thus, these policies reemerged when Lula took over the presidency in 2003. His government launched the *Política Industrial, Tecnológica e de Comércio Exterior* (PITCE) (Industrial, Technological and Trade Policy) plan in November 2003. A program that "... aimed to promote exports of value-added goods and services, increase the technological content of domestic production, and stimulate Brazilian companies' activities on international markets." This program focused on three aspects: first, the stabilization of the macroeconomic variables; second, "... to overcome Brazil's lack of competitiveness in some manufacturing sectors such as semiconductors, software and capital goods, where the technology was clearly outdated, third [...] open a window of opportunity to affordable developments in scientific and technological systems by focusing on sectors like oil and gas, agricultural and pharmaceuticals." This program led to the enactment of a series of regulations such as the Innovation Act (Law 10.973), the *Lei do Bem* (Law 11.196), the Biosecurity Act (Law 8.974), and the Biotechnology Development Policy (Decree 6.041). Within PITCE, government institutions for the promotion of industrial development, such as the Council for National Industrial Development

(CNDI) and the Brazilian Industrial Development Agency (ABDI), were founded. Finally, the PITCE required the developed new financial instruments and institutions: the financial programs for the pharmaceutical industry (Profarma) and for software (Prosoft) were both created by the BNDES (Santarcángelo et al. 2017: 27–28).

In response to the global economic crisis of 2008, the Brazilian government implemented, a new industrial plan called the Productive Development Policy (PDP), which, according to Santarcángelo, Schteingart, and Porta went even further in a developmentalist direction that the PITCE. This plan had four goals: "…to expand supply capacity, improve the balance of payments dynamics, increase innovation, and strengthen small and medium size enterprises" (Kupfer 2012: 17, cited by Santarcángelo et al. 2017). The PDP fixed quantitative targets, "…contemplated an increase in gross fixed capital formation, a rise in private spending on R&D, an increase in Brazil's share of international exports, and a higher number of exporting SMEs" (Ninomiya 2015: 67, cited by Santarcángelo et al. 2017). "The PDP designed three different types of programs. The first one was centered in strengthening competitiveness in sectors where Brazil has many enterprises and productive capabilities but problems to sustain productivity and exports growth (automotive, capital goods, textiles and clothing, wood and furniture, personal care, perfume and cosmetics, civil engineering, services, shipping, hides, leather and handcrafts, agro-industry, biodiesel, plastics, wheat, consumer electrical goods and toys). The second program was focused on those leading sectors of Brazil's productive structure, attempting to consolidate and expand their leadership. Branches such as the aeronautics industry, petroleum and gas, bioethanol, meat processing, mining, iron and steel, and cellulose and paper were the main targets of this second program. The third program was directed to strategic areas, such as the health industry, IT, nuclear energy, defense industry, nanotechnology, and biotechnology" (Kupfer 2012: 18, cited by Santarcángelo et al. 2017). Nonetheless, "the outbreak of the international crisis made the implementation of the PDP much more defensive than its original design" (Santarcángelo et al. 2017: 29–30).

Against the slowdown of the economy at the end of the Lula Da Silva presidency, Dilma Rousseff implemented the *Plano Brasil Maior* (PBM) in 2011. The objective of the plan was to build and strengthen different competencies in the national economy, to enhance productivity and technological density within value chains, to expand the domestic and external markets of Brazilian companies, and to ensure socially inclusive and environmentally sustainable growth (Kupfer 2012: 23, cited by Santarcángelo et al. 2017). The first stage of the PBM was launched in August 2011, and included almost 40 measures including financial and fiscal incentives, new regulations, and a group of new institutions. According to Kupfer (2012), the PBM was intended to "... generate investments and innovation [...] by tax relief, financing for investment and innovation and a new legal framework of innovation, improve foreign trade through a battery of tax relief on exports, trade remedies, financing and guarantee for exports, and trade promotion; finally, to defend industry and domestic market with a new special automotive regime, tax exemptions on payrolls, government procurement and harmonization of funding policies" (Governo Federal do Brasil 2011: 9, cited by Santarcángelo et al. 2017).

Equally facing the crisis, the government of Lula amplified the *Programa de Aceleração do Crescimento* (PAC), a plan to incentivize the internal market through State investment. The PAC that had already been launched since the beginning of 2007 projected an investment of around 500 billion *reais* oriented to credit reforms in the taxing system, but especially to infrastructure investment (Neto and Coelho 2008). The BNDS was central in this policy, as the global crisis had significantly cut access to international financial resources. It became the main funder of the Brazilian economy, with 37% of the total of credit and 17% of GDP (Ferraz, 2010: 20, cited by Actis, 2011). The loans given out by the BNDS increased by 468% from 2007 to 2009 (PAC 2010: 24, cited by Actis 2011). According to the government, by 2016, nine years into the program, the PAC had invested 1.3 trillion reais.[29] In addition, during the 2008 global crisis, the Brazilian Central Bank gave assistance to farming exporters (Bouët and Laborde 2009); it anticipated a 12% increase in minimum salaries from April to February 2009. It also announced tax reductions on consumer financial operations from 3 to 1.5%, the elimination of a tax on industrialized products, mainly affecting cars, and a tax exemption of individuals earning less than 875 dollars per month (CEPAL 2010: 12–14).

"In April 2012 the second stage of the *Plano Brasil Maior* was launched after the recognition of the worsening of the competitiveness gap of Brazilian industry and the need to change the target for the industrial policy from productive chains to productive systems"

[29] http://www.pac.gov.br/noticia/68777baf.

(Ninomiya 2015: 73, cited by Santarcángelo et al. 2017: 30–31). It included "… a mixture of fiscal incentives for labor-intensive industries, loans to the automotive and IT industries from the Brazilian Development Bank (BNDES) at preferential rates, expansion of export financing programs and tax relief for Internet broadband access, and measures for stimulating the national industry through Government procurement, where national goods and services will take priority over imported goods" (UNCTAD 2013: 61). An example of one of the most significant actions of this plan is the new Automotive Regime Innovar-Auto, intended to boost investment by transnational companies (that dominate the sector) in the auto industry. It imposed a 30% tax on industrialized products for all light vehicles and light commercial vehicles, which can be deducted if automakers use local manufacture production and inputs, and carry out a certain number of manufacturing processes in Brazil (i.e., investment in R&D, engineering, industrial technology and supplier capabilities, and participation in the Vehicle Labeling Scheme, which is required to ensure a vehicle's efficiency) (Ninomiya 2015: 73, cited by Santarcángelo et al. 2017: 30–31; UNCTAD 2013: 61). This industry has benefited from long-term financing from BNDES, amounting to 6% of all the bank's loan disbursements between 2002 and 2012. These measures increased FDI in the automobile industry (assembly and auto parts), which grew from an annual average of $116 million in 2007–2010 to $1.6 billion in 2011–2012 (UNCTAD 2013: 61).

One last element to be mentioned is the amount of investment in what the OECD calls knowledge-based capital (KBC)—software, data, R&D, firm-specific skills and organizational capital, as well as what the World Bank catalogues as R&D. However, these types of investments are low in Latin America, in comparison with countries such as the USA or China, and especially Korea; while the USA later invested 7.5% of GDP in such assets, Brazil invested about 4% of GDP over the past decade, while in India it was around 3% of GDP in 2007 (OECD, WTO, and WB 2014: 38). According to World Bank data, while Brazil spends 1.15% of GDP in R&D, Mexico spends 0.55% of GDP, Argentina 0.59% of GDP, Chile 0.37% of GDP, Colombia 0.24% of GDP, and Peru a mere 0.12%.[30] In contrast, Korea spends around 4%, Japan 3.5%, and the USA and Germany around 2.8% (Ibid.).

[30] World Bank Data.

Facing the most recent crisis, there was a sustained will to reinforce the internal market. The Fernandez–Kirchner government invested massively to try to counteract the social effects of the crisis; in the first trimester of 2009, it increased its public investment by 5.7% in relation to GDP. It also announced a 15.5% salary increase for government employees and increased the unemployment benefits as a way to incentivize employers to retain their personnel throughout the crisis (Palomino and Trajtemberg 2006: 56). But the most significant measure was surely the renationalization, in 2008, of the pension funds that had been partially privatized during the Menem presidency. The government unified the system under a State-controlled regime, eliminating the segment of capitalization administered by the AFJP (Administradoras de Fondos de Jubilaciones) (CEPAL 2010: 8–9). According to some analysts, all these measures signal a decisive shift to a development mode that attempts to equilibrate the external and the internal market and that articulates economic and social policies in order to develop the latter (Novick et al. 2009: 272). Nevertheless, the data on the relation between salaries and productivity, as well as the structural analysis of the economy show how the economic structure has hardly changed (Fernandez Bugna and Porta 2008: 223).

While in the case of Argentina, industrial policy was basically horizontal during the 1990s and beginning the 2000s, it shifted to a vertical policy after the global crisis; it has again been reversed since the arrival of Macri to the presidency. After the abysmal 2001–2002 crisis, the government of Kirchner (2003–2007) and then of Fernandez (2007–2015), in many respects retraced the path treaded by Menem's administration, enhancing the intervention of the State in the economy. The government of Kirchner adopted a policy of managing the exchange rate so that the relative prices could continue favoring the limited process of re-industrialization that had begun after the crisis, when the peso was strongly devalued and the country was cut from external loans and imports were drastically reduced (Wylde 2010). On the other hand, the State has achieved increasing its financial capacity by imposing higher and variable taxes on the exports of agricultural products; albeit, at some moments, in a very un-political manner.

Both Kirchner and Fernández governments' interest "…shifted from strengthening sectors where Argentina had a static comparative advantages (such as mining, forestry or fishing), as it happened in the 1990s, to foster competitiveness in sectors where comparative advantages were low (such as auto parts, electronics or capital goods, among others) or even to create new sectors (such as aerospace, biotechnology or nanotechnology, among others)" (Santarcángelo et al. 2017: 23). Nonetheless, industrial policies in this country were less effective than in Brazil because Argentina "... has had greater institutional disorders than Brazil, partly because the dismantling of the State during the last quarter of the twentieth century was significantly higher. Second, financial resources to industrial policy have been much lower, despite a significant increase in recent years. One of the main reasons for that is that Argentina has not had a development bank like the Brazilian one" (Bizberg 2014). Finally, although the Argentinean State devised two development plans in 2011 (the Strategic Industrial Plan 2020 and the Innovative Argentina Plan), they were "... more wishful thinking than a realistic option" (Santarcángelo et al. 2017: 23). Nonetheless, the Kirchner administration did invest considerably in the national scientific and technological system, created new fiscal incentives to sectors such as capital goods and software, and kept those created in the 90s for the automotive sector (Lavarello and Sarabia 2015, cited by Santarcángelo et al. 2017: 23). Finally, in 2012, the government imposed a regulation on domestic and foreign capital, and it established a committee to supervise investments by insurance and reinsurance companies as part of its Strategic National Insurance Plan that intended to force insurance companies to use part of their funds for investment in the real economy (UNCTAD 2013: 94).

"Compared to Argentina, Brazil, and even Chile, Mexico has experienced little changes in its industrial policy since the 1980s. In fact, despite the fact that the term "industrial policy" has regained some importance in the public agenda, the continuities with the period opened in the 1980s are much more pronounced than its ruptures. Actually, the Mexican industrial policy has continued rejecting the use of vertical instruments, and it has preferred the market failures approach, where the State has a very limited role in the economy. Moreover, resources to fund industrial policy have continued to be weak, and the same happened with Mexico's institutional capabilities. That is why the firepower of the (restricted) industrial policy has been very low. It should be noted that there were many national development plans, but they have been rather generic and limited to a few objectives related to social welfare. This is in sharp contrast with the Brazilian development plans (such as the PITCE, the PDP and the PM), and even more with those of the ISI" (Santarcángelo et al. 2017: 24).

And, in fact, even confronted to the global crisis of 2008 that resulted in a very deep recession of around 5% of the GDP, the Mexican government did not react. The measures it took were destined to merely mark time while waiting for the recovery of the USA. It reacted timidly and, in some cases, inconsistently. In October 2008, the government announced a program to support growth and employment on the scale of 6390 million dollars for infrastructure and 11,680 million dollars to finance private investment. Nevertheless, at the same time, it proclaimed a reduction of 6 billion dollars in public expenditure, owing to the decline of public finances due to the decrease in economic activity and lower oil prices (40% of the government's resources; CEPAL 2010: 34). Most of the infrastructure projects had enormous implementation difficulties; some non-official sources stated that up to 28% of the resources were not used.[31]

Since in Mexico there is no unemployment insurance, in 2008 the government decided to implement a program for the preservation of jobs in the export sectors (automobile, auto parts, electronic, electric, and capital goods) that had seen a reduction of 11.6% in their production by May 2009. The government would compensate the salaries of the workers affected by production stops in exchange for a promise from the enterprises not to fire them (Galhardi 2009a). It also extended the existing program of temporary employment (which hires workers for communitarian projects in education and health) directed to rural and urban areas where unemployment is very high (Galhardi 2009b). Although these two programs were supposed to cover 500,000 workers, they were assigned a mere 140 million dollars and 165 million dollars, respectively. An indicator that this program was not working is that six months later, in March 2009, the government announced that the rules of access would be eased. In addition, the minimum salaries were raised by a mere 4.6% and the government allowed workers to use part of the individual pension funds (CEPAL 2010: 35–37).

In the last decade or so, we have seen an increasing number of subsidiaries of transnational companies settling in the country. This is nonetheless not due to any governmental action, but due to a process of nearshoring "…which is boosted by the rapid growth of labor costs in China and the volatility of rising fuel costs, which have made the shipment of goods across the Pacific less attractive." According to the UNCTAD "Companies are now more likely to diversify their manufacturing presence to serve regional markets, as transportation costs increase and markets become more regionally focused. Mexico will always have the advantage of its proximity to and trade agreement with the United

[31] http://www.milenio.com/node/372874.

States" (UNCTAD 2013: 62). However, China offers other advantages that do not guarantee that this process will continue, as their industry has upgraded, and their supply chains are deeper than those existing in Mexico. In Mexico, "international companies have trouble finding local suppliers for parts and packaging. Unlike in China, where the Government identifies 'pillar industries' and supports them, smaller companies in Mexico that are eager to start or grow businesses and establish linkages with foreign companies suffer from a lack of affordable access to financing" (UNCTAD 2013: 62).

Another disadvantage of the Mexican economy is the weakness of the State's regulatory capacity. Although the Mexican State was set to become a regulatory instance, the manner in which it proceeded with the privatizations of its enterprises and the way it conceived the retreat from economy weakened its regulatory capacity considerably. This is why the Mexican economic structure is plagued by monopolies and oligopolies that have formed in several areas such as telephone, banking, media, the cement industry, and commercial distribution.

Until the beginning of the 1980s, the case of Chile resembled that of Argentina when the military was demolishing the interventionist State, and that of Mexico of the 1980s and 1990s. Nevertheless, after the economic crisis of 1983–1984, the government abandoned the purely monetarist approach that had dominated until that moment with the influence that the radically liberal "Chicago Boys" exerted upon the government and began to apply a less orthodox economic policy. The government sustained an economy based on the industrialization of commodities (copper, agro-industry—fish, wine, dried fruits—wood pulp) with a considerable support of the State (Rodrik 2010). Forest products started to be subsidized under Pinochet, and the government financed R&D for the development of the wine industry, while the salmon industry owes much to the support of *Fundación Chile*, a semi-public venture fund. Finally, the Pinochet government preserved the copper industry under control of the State (Boschi and Gaitán 2017: 11). Under the governments of the *Concertación*, in the 1990s, the State imposed controls on the entry of capital, in order to reduce the instability of portfolio capital. It also constituted a stabilization fund with part of the resources of the copper exports, to be used anti-cyclically in times of crisis. In this way, the Chilean State of the 1980s and 1990s implemented what some have characterized as an autonomous State with a cooperative relationship with the private sector (Silva 2007: 79).

Excepting these examples, industrial policy in Chile has been mostly horizontal. Its main mechanisms have been "… a relatively competitive real exchange rate, the development of infrastructure (ports, airports, roads, electricity or telecommunications), the signature of multiple free trade agreements (with the aim of opening new export markets) and the availability of credit for SMEs" (Moguillansky et al. 2013, cited by Santarcángelo et al. 2017: 23). Nonetheless, Chile again turned being an exception in this aspect, as "…it created two institutions which in an incipient form aimed to generate some selective 'niches'. First, the National Innovation Council for Competitiveness was founded emphasizing that Chile needed to develop productive clusters in sectors where the economy was already quite competitive (for example processed food, fruit, financial services, construction, aquaculture, mining or tourism, among others). Second, the government created the Regional Productive Development Agencies (ARDPs), with the aim of minimizing the large territorial inequalities" (Moguillansky et al. 2013, Benavente and Price 2014, cited by Santarcángelo et al. 2017: 23). However, the Piñera government (2010–2014) returned to a mainly horizontal industrial policy (Goya 2014). But even during the *Concertación* governments "…industrial policy firepower was intermediate, achieving many goals but leaving much to do. For example, progress was made in infrastructure, but that was not quite enough to satisfy the current needs of the country. In sum, the Chilean State intervened less than in Argentina or Brazil, but its intervention had positive impacts since the goals were clearer and its institutional capabilities were quite sound" (Santarcángelo et al. 2017: 24).

The rest of our countries, Colombia, Peru, Ecuador, and Bolivia, are either too liberal to have an industrial policy other than one similar to that Mexico's, or too dependent on commodities and too weakly industrialized to have more than a general, horizontal industrial policy. Nonetheless, as we will be able to see, some countries have tried to limit the rights of foreign capitals. The case of Colombia is very representative in terms of a horizontal industrial policy, as its main and favorite instrument for inciting foreign investment is the installation of free economic zones, of which there are 108 in operation. In fact, Colombia "… concentrates 25% of the 400 free zones of Latin America and is the country with the largest number of industrial parks in the continent" (Mouthón 2017). In 2016, the Colombian government modified its free zone regime in order to unify existing regulations, making investments more flexible.[32] Also in Peru, the installation of free economic zones also seems to be a priority in terms of industrial policy. According to the Plan for Industrial Diversification, industrial parks "…facilitate the orderly access of producers to an industrial zone with low real estate costs, as well as public services of better quality and lower prices (broadband, electricity)."[33]

Bolivia and Ecuador have a much more ambitious industrializing performative agenda. The government of Correa proposed a return to industrial policies in the following terms: "Since the 1980s, structural adjustment programs and liberalization or trade liberalization have been implemented, proclaimed by the Bretton Woods institutions, under the support of the Washington Consensus, which had as its priority objectives for economic reactivation, adjustment and stabilization, causing a significant reduction of the State as a planning and regulating entity of economic and productive activities […] The Ministry of Industries and Competitiveness, aware of the need to have explicit public policies for the development of the Ecuadorian industrial sector, has developed the Industrial Policy, which establishes principles, strategies and objectives, action plans, programs and projects, and contemplates an important participation and articulation of the public and private sectors, as well as the academic sector, which will start a new stage of industrialization, in harmony with the economic, social and political transformation that the country is undergoing."[34]

The Bolivian government of Evo Morales declared equally ambitious goals in its *Plan de Desarrollo Bolivia digna, soberana, productiva y democrática para vivir bien*. In order to attain its central objective, to end social inequality, the country "…requires changing the pattern of primary export development, which is characterized by the exploitation and export of natural resources without added value, in order to establish a new pattern of integral and diversified development, which consists in adding value and in the industrialization of renewable and non-renewable natural resources. […] Productive Bolivia has

[32] Agencia EFE. (January 6, 2017). "Colombia improves the free zones regime to increase its competitiveness." *El Heraldo newspaper*. Accessed October 19, 2017, https://www.elheraldo.co/colombia/colombia-mejora-regimen-de-zonas-francas-para-aumentar-su-competitividad-317458.

[33] Ministerio de la Producción, *Plan Nacional de Diversificación productiva*, Lima, 2014, p. 30.

[34] Ministerio de Industrias y Productividad, Política Industrial del Ecuador 2008–2012, p. 11, http://portal.uasb.edu.ec/UserFiles/381/File/POLITICA%20INDUSTRIAL%20DEL%20ECUADOR%202008-2012.pdf.

transformed, integrated and diversified its productive matrix within the framework of a new pattern of development, that it extends to the entire territory and has achieved the development of productive complexes; it is a country that creates material and intellectual products with a Bolivian brand, has reached the industrialization of its natural resources and increased added value to its exports, with the support of the State as promoter and protagonist of development."[35]

Nonetheless, they have lacked both the State capacity and the resources to propose and much less to embark upon such a process of industrializing the commodities they export (oil, gas, lithium). Moreover, they have been much less incapable of building a technological core that would allow them to upgrade their productive structure and develop technologically. According to the CEPAL, in a diagnosis that serves for all these countries, the least, as well as the most developed ones, is that although the favorable international prices of commodities encouraged economic growth and, in the case of the redistributive countries, the reduction of inequality and poverty, the profitability of the primary sector and the dollarization has discouraged productive diversification (Calderón Hoffmann and Stumpo 2016: 13), which has negated these countries' most promising development projects.

References

Actis, E. (2011). La estrategia "híbrida" de desarrollo del gobierno de Lula: neodesarrollismo Heterodoxo. *Temas y Debates, 22,* 115–135.

Bachiller, J. V. (2012). *El BNDES y las estrategias de desarrollo económico en Brasil. Banca pública de desarrollo, instituciones gubernamentales y trayectorias de intervención estatal (1952–2010).* Tesis doctoral del Programa de Doctorado Procesos Políticos Contemporáneos, Universidad de Salamanca.

Beck, U. (2002). *Poder y Contrapoder en la Era Global, La nueva economía política global.* México: Paidos.

Boschi, R., & Gaitán, F. (2017). El Estado desarrollista en Brasil: Crisis, continuidad, incertidumbres. In C. Alba Vega & I. Bizberg (Eds.), *Dimensiones sociopolíticas y económicas de la crisis global y su impacto en los países emergentes.* México: El Colegio de México.

[35] Plan de Desarrollo Bolivia digna, soberana, productiva y democrática para vivir bien, p. 3, https://extranet.who.int/nutrition/gina/sites/default/files/BOL%202006%20-%20Plan%20Nacional%20de%20Desarrollo.pdf.

Bouët, A., & Laborde, D. (2009). The potential cost of a failed Doha round. *SSRN Electronic Journal.* Available at SSRN: https://doi.org/10.2139/ssrn.1396335.

Bourdieu, P. (2013). *La nobleza de Estado.* Buenos Aires: Siglo XXI.

Bresser-Pereira, L. C. (2018). *Rentier-financier capitalism* (Unpublished manuscript to be published in the *Revue de la Régulation*).

Calderón Hoffmann, A., & Stumpo, G. (2016). La evolución económica y social del Ecuador: las restricciones de la estructura productiva. *Los desafíos del Ecuador para el cambio estructural con inclusión social* (pp. 11–58). Santiago: CEPAL, LC/L. 4281.

Cardoso, F. H., & Faletto, E. (1969). *Dependencia y Desarrollo en América latina.* México: Siglo XXI.

Castillo Torres, M. (2005). Evolución, perspectivas y diseño de politicas sobre la banca de desarrollo en el Perú. *Serie financiamiento del desarrollo (174).* Santiago de Chile: CEPAL.

CEPAL. (2010). *La reacción de los gobiernos de las Américas frente a la crisis internacional: una presentación sintética de las medidas de política anunciadas hasta el 31 de diciembre de 2009.* Santiago de Chile: United Nations.

Conaghan, C. M. (2008). Ecuador: Correa's plebiscitary presidency. *Journal of Democracy, 19*(2), 46–60.

De la Torre, A., Ize, A., & Schmukler, S. L. (2012). *Financial development in Latin America and the Caribbean. The Road Ahead.* Washington, DC: IBRD, World Bank.

De Olloqui, F., & Palma, C. (2013). Panorama y evolución reciente de los bancos públicos de desarrollo. In F. De Olloqui, M. D. Chrisney, J. J. Gomes Lorenzo, A. Maffioli, R. Monge-González, M. Netto, F. Nieder, C. Palma Arancibia, & C. M. Rodríguez (Eds.), *Bancos públicos de desarrollo: ¿hacia un nuevo paradigma?* (pp. 1–19). Washington, DC: BID.

De Souza Keller, W. (1994). Neocorporativismo y relações de trabalho: elementos para um debate sobre a experiência brasileira recente. *Boletim de Conjuntura: Política social, 14,* 31–40.

Diario La Información. (2012, April 16). Empresas estatalizadas o nacionalizadas en Argentina. *Diario La Información.* https://www.lainformacion.com/politica/nacionalizacion/empresas-estatalizadas-o-nacionalizadas-en-argentina_FnN4HbzqLRMe9znUxHddp1/. Accessed 16 October 2017.

Eslava, M., Meléndez, M., & Perry, G. (2014). *Notas sobre Política de Desarrollo Productivo en Colombia.* Bogotá: Centro de Estudios sobre Desarrollo Económico, Universidad de los Andes.

Evans, P. (1995). *Embedded Autonomy. States and industrial transformation.* Princeton, NJ: Princeton University Press.

Fernandez Bugna, C., & Porta, F. (2008). El crecimiento reciente de la industria Argentina: Nuevo Régimen sin cambio estructural. In M. R. Soares de Lima (Ed.),

Desempenho de Governos Progressistas no Cone Sul: Agendas alternativas ao Neoliberalismo. Rio de Janeiro: Edições IUPERJ.

Ffrench-Davis, R. (2008). *Chile entre el neoliberalismo y el crecimiento con equidad. Reformas y políticas económicas desde 1973*, Santiago: J.C. Sáez editor.

Galhardi, R. (2009a). México. Programa para la preservación del empleo. *OIT Notas sobre la crisis*. Santiago de Chile: OIT.

Galhardi, R. (2009b). Programa de empleo temporal ampliado (PETA). *OIT Notas sobre la crisis*. Santiago de Chile: OIT.

Goldstein, A., & Lemoine, F. (2013). *L'économie des BRIC: Brésil, Russie, Inde, Chine*. Paris: La Découverte Editions.

Golonbek, C. (2008). Banca de desarrollo en Argentina: breve historia y agenda para el debate. *Documento de Trabajo Nº 21*. Buenos Aires: CEFID-AR.

Goya, D. (2014). *Industrial policy: What is it, why it is necessary, and its past, present and future in Chile* (MPRA Paper No. 64881). Munich: Munich Personal RePEc Archive.

Haggard, S. (1990). *Pathways from the Periphery. The politics of growth in the newly industrializing countries*. New York: Cornell University Press.

Hochstetler, K., & Montero, A. (2012, May 23–26). Inertial statism and the new developmentalist state in Brazil. In XXX *International Congress of the Latin American Studies Association*, San Francisco.

Kennemore, A., & Weeks, G. (2011). Twenty-first century socialism? The elusive search for a post-neoliberal development model in Bolivia and Ecuador. *Bulletin of Latin American Research, 30*(3), 267–281.

Kupfer, D. (2012). *Case Studies of Successful and Unsuccessful Industrial Policies: The Case of Brazil*. New Thinking on Industrial Policy International Economic Association (IEA)-World Bank Roundtable, Washington, DC, May 22–23.

Lavarello, P., & Sarabia, M. (2015). *La política industrial en la Argentina en la década de los 2000. Serie Estudios y Perspectivas de la CEPAL*. CEPAL: Buenos Aires.

Manrique, C. (2007). Banca de desarrollo en México: un futuro necesario. In J. L. Calva, *Agenda para el Desarrollo, Vol. 6: Financiamiento del crecimiento económico* (pp. 100–116). México: Porrúa-UNAM.

Maradona, S. (2012, May 4). Seis años de nacionalizaciones forzosas en América Latina. *Sección 5 Días, Diario El País*. https://cincodias.elpais.com/cincodias/2012/05/04/empresas/1336298336_850215.html. Accessed 16 October 2017.

Moguillansky, G., Ramírez, E., & Furnaro, A. (2013). *Las políticas de desarrollo productivo en Chile, 1990–2012*. Programa de Cohesión Territorial para el Desarrollo Rural-RIMISP.

Moore, B. (1969). *Social origins of dictatorship and democracy lord and peasant in the making of the modern World*. London: Penguin Books.

Mouthón, L. (2017, May 2). Colombia, the country with the most free zones in Latin America. *El Heraldo newspaper*. https://www.elheraldo.co/economia/colombia-el-pais-con-mas-zonas-francas-en-america-latina-355483. Accessed 19 October 2017.

Muniesa, F., & Callon, M. (2013). 8. La performativité des sciences économiques. In P. Steiner & F. Vatin (Eds.), *Traité de sociologie économique* (pp. 281–316). France: Presses Universitaires de France.

Neto, O. A., & Coelho, C. F. (2008). Brasil en el 2007: el desencuentro entre la economía y la política. *Revista de ciencia política (Santiago), 28*(1), 81–102.

Niemetz, K. (2009). La nacionalización de los fondos de jubilación privados en Argentina. *Economic Affairs, 29*(1), 49–53.

Ninomiya, Y. (2015). Industrial policy and the post-new Brazil. In R. Konta (Ed.), *The post-new Brazil*. IDE-JETRO: Chiba.

Novick, M., Lengyel, M., & Sarabia, M. (2009). De la protección laboral a la vulnerabilidad social. Reformas neoliberales en la Argentina. *Revista Internacional del Trabajo, 128*(3), 257–275.

OECD, WTO, & WB. (2014). *Global value chains: Challenges, opportunities, and implications for policy*. Report prepared for submission to the G20 Trade Ministers Meeting Sydney, Australia.

Palomino, H., & Trajtemberg, D. (2006). Una nueva dinámica de las relaciones laborales y la negociación colectiva en la Argentina. *Revista de Trabajo, 2*(3), 47–68.

Puyana, A. (2008). El manejo del petróleo mexicano: ¿política o economía? *Perfiles latinoamericanos, 16*(32), 67–102.

Quispe, M. U. (2017). La desigual capacidad del Estado en América Latina. *Política y gobierno, 24*(2), 435–457.

Rodrik, D. (2010, April 12). The return of industrial policy. *Project Syndicate*. http://www.project-syndicate.org/commentary/rodrik42/English. Accessed 15 May 2018.

Rodriguez Salazar, O. (2015). Prologo. In D. Restrepo Botero (Ed.), *Procesos de descentralización en Bolivia y Colombia, 1980–2005. Una propuesta de economía política comparada* (pp. 11–22). Bogotá, Colombia.

Santana, C. H. V. (2011). Conjuntura crítica, legados institucionais e comunidades epistêmicas: limites e possibilidades de uma agenda de desenvolvimento no Brasil. In R. Boschi (Ed.), *Variedades de Capitalismo, Política e desenvolvimento na América Latina*. Belo Horizonte, MG: Editora UFMG.

Santarcángelo, J. E., Schteingart, D., & Porta, F. (2017). Industrial policy in Argentina, Brazil, Chile and Mexico: A comparative approach. *Revue Interventions économiques, 59*. http://journals.openedition.org/interventionseconomiques/3852. Accessed 13 June 2018.

Schneider, B. R. (2013). *Hierarchical capitalism in Latin America: Business, labor, and the challenges of equitable development*. New York: Cambridge University Press.

Sikkink, K. A. (1988). *Developmentalism and democracy: Ideas, institutions and economic policy making in Brazil and Argentina 1954–1962.* Ph.D. Dissertation, Columbia University, New York.

Silva, E. (2007). The import substitution model: Chile in comparative perspective. *Latin American Perspectives, 34*(3), 67–90.

Skockpol, T. (1984). *Los Estados y las revoluciones sociales.* México: Fondo de Cultura Económica.

Steinmo, S. (2010). *The evolution of modern states: Sweden, Japan, and the United States.* New York: Cambridge University Press.

Théret, B. (1995). *L'État, la finance et le social. Souveraineté nationale et construction européenne.* Paris: La Découverte.

Théret, B. (2002). *Protection Sociale et Fédéralisme. L'Europe dans le miroir de l'Amérique du Nord.* Montréal: Presse de l'Université de Montréal - Peter Lang.

Torres Gutiérrez, C. (2014). *La privatización parcial y su efecto en el crecimiento de las ventas y el activo de Pemex: evidencia en Petrobras y Ecopetrol.* Tesis de Doctorado. Nuevo León: Universidad Autónoma de Nuevo León Facultad de Contaduría Pública y Administración.

UNCTAD. (2013). *World investment report, global value chains: Investment and trade for development.* New York & Geneva: United Nations Publication.

Wylde, C. (2010). *Argentina, Kirchnerismo, and Neodesarollismo: Argentine Political Economy under the Administration of Nestor Kirchner 2003–2007. Documento de Trabajo n°44.* Buenos Aires: Área de Relaciones Internacionales, Flacso-Argentina.

CHAPTER 6

The Dominant Social Coalition: Transformations and Present Configuration

As Haggard has written (1990), what a country manufactures is not necessarily what it is more efficient in producing; if that were true, we would live in a perfect Ricardian world, where all countries would accord their productive structure on their main comparative advantages, in other words, what by nature it is destined to produce, its factor endowments. The reason why factor endowments do not totally predispose a country is that the conflicts and agreements of social actors and the State orient the economy toward certain products for which a country does not have competitive advantages, and this for many reasons that have been discussed in the literature. What a country produces and exports, as well as the way in which the benefits of development are distributed and consumed, the character of the action of the State, and the international insertion of an economy are, in many respects, determined by the composition of the dominant social coalition.

This idea has a long tradition. Cardoso and Faletto, as well as Haggard, make a point on how a strong and cohesive industrializing coalition (that includes the State) explains the depth of industrialization (Cardoso and Faletto 1969; Haggard 1990). Esping-Andersen (1990) and Bruno Théret (2011) emphasize the role of coalitions and their relation to the State in shaping the characteristics of the national social protection systems. Crouch elucidates the cooperative or contentious character of unionism by the relationship and coalitions around the State and the church (and the guilds) during the formation of the nation-states in the nineteenth century (Crouch 1993). Bresser-Pereira considers that

I. Bizberg, *Diversity of Capitalisms in Latin America*,
https://doi.org/10.1007/978-3-319-95537-7_6

the variety of capitalisms and the possibility of development of peripheral countries are at present determined by whether the dominant social coalition is formed by rentiers and financiers or by industrialists and a developmental State (Bresser-Pereira 2018). Finally, the French school of regulation defined Fordism (1945–1973) as a type of capitalism characterized by the redistribution of the benefits of growth among workers and business, accomplished through the participation of the salaried class in a coalition with the employers and the State (Aglietta 1979; Amable 2005; Boyer 2015).

The four countries that have served us most closely to formalize the typology of the diversity of capitalisms in Latin America traversed different trajectories in what concerns the relationship between the State and the domestic social sectors, and the national and international capitalistic groups. In the 1980s and 1990s, new coalitions arose in almost all the countries in Latin America. Most of the countries went through a democratization process, transiting from a dictatorship (typically military), that had taken power in the 1960s or 1970s, to a government holding elections and the legalization of unions and social movements. The way in which each country transited this process, whether it democratized due to the action of civil society, or if did so through a compromise between the governmental and the opposition elites, was crucial to define the strength of civil society and the social coalition that dominated the post-transition. Whether social actors had the force to impose themselves, to continue strongly organized after democratization, was also crucial, as it was equally decisive how the social actors reacted and their capacity to impose themselves during the process of liberalization that swept the continent as a result of the debt crisis that burst with the Mexican default of 1982.

While in the countries where civil society had a major role in democratization, liberalization was implemented after this process, in the countries where social actors were weaker, liberalization was imposed prior democratization. This meant both a more orthodox liberal program (because less contested), and a more severe undermining of the social actors, especially the unions. *In fine*, the periodicity between the political and the economic transition was dependent on the capacity of civil society to oppose the dictatorial or authoritarian governments and initiate democratization. In the case of Brazil and Argentina, liberalization of the economy occurred after democratization, which determined that it was less radical (although in the case of Argentina it was radicalized during the *peronista* government of Menem with the complicity of a sector of the labor movement) and less aggressive against labor and the social security regime. Although in both Mexico and Chile, civil society was also present and active, it was not able to become a central actor of democratization. The PRI, in Mexico, had the capacity to limit the emergence of social actors of the opposition through its control of the popular organizations. In Chile, the numerous manifestations against the Pinochet regime that burst in the mid-1980s were demobilized as soon as the political opposition accepted the rules set by the 1980 Constitution, with regard to the plebiscite of 1989. Thus, in both of these latter cases, democratization was accomplished without the action of civil society and the liberalization of the economy found little resistance of the social and political opposition, as it was imposed by an authoritarian government. And orthodox liberalization further weakened the unions and other social actors.

Each of these situations gave way to a different management of the crisis of the 1980s and to a different social pact once the crisis was over. In the countries where democratization occurred after the government liberalized the economy, the retreat of the State and the weakening of the unions and other social actors that had been part of the industrializing coalition during ISI were more radical. This situation led to a dominant social coalition post-ISI where the popular sector was absent. In the countries where social actors pervaded and democratization happened during the crisis, such as Brazil and Argentina, but also Bolivia and Ecuador, civil society was a significant partner of the post-ISI dominant coalition.

On the other hand, in the countries under authoritarian regimes, the cost of the crisis was payed solely by the middle and working classes, and even if there occurred an inflationary situation, the debt crisis did not lead to a monetary crisis since the governments had the capacity to impose austerity policies through the control of unionism (Mexico) or through repression in the case of Chile (Marques Pereira and Théret 2004). In countries where civil society gave the democratic impulse, the governments that emerged were forced to arbitrate between the needs of society and the interests of creditors, to pay their debts while protecting their society, by applying heterodox plans. Civil society demanded a compensation of the social debt accumulated by anti-popular economic and social policies during the years of authoritarian governments. The monetary crisis that ensued the debt crisis and expressed itself as hyperinflation resulted, in large part, from the fact that the crisis had to be managed in democracy, *post facto*, and thus with strong distributive conflicts (Marques Pereira and Théret 2004).

The strength of civil society has also had a significant impact on State capacity. In most of our cases, facing a weak civil society there is a weak State. On the one hand, where civil society was very weak, as a result of the subordination to the demands of creditors (Mexico and Chile), the State withdrew from the economy and reduced social security. This led to a vicious cycle, where civil society weakened further and democracy became more and more formal, particratic or technocratic. On the other hand, where civil society was able to pressure for democratization and force the State to mediate between the interests of the population and those of the creditors (Brazil and Argentina), the State was reinforced, did not abandon its economic intervention, nor reduce social security, and both civil society and democracy strengthened.

The sociopolitical coalition that dominates both groups of countries is defined basically by the presence or absence of a strong civil society that is able to defend the interests of the popular classes. In the ***international outsourcing capitalism*** and ***liberal rentier capitalism***, the dominant coalition is constituted by multinationals, large national entrepreneurs, financial capital, together with a small middle class that profits from the establishment of the foreign enterprises, and the commercial and service sectors that these enterprises require. In these cases, the State basically acts as an agent of the foreign and national multinationals. In addition, as we will discuss in the next chapter, because civil society was basically absent in democratization, this process gave rise to a pluralistic, purely electoral, democracy that is either characterized by a strong particratic tendency, where these parties are institutionalized (Mexico and Chile), or to a de-institutionalized political system, where the political parties and the social actors are very weak or totally disarticulated, and the State is led almost exclusively by technocrats—a technocratic State (Peru, Colombia). In both cases, the political system is impervious to the interests of the popular classes. In these cases, productivity or rentier gains are mostly oriented toward profits.

On the contrary, where social actors are strong enough to force the State to include them as part of the coalition, the coalition is broader, including industrialists, middle classes, in a compromise with agro-exporters and financial sectors. In this case, we have either a

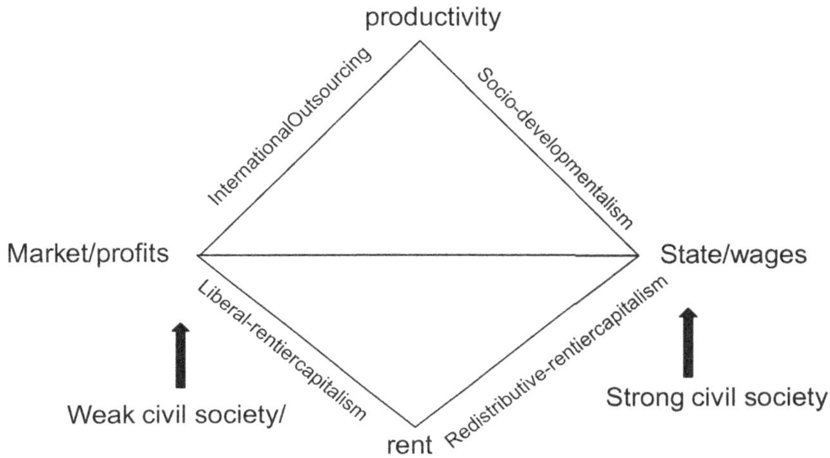

Fig. 6.1 Mode of accumulation, state vs. market coordination and strength of civil society. *Source* Own elaboration

socio-developmentalist type of capitalism if based on productivity gains (Brazil and Argentina) or a ***rentier redistributive capitalism*** if based on rents (Bolivia and Ecuador) (Fig. 6.1).

6.1 Entrepreneurs and Multinational Companies

The coalition that dominated most of Latin American countries during the time of ISI was, as Cardoso and Faletto have written, a national-popular coalition, where popular interests, the State, national industrialists, and middle classes dominated. Since the crisis of the 1980s, the scope of the State was reduced and the popular classes, especially unions, have been weakened. Big national groups, multinationals, allied with international financial interests have come to the fore. Accepting that the State was the dominant actor during ISI, Schneider characterizes the present situation of the Latin American economies in the following terms: "...economic activity in Latin America is still largely subject to planning, rather than to the spontaneous free play of market forces, but the planning shifted after the 1990s from ministry offices to corporate boardrooms" (Schneider 2013: 11). Although we believe this may be the case for the countries where civil society is weak and an outsourcing or a liberal capitalistic mode have been implemented, where social actors were empowered in the democratization process, the domination of the business interest has not been so unilateral. In the countries where a redistributive social pact has been convened, and either a social-developmentalist or a rentier distributive capitalism has been intended, what we have seen is a compromise between the interests of the financial, industrial, agro-business, and MNCs, on the one hand, and the popular sectors, represented in government, on the other.

The effect of the crisis of the 1980s and liberalism is that in most countries of Latin America, the entrepreneurs are very well organized and have been able to establish a very close relationship with the government. According to Schneider, "countries like Mexico, Chile, and Colombia follow a more European or Japanese model of business organization compared to a more 'American' style of fragmentation in Brazil and Argentina" (Schneider 2004: 6). In both Mexico and Chile, "... strong business associations collaborate closely with government negotiators in devising the terms of regional integration. In Mexico representatives of government and business associations met literally thousands of time to exchange information, reconcile conflicting preferences, and work to reach consensus positions for Mexican officials to take into the negotiations over NAFTA" (Schneider 2004). In effect, in the case of Mexico this is especially true beginning with the negotiation of NAFTA in 1992, with the well-known "*cuarto de al lado*" ("the room next door"), where the main organizations of the employers, basically those of the big entrepreneurs: Concamin and CCE (the Canacintra, which represents the small and medium-sized entrepreneurs were not present) were taking part in the negotiations. The official government negotiators came in once in a while to ask the entrepreneurs what they thought of a specific question that was being negotiated (Alba 2005). One can also consider that the Mexican stabilization program of the second half of the 1980s, when inflation peaked around 150% in 1987, the government of De La Madrid imposed a limit of both salary and price hikes on unions and employers, proves not only the effectivity of the corporatist control upon the unions, but also the close relation with the employers (Schneider 2005: 25). Consultative boards are also common in recent periods in Colombia, Chile, Costa Rica (ibid.: 29). At one point of the deep economic crisis of the 1980s, in 1983 the Pinochet government adopted a more pragmatic economic perspective that departed from the very ideological "Chicago Boys," and approached the business associations, through consultation in policy forums (ibid.: 29).

An indicator of the strength of the associations of entrepreneurs is their actual staff: in Mexico, Coparmex has 30 functionaries and the CCE 80; in Chile, the CPC has only 8, but the Sofofa has 50; in Colombia, *Federacafe* has 3500 and ANDI 150 (ibid.: 7). In Colombia, the "coffee confederation, Federacafe, has control over an export tax and other resources and is responsible for financing, promoting, and marketing Colombian coffee" (ibid.: 10). Other countries like Peru and Venezuela have fairly well-organized economy-wide encompassing associations: Confiep and Fedecamaras, respectively. "Almost all the smaller countries, with the significant exception of Uruguay, have economy-wide encompassing associations" (ibid.: 6).

It is also very common that governments integrate business people into government in Latin America. This happens very often in the case of Colombia and Peru, but also in Argentina and Brazil (ibid.: 5). Although Schneider rightly considers that in Mexico and Chile the government did not call upon entrepreneurs to become functionaries in the past, it is possible to temper this information as the current president of Chile is one of the richest men in the country, previous owner of the principal airline. In the case of Mexico, while in the PRI governments before the 1980s there were no business appointees, but rather economists and lawyers, although the biggest entrepreneurs were all linked to the PRI. In the last years we have seen a close relationship between government and business, as former politicians have gone over the business circles, while keeping their contacts in government. On the other hand, the most relevant officials of the economic institutions come from a private university, the ITAM; many of them have been students or colleagues of the officers of the Minister of Finance at the time of Salinas de Gortari, who signed NAFTA and implemented the neoliberal model. Pedro Aspe, the finance minister of Salinas de Gortari (1988–2004), is Chairman of Evercore Casa de Bolsa, S. A, and Francisco Gil Diaz, who was finance minister of Fox (2000–2006), is at present representative of the Spanish Telefonica. During the last two PAN administrations, especially during the presidency of Fox (2000–2006) who was a high functionary of the Coca-Cola Company, business people were recruited into government, most of them from small and medium enterprises. It also well known that some deputies in Congress are very near different sectorial interests; it is, for example, well known that the telecommunications interests have a group of deputies.[1]

Data on the appointees coming from the private sector in high posts in the government of the more liberal countries of Latin America are very telling. In Mexico, during the Fox presidency, there were 5 functionaries coming from the private sector—that is 25% of the total. In Colombia, during the Uribe presidency, there were 7 functionaries coming from business—54% of the total of his government. In Peru, during the Toledo government, there were 7 or 27%. In Chile, there were none due to the fact that at that moment it was Lagos, a socialist, who was president (Schneider 2004: 15). The situation has changed considerably during the two Piñera presidencies, as he included various entrepreneurs in his government.[2]

The fact that although the Mexican government mandated that businesses incorporate into the different corporations, these organizations were excluded from the post-revolutionary corporatist arrangement that created the PRI, which only comprised workers, peasants, and other popular organizations, resulted in that the leading businessmen have had direct access to the president or to his finance and economic ministers since the 1950s (Alba 2005). For example, the *Consejo Mexicano de Hombres de Negocios* (CMHN), which incorporates the 50 or so most important entrepreneurs of Mexico, hosted monthly luncheons, where it invited top functionaries to discuss the economic situation of the country (Schneider 2005: 10). In addition, with democratization, business people began to actively try to influence deputies and senators in Congress in order to get them to either block or pass legislation that hurts or favors them, through active lobbying (Alba 2005).

While in the case of Colombia the relation between business interests and the government has not been so well studied, "...public and private elites in Colombia seem in most periods to be thoroughly networked and interconnected [...] most political elites in Colombia follow careers that weave in and out of government and private firms or business associations" (Schneider 2005: 14). In the other smaller countries that were not able to considerably industrialize, business associations are incipient. Nonetheless, one could make a case of the strength of the agro-exporters

[1] http://www.sinembargo.mx/09-07-2012/291704.

[2] https://www.laizquierdadiario.com/Chile-Pinera-presento-su-gabinete-con-varios-empresarios-y-mayoria-de-independientes.

of Santa Cruz that have been empowered with the autonomy they won after the Constitution of 2009, in Bolivia.

Both Alba and Schneider have signaled the relative weakness of the business organizations in Brazil. Contrary to what we have mentioned for the cases of Mexico and Chile, in the case of Brazil and Argentina, the relationship between the entrepreneurs and the State is weaker (Schneider 2013). In the first place, in both Brazil and Argentina, the business associations are weak and unrepresentative (Alba 2004). "Brazil gave industry federations the appearance of institutional strength, but behind the façade they were much weaker, in large part due to State controls on internal organization. These controls were especially debilitating in Brazil where the regional structure of representation gives marginal industry federations from states in the rural northeast control of the national industry confederation, CNI" (Schneider 2005: 8). In terms of the size of staff, compared to what we already mentioned for the other countries, in Argentina the CGE has 10 employees, the UIA 50, while in Brazil the UBE has none, and the IEDI 8 (Schneider 2005: 7). In contrast to what happened in Mexico with the negotiations of NAFTA, where business was in the "*cuarto de al lado*," the Brazilian government officials negotiated Mercosur in isolation from the entrepreneurs (Schneider 2004: 5). Nonetheless, the lobbying of the Brazilian entrepreneurs is quite sophisticated and precedes the Mexican (ibid.: 11). This is obviously a result of the earlier democratization of Brazil in comparison with that of Mexico. Nonetheless, as Carlos Alba has analyzed, Mexican entrepreneurs have recovered terrain in the years 2000 (Alba 2005).

Another indicator of the power of business is the concentration of economic activity in a few enterprises, the oligopolization of the economy. While in the case of Mexico, in 1990 the 59 largest groups represented 15% of GDP, in Chile the 11 largest groups concentrated around 300 firms, and the 20 largest ones produced 50% of GDP. Colombia is even more concentrated; the four largest groups concentrated 20% of GDP and controlled 278 firms in 1998 (Schneider 2005: 45). "In Mexico, 31% of total household spending is in markets that are monopolized or suffer from limited competition..." (OECD, cited by Schneider 2013: 68–69). In selected sectors, such as candy, chewing gum, beer, wine, tobacco, textiles, insurance, packaged bread, mobile phone, cement, in Argentina, Brazil, Chile, Colombia, Mexico, the concentration of one single company goes from a low of 35 to 98% (Schneider 2013: 69).

In addition, notwithstanding the great importance of the domestic groups, "...the MNC's are boxing out the national ones from the more dynamic manufacturing sectors" (ibid.: 82). We thus have to turn our view to these foreign companies in order to have a complete picture of who dominates the economy.

Economic concentration in the hands of the MNCs is strong, or even stronger that of domestic capital. According to Schneider, in most countries, these enterprises represent between a third and a half of the largest firms (Schneider 2013: 73). At the beginning of the years 2000, the stock of FDI with respect to GDP was 16%, in average, for the four largest countries in the continent, while, for example, in Korea it was 2%, and in Thailand it was 10%. In addition, "...the share of MNC's in the sales of the 500 largest companies in the region ranged from 30 to 40% for most of the 1990s and the MNC share of the top 200 exporters grew to nearly half in 2000 before dropping back to a third in 2004" (Schneider 2013: 11). In addition, according to Amsden, the evolution of the dominance between national and multinational companies has been leaning against the first. "Between 1990 and 1996, the share of national firms in the sales of Latin America's 100 largest industrial enterprises fell from 46 percent to 40 percent, while the share of multinationals rose from 46 to 57 percent" (Amsden 2001: 213). In addition, MNCs have been continuously dominating exports, especially in an outsourcing economic model like the Mexican. In this case, 20 of the largest companies (10 automobile, 5 *maquiladoras*, 4 electronics and metallurgical) concentrate 32.5% of all exported value, and all but one are foreign; 45 enterprises export 50% of the total, none are small or medium sized. In effect, three enterprises, General Motors, Chrysler, and Ford, export 9.3% of the total.[3]

The same situation, although not as extreme, concerns the other countries of Latin America. Since the 1970s, concentration of manufacturing in MNC's is high: 24% in Argentina, 50% in Brazil, 30% in Chile, 43% in Colombia, 44% in Peru. MNCs in Brazil exported 70% more than the national firms in the late 1990s (Schneider 2013: 82). In the years 2000, MNCs installed in Brazil, added 63% of total exports and 57% of imports. Intrafirm trade between large multinationals is also an indicator of this same situation: in 2000, 38% of total exports and 33% of imports

[3] http://www.eluniversal.com.mx/articulo/cartera/economia/2017/01/18/trasnacionales-concentran-un-tercio-de-exportaciones.

were intrafirm in Brazil (ibid.). In addition, the domestic groups are located in the low value added, low skill, low technology sectors, while the MNCs are in the more complex ones (ibid.: 83). An example from the Mexican case, the only Mexican company that is among the utmost exporting companies is Pemex, which occupies the first place, with 4.9% of exports.

In the banking system, a comparable situation prevails. The Argentinian banking system denationalization of the 1990s was radical, amounting to 61% of the total. Although Mexico resisted mass denationalization of banks until the crisis of 1994–1995, thereafter national banks were bought by foreign financial groups to 85%. In Brazil, the percentage of banks in foreign hands is only 49% (Boschi and Gaitán 2017). Finally, the banking system in most of the Latin American countries is very condensed: five of the most important banks aggregate between 57 and 100% of all bank assets (Jeanneau et al. 2007: 20).

Thus, although there are significant differences in terms of the power of the business organizations, in all of Latin America, capital, both national and foreign, has gained power both in its relation with government and in economic terms. They thus have nowadays a very significant weight on the economic decisions. The main difference that defines the composition of the dominant coalition in these countries, is the place occupied by the interests of the popular sectors, which is determined by the power of civil society. Where it is strong and mobilized, the State has had to compromise with it. Where it is weak and atomized, the State is fundamentally linked to business. We will now discuss the situation of civil society in our different countries.

6.2 From a Corporatist Redistributive Pact, to an Oligarchic Alliance

Mexico, which we have considered as the closest example of an international outsourcing economy, which bases its existence on low costs of labor (in terms of both wages and social protection), can only be explained by very weak labor unions and civil society and a coalition between the State and domestic and foreign capital. To which, we have to add a political system that gives little room for an anti-liberal coalition to emerge, a particracy—something we will analyze in the next chapter. And in this respect, because what characterized the history of Mexico was a long enduring corporatist system, where a coalition between the State and the popular classes was maintained by redistributive policies, we must analyze how this change came about.

In Mexico, Argentina, Brazil, and to a lesser degree Bolivia, there existed a corporatist pact where the State gave priority to its relation with the popular sectors. In Mexico and Bolivia, this pact resulted from a revolution. In Mexico, a peasant revolution compelled the new emerging State to organize the peasants, the workers, and other social sectors in order to achieve political stability. In addition, it had to insure that economic development benefits these sectors and that growth had to be accompanied by redistribution. This is why it proceeded to a radical agrarian reform and to constant concessions to the unions, workers, and functionaries that were included in the formal economy. It also nationalized the oil companies and implemented a State-led industrialization project. In Bolivia, after the 1952 Revolution, the State, under the MNR, distributed the land that was occupied by the Indian population of the *altiplano* (the highlands), the west of the country (without affecting the lowlands of the east), and approached the labor movement, the miner's *Confederación Obrera Boliviana*, in a State-popular alliance that organized peasant and workers under its helm. It also nationalized the main tin mines that were in the hands of three families.

In Brazil and Argentina, the corporatist pact was achieved without a social revolution, by two authoritarian (military) governments, inspired on the relation between the State and the popular classes in fascist Italy. Nonetheless, in order to maintain its popular base, the government of Vargas and of Perón had to allocate significant concessions to the unions and the workers, which are the basis of the present social security regime. The State also advanced an industrializing project where the national entrepreneurs, the workers, and the urban middle classes were the main beneficiaries. In these two cases, in contrast to the former ones, there was no agrarian reform and thus no organization of the peasants. The Mexican revolution was a "classical" peasant revolution while the Bolivian one originated in the arrival to government of a political party (the *Movimiento Nacional Revolucionario*—MNR), representing the workers and peasants, which defeated the army (weakened by the Chaco war) and led Bolivia to radical political, social and economic changes. The Brazilian and Argentinian corporatisms were top-down, conservative revolutions that had nonetheless equally significant impacts on the worker's organization and the social security system.

The corporatist pact in Mexico was the most stable of them all. It had the ability not only of including all the social forces that existed at the moment (comprising the military) in which the revolutionary party, the Partido Revolucionario Institucional (PRI), was created, but to organize a vast political apparatus (only surpassed by the Communist Party in Russia and China) that served to control, overlook, and preempt any dissidence. The PRI had the capacity to distribute political and economic concessions to all groups in order to control them, coopt any dissidence before it became opposition, and repress those movements that did not accept to cooperate. It had a commandment chain that served to transmit orders and directives in all domains, and serve as a space where decisions were discussed and taken, through a pragmatic and instrumental consensus that allowed this organization to rule the country without interruption for seventy years. That is the reason why, in contrast to Brazil, Argentina, and Bolivia, Mexico did not suffer a military (or for that effect, a civilian) coup and always held elections that were unceasingly won by the ruling party.

Nonetheless, this corporatist pact did not survive the 1982 debt crisis. Facing this crisis that led to the so-called lost decade, the Mexican State opened the economy to productive as well as to financial capital, privatized its enterprises, abandoned subsidies to industry and to the *ejidos* (communal land property), decentralized education and health services, and shifted its social policy toward assistance (Barba Solano 2007; Valencia Lomelí 2008; Barba Solano and Valencia Lomelí 2013). It was able to do so without social or political resistance as it had retained the authoritarian structure of the regime: social organizations were under the hold of the PRI and the democratization process began until the end of the decade. The PRI suffered a scission that provoked the founding of a new center-left party, the PRD, when a group of the more traditional politicians left it, due to the fact that it had been taken over by technocrats implementing liberal policies that contradicted the interests of its social base. Almost simultaneously, the PRI lost its first governorship, that of Baja California, in 1989, to the center-right party, the PAN.

In the economic scenario, the default of the Mexican government on its external debt forced it to a negotiation with the IMF and the imposition of drastic measures of austerity resulting in rising unemployment, the plummeting of the minimum wage (from an index of 100 in 1980 to 46 in 1990 in real terms), and the reduction in social spending (Marichal 2003: 472). Indeed, the public deficit was cut from 16.9% of GDP in

1982 to 8.6% in 1983 (Romero Tellaeche 2003: 192). As a result of these policies, the economy grew at a mere average annual rate of 0.2% between 1982 and 1988 (Ibid: 191). Finally, toward the end of the crisis, in 1987, when the country was confronted with an inflationary surge caused by the drop in oil prices and the intensification of the distributive conflict that accompanied democratization, it abandoned the import substitution model and opened the economy, oriented it toward exports, and liberalized finances.

The insertion of Mexico into the General Agreement on Tariffs and Trade (GATT), and then the signing of NAFTA with the USA and Canada, anchored the indiscriminate opening of the Mexican economy to foreign goods and capital and in a great sense affixed a model that, as we have been discussing in this book, greatly depends on foreign capital investment and on the repression of labor costs, as this is one of the main factors of its competitivity. This implied a turnabout of the alliance from a State-corporatist pact with popular sectors, to a coalition with financial and manufacturing foreign and domestic capital, and the middle classes that profit from this investment. The State assumed the role of an agent of these interests, which meant that the old alliance that existed since the end of the revolution and the founding of the PRI had to be dismantled, or rather, as the Mexican State did, re-instrumentalize it in order to politically sustain the new model.

Indeed, facing the 1982 crisis, the response of the Mexican State was to make its population pay for the excesses of the governments' indebting itself during the 1970s in order to build its oil productive structure and continue distributing resources to its political bases: in brief, internal adjustment was the condition for external adjustment (Marques Pereira and Théret 2004). This was only possible due to the corporatist control exerted by the government upon unions and other social organizations. In contrast to Chile, where deregulation of the industrial relations was achieved with the disappearance or murder of hundreds of union leaders and a reform of the labor legislation, in Mexico it was accomplished under the same political regime and under practically the same law—in many cases by circumventing it. During the 1980s and 1990s, the internal relations of most of the medium-sized enterprises were radically flexibilized. On the other hand, while the workers in the most strategic and dynamic sectors (oil, education, health, telephone, automobile) still have the protection of unions, in the vast majority of the workplaces (*maquiladoras*, construction, commerce, services, small and medium enterprises, the spare parts auto-industry), there are no unions or they only exist on paper (they are protection unions). Although labor legislation was modified in 2012, the federal labor law still preserves corporatist mechanisms: such as the closed shop, the compulsory legalization of unions, of elections, of strikes. On the other hand, collective negotiations in Mexico, Chile, as well as Peru and Colombia, occur mostly by enterprise and not by branch as in Argentina and Brazil. Unionization rate of the total of salaried earners is 11.5% in Chile and 17% in Mexico, while collective bargaining rate among salaried employees is 9.6% in Chile and 10.5% in Mexico (Hayter and Stoevska 2011, cited by Bensusán 2016). In Peru and Colombia, union density is even lower: 5.3%[4] and 3.4%[5] respectively.

In this way, the instruments of control were still in the hands of the State, through the threat of privatization of many State-owned companies, or the closure of private companies in the context of the crisis of the 1980s, together with the "pragmatism" of the corporate leaders who preferred to accept flexibilization, the reduction in union power, and the emergence of protection unions, in exchange of the benefits that the State still granted them for their loyalty. The fact that the traditional unions occupied the terrain and that the government kept its capacity of control prevented the emergence of independent unions that may have resisted the implementation of economic and State reforms. Although there were some outbreaks of autonomous unionism, in the telecommunications sector, some automotive companies, and universities, flexibilization, de-unionization, and protection trade unionis were to a large extent imposed (Bizberg 1999; Bensusán and Middlebrook 2013).

Although Mexico underwent a process of electoral democratization that led to the triumph of Vicente Fox to the presidency in 2000, this government did not fulfill its promise to be more open to the registering of new independent unions, or for that matter peasant and other popular organizations that were under the hold of the corporatist pact. It maintained a status quo with the corporative organizations he had promised to dismantle. Thus, neoliberalism and democratization continued

[4] http://www.redlat.net/site/wp-content/uploads/2016/06/peru-trabajo_decente.pdf.

[5] http://www.urosario.edu.co/urosario_files/76/7692c2f4-e5dd-46bd-aafa-2f505d-6dcff2.pdf.

weakening union corporatism while the emergence of independent social organizations remained being hampered.

On the other hand, after the 1985 earthquake in Mexico City, as a consequence of the protracted and inefficient government reaction (Verduzco Igartúa 2005), there was an upsurge of social organizations and movements, mainly NGOs, that emerged to ease the catastrophic situation. For years after this humanitarian crisis, they continued to proliferate in order to alleviate the growing absence of the State, the rise of inequality, and poverty that the neoliberal model generated. With the electoral alternation, first in Mexico City (in 1997) and then at the federal level (in 2000), a window of opportunity that did not exist at the time of the PRI (that channeled all of its initiatives through governmental agencies or their own corporate organizations) opened for the NGOs, as both the PAN and the PRD, promoted greater participation of these organizations. On many occasions, these two parties used these organizations to alleviate the shortcomings of an underdeveloped party apparatus and because they were closer to the population. In consequence, these NGOs began to be funded by the government. In the case of Chile, the democratic governments succeeded in recuperating the civil society organizations that emerged during the dictatorship to deal with the economic and social problems of the poor and marginalized that were at the center of the mobilizations of the 1980s in the marginalized areas of the cities.

This evolution resulted in a gradual transformation of the role of these organizations in both countries: instead of being proactive actors and social promoters, they became enablers and consultants of the government's social policy. Governments succeeded in converting autonomous and combative organizations that had fought for a more just society, into associations that disseminate a conception of citizenship based on the market and the individual, that matches the neoliberal model. Most of the organizations that now help the poor and the indigenous receive their resources from the State and have modified their conception of citizenship from one that was based on rights, to another that focuses on the human condition, which needs charitable help either by the State or by social organizations—a conception based on social responsibility and individual moral solidarity (Dagnino 2003: 27). As De la Maza affirms for Chile, this had as a consequence that the participation of civil society became purely instrumental, fragmented, without networks, oriented toward the poor, and dependent on governmental financing (De la Maza 2010, cited by Oxhorn 2011: 126). In a sense, the NGOs were victims of their own success and suffered a collateral effect of democratization, as they went from a situation in which they defined their agenda autonomously to one of collaboration or even cooptation by the State.

Notwithstanding that this is the general situation of social movements in Mexico, every single day there are a myriad of demonstrations in Mexico City and other parts of the country that raise all kinds of demands: for protection against violence of drug cartels, the police and the army, against a political authority, to reject a mining project, among many others. There have also been very significant social movements that raise very noteworthy ethical issues, like one of the student movements #YoSoy132 and that of the victims of violence, the *Movimiento por la Paz con Justicia y Dignidad* (MPJD), two of the country's most original movements (Bizberg 2014). Nonetheless, these countless movements are atomized, they pose in general very specific and localized demands that do not allow them to connect with other movements or actions in order to become movements that jeopardize the status quo.

6.3 From an Oligarchic Pact to a Compromise Between the Popular Sectors and the Financial and Extractive Rentier Sectors

As we have already mentioned above, similarly to the Mexican case, both in Brazil and in Argentina, a corporatist pact was established in the 1930s. Nonetheless, in these two countries, the corporatist pact was not institutionalized in a State party that maintained itself in power uninterruptedly for more than 70 years. The corporatist pact in Brazil lasted until the coup d'état against Joao Goulart in 1964 and in Argentina until the coup against Peron in 1955. In these two countries, there was no popular revolution, although both Vargas and Perón considered their movement as one and made profound changes to the social and political regime of their countries. In both countries, as in Mexico, State leadership coopted or even crafted the unions, and then exchanged benefits against support of the government. Yet, in contrast to Mexico, where peasant and other popular sectors were organized and mobilized, in Brazil and Argentina, the pact was much more narrow, as it was restricted to the workers and public functionaries. Both the Brazilian and the Argentinian unions gained autonomy from the State when the military took over and succeeded in exerting pressure on the government in opposition. In contrast, the Mexican social organizations were rarely opponents, they were included in the PRI since their birth and were always associated with the party in power until the years 2000.

In the 1970s, the Mexican economy went through ten years of a total re-orientation from import substitution industrialization to an oil exporting economy (at the end of the 1970s Mexican exports were around 80% dependent on petroleum; the foreign exchange that poured into the country from oil exports and external debt generated the Dutch disease that in its turn led to de-industrialization). In contrast, the Brazilian military government, that was also heavily indebted, had concentrated its investments in infrastructure and in expanding its capital and intermediary goods production. Facing the crisis, the Brazilian State was less prone to the pressure of the FMI and thus had less external pressure to liberalize. Concurrently, the Brazilian democratization process was in its apex. This process had begun with the union strikes of the end of the 1970s, continued with the movement to elect a civil president directly, the *diretas ya*, and culminated with the drafting of a new constitution, between 1986 and 1988, where a myriad of social movements and actors intervened.

These divergent situations explain the most significant differences between the Mexican pact and the ones we will now begin discussing. They explain the endurance of the Mexican social contract, the fact that the social organizations in Mexican pact had less autonomy from the State, and that they were significantly weakened by neoliberalism. This is what explains that while the PRI maintained political control throughout the period of economic liberalization, in Argentina and Brazil, civil society was central to push for democratization and resist economic liberalization (Bizberg 2010; Bensusán 2016).

In Brazil, the periodization between democratization and liberalization was the contrary, as the country democratized before the implementation of neoliberal policies. This meant that when neoliberal policies began to be executed at the end of the 1980s and beginning of the 1990s, the unions and other social actors were strong enough to confront the government and stop it short from imposing purely orthodox measures. The presence of a trade union movement, the CUT, together with a disciplined political party (the Workers' Party) and a very active civil society opposing the Washington Consensus, were crucial to determine the social, political, and economic trajectory of the country. On the other hand, the fragmented and decentralized political system of Brazil prevented the materialization of a political coalition capable of executing a radical dismantling of the interventionist State. In this manner, resistance and lack of cohesion of the actors applying neoliberal policies led Brazil to be the Latin American country that had better preserved the powers of State through the liberal wave of the 1980s and 1990s.

The first democratic government (Sarney 1985–1990) was pressed to take into account the interests of the popular sectors which had suffered from the measures of the military regimes and had triggered the process of democratization, carried out an heterodox plan (the Cruzado Plan) that intended to recuperate growth and curb inflation. The country actually began growing again at a rate of 4.3% per year during the *Nova República*, and unemployment fell from 4.4 to 3.8% in the first four months of 1986 (Barros de Castro 2005: 126). This growth was possible owing to the maturation of the investments made during the military regime (especially the plan PNDII) (ibid.: 132). In contrast to most Latin American countries, Brazil's economy (along with Colombia and Panama) managed to grow its per capita product at significant rates during the first period of the new Republic: 7.9% (1985), 8% (1986), 3.6% (1987), −0.1% (1988), 3, 3 (1989), −4, 3 (1990) (World Bank Data base: https://data.worldbank.org; Hermann 2005a, b; Barros de Castro 2005). Notwithstanding, the Cruzado Plan, like the others that followed it until the Real Plan, failed to control inflation as it did not succeed in blocking prices and wages, as evidenced by the average of 471% price increase in the period of the *Nova República*. On the other hand, although Brazil accepted the constraints of the IMF and applied austerity measures, it neither reduced social spending, nor undertook privatizations until after 1990, under the Collor and Cardoso governments. In fact, social spending only declined in 1984 and 1985, but then rose sharply since the adoption of the 1988 Constitution (Lautier 2009; Haggard and Kaufman 2008: 388–390). Finally, according to Marques Pereira and Théret, although inflation had a very negative effect on the poor that did not have formal jobs where wages were indexed, the country managed to better preserve its industry as "The creeping nature of hyperinflation [...]operated de facto as an instrument of resistance to the de-industrialisation that tends to provoke any financial liberalization under external constraint ..." (Marques Pereira and Théret 2004).

Analysts have repeatedly claimed that most of the Latin American social and union movements that emerged during democratization demobilized once the regime change occurred (Arato 2000;

Berins Collier 1999; Sallum 1996, 2010; Riethof 2004). It has been even proposed that Brazil was no exception if one takes into account the number of strikes and strikers: in effect, while the 1978 strikes mobilized about a quarter of a million workers for nine weeks and about half a million by the end of the year and in 1979 more than three million workers participated in more than 100 strikes (Berins Collier, op. cit.: 135), once the new regime was established, there was a clear decrease, from 3,943 strikes and 18,4 million strikers in 1989 to 382 strikes and 1.57 million strikers in 1998 (Invernizzi 2006: 105). On the other hand, since 1983, the union leaders dedicated themselves to organize both the *Central Única dos Trabalhadores* (CUT) and the *Partido dos Trabalhadores* (PT) (Sallum 1996: 85).

Nonetheless, unionism in Brazil was not the sole key player in democratization, although it contributed to the creation of one of the fundamental political parties that emerged from this process: the PT. In addition, it differs from Peronism and other parties such as Solidarity in Poland, where trade unionism was an actor of democratization but intervened directly (as in Poland) or reached agreements with the government that imposed the new economic model (as in Argentina), something that weakened and de-legitimized it. On the contrary, in the case of Brazil, trade unionism remained in opposition until the beginning of the 2000s, when the PT arrived to power. Indeed, the CUT/PT opposed the more liberal aspects of the governments of Collor and Cardoso, and managed to resist the most radical neoliberal measures, such as privatizations and the reform of the pension system.

Thus, although, as in the rest of the continent the industrial relations were flexibilized in the 1990s, unionism managed to retain an important degree of autonomy and capacity of action. This is partly due to the fact that the labor movement in Brazil was a central actor both in the democratization process and in the discussions leading to the 1988 Constitution, but also because it never lost its character as an interlocutor of the successive governments, even with the more liberal ones. During the presidency of Cardoso, the government promoted negotiations between employers and labor (the *Cámaras sectoriais*) in order to set conditions for the modernization and increase in production in several branches of the economy. Both the CUT and *Força Sindical* were included in a tripartite association together with the employers of various union branches (automotive, textile, electronics, among others) and the State: the so-called *camaras sectoriais* that served to negotiate salaries, prices, and taxes with a view to stimulate the growth of the most strategic economic branches (De Souza Keller 1994). During the Lula government, the tripartite relationship was further strengthened, several temporary and permanent tripartite councils were created with the aim of discussing certain laws and measures that affected the interests of the workers, such as the Socioeconomic Council and the forums to discuss the reforms to the pension system and the labor law (Riethof 2004; Cardoso and Gindin 2009). In addition, union leaders were promoted to the head of different State companies (ibid.: 12). Finally, since the 1980s, unions have managed to impose local representation, through delegates, in some of the largest companies. They also accomplished to unionize previously non-organized sectors such as the peasants (Bizberg 2004). In fact, although it is true that unions are smaller, the total number of unions has increased considerably, and trade union density is quite high in comparison with that of the rest of Latin America: 20.9% (Hayter and Stoevska 2011).

The arrival of the PT to government could have forced the unions into a State corporatism similar to that established by the PRI with the CTM or Peronism with the Peronist Party in the Perón era. However, the relationship between the CUT and the PT government was far from resembling the support given by the Mexican official unionism to the government of Salinas or that of the CGT to the government of Menem, two rulers who imposed neoliberal measures on unionism. The CUT adopted a position it called "critical solidarity," a position that we could describe as neo-corporativism, as did Etchemendy and Collier for the Argentine case.

Other social movements also contributed decisively to the process of democratization and participated very actively in the drafting of the 1988 Constitution, which has been the most open of all the constitutional revisions in the continent. In this country, the mobilization of civil society survived the process of democratization for three main reasons: the strength of social mobilization, due to the fact that shortly after the arrival of a civilian president a very open process of drafting a new constitution took place, which re-mobilized civil society, unlike what happened in Chile or Mexico, where there was no such process and where everything contributed to demobilization. On the other hand, in its strategy to win supporters and move toward national power from the localities, the PT developed new ways of defining public policies, especially the participatory budget, which involved a strong participation of local populations through social organizations and a frontal struggle against patronage so characteristic of Brazilian political life.

The constitutional process that lasted almost three years, between 1986 and 1988, had such an impact on civil society that "… in all the localities of the country, spaces for discussion, forums, committees and plenary meetings were created to articulate the demands in order to present them to parliamentarians" (Chaves Teixeira et al. 2002: 55). Consequently, for the first time in Brazil, different sectors of the population participated effectively in the elaboration of the constitution and not only the political elites (Chaves Teixeira et al. 2002: 57). Several authors consider that the idea of democratizing existing decision-making arenas began to gain ground, as well as creating new ones to stimulate the participation of civil society, especially among the sectors of society that had been marginalized in the decision processes of the past (Chaves Teixeira et al. 2002: 55). All this led to the inclusion in the constitution, in addition to the universality of social rights, the right to plebiscite and popular referendum, public hearings, as well as the creation of councils responsible for defining and monitoring the execution of public policies at the federal, state, and municipal levels (Chaves Teixeira et al. 2002: 57). Finally, the great innovation of the participatory budget and the enormous network of institutionalized participation that exists in Brazil allows us to consider that this country had been establishing a path toward participatory democracy until the recent events that resulted in the impeachment of Dilma Roussef and the election of Bolsonaro in October 2018. Even as recently as 2013, at the dawn of the World Cup, there were a series of demonstrations promoted by "Free Pass" social movement against increases in metro rates, which were joined by protesters who demanded the improvement in public services. And more recently, the movements of the middle classes against Dilma Rousseff that demanded her impeachment and the continuation of the corruption investigations known as *Lava Jato*. Both movements, however of contrary political sign, witness a very active civil society, ready to mobilize when it finds reasons to do so.

Argentina also democratized in the midst of the debt crisis, in 1985. The first democratic government that of Alfonsin also applied heterodox plans to fight the crisis, as a manner of beginning to pay the 'social debt' accumulated by so many years of dictatorship where social demands had been repressed (Marques Pereira and Théret 2004). But their heterodox plans also failed to curb inflation arising from distributive conflicts in an inflationary and democratic context. However, the traditional polarization between the agro-export sector (allied with finance) and the industrial sector, as well as between Peronism and entrepreneurial interests, combined with the weak power of the Argentine State and the weak institutionalization of the political system, resulted in a much more intense and uncontrollable distributive conflict than that of Brazil (Bizberg and Théret 2012). On the other hand, while in Brazil at the beginning of the 1980s the debt was mostly public and had been invested in productive assets, in Argentina a large part was private and had been used for speculation and capital flight; it is for this reason that the assumption of this debt by the Argentine State in 1981 was considered illegitimate and generated a strong dissatisfaction (Welch 1991: 10; Cortés Conde 2007: 299). This polarization and lack of confidence in the Argentine State explain why, while the Brazilian inflation was "... characterized by its highly inertial character which gave it a relative regularity [...] inflation was erratic in Argentine, witnessing a succession of periods of acceleration and deceleration, ending with two episodes of hyperinflation in 1989 and 1990 and averaging a higher level than in Brazil" (Baldi-Delatte 2004: 4).

Because Argentinian unionism was more social and weakly rooted at the plant level, as it controlled the health and pension benefits and negotiated the general conditions of the workers at the branch level, internal plant flexibility was implemented without modifying the legislation. Moreover, in order to abate the labor movement, in the 1990s the Menem government tried to impose local-level negotiations and wage increases linked to productivity growth by decree. He also intended to "privatize" health services, the so-called *Obras sociales* administered by the unions. Nonetheless, the unions were successful in resisting the latter. Although flexibility passed, neither negotiations at the local level nor privatization of the health services went too far, partly due to a compromise between the main union confederation, the *peronista* CGT, and Menem, by which the confederation accepted flexibility (and other measures such as privatization of public enterprises) in exchange for preserving control of the *Obras Sociales* (Murillo 2000; Munck 2004). The issue that the Menem government had to negotiate with the unions paradoxically led to a very radical privatization program but concurrently to the preservation of the force of the unions that were re-activated in the Kirchner and Fernandez governments (Etchemendy and Collier 2007). Indeed, in comparative terms, the Argentinian labor movement has been relatively well preserved at around 37% of union density, the highest in Latin America. Nevertheless, the support given by unions to the Menem government did result in the division of the *peronista* union and a decrease in the proportion of the active working class that it organizes (Palomino 2000).

The crisis of 2001–2002 considerably modified the context, as it gave rise to a wave of protests and more or less spontaneous social movements unprecedented in Argentina. With the deepening economic, political, and social crisis that resulted with the end of "convertibility", trade unionism, together with a myriad of other social actors (*piqueteros*, human rights, the children of the disappeared), reemerged with great force. In the context of this generalized social mobilization, unionism and *piqueteros* appeared as the main organized actors and became the principal support for the Kirchner and the Fernández de Kirchner governments that began in 2003 (Palomino and Trajtenberg 2006). As a result, their government was forced to orient itself toward workers' interests in search of popular support and legitimacy.

The remobilization of the Argentinian society gave birth to a series of movements protesting against politicians and defending the rights of the small bank savers, factory occupations, and the *piqueteros*. Together with the human rights movements, the latter may be considered the most significant as they survived the most serious moments of the crisis. The *piquetero* movements began with protests against the closure of State enterprises during Menem's government in the south of the country (Neuquén, Salta, and Jujuy), which, in many cases, were the only source of employment of a locality. The workers protested by blocking the streets and highways of the regions; in many cases, they led to widespread revolts of the inhabitants of the towns. These actions increased together with the impressive growth of unemployment from the 1990s to 2001: from 15% in 1992 to 40% just prior the outbreak of the crisis. In those years, but especially during the government of De la Rua, the movements spread to the whole of the country, arriving at the region of Buenos Aires, where convertibility had been disastrous and was impacting especially private-owned companies (Svampa and Pereyra 2004). This situation also led to a broad movement of the occupation of hundreds of plants that were closed by their owners and organized by their workers to continue making them function.

The *piquetero* movements, unlike the other spontaneous movements that arose in the crisis, consolidated in permanent organizations and came to terms with the Kirchner government. His government increased social policies destined to these movements and allowed them to administer and distribute them directly—something that resulted in a decrease in the *piquetero* actions and aligned the organizations to the government (Cheresky 2004: 15). This, in its turn led to the strengthening of the piquetero organizations: membership increased from 1000 in 1997 to more than 200,000 in 2004. The most important association was the Land and Housing Federation, with 125,000 members, headed by Luis D'Elia, which joined a union confederation, the CTA, and managed 75,000 temporary work programs (Franceschelli and Ronconi 2005: 15). This organization had a crucial role during the Fernandez de Kirchner presidency, especially in the conflict that opposed her government to the agricultural producers in the summer of 2008, concerning new fiscal measures.

Although, following the crisis of 2001–2002, the huge rise in protest and mobilization was mainly led by the *piqueteros* and other spontaneous groups, led to think that these movements had completely displaced unionism, as of 2004, the trade union movements once again dominated the social action field (Etchemendy and Collier 2007: 370). Whereas until 2003 nonunion conflicts were greater than union conflicts (60% against 40% and 58% against 42% in 2002 and 2003 respectively), in 2005 there were almost 80% union conflicts (ibid.: 371).

With the arrival to the presidency of Néstor Kirchner in 2003, the Argentinian government reaffirmed its alliance with the *peronist* unions. Its social and labor policies changed radically with respect to the Menem and Alfonsín years: it named a renowned labor lawyer at the head of the Ministry of Labor that, contrary to what was current during the Menem years, began promoting branch rather than enterprise level collective negotiations (Palomino and Trajtemberg 2006: 49). In addition, union action and increased inspection by the Ministry of Labor led to a substantial increase in registered labor in contrast to the previous tendency to outsourcing and informalization; the coverage of collective bargaining went from 1.6 million workers in 2003 to 3.5 million in 2006.[6] The government also raised minimum salaries, strove to reduce the gap between low and high salaries, and increased the resources of the pension funds—all of this a result of higher salaries and of a larger extension of coverage, which we will discuss in Chapter 8 (ibid.: 52–55; Novick et al. 2009: 272).

Most authors emphasize that the change came "from above," which is to say that it was the attitude of a more pro-labor government, a more traditional Peronism, that amended the anti-union attitude of the previous government of Menem, to seal an alliance with the Kirchner government. Other studies emphasize, on the contrary, that it was the mobilization of both nonunion and grassroots workers, which led the government to renew its alliance with the CGT, controlled by Hugo Moyano, the most notable anti-Menem leader, under whom, the CGT reunified in 2004 (Cardoso and Gindin 2009: 12).

The interpretation 'from above" states that the presidency of N. Kirchner re-established relations with organized syndicalism based on the traditional Peronist identity, especially the recognition of traditional structures and leaderships, as well as with State policies aimed at the revitalization of collective bargaining, which had been restricted by the Menem government (Cardoso and Gindin 2009: 12). The interpretation "from below" emphasizes the increase in union conflicts that obliged both the Peronist unions and the government to come to terms in order to prevent the overpowering of the institutional union system. Varela (2013) and Duhalde (2013) analyze the emergence of grassroots unionism that was acting "... independently of, or in open opposition to the union leadership" (Varela 2013: 80–81). The conflicts were both owing to formal and outsourcing workers. The first movement of this type, in 2004, was that of the outsourcing metro workers who united with the regular workers on five subway lines to strike; it was led by union delegates independent or in opposition to the official unions. The result of

[6]Varela rightly considers that the official statistics during the government of Cristina Fernández have little credibility, and contests these data. According to this author, while at the beginning of the decade of the 1980s the unregistered work rate was 25% and by the end of the 1990s it had risen to 40%, notwithstanding "... nine years of growth at 7.6 average (from 2002–2010), the unregistered work rate is at levels close to those reached after the neoliberal counter-reforms" (Varela 2013: 88).

this "wild" strike was an improvement in working conditions, but above all "... the recognition of the body of delegates opposed to the direction of the UTA (Automotive Tramway Union). At the end of the same year, there was a movement of the outsourced workers of a company that gives maintenance to the subway. These movements and the subsequent mobilizations resulted in the inclusion of all the outsourcing workers in the collective convention signed by the UTA" (Varela 2013: 80).

In any event, unions were forcefully re-activated during the Kirchner and Fernandez governments and became significant sociopolitical actors to the extent that Etchemendy and Collier (2007) qualified the relationship between these two governments with labor as socio-corporatist. Although they are now under pressure in the Macri government, the final result is uncertain. The CGT has organized vigorous social movements, among them a couple of general strikes. On the other hand, union density, which is an indicator of the force of this movement, is one of the highest in Latin America: 37.6% (of the salaried earners), while the coverage of the collective contracts is 60%. In Brazil, the percentages are 20.9% and 60%, respectively, in Uruguay it is 19% and 83%[7] (Hayter and Stoevska 2011).

6.4 The Imposition of a Liberal Rentier Pact

The cases of Chile, Peru, and Colombia are similar to each other and to the Mexican one, especially because both unions and social organizations are very weak. This does not mean that there are no frequent protests and manifestations that occur at the local level, or even very significant social movements as one of the students in Chile and in Mexico, of the victims of violence in the case of Mexico, and even large and massive movements such as the student or the pensioner's movement in Chile. Nonetheless, all these movements are disconnected and unable to pose a real challenge to the *status quo*.

The weakness of organized civil society in these countries is the consequence of violence in the case of all three and the exhaustion of the party system in Peru and Colombia. Violence was the way in which the Pinochet regime tore apart the ancient political system during the fifteen years in which the military regime reigned. The military regime killed or disappeared numerous union and political leaders, illegalized parties and unions, proclaimed a new constitution, and passed labor laws that

[7] There are no accessible data for collective bargaining coverage for Uruguay.

were intended to institutionalize the weakness of the social and political organizations that was accomplished through violence; in many respects, it served its purpose. In the case of Colombia, violence has been imbedded in the system since at least the 1950s, with the emergence of guerilla warfare and then the appearance of the drug cartels and their imbrication with the guerrilla groups. On the other hand, the old party system, based on a pact between the two major parties, called the *Frente Nacional*, according to which they divided among them the different governmental posts, ruined the legitimacy of both parties, exhausted the pact, and resulted in a profoundly atomized system. Both extreme violence and the closing of the party system were totally negative for the existence of a strong organized civil society. Suffice it to mention the fact that every year, there are a myriad of unionists and social activists killed and that union density is almost negligible, 3.5%. In Peru, although violence was never as extended as in Colombia, it was very significant in the 1970s and 1980s, when the radical and very violent Maoist group *Sendero Luminoso* wreaked havoc in the countryside and in some cities. This situation was totally unfavorable for the existence of a more reformist left, which was divided with regard to the position to adopt toward this movement. Finally, the election of Fujimori, the *auto-golpe* and his ten years in power (1990–2000), repressed the parties and the social organizations and destroyed what was left of them and of the unions.

In the case of Chile, the cause of the extreme weakness of civil society in the aftermath of the democratization process was the fact that the military coup against the elected government of Allende, on September 11, 1973, broke not only with democracy and the developmentalist economic model, but also with the net of social and political organizations that had existed in that country for decades. During the 1980 crisis, the Pinochet regime, like the Mexican, imposed on its population drastic austerity measures. The Pinochet government made the payment of the debt the absolute priority; in order to preserve its international reputation, it did not try a compromise between the external financial interests and its population. First, the State absorbed private obligations, which raised the government's debt from 36% of GDP in 1981 to 86% in 1987 (Ffrench-Davis 2008: 210). Second, it imposed strict orthodox measures that resulted in a 25% decrease in domestic demand per capita and a 14% fall in GDP (Ffrench-Davis 2008: 196). Nevertheless, faced with the gravity of the crisis, in 1983 it abandoned the ultra-liberalism of the

"Chicago Boys" to pursue more "pragmatic" policies, such as subsidizing exports and raising taxes on imports and abandoning the absolute fiscal equilibrium policy. Faced with the fiscal crisis caused by the debt crisis, the Pinochet government saved the banks and then imposed very strict bank regulations (ibid.: 196, 216). Whereas during the years 1982–1985 the deficit was of 3.1% on average, with a high point of 3.7% in 1985, in 1987 it reached a surplus (ibid.: 216). On the other hand, the need to generate a trade surplus to pay the debt forced the government to enforce different policies to stimulate the development of certain economic sectors (forest products, wine, fruit, salmon) that would become central to maintain the country's growth (ibid.: 231–238). With regard to wage and social policy, orthodoxy was the absolute rule: it imposed wage restrictions and significantly reduced social spending (Haggard and Kaufman 2008: 388). As a result, the productivity/wage ratio became very favorable to capital (Graña and Kennedy 2008), and the level of poverty and income inequality increased dramatically (Ffrench-Davis 2008: 283).

But the coup had even longer-term, foundational, intentions that went beyond the modification of the economic model or what the military called the "restoration of order," it defined its role as "... a total war directed against an enemy that had infiltrated (sic) more than half of the population." Under this perspective, it was necessary to destroy both the left political parties and the unions (Valenzuela 1995: 98). Thus, the logic behind and the main objective of the Pinochet government were, as the Argentinian junta defined it, the "de-politicization of the State." This implied a political offensive against leftist political parties and unionism intended to break the ties between politics and social actors, with unionism in foreground. And truly, under the dictatorship of Augusto Pinochet, the relationship between social organizations and political parties was practically annihilated (Munck 2004: 7).

The relationship between Chilean unionism and the political parties that had been its main strength in democracy became its greatest weakness in a dictatorship. Unionism was easily beheaded by the military government when it repressed and banned political parties (Barrera 1994: 116). Indeed, the capacity of the military regime to uproot trade unionism both politically and socially was due in part to the violence exercised and, on the other, to the fact that Chilean unionism, as its party system was, like in Europe, closely linked to the socialist and communist parties, so the destruction by the Pinochet regime of this linkage led to a lasting weakening of the unionism itself. Unlike the trade unions closely linked to the State, connected to pluri-classist parties characterized by a nationalist and anti-imperialist ideology—like the Mexican, the Brazilian, the Argentine and the Venezuelan—the Chilean union movement was more autonomous of the State, more radical, and more ideological. This is explained by its origin, in an enclave economy dominated by foreign capital and based on the exploitation of saltpeter first and copper after, in isolated regions of the country (Bergquist 1986).

In addition, the Pinochet regime transformed profoundly practically all spheres of social and political life, to a certain extent "refounded" the Chilean institutions: economic (orthodox liberalism), social (unions, privatization of pensions, health, and education), and political (the binominal system, the life senators, the role of the army). Furthermore, it managed to institutionalize these changes in the 1980 Constitution and the labor laws of 1979. The Labor Plan restored some rights that had been suspended, such as the election of union leaders and collective bargaining, albeit under a highly restrictive framework, as it imposed the prohibition of political party involvement in union affairs and shifted collective negotiations from the branch to the local plant level. The law determined, among other things, that wage and working conditions should be negotiated without external intervention (which pointed to the political parties that had dominated union life before the coup (Barrera, op. cit.: 117)) and among several unions within each company, which ensured their division (Zapata 1992: 706). The law also imposed very flexible industrial relations: workers could be fired without any reason and with a minimal compensation, and employers could substitute striking workers. This had a lasting effect because even if after democratization the number of unions has increased considerably, they are smaller compared to those that existed before the coup (Barrera 1994: 117) and unionization rate of the total of salaried earners is very low: 11.5% (Hayter and Stoevska 2011).

The weakening of civil society did not concern only unions, but most authors coincide in emphasizing that the way the transition took place (almost exclusively through the electoral process, as in Mexico), implied the demobilization of the civil associations that had been very active in the mid-1980s. The actors of the Chilean democratization (both government and opposition) were very careful to limit it to the political system. For Maza, the main characteristic of the Chilean democratization process was the "...identification between democracy and political system" (De la Maza, op. cit.: 225). The political actors that negotiated the transition with Pinochet were careful not to endanger the possibility that the military call off the plebiscite, and were conscious of the fact that the political and social polarization that prevailed in the 1960s and the early 1970s was part of the scenario that had allowed for Pinochet's coup d'état, and something which was less explicit, considered as a success the economic model of the dictatorship. That is the reason why the process of democratization in Chile took place through the demobilization of civil society that had begun to activate in the middle of the 1980s and that had triggered the process. While neither in Argentina nor in Brazil the social groups that had begun the process were demobilized, during or after democratization, once the Chilean parties had decided to participate in the Pinochet plebiscite in 1988 (Oxhorn 1994), the groups of settlers of the poor sectors of the cities, especially Santiago, that were organizing the *Jornadas Nacionales de Protesta* since 1983, were stopped by the political parties.

On the one hand, in spite that the mobilizations of the settlers continued until 1986, they did not succeed in modifying the attitude of the government, that responded with increasing repression. On the other hand, the traditional political and social actors felt a certain distrust toward the direct manner of doing politics of the settlers (Doran 2000); the memory (trauma) of the polarization generated during the Popular Unity government played a significant role. That is why, despite the fact that the National Days of Protest had crystallized around the social and political actors, they began to question the effectiveness of these actions. It was also argued that the violence that accompanied the protests, more and more frequently, had generated a climate of uncertainty and fear that served to legitimize the repressive actions of the military regime (Oxhorn, op. cit.).

As the date for the plebiscite set by the 1980 Constitution approached, the options offered to the opposition became clearer. The political parties were inclined to accept the rules of the game of the regime (which implied giving it a certain legitimacy) and prepared to participate in it. The alternative was too risky, because it meant rejecting the institutions of the military regime, continue with the protests, boycott the plebiscite, and face the inevitable victory of the candidate of the *junta* (Oxhorn, op. cit.: 54). With the exception of the Communist Party and extreme left groups, the opposition opted to participate.

This had as a consequence that, from that moment on, the traditional forms of political–electoral participation began dominating; which meant that the protest action of the popular sectors to put pressure on Pinochet would have to give way to electoral action (ibid.: 59).

This not only led to the "structural" weakness of Chilean civil society, but also to the protection of the economic model and the preservation of the institutions of the old regime, which became "authoritarian enclaves" (Garretón 1991). Although the successive governments of the *Concertación* set out to modify the most socially unjust aspects of the economic, social, and political model adopted by the military government, in order to promote a process of "growth with equity," their intentions did not have significant changes for the unions and social movements. On the one hand, the labor law has, up to the present, still not been profoundly modified, and on the other, the reforms carried out maintain the equation of cheap labor and reduced rights for collective action (Taylor 2004: 76). First, in the 1990s, the *Concertación* governments proposed promoting greater organizational capacity and the protection of labor rights. The government of Aylwin (1990–1994) promised to ensure stability through cooperation; however, changes to the labor law negotiated between 1990 and 1993 were not significant. The same can be said of the reforms of Lagos and Bachelet. The reforms gave some marginal rights to workers, but did not restore branch collective negotiations, nor loosen considerably the right to strike, which is still very constrained in this country and gives ample capabilities to employers to replace striking workers (Cerdas Sandí 2017).

The cases of Perú and Colombia were different from Chile in that neither country had to cope with such a brutal and long-term dictatorship. Truly, in the case of Peru, the coup d'état that installed a military junta in 1968 was led by a nationalist, popular, and anti-imperialist sector of the army. In Colombia, there was no military government since the coup of 1953. On the other hand, the unions and civil society organizations were never as strong in these two countries as in Chile. Furthermore, in the 1990s, when the liberal economy was imposed, the social organizations of both countries had been severely weakened.

In the case of Peru, between the coup of 1968 and 1975, there was a belated and short corporatist interlude that did not last enough to consolidate like it did in some of the other countries in Latin America that we have discussed. It was a military government that, contrary to the others that took power in the continent, implemented a statist, leftist, and corporatist socioeconomic policies. The government of Velasco Alvarado (1968–1975), as other national-popular governments before him, motivated the labor, peasant, and squatter organizations, to control them and build a social base for his government (Stepan 1978, cited by Silva 2009).

Although the military did not try to create a political party, they did create an organization that was charged with the functions of the PRI in Mexico, the *Justicialista* party in Argentina, the *Partido Travaillista* in Brazil, and the MNR in Bolivia: the *Sistema Nacional de Apoyo a la Movilización Social* (SINAMOS). The government increased State intervention in the economy from 1% of GDP in 1968 to nearly 20% in 1975. It set up State banks, nationalized oil and mining firms and expanded the State companies in steel, electricity and mining, and invested in infrastructure. It also protected industry and controlled prices, all in an effort to develop the country through a model that in other nations was about to enter its final crisis (Silva 2009), but that in this country had been always blocked by an agrarian oligarchy (Contreras and Zuloaga 2014). This leftist military government also engaged in an agrarian reform that was neither as ample as the Mexican, nor as the Bolivian, because it only benefited between 10 and 15% of the Peruvian peasants that lived in the coastal lands, while it ignored those that were in the highlands; but it nevertheless serve to weaken the agrarian oligarchy and create a quite ample constituency that was assembled in peasant organizations (Silva 2009). These policies had two other intentions: it was a strategy to isolate and replace the nationalist-popular party that had emerged in the 1930s, the APRA, that was linked to the workers' organization, the *Confederación de Trabajadores Peruanos*; indeed, with this in mind, the government of Velazco Alvarado not only created its own unions, but guided them to be included in the *Confederation General de Trabajadores del Peru* (CGTP), a communist confederation that was strengthened and soon outflanked the *Aprist* confederation. Regarding the beneficiaries of the agrarian reform, mostly indigenous, they were integrated into the communist-controlled Peruvian Peasant Confederation and the *Confederación Nacional Agraria*, as a way in which the government tried to "...restructure ethnic relations in Peru [...] by redefining Indians as peasants" (Silva 2009: 232–233).

Nonetheless, this nationalistic, industrialist, corporatist military government soon found its limits in a context defined by the world economic crisis that began with the hike of oil prices in 1973, that nourished the division of the military regarding its relation with the mobilized social movements. While Mexico was able to endure the crisis of the 1970s because it discovered vast reserves of oil and Brazil had the possibility of contracting debt and attracting investments for its industry, Peru had neither of these; it thus continued promoting a national economy through State expenditure, a situation that soon became untenable. With these two tribulations, in the mid-1975 a rightist sector of the military decided to give a house coup against Velasco and force into power Morales Bermudez, who imposed austerity measures and tried to weaken and dismantle the popular organizations that had been organized by his predecessor (Silva 2009).

This radical modification was the signal for the start of mobilizations of the social sectors that saw their economic and political position at risk. The mobilization was very ample, although it extended beyond the labor movement; one of the main organizations deployed was the communist CGTP, which declared its first general strike ever in 1977 and then another one in 1978; both of which had the support of many of other popular organizations. The movement was so successful that it was interpreted as a pre-revolutionary situation by the left. Paradoxically, not only did it not lead to a revolution, but on the contrary it headed to the displacement of the military; they were weakened by the economic situation of the country and by the rift in their ranks. The military announced a transition to democracy, which would have as its first step the convocation of a constituent assembly that would be charged with drafting a new constitution. The 1978 Constitution gave ample power to the State in economic and social matters; it also expanded considerably the electorate by allotting the illiterate the right to vote. The second step were the elections of 1980 (Silva 2009; Contreras and Zuloaga 2014: 257–259).

The transition to democracy coincided with the economic crisis that struck all of Latin America in the 1980s. In the case of Peru, the first democratic government of Belaunde imposed an orthodox stabilization policy, reducing the weight of the State, liberalizing the economy, reducing tariffs, subsidies, and taxes, as well as imposing limits to wage increases. These policies led to an opposition that this time did not result in such an ample mobilization as the one that had displaced the military, but that was channeled electorally as the new constitution had legalized the leftist parties (Contreras and Zuloaga 2014: 257–259). In the elections of 1985, the nationalist-popular party APRA that had been inspired by the other popular parties of Latin America in the 1930s (especially the PRI), won the election with Alan García. This government reversed the policies that had been imposed during the previous one and implemented a more active developmentalist policy. One of the main actions it took was to set a limit to the payment of the debt, set at a maximum of 10 percent of the total of exports. As no other country in Latin America went along with Peru, the country was cut off the international financial circuits that considered it had defaulted its debt (Contreras and Zuloaga 2014: 261). This led the García government to incur in an enormous fiscal deficit that increased from an already large 46% of GDP in 1983 to 61% in 1990, which, in its turn, drove Peru to hyperinflation, as many other countries in Latin America (Silva 2009: 237).

The fact that the military regime governed Peru for more than a decade and the deep economic crisis that coincided with the transition to democracy had a very disruptive effect on the party system. But what had a definite impact in demolishing it was its convergence with the appearance of an increasingly powerful radical and violent guerilla movement, *Sendero Luminoso*, that had its strongholds in the highlands, where the agrarian reform had not progressed. This movement was one of the causes of the demise of the social movements and leftist parties in Peru. The fact that the democratic governments proved unable to neutralize this movement increased the popular defiance to government and parties, and resulted in what Tanaka has called a democracy without parties (Tanaka 2005).

In addition, we can also call the Peruvian (and the Colombian, as we will see next) as an empty democracy, as it is lacking social organizations. Actually, the class organizations that were promoted during the 1970s by the government of Velasco decayed. This was a consequence of a profound transformation of the class structure: during the 1980s, the last barriers to universal suffrage were eliminated, there was a strong rural migration to the cities, and the informal sector expanded to comprise more than 50% of the active population (Levitsky and Cameron 2003: 6). In addition, "...in the 1980s the union movement entered a process of fragmentation of their interests and their organizations due in part to the return to democracy, as the main organizations no longer had a common enemy" (Ibid.). Along with the sociopolitical situation, the economic situation turned critical, with high unemployment rates, a considerable fall of real wages, and an increasing conflict between employers and unions (Huber 1983: 78) as the business sectors pushed for a flexibilizing labor reform (Cook 2007: 116). Lastly, "...the advance of the terrorism of the Shining Path demobilized the social and autonomous protest movement of the previous decade, because any protest movement was automatically accused of being terrorist" (Gil and Grampone 2014: 10).

All of this helps to explain why in 1990, Alberto Fujimori, a totally unknown candidate, with little more than 1% of the voting intentions in February 1990, reached the presidency and inaugurated a decade during which he accumulated unprecedented power in Peru together with his advisor Vladimiro Montesinos (Degregori 2003: 243). Fujimori arrived to power without a party and was obliged to construct majorities for every issue. Between August 1990 and March 1992, the traditional political parties, in order to survive, collaborated with his government; indeed, both the APRA and the left in Congress reacted very cautiously to its liberal reforms. In 1992, when the presidency and Congress disputed first over the anti-subversive strategy against *Sendero Luminoso* and then tried to curb the president's powers, Fujimori opted to dissolve Congress on April 5, 1992, and place under his direct control the regional governments, the judiciary, the electoral tribunal, and the constitutional court. The executive imposed an emergency government of national reconstruction (Degregori 2003: 246–247). The population basically accepted these measures as Fujimori had managed to control inflation, had implemented a clientelistic social policy, and was defeating the Maoist guerrilla.

After this "self-coup" *(auto-golpe)*, Fujimori's government did not invest efforts in the organization of a party or on the construction of a social base. His organization of origin, *Cambio 90*, had no program, no national organization, nor activists. He could have used his popularity to transform it into a consolidated party but, instead, did everything possible to avoid it: he replaced the party with State agencies and continued using the media to address the masses directly (Levitsky and Cameron 2003: 10–12). In addition, the parties and civil organizations on the left were practically eliminated from the political scene as they never achieved to deal with the *Sendero Luminoso* question (Tanaka 2004–2005: 65–88). They were always vacillating between supporting it as a possibility of attaining a social revolution and condemning its excesses and its project as too radical. This led to the demise of not only the party system but also of the organizations of civil society.

More specifically on labor, until the Fujimori period, the regulation of the labor market was "…characterized by a general system with limited exception regimes, absolute labor stability, large presence of collective bargaining by branch of activity, active minimum wages, State intervention in the increase of remuneration of workers without collective bargaining, among other aspects" (Vidal Bermúdez et al. 2012: 13). The elimination of these features and the transition to a highly flexible labor regime were based on two main reforms via decrees, in 1991 and 1992, thus after the presidential coup; they established union pluralism at the plant level, promoted the decentralization of collective bargaining, increased restrictions on the right to strike, and granted more power of intervention to the State for the registration of new unions and the control of union activities (Cook 2007: 122). These modifications will be consolidated in the 1993 Constitution. As a consequence, the union movement was almost completely disarticulated and turned into a political actor without relevance (Gil and Grampone 2014: 27).

These reforms as well as the privatizations of State enterprises, the opening of the economy and price deregulation, awakened little opposition from the main trade union organizations, the CGTP and the CTP, partly because of their dwindling power, but also because the Fujimori government frequently used repression against them. The union movement does not seem to have recovered its force after more than 15 years (Gil and Grampone 2014: 17). Peru's organizations of civil society as well as its party system seems totally bereft of any force; in this context, the power of the government technocrats and the employers is dominant.

The case of Colombia is distinctive for Latin America, although the results in terms of the characteristics of the dominant coalition that, to a great extent determines the economic model, are very similar to the other two we have discussed in this section of the book. We can summarize the reasons for the weakness of civil society and of the workers' organizations in particular, by the fact that the political life of this country has been dominated by violence. The civil war between the liberal and the conservative parties lasted, with ups and downs, from the nineteenth century until 1958, when the National Front between the two contenders was established. It was then substituted by guerilla warfare and paramilitary violence, since the mid-1960s, which has persisted until the present,[8] and then by the violent action of the drug cartels from the 1970s to the years 2000.

[8] A peace treaty has just been signed in 2017 between the guerilla and the government of Santos.

Although we cannot absolutely affirm that drug cartel violence was a continuation of the other two types of violence; while the guerilla did have links to the drug business and trafficked drugs, there also seems to be a historical link between the liberal armed forces that intervened in what is called "The Violence," and the leftist guerilla that emerged in the 1960s and 1970s (Restrepo Botero 2015: 299).

In such a scenario, where social activists were killed by either one of the contending parties, by the guerrilla, by the drug cartels, or repressed by the government when their actions were seen as being sympathetic to the guerrilla, or just because it contributed to social unrest in a war situation, social actions did not find fertile ground, on the contrary. As Restrepo Botero has affirmed, in a situation where counterinsurgency policies are dominant, "…many social manifestations fell under the concept of 'public order' unrest under a State of siege and of exception and mechanisms directed to the enemies of peace and the State we applied to them. Pacification of the National Front rapidly became the militarization of social conflicts" (Restrepo Botero 2015: 274).

The political effect of this pact that ended *La Violencia* implied that the ideological differences between the parties disappeared, and both elections and the party system became irrelevant: first due to guerilla warfare in the years 1950s and 1960s, when the attraction exerted by the Cuban Revolution and its *foquista* politics was prevalent, and then, in the years 1990, when all parties implemented the same liberal economic policies. This situation eventually ensued in an ever higher abstention, the emergence of apolitical leaders and movements, and *in fine*, the destruction of the traditional parties in Colombia. A similar evolution occurred in the other countries we are discussing in this section and in the next (Bolivia and Ecuador).

The question is why the guerilla in Colombia abided until the present, when in all the other countries where it appeared it was defeated in the 1980s or 1990s. One part of the explanation lies in the armed conflict of the rural guerilla, during the nineteenth century, but especially during *La Violencia* of the end of the 1940s and early 1950s, when armed peasants organized in the liberal guerillas in order to defend their communities. According to Melo, many of the founders of the FARC had participated in the liberal and communist armed groups in the 1950s. A second factor is that guerilla emerged in the regions where in the 1920s and 1930s, the peasants had occupied latifundia; they then had to defend themselves against the army and the landowners' armed militias (Melo 2017: 247; Restrepo Botero 2015: 297). This author also mentions how the peasants that were involved with the FARC were the protagonists of the most massive manifestations of the 1990s and 2000, and how other guerilla groups, like the EPL and ELN, buttressed the peasant organizations in their struggle against the entrepreneurs in regions like Urabá, as well as the way in which, in turn, union conflict was substituted by local proprietaries arming themselves (Melo 2017: 248). Restrepo Botero adds the fact we mentioned above: the *Frente Nacional*, that consisted in the allocation of political posts among the liberal and conservative parties, made political action irrelevant, and in this manner, non-attended social demands shifted toward illegality (Restrepo Botero 2015: 297). Finally, Melo adds a geographical explanation, the guerilla groups evolved in territories with geographic and social conditions that protected them—in mountainous and jungle regions where the regular army had enormous difficulties to perform (Melo 2017: 247). Thus, the guerilla had a strong social base in isolated localities, to which in the 1980s and 1990s it added the peasants that cultivated coca.

This context explains why the case of Colombia's labor unions is one of the gloomiest in the region. Despite the peace process that was concluded in the 1991 Constitution, violence against social organizations in general and trade unions in particular was particularly brutal in the 1980s and 1990s, where assassinations, persecutions, and disappearances of leaders reached higher levels than in many countries under dictatorships (López Pacheco and Hincapié Jiménez 2015: 1082–1083). One of the most significant actions of the M19 that, in contrast to the other guerilla groups, was embedded in urban centers, was the assassination of the main leader of the *Confederación de Trabajadores Colombianos* (CTC), the liberal labor confederation, arguing he was a traitor to the cause of the people (Melo 2017: 252). In addition, administrative obstacles set upon unions by the Colombian government are considerable: a 1996 study by the OECD (cited by Aidt and Tzannatos 2002: 3) situates this country in group 3 of 4, according to the presence of restrictions on the freedom of association. Another indicator of the situation of unionism in this country is that unionization rates (of the total employed population) that were already at a low of 9% in 1984 went down to 7.8% in 1990 and have fallen to 4.5% in 2005 (Pineda Duque 2015: 131).

Thus, social movements and organizations were threatened from both sides: their relation with the guerillas led to armed confrontation with the landowners and their paramilitary bands. On the other hand, the fight of the government against guerilla and then the cartels led to the repression of social conflicts in the name of the maintenance of the public order. This situation led to civil actions expressed as local and occasional actions that contested particular governmental policies in the 1970s. There was no national or even regional permanent coordination to agglutinate these struggles and extend them temporally. When they began to coalesce in regional organizations in the 1980s, the government started implementing the neoliberal economic measures and the decentralization of the public policies, something that destroyed these intentions to unite and re-atomized social action (Restrepo Botero 2015: 293). On the other hand, the political left has been traditionally divided into all sorts of parties: communists, Trotskyists, Maoists, castrists; some favorable to, others against guerilla warfare; none of them ever got more than 5% of the votes. In the 1982 elections, the left finally united around a nonviolent program; nevertheless, the fact that the M19 guerilla covertly supported violence led to its demise after a bad electoral result (Melo 2017: 254).

In this manner, in all the three countries that we have considered as approaching the rentier liberal capitalism type, the main factor that determines whether an economy is more or less redistributive, the organization of civil society, is absolutely lacking. Hence, the alliance between the State and the rentier capital (mining, agrarian, financial, and even real estate) dominates, without any other force being capable of restoring social balance. In the next chapter we will see that this situation is reinforced and made more lasting, more impervious to the actions of civil society, by a type of State structure and of political regime, as political regimes can be more or less permeable to social actions. State structure also plays a role: decentered federalism (like Brazil, Argentina) is more open to pressures coming from society, while centered federalisms (like Mexico) or centralized States (like all the Andean ones) are more impervious to civil society.

6.5 From a Rentier Liberal to a Redistributive Social Pact

In the two countries that embraced a rentier redistributive capitalism, civil society movements were constantly defying liberalism during the 1990s and beginning of the years 2000, and continue to be very active nowadays. While in the cases of Argentina and Brazil, the strongest actors were the labor and the social movements, in the case of the

Andean countries, the social sector that gained political power since the beginning of the present century was the indigenous movement. In Bolivia, the most significant social actor between the 1950s and the 1990s was the mining workers' *Confederación Obrera Boliviana*. During the 1980s and 1990s, the COB lost influence compared to the indigenous organizations and coca producers of the Chaparé, who are the base of the *Movimiento al Socialismo* (MAS) that led Evo Morales to the presidency (Mayorga 2011). As in most regimes based on a national-popular political movement, at the end of the 1952 revolution, the State undertook the organization of a party, in this case the Revolutionary Nationalist Movement (MNR) that fashioned a corporatist relation with the Bolivian Workers' Confederation (COB). Since the mid-1980s, the bases of the COB were sapped by liberalism, the decline of tin mining, unemployment, and informalization of labor; all of which marginalized this confederation and reduced its capacity for confrontation and for exerting pressure (Torrico Terán 2006: 244).

In the case of Ecuador, there was neither such a corporatist regime, nor a strong union movement previous to the application of neoliberal measures. Indeed, although existent, nationalist-popular politics were weaker in this country due to regionalism, elite conflicts, political fragmentation, in addition to a much weaker industrialization process and the absence of a single product as tin in Bolivia (Silva 2009: 148). Although in the 1970s the major confederations merged into a single unitary organization, the *Frente Unitario de Trabajadores* (FUT), and while it actually managed to unleash a considerable number of general strikes, its real force came from the support it received from the indigenous movement; the Confederación de Nacionalidades Indígenas del Ecuador (CONAIE) was an enduring movement that expressed itself through local and regional mobilizations, blocking highways and leading manifestations all over the country (Silva 2009: 149).

In effect, one of the most significant characteristics of the indigenous movements in both Bolivia and Ecuador is that they demand the recognition of their distinctive identity, as a right to be different from the other groups of their respective national societies; they questioned the ethnic boundaries of a model based on homogeneity (Le Bot 2009). They have, in most cases, been exemplary insofar as they affirmed their identity without excluding the others, in contrast to other such movements in other parts of the world that define themselves in opposition and in exclusion to other groups this latter, an attitude that is conducive to nationalism and war (Gellner 1983). Although indigenous movements gained international recognition with the 1994 Zapatista rebellion in Mexico, social actions that rejected the assimilation policies that Spanish- or Portuguese-speaking Latin American governments imposed during most of the twentieth century began in the 1970s in Bolivia and Ecuador. In most cases, these movements were embraced by the local churches that participated in the Liberation Theology movement. In the Amazonian region of Ecuador, what began as a movement against the intervention of oil companies in indigenous territories, became a cultural movement that organized nationally in the Confederation of Indigenous Nationalities of the Ecuadorian Amazon (Confeniae) that according to Albó and Le Bot was the first indigenous organization to adopt the term "nationality" (Albó 2008: 127, Le Bot 2009). In Bolivia, the Katarista movement (Túpac Katari) was propelled by young leaders with an indigenous rather than a class/peasant ideology, since 1976. By the end of the 1970s, they had managed to gradually take control of the official peasant organizations and created their own: the *Confederación Sindical Única de Trabajadores Campesinos de Bolivia* (CSUTCB) (Klein 2015: 313). This organization concentrated on ethnic as well as peasant demands and would gain importance within the labor confederation, the COB, when this miner's union named a peasant and a member of the Katarist movement as its leader in 1981 (Klein 2015: 325). This movement would be crucial, 20 years later, to ensure the election of Evo Morales as the first indigenous president of Bolivia (Albó 2008). In this way, in both Bolivia and Ecuador, protests against the economic model transcended the economic sphere and served, in fact, as an instrument to affirm indigenous identity and their socioeconomic, cultural, political, and, in some cases, territorial rights (Le Bot 2009).

According to Edwin Cruz, the indigenous movement appeared earlier in Ecuador than in Bolivia, and while in the latter it was empowered with the "water war," in Ecuador it was in franc decline owing to its support to the failed military coup of the years 2000, and then its inclusion in the elected government of Gutierrez (the general that directed the coup) in 2003. On the other hand, while in Ecuador the indigenous movement was always more intense and extra-institutional, in Bolivia it managed to have a greater institutional impact by being able to negotiate the recognition of the territoriality of the first peoples and pass the Law of Popular Participation that ensured the indigenous population a higher degree of representativity and of capacity to defend its collective rights. The explanation offered by Cruz to these differences is paradoxical: on the one hand he stresses the greater organizational and discursive articulation of the Ecuadorian indigenous peoples, under the concept of plurinationality, in contrast to the fragmentation of the Bolivian indigenous, on the other hand, a more repressive Bolivian State than the Ecuadorian explains the extra-institutional mobilization dynamics in the latter (Cruz, cited by Ortiz Crespo and Mayorga 2012: 15).

In association with the COB, and in a corporatist alliance with the military, the movement that gathered the peasants that had been favored by the agrarian reform that followed the 1952 revolution unified in a confederation: the CSUTCB. The Katarist indigenist movement that surfaced at the end of the 1960s and 1970s, promoting an indigenous rather than a peasant identity, took control of this confederation. Under the control of this political group the CSUTCB, together with the COB, staged two general strikes, in 1979 and 1982, that were crucial for the ouster of the military. This organization was not only crucial for the democratization process, but also for the arrival of the MAS to power, nonetheless, at some moments in the 1990s and 2000, it has been defiant of Evo Morales as it defends a more fundamental conception of indigenism; especially when it was presided by Felipe Quispe. With the decline of the COB, the CSUTCB has become even more autonomous (Silva 2009: 105–106).

Although labor was weaker in Ecuador than in Bolivia, where tin miners were a very powerful social and political actor, labor also managed to unify in a single federation in 1974. The FUT organized strikes against the government, joining congressional opposition against certain laws threatening the interests of the workers and peasants during the first post-transition government of Febres Cordero (1984–1992) (Silva 2009). On the other hand, the CONAIE was formed during the presidency of Febres Cordero with the fusion of two indigenous organizations, one of the highlands (ECUARUNARI) and another of the lowlands/Amazonia (CONFENIAE). It became the most important social movement of Ecuador after the first National Indian Uprising in 1990, dominating the social life of this country both through its social actions and through its political party the Pachakutic. The labor federation and the CONAIE frequently coincided in their active opposition against liberalization in the 1980s and 1990s. But, contrary to the case of Bolivia, the alliance of Ecuadorian labor and the peasant/indigenous organizations was not organic; the CONAIE upheld some of the strikes of the FUT with road blockades in the provinces that created significant difficulties for supplying the capital and other large cities in the 1990s (Silva 2009).

In Bolivia, the unions of the coca producers of the *Chaparé* region, presided by Evo Morales, were the central social movements of the 1990s and 2000: they backed his first incursion in politics, his candidature to Congress. As coca was legal before the 1990s, many miners that had lost their jobs because of the decline of tin mining, migrated from the *altiplano* to the lowlands of the *Chaparé* to cultivate it. Imbued with their labor movement tradition, they organized into a myriad of unions that eventually joined the peasant confederation, the CSUTCB, and managed to displace the *Kataristas*, substituting the indigenous identity with a more class-oriented posture and taking control of a social organization that will prove crucial for the ambitions of Evo and his followers. The organization of the coca growers was empowered by the struggle against the efforts of the US government to force the Bolivian authorities to destroy the coca plantations in order to reduce the supply of cocaine to the USA. When in the 1990s, the government of Paz Estenssoro not only implemented radical liberalizing actions, but accepted the viewpoint and the aid of the USA to crush coca production, the growers of the Chaparé responded with great force, defending coca both as a traditional cultural good and as livelihood for thousands of peasants. From this moment on, the peasants of the Chaparé and their organization, within the unitary confederation, became the center of the social mobilizations against the established governments (Silva 2009: 113–115).

The conflict concerning the coca plant was crucial for the continuation of the movement, as it fused two different significations: on the one hand, the fight of the peasants for their livelihood, a class struggle, led by peasant unions, and on the other hand, the defense of a plant that has cultural/symbolic significance for the indigenous populations: in religious, medical, and traditional aspects. It thus fused the two strands of the Bolivian social struggle: the popular and the indigenous, something that neither the labor movement nor the exclusively indigenous *Movimiento Indigenista Pachakuti* (MIP) was able to represent. That is why this movement endured and became empowered, while the COB and the more "fundamentalist" indigenous movement, the MIP, were marginalized. While Felipe Quispe got 6% of the vote in 2002, Evo Morales got elected in the first round in the 2005 elections with 53.7% of the votes (Silva 2009: 118). The MAS candidate prevailed over the

Bolivian ethnic movement that proposed the end of the postcolonial Bolivian State, the westernization of the country, and its re-indianization. For Evo Morales and the MAS, the priority was equality and justice, and the State the basic instrument to achieve that goal (Mayorga 2011: 256–257).

The MAS relied on these movements that were radicalized and invigorated by two governmental decisions they set in motion the "Water War" and the "Gas War." The first movement, the "Water War," initiated with the abrupt increase in water rates in the city of Cochabamba in 2000, resulting from the privatization of water services; it gave rise to massive manifestations of the population of the Alto that were repressed by the force of order. After a week of confrontations, the army refused to continue applying the State of siege decreed by the government; a situation that led the latter to rescind the privatization of the water services. Between September and October of the same year, there was another movement, this time peasants blocking the access to La Paz, the capital, causing food shortages. Once again, the government decreed the State of siege and again, after the clashes, the armed forces withdrew. The succession of mobilization, repression and retreat, strongly affected the legitimacy of the government and seriously upset the party system of what was called the "*democracia pactada*"[9] (convened democracy), and heightened the reputation of the social leaders that commanded the actions; mainly of those who had gathered around the MAS (Torrico Terán 2006: 88).

The "Gas War" that erupted against the privatization of the gas industry and a settlement with the Chilean government to build a gas pipeline passing through its territory in order to export it, resulted in the ousting of Sánchez de Lozada. Gas had become one of the principal exporting products of the country and, according to the opposition, after the privatization of tin, silver, nitrates, was the only product upon which one could attempt to develop the country (Silva 2009: 138). Most of the social organizations (MAS, CSUTCB-Movimiento Indigenista Pachakuti, the COB, and the organizations of the inhabitants of El Alto) gathered round the opposition to privatize gas and succeeded in blocking numerous highways throughout the country. The government tried to deblock the roads by calling the army. One of these actions, the

[9]We will talk about this question in the next chapter.

attempt to liberate a tourist car that was being detained in the Titicaca region, resulted in the death of five peasants; an event that led to the intensification of the protests and of the roadblockings. Once again, the government called the army, this time to deblock the road from El Alto to La Paz, with more catastrophic results, as 30 people were killed. The result was an escalation of blockings and a march of 150,000 inhabitants of El Alto to the center of La Paz. A few days later, when they were joined by miners and protesters from Oruro and Potosí, coca growers from Chaparé, middle classes from different organizations (NGO leaders, intellectuals, students, professors), they forced Sanchez de Lozada to resign in October 2003, after only 13 months in the presidency (Silva 2009: 132–142).

In addition to the social dynamics, since the 1997 elections, four of the main leaders of these different social organizations had been elected to Congress, among them Evo Morales. In these elections, the MAS, which proposed to re-found the Bolivian State based on the values and conceptions of the original nations, the end of neoliberalism and granting the rightful place to indigenous regions and popular leaders, obtained a little more than 20% of the votes. Together with the Indigenous Movement Pachakuti (MIP), that obtained 6% of the votes, who fought for the end of the political and cultural discrimination of the indigenous people (what they called the end of the "two Bolivias"), for the adoption of participatory democracy and the preservation of the culture of the coca leaf, they occupied a third of the seats in Congress. For the first time in Bolivian history, peasants and indigenous people had an important presence in the political life of the country (Torrico Terán 2006).

This presence in Congress was fundamental to allow these leaders to express their opposition to the agreement between the Bolivian government and the USA for the eradication of the coca leaf, as well as against the neoliberal project implemented by all the parties that had arrived to power with the "*democracia pactada.*" One of the events that enhanced Morales's popularity was his exclusion from parliament after the violent demonstrations in the Chaparé between the *cocaleros* (coca leaf cultivators) and the armed forces in 2002. It also strengthened the movement against the traditional parties and nurtured the idea of convening a constituent assembly to transform the structure of the State and of the political system; to "re-found the country." In addition, since the years 2000, economic conditions worsened. It was in this context that the elections of 2002, where Evo Morales won the presidency, took place (Torrico Terán 2006: 89–90).

There was no such unitary organization that represented both class and indigenous demands in Ecuador. Nonetheless, there were moments where both labor unions and indigenous organizations proceeded in unison. In the 1970s and 1980s, there was an upsurge of the labor movement, first with the *Frente Unido de Trabajadores* (FUT) and then with the Coordinadora de Movimiento Sociales (CMS), that coalesced the unions of oil, electrical, and cement sectors, the teachers and university professors, as well as informal workers. When in the 1990s the worker's organizations weakened, the main indigenous organization, the CONAIE, came to the fore. Although none of these movements succeeded in stopping the austerity measures, the privatizations, not even the dollarization of the economy, and while the CONAIE made the grave political error of supporting a failed *coup d'état* by Colonel Lucio Gutierrez, it gained two pyrrhic triumphs—forcing the resignation of two presidents.

The events that finally led to the election of Rafael Correa in 2007 were triggered by the policies implemented during the government of Jamil Mahuad (1998–2000). The political scenario was set a few years before with the dismissal of President Bucaram that was impeached by Congress after numerous manifestations. After this event, Congress called for a Constitutional Convention in the hope of calming the social turmoil. Nonetheless, the resulting constitution did not satisfy anybody, because on the one hand it facilitated the deepening of neoliberalism and, on the other, "...although it did advance in the indigenous agenda, it fell short of declaring Ecuador a pluri-national state." In addition, President Mahuad pushed forward very orthodox neoliberal measures and more privatizations. This, together with the aggravation of the economic situation, awoke the popular manifestations that were once again led by the CONAIE. Facing an ever deteriorating social, political, and economic situation that was aggravated by a crisis of the banking system, the government decided the dollarization of the Ecuadorian economy, substituting the sucre by the US dollar. This was the final straw. The CONAIE not only radicalized its manifestations but conspired with a group of militaries to support the failed coup d'état of Colonel Lucio Gutierrez. In the next elections that were won by Gutierrez, the CONAIE committed his second grave political mistake, that of participating in his government through its party, the Pachakutic (Silva 2009: 175–188). These two mistakes explain why the indigenous movement declined, as Ortiz Crespo and Mayorga (2012) write. Nonetheless, the fact that this movement was so powerful for decades and that it still maintains a non-negligible force, imposed part of the agenda of the Correa presidency, and its need to balance between the needs of capital and those of the popular classes, although the relation was by no means smooth.

In both Ecuador and Bolivia, there was a similar situation of a highly mobilized civil society that tried to resist the imposition of the neoliberal program during the 1980s and 1990s. Although in neither country did they succeed in stopping privatizations, austerity measures, the retreat of the State from the economy, these movements accomplished to force a change of government in the mid-2000. Both in Bolivia and Ecuador, the pressure of the organized movements, assisted by the catastrophic results of the liberal policies of the successive governments, led to the collapse of the old party system (a characteristic of all the Andean political systems, except the Chilean). But in these two countries the collapse did not result in a durable political vacuum, like in the case of Peru or Colombia, because of the presence of strong social actors, and in the case of Bolivia, an organization that translated their projects led Evo Morales to power, and Correa in Ecuador.

The following two tables summarize the characteristics of the different pacts that have determined the four countries that best exemplify the types of capitalism in time (Tables 6.1 and 6.2).

Table 6.1 Main characteristics of the dominant social coalition in four moments in four exemplary countries of our typology 1

Period	*Mexico*	*Brazil*	*Chile*	*Bolivia*
Import substitution industrialization	State, industrialists, middle classes, unions, peasants	State, industrialists, middle classes, unions, in a compromise with the agrarian oligarchy, from 1964 to 1985, the unions from the past	State, industrialists, middle classes, unions	State, mining unions, peasants, middle classes
Neoliberal (mid-80s and mid-90s)	Imposition of a new pact between state, multinationals, large domestic capital, and financial capital	Intent to impose a neoliberal pact between State, multinationals, large domestic capital, financial capital, and agro-exports. Resistance of the unions, opposition parties, and social movements	(Beginning with the coup in 1973) Imposition of a new pact between State, multinationals, large domestic capital, and financial capital	Intent to impose a neoliberal pact between state, multinationals, large domestic capital, financial capital, and agro-exports. Resistance of indigenous population

Source Own elaboration

Table 6.2 Main characteristics of the dominant social coalition in three moments in four exemplary countries of our typology 2

Period	*Mexico*	*Brazil*	*Chile*	*Bolivia*
Super commodity and financial resources boom	State, multinationals, large domestic capital, and financial capital	State, middle classes, unions, industrial capital **in a compromise with** rentier and financial capital	State, multinationals, large domestic capital, rentier and financial capital, and middle classes	State, indigenous population, peasants **in a compromise with** rentier and financial capital
First changes due to the end of the boom	The social pact is challenged from the exterior (Trump). Opportunity for an internal modification of the social pact?	Intent of the rentier and financial capital to exclude the popular classes. Do the latter have the capacity to resist?	Reduction of growth	Reduction of State resources. Reduction of redistribution?

Source Own elaboration

References

Aidt, T., & Tzannatos, Z. (2002). *Unions and collective bargaining: Economic effects in a global environment*. Washington, DC: World Bank.

Aglietta, M. (1979). *Régulation et crises du capitalisme*. Paris: Calmann-Lévy.

Alba, C. (2004). Los dirigentes económicos de Brasil y México en el cambio económico y la transición política. Notas para una comparación. In C. Alba Vega & I. Bizberg (Coords.), *Democracia y globalización en México y Brasil*. Mexico: El Colegio de México.

Alba, C. (2005). Relaciones entre los empresarios y el Estado. In I. Bizberg & L. Meyer (Coords.), *Una Historia Contemporánea de México, Tomo 2. Actores*. México: Océano.

Albó, J. (2008). *Movimientos y poder indígena en Bolivia, Ecuador y Perú*. La Paz: CIPCA.

Amable, B. (2005). *Les cinq capitalismes*. Paris: Editions du Seuil.

Amsden, A. H. (2001). *The rise of "the rest": Challenges to the West from late-industrializing economies*. New York: Oxford University Press.

Arato, A. (2000). *Civil society, constitution, and legitimacy*. Lanham, MD: Rowman and Littlefield.

Baldi-Delatte, A. L. (2004). La stabilité monétaire après les crises argentine et brésilienne. *Rapport d'étude pour la Caisse des Dépôts et Consignations*, manuscrit, avril.

Barba Solano, C. (2007). Claroscuros de la reforma social en México y América Latina. *Espiral (Guadalajara), 13*(39), 35–76.

Barba Solano, C., & Valencia Lomelí, E. (2013). La transición del régimen de bienestar mexicano: entre el dualismo y las reformas liberales. *Revista Uruguaya de Ciencia Política, 22*(2), 28–54.

Barrera, M. (1994). Política de ajuste y proceso de democratización en Chile: sus efectos sobre los trabajadores. *Revista Mexicana de Sociología, 56*(1), 105–129.

Barros de Castro, L. (2005). Esperança, Frustração e Aprendizado: A Historia da Nova República. In Giambiagi, et al. (Eds.), *Economía Brasileira Contemporânea (1945–2004)* (pp. 116–140). Rio de Janeiro: Elsevier.

Bensusán, G. (2016). Organizing workers in Argentina, Brazil, Chile and Mexico: The authoritarian-corporatist legacy and old institutional designs in a new context. *Theoretical Inquiries in Law, 17*(1), 131–161.

Bensusán, G., & Middlebrook, K. (2013). *Sindicatos y Política en México. Cambios, continuidades y contradicciones.* México: UAM, Flacso y Clacso.

Bergquist, C. (1986). *Labor in Latin America. Comparative Essays on Chile, Argentina, Venezuela, and Colombia.* Stanford, CA: Stanford University Press.

Berins Collier, R. (1999). *Paths toward democracy: The working class and elites in Western Europe and South America.* New York: Cambridge University Press.

Bizberg, I. (1999). Le Syndicalisme Mexicain face à la mondialisation et à la recomposition du régime politique. *La Revue de L'IRES, 29,* 131–164.

Bizberg I. (2004). Trayectorias políticas e institucionales de México y Brasil: el caso de las relaciones entre el Estado y el sindicalismo. In C. Alba Vega & I. Bizberg (Coords.), *Democracia y globalización en México y Brasil.* Mexico: El Colegio de México.

Bizberg, I. (2010). La democracia vacía. In I. Bizberg & F. Zapata (Eds.), *Los Grandes Problemas de México. Los movimientos sociales.* México: El Colegio de México.

Bizberg, I. (2014). Los nuevos movimientos sociales en México: el movimiento por la paz con justicia y dignidad y #YoSoy132. *Foro Internacional 55*(217): 262–301.

Bizberg, I., & Théret, B. (2012). La diversité des capitalismes latino-américains: les cas de l'Argentine, du Brésil et du Mexique. *La Revue de la Régulation,* (1). Paris.

Boschi, R., & F. Gaitán. (2017). El Estado desarrollista en Brasil: Crisis, continuidad, incertidumbres. In C. Alba Vega & I. Bizberg, *Dimensiones sociopolíticas y económicas de la crisis global y su impacto en los países emergentes.* México: El Colegio de México.

Boyer, R. (2015). *Économie politique des capitalismes. Théorie de la régulation et des crises.* Paris: La Découverte.

Bresser-Pereira, L. C. (2018). *Rentier-financier capitalism* (Unpublished manuscript to be published in the *Revue de la Régulation*).

Cardoso, A., & Gindin, J. (2009). *Industrial relations and collective bargaining: Argentina, Brazil and Mexico compared* (Working Paper No. 5). Geneva: Industrial and Employment Relations Department, International Labour Office.

Cardoso, F. H., & Faletto, E. (1969). *Dependencia y Desarrollo en América latina*. México: Siglo XXI.

Cerdas Sandí, D. (2017). *La Disputa por el Poder de Asociación de los Trabajadores: Veto Empresarial y Democracia Restringida en América Latina*. Tesis doctoral del Programa de Doctorado en Investigación en Ciencias Sociales, con mención en Ciencia Política. México: Facultad Latinoamérica de Ciencia Sociales.

Chaves Teixeira, A. C., Dagnino, E., & Almeida Silva, C. (2002). La constitución de la sociedad civil en Brasil. In E. Dagnino (Coord.), *Sociedad civil, esfera pública y democratización en América Latina: Brasil* (pp. 21–76). México: Unicamp-Fondo de Cultura Económico.

Cheresky, I. (2004). Argentina. Cambio de rumbo y recomposición política. *Nueva Sociedad, 193,* 4–16.

Contreras, C., & Zuloaga, M. (2014). *Historia mínima de Perú*. México: El Colegio de México.

Cook, M. L. (2007). *The politics of labor reform in Latin America: Between flexibility and rights*. University Park: The Pennsylvania State University Press.

Cortés Conde, R. (2007). *La economía política de la Argentina en el siglo XX*. Buenos Aires: Edhasa.

Crouch, C. (1993). *Industrial relations and European state traditions*. Oxford: Oxford University Press.

Dagnino, E. (2003). Citizenship in Latin America. *Latin American Perspectives, 30*(2), 211–225.

De Souza Keller, W. (1994). Neocorporativismo y relações de trabalho: elementos para um debate sobre a experiência brasileira recente. *Boletim de Conjuntura: Política social, 14,* 31–40.

Degregori, C. I. (2003). Perú: el desvanecimiento de un régimen y el desafío de la reconstrucción democrática. In J. I. Domínguez & M. Shifter (Eds.), *Construcción de gobernabilidad democrática en América Latina*. México: Fondo de Cultura Económica.

Doran, M. C. (2000). La Palabra Soberana: Los pobladores Chilenos frente a la Política. *Versión, 10,* 287–329.

Duhalde, S. (2013). Organización y acción en el sindicalismo de base en Argentina: un abordaje Conceptual. *Revista de Sociología e Politica, 21*(48), 161–177.

Esping-Andersen, G. (1990). *The three worlds of welfare capitalism*. Princeton, NJ: Princeton University Press.

Etchemendy, S., & Collier, R. B. (2007). Down but not out: Union resurgence and segmented neocorporatism in Argentina (2003–2007). *Politics & Society, 7*(3), 363–401.

Ffrench-Davis, R. (2008). *Chile entre el neoliberalismo y el crecimiento con equidad. Reformas y políticas económicas desde 1973*. Santiago: J.C. Sáez editor.

Franceschelli, I., & Ronconi, L. (2005). Clientelism, workfare and the emergence of the *piqueteros* in Argentina. LACEA Conference. http://depot.gdnet.org/gdnshare/pdf2/gdn_library/annual_conferences/seventh_annual_conference/Franceschelli_Parallel_1_4.pdf. Accessed 15 May 2018.

Garretón, M. A. (1991). La redemocratización política en Chile. Transición, inauguración y evolución. *Estudios Públicos, 4*(1), 101–133.

Gellner, E. (1983). *Nations and nationalisms*. Paris: Payot.

Gil, R., & Grampone, A. (2014). Sindicalismo y política en el Perú: una breve aproximación en perspectiva comparada. *Documento de Trabajo N°2. Serie de Documentos de Trabajo*. Lima: Asociación Civil Politai.

Graña, J. M., & Kennedy, D. (2008). *Distribución funcional del ingreso, salario real y productividad en Argentina en perspectiva latinoamericana. Desde mediados de los setenta hasta la actualidad*. Buenos Aires: CEPED, Universidad de Buenos Aires. Available at: http://209.177.156.169/libreria_cm/archivos/pdf_981.pdf.

Haggard, S. (1990). *Pathways from the periphery. The politics of growth in the newly industrializing countries*. New York: Cornell University Press.

Haggard, S., & Kaufman, R. (2008). *Development, democracy, and welfare states: Latin America, East Asia, and Eastern Europe*. Princeton: Princeton University Press.

Hayter, S., & Stoevska, V. (2011). *Social dialogue indicators. International statistical inquiry 2008–09. Technical Brief*. Geneva: ILO.

Hermann, J. (2005a). Reformas, endividamento externo e o 'milagre' econômico. In F. Giambiagi, A. Villela, L. Barros de Castro, & J. Hermann (Eds.), *Economia brasileira contemporânea* (1945–2004) (pp. 69–92). Rio de Janeiro: Elsevier.

Hermann, J. (2005b). Auge e Declínio do Modelo de Crescimento com Endividamento: O II PND e a Crise da Dívida Externa (1974–1984). In F. Giambiagi, A. Villela, L. Barros de Castro, & J. Hermann (Eds.), *Economia brasileira contemporânea* (1945–2004) (pp. 93–115). Rio de Janeiro: Elsevier.

Huber, E. (1983). The Peruvian military government, labor mobilization, and the political strength of the left. *Latin American Research Review, 18*(2), 57–93.

Invernizzi, N. (2006). Disciplining the workforce: Controlling workers in the restructuring of production. *Latin American Perspectives,* 33(3), 89–110.

Jeanneau, S., Tovar, C. E., & Moreno, R. (2007). Introduction. In S. Jeanneau & C. E. Tovar (Eds.), *Evolving banking systems in Latin America and the Caribbean: Challenges and implications for monetary policy and financial stability* (BIS Papers No. 33) (pp. 1–2). Basel, Switzerland: Monetary and Economic Department, Bank for International Settlements.

Klein, H. S. (2015). *Historia Mínima de Bolivia*. México: El Colegio de México.

Lautier, B. (2009). Gouvernement moral des pauvres et dépolitisation des politiques publiques en Amérique Latine. In N. Borgeaud-Garciandía, B. Lautier, R. Peñafiel, & A. Tizziani (Eds.), *Penser le politique en Amérique Latine* (pp. 19–36). Paris: Karthala.

Le Bot, Y. (2009). *La Grande révolte indienne*. Paris: Robert Laffont.

Levitsky, S., & Cameron, M. A. (2003). Democracy without parties? Political parties and regime change in Fujimori's Peru. *Latin American Politics and Society, 45*(3), 1–33.

López Pacheco, J. A., & Hincapié Jiménez, S. (2015). De la movilización tradicional a las redes de presión transnacional: violencia antisindical y derechos humanos en Colombia. *Foro internacional, 55*(4), 1082–1114.

Marichal, C. (2003). La deuda externa. In I. Bizberg & L. Meyer (Eds.), *Una historia contemporánea de México, Tomo 1. Transformaciones y permanencias* (pp. 451–491). México: Océano.

Marques Pereira, J., & Théret, B. (2004). Mediaciones institucionales de regulación social y dinámicas macroeconómicas: los casos de Brasil y México. In C. Alba & I. Bizberg (Eds.), *Democracia y Globalización en México y Brasil*. México: El Colegio de México.

Mayorga, F. (2011). *Dilemas. Ensayos sobre democracia intercultural y Estado plurinacional*. La Paz: Centro de Estudios Superiores Universitarios, Universidad Mayor de San Simon and Plural Editores.

Melo, J. O. (2017). *Historia minima de Colombia*. México: El Colegio México.

Munck, R. (2004). Introduction. *Latin American Perspectives, 31*(4), 3–20.

Murillo, M. V. (2000). From populism to neoliberalism: Labor unions and market reforms in Latin America. *World Politics, 52*(2), 135–174.

Novick, M., Lengyel, M., & Sarabia, M. (2009). De la protección laboral a la vulnerabilidad social. Reformas neoliberales en la Argentina. *Revista Internacional del. Trabajo, 128*(3), 257–275.

Ortiz Crespo, S., & Mayorga, F. (2012). Introduction to the dossier: Movimientos sociales, Estadoy democracia en Bolivia y Ecuador en el tránsito del neoliberalismo al postneoliberalismo. *ÍCONOS, Revista de Ciencias Sociales, 44*, 11–17.

Oxhorn, P. (1994). Where did all the protesters go? Popular mobilization and the transition to democracy in Chile. *Latin American Perspectives, 21*(3), 49–69.

Oxhorn, P. (2011). *Sustaining civil society*. University Park: Penn State University Press.

Palomino, H. (2000). Los sindicatos en la Argentina contemporánea. *Nueva Sociedad, 169*, 121–134.

Palomino, H., & Trajtemberg, D. (2006). Una nueva dinámica de las relaciones laborales y la negociación colectiva en la Argentina. *Revista de Trabajo, 2*(3), 47–68.

Pineda Duque, J. (2015). Colombia: el sesgo antilaboral del modelo de desarrollo y las políticas de formalización. *Cuadernos del CENDES, 32*(89).

Restrepo Botero, D. (2015). *Procesos de descentralización en Bolivia y Colombia, 1980–2005*.

Riethof, M. (2004). Changing strategies of Brazilian labor movement—From opposition to participation. *Latin American Perspectives, 31*(6), 31–47.

Romero Tellaeche, J. (2003). Crecimiento y comercio. In I. Bizberg & L. Meyer (Eds.), *Una historia contemporánea de México, Tomo 1. Transformaciones y permanencias* (pp. 155–221). México: Océano.

Sallum, B., Jr. (1996). *Labirintos. Dos generáis à nova república*. São Paulo: Universidade de São Paulo-Editora Hucitec.

Sallum, B., Jr. (2010). El Brasil en la 'pos-transición': la institucionalización de una nueva forma de Estado". In I. Bizberg (Ed.), *México en el espejo latinoamericano. Crisis o Democracia*. México: El Colegio de México-Fundación Konrad Adenauer.

Schneider, B. R. (2004). *Business politics and the state in twentieth-century Latin America*. Cambridge: Cambridge University Press.

Schneider, B. S. (2005). *Business politics and policy making in contemporary Latin America*. Available at: http://www.oecd.org/dev/devcom/35496225.pdf.

Schneider, B. R. (2013). *Hierarchical capitalism in Latin America: Business, labor, and the challenges of equitable development*. New York: Cambridge University Press.

Silva, E. (2009). *Challenging neoliberalism in Latin America*. Cambridge: Cambridge University Press.

Svampa, M., & Pereyra, S. (2004). La política de los movimientos piqueteros. *Revista da Sociedade Brasileira de Economía Política*, (15).

Tanaka, M. (2004–2005). Révolutionnaires, réformistes ou 'hommes politiques traditionnels'. Montée en puissance et effondrement de la gauche au Pérou. *Problèmes d'Amérique Latine*, (55), 65–88. http://eska-publishing.com/fr/1328-problemes-d-amerique-latine.

Tanaka, M. (2005). *Democracia sin partidos. Perú 2000–2005: los problemas de representación y las propuestas de reforma política*. Lima: Instituto de Estudios Peruanos.

Taylor, M. (2004). Labor reform and the contradictions of 'Growth with Equity' in post dictatorship Chile. *Latin American Perspectives, 31*(4), 76–93.

Théret, B. (2011). The place of national systems of social protection and political representation in socio-economic regulation: A morphogenetic structuralist view on institutional change in comparative perspective with special references to Japan and France. *Evolutionary institutional economic review, 7*(2), 177–208.

Torrico Terán, M. (2006). ¿Qué Ocurrió Realmente en Bolivia? *Perfiles Latinoamericanos, 13*(28), 231–261.

Valencia Lomelí, E. (2008). Las transferencias monetarias condicionadas como política social en América latina. Un balance: Aportes, límites y debates. *Annual Review of Sociology, 34*, 499–524.

Valenzuela, A. (1995). Chile: Origins and consolidation of a Latin American Democracy. In L. Diamond et al., (Eds.), *Politics in Developing Countries: Comparing experiences with democracy*. Boulder: Lynne Rienner.

Varela, P. (2013). Los sindicatos en la Argentina Kirchenerista: entre la herencia de los 90 y la emergencia de un nuevo sindicalismo de base. *Archivos de Historia del movimiento obrero y la izquierda, 2*, 77–100.

Verduzco Igartúa, G. (2005). Las organizaciones solidarias en México. In I. Bizberg & L. Meyer (Coords.), *Una historia contemporánea de México, tomo 2, actores* (pp. 367–402). México: Océano.

Vidal Bermúdez, Á., Cuadros Luque, F., & Sánchez Reyes, C. (2012). *Flexibilización laboral en el Perú y reformas de la protección social asociadas: Un balances tras 20 años. Serie de Política Sociales N° 175*. Santiago de Chile: CEPAL.

Welch, J. H. (1991). *Hyperinflation and internal debt repudiation in Argentina and Brazil: From expectations management to the "Bonex" and "Collor" plans* (Research Paper No. 9107). Dallas: Federal Reserve Bank of Dallas.

Zapata, F. (1992). Transición democrática y sindicalismo en Chile. *Foro Internacional, 32*(5), 703–721.

CHAPTER 7

State Structures and Political Systems

The effect of the action of civil society on the economic regime is mediated by the political system. While in the last chapter we analyzed the trajectory of civil society in the democratization and liberalization processes, we will now address the question of the trajectory of the political regime after democratization and liberalization in order to analyze the effect of the existence of an active and autonomous civil society on the type of capitalism. Civil society can have an impact on the economic mode through State structure and the political system. As Tilly has well established in his book *Democracy*, a democratic regime depends on one part on the openness of the political system to societal demands, as well as on the capacity of the State to implement them. In some countries, the political system is closed and does not accept the pressure of civil society. In others, the State is too weak and cannot implement the decisions. But rather than talking about weakness and strength of the State that we have seen to be not too accurate, we will focus on the analysis of the structure of the State from the perspective of federalism of Bruno Théret. According to this author, some forms of the State are more open to civil society than others, depending first on whether a State has a federal or centralized structure, and then on whether federalism is decentered or centered; while some federalisms are very centralized, almost as centralized countries, others are decentralized. In the case of centralized countries, we will discuss the effects of decentralization that most Latin American countries underwent. On the other hand, we can typify different political regimes, (in this case we only

I. Bizberg, *Diversity of Capitalisms in Latin America*,
https://doi.org/10.1007/978-3-319-95537-7_7

take into consideration democracies) whether they are more or less institutionalized, more or less representative, and more important for our purpose, if they are more or less determined by the action of civil society (Table 7.1).

7.1 State Structure: Federalism, Centralism, and Decentralization

To begin with, some State structures may be more or less open to social actors, depending on both their character as federalist or centralist/unitary States and their degree of decentralization. A federal State allows for more space for the emergence of new political and social actors and for social, political, and economic innovation. On the contrary, more centralized/unitary State systems allow less space for social action and innovation. In addition, more decentralized systems encourage greater redistribution and more egalitarian wages, while more centralized systems are more elitist, less redistributive, and more unequal.

Following Bruno Théret (2015), we will differentiate between federal or non-centered systems and unitary systems that decentralize because while "...decentralization is not a characteristic of federative political orders, non-centralization (or decentering) is, because it establishes the conceptual distinction between a federation and a unitary State: federations can be differentiated by their degree of non-centralization, which is nothing more than a degree of conformation of the global political order to the principles of the political philosophy of federalism" (Théret 2015: 254). In our cases, we have three federal States and five unitary States. Some federal States are more or less decentered, while the unitary States are more or less decentralized.

7.2 The Federal States

Mexico is surely the least decentered of the three federalisms, as Théret writes, Mexican "...federalism is reduced in practice to zero despite its possible formal conservation in the constitutional field." Mexican State structure is "...1) almost totally focused on the federal state that can be assimilated to a central State, 2) devoid of any program of unconditional financial compensation for the budgetary capacities of the federated entities [...] and 3) endowed with a weak political representation of the

Table 7.1 Dominant social coalition, state structure and type of political regime

	International outsourcing	*Socio-developmentalist*	*Rentier/Liberal*	*Rentier/Redistributive*
Dominant Social Coalition	*Oligarchic*: State, multinationals, large national entrepreneurs, financial capital, middle classes	*Compromise between oligarchies and popular classes*: State, middle classes, unions in a compromise with agro-exporters and financial capitalism	*Oligarchic*: State, multinationals, big national entrepreneurs, financial capital, middle classes	*State/Civil Society Alliance*: State, Popular sectors, lower middle classes
State structure	Centralized federalism	Decentralized federalism	Decentralized centered State	Decentralized centered State
Type of democracy	Weak representativeness and civil society; strong parties; particracy	Strong representativeness, strong civil society; institutionalized parties; participatory democracy	Weak representativeness; weak civil society; institutionalized parties or weak parties; particracy or destructured political system	Strong representativeness; strong civil society: movementist/delegative democracy

Source Own elaboration

federated entities due to a very weak Senate, especially in what concerns its elaboration of the Budget, which is the exclusive faculty of the assembly of deputies" (Théret 2015: 255). An additional centralizing feature of Mexican federalism was the corporatist political party system that concentrated political power for more than 70 years, where all governorships, municipal presidencies, national and local congresses, and national and local social organizations were controlled by the PRI, exerting a very powerful centripetal force.

Although the PRI was weakened by democratization and the State structure has decentralized, the process was obstructed due to its particular sequence, as defined by Falleti (2010). The process began with administrative decentralization promoted by the federal State, followed by political decentralization upheld by the federated entities in the course of democratization, when opposition parties won the local governments, and then by the blocking of fiscal decentralization by the federal State, in order to resist both stronger autonomy of the federated entities and further democratization. In addition, in this case, "…decentralization served as a tool that allowed the PRI a slow and orderly retreat" (Meyer, cited by Falleti: 188), permitting this party to maintain some of its power by controlling especially governorships; that is the reason why the reforms gave more power to federated States than to municipalities.

In contrast to the Mexican case, Brazil "…presents a high level of non-centralization of the Federation (similar to the Canadian, Swiss and German federations); but also a high level of unconditional compensation of the budgetary capacities of the states (similar to Canada, the Federal Republic of Germany, Australia and Spain); finally a high level of power of the Senate." In addition, Théret signals the importance of the municipal orders of government that "… have been the central places of political and social innovations (participatory budgets, social minima), where the dynamic force of Brazilian civil society is exerted" (Théret 2015: 256–257).

Diverging from Mexico, where administrative decentralization was as a process of "…off-loading responsibility on provinces and states, in Brazil the demands for decentralization (even administrative decentralization) and democratization were tightly linked together in the political discourse of politicians and societal actors" (Falleti 2010: 163). In this manner, the sequence of decentralization was different, and all forms reinforced each other. And especially, Brazil decentralized fiscally and was transformed "… into one of the world's most fiscally decentralized systems" (Samuels and Mainwaring 2004: 95).

"Finally, Argentina is a centered corporatist federalism that has decentralized, which occupies an intermediate position between the centralized Mexican centered corporatist federalism and the decentralized Brazilian decentered individualist federalism. The central mediating role played in Argentina by the party system to ensure the cohesion of the Federation, together with the federal-provincial ambivalence of this system determines its position close to Mexico, in terms of the degree of (low) power of the Senate and centering of the Federation, and on the other hand close to Brazil, for the degree of unconditional fiscal compensation" (Théret 2015: 258). In addition, fiscal federalism in Argentina is institutionalized in the constitution and in the laws, and the intergovernmental financial transfers are not tagged and are discretional. On the other hand, they are oriented (in principle) to decrease the interregional inequality with respect to the budget of the federal entities (Théret 2015: 253). All of this is not the case in Mexico.

7.3 Decentralization of Unitary States

In the case of the Andean countries, which are all centered State forms that have undergone a decentralization process, we have seen different degrees of decentralization: While Bolivia reached very high levels of political, fiscal, and administrative decentralization, the case of Colombia is intermediate and those of Peru and Chile achieved a lesser level.

While before 1994, the year of the enactment of the "Ley de Participación Popular" (Law of Popular Participation-LPP), Bolivia was one of the most centralized countries in the world. Due to decentralization this country experienced dramatic changes. "The spatial distribution of resources across Bolivia became far more equitable. And local governments proved far more responsive to objective indicators of local needs than central government had been before in all sectors examined: education, agriculture, water and sanitation, health, urban development and transport. These shifts were disproportionately driven by Bolivia's smaller, poorer districts, which benefited from a massive transfer of resources at the expense of the center and cities" (Faguet 2012: 271).

Then again, the LPP empowered the social movements, especially the indigenous, and was instrumental for the arrival of the MAS to power. Previous to the LPP, the Bolivian State was a weak centralized State. It was weak, as it only had control of about half of the territory. This law allowed the State, for the first time in history, to exert its power in the rural regions that concentrated 42% of the country's population

(Oxhorn 2001: 7–9). It was, paradoxically, extremely centralized, as it was organized by departments with prefects appointed by the center. The law, promoted by Vice President Víctor Hugo Cárdenas, created 311 municipal governments that not only had the possibility of electing their own authorities but also considerably increased their economic resources. On the other hand, the law substantially increased the power of thousands of local indigenous organizations that had, thanks to isolation, survived and preserved a strong indigenous culture. They were ratified as Territorial Base Organizations (*Organizaciones Territoriales de Base*), designed to supervise the use of the resources that the new law allocated to the municipalities (Oxhorn 2001: 7–9).

Furthermore, by opening up the local sphere that was narrowly restricted by the centralization of Bolivian politics, the LPP expanded the possibilities of political participation. It favored the political integration of new social sectors and of new political personnel insofar as it oriented politics toward the local level and "...ruralized and indianized politics by weakening the conventional partisan mechanisms of recruitment of candidates and promoting a strategy of alliances with social organizations prompting a change of political elites at the municipal level as the start of the "ruralization of politics" that reached its climax with the electoral victories of the MAS in 2005 and 2009" (Zuazo Moira, 2008, cited by Mayorga 2011: 21). The law helped the new associations to distance themselves from the corporatist organizations such as the civic committees and unions, which had dominated the sociopolitical scene since 1952. The LPP radically shifted the organization of Bolivian civil society from being based on union and peasant corporations, to the territory (Oxhorn, op. cit: 13). "Since 2010, this expansion has spread to another subnational area with the creation of departmental legislative assemblies, to which the creation of governments in the indigenous autonomies in some municipalities has been added" (Mayorga 2011: 22).

Finally, the LPP "...marked the formal incorporation of civil society into the governance process as a governing institution, via the oversight committees. The OC's are charged with the supervision of all municipal activities on behalf of grassroots organizations, and can effectively paralyze the administration if it objects it" (Faguet 2012: 206). Studying two different communities, Faguet found that the existence of an organic civil society is crucial to make the OC's function, that is, for decentralization to have a beneficial effect on the population. "In Charagua, a civil society that functioned organically essentially took over local government and made it work" (Faguet 2012: 208).

The contrasts with Chile, Peru, and Colombia are manifest, because in these countries decentralization has had the contrary effect, closer to what Restrepo Botero describes for Colombia. The reason for this difference is, as we have analyzed in the previous chapter, the characteristics of civil society. Decentralization with a dense and active civil society, as has existed historically in Bolivia, resulted in turning "...passive residents into engaged citizens, many of whom became deeply involved in local affairs, and most of whom voted" (Faguet 2012: 280). In the liberal countries it has not, on the contrary, it has been instrumentalized to further weaken civil society. This is because decentralization leads to the atomization of the demands of the population and of their social organizations, making it difficult to organize social movements at the regional or national levels; demands are raised and treated at the municipal or state level. In these situations, decentralization creates the opportunity for focalized social assistance programs that divide the territory and the population, inducing them to pose dissimilar demands, to which different policies may be applied; it also increases opportunities for clientelism (Restrepo Botero 2015).

Actually, one of the main objectives of the government of Pinochet—which it shared with other Latin American dictatorships—was the depoliticization of the State. The construction of a new way of organizing social policy was central to achieving this goal. The neoliberal social policy of the dictatorship had as its objective the depoliticization of social policy, neutralizing the repercussion that it had on political participation before the coup, where social policy was a social response to the demands that the population conveyed through the political system. The Pinochet government decentralized health and assistance, shifting administrative responsibility toward the municipal authorities and severely limiting their ability to take decisions and generate resources. This led to the concentration of social policy in the hands of technocrats in order to distance it from social pressure. This policy cut relations between political parties and their social bases (Posner 2005: 63). The result of technocratic decentralization in the case of Chile can be synthesized as "... insufficiently dynamic. A few policies stand out—the creation of municipalities (1989), the direct election of mayors (1992), and laws addressing local civil servant incomes and local personnel management—but on the whole, the decentralization process can be characterized as a sum of relatively isolated, formalistic and low-impact initiatives" (Inostroza Lara and Fuenzalida Aguirre 2015: 43). On the other hand, the level of expenditure by the subnational governments is the lowest of all our countries, 14%, and in addition, they have little autonomy regarding their use.

One of the principal reasons why decentralization in Bolivia was effective and enhanced social and political participation is that it entailed the decentralization of fiscal resources to be used unconditionally, and that it "...built enhanced accountability measures into decentralization via municipal oversight committees, which operate alongside the formal institutions of power [...] their power resides in their ability to suspend central transfers to local authorities..." (Faguet 2012: 286). These characteristics would have most probably not had the same results had they not been accompanied by an organized and active civil society.

In Peru, there exists a fiscal structure considerably different to the Bolivian; in contrast to the latter, it does not pretend to be equalizing, "... in Peru regional governments do not receive unconditional equalization transfers, and at the local level the governments are not given equalization transfers for capital spending" (Brosio and Jiménez 2012: 284); most governmental resources come from oil and gas revenues. 70% of the total transfers to regions (*recursos ordinarios*) are allocated on a discretionary basis, decided by the central government on a case-by-case basis, with a political rationale (Letelier and Neyra 2013: 148). The remaining 30% of the transfers pretend to be equalizing,[1] as they are apportioned according to population and level of poverty. On the other hand, there is the *canon minero*, a transfer of 50% of the taxes payed by the mining companies that goes directly to the regions and municipalities where extraction takes place. These taxes have been so substantial and have been distributed so unequally that they have transformed the fiscal structure of the country (Arellano Yanguas 2014: 39).

On the other hand, while in Bolivia resources are given unconditionally and their use is defined by the local authorities, with the surveillance of civil society, in Peru, because decentralization was done progressively and began with fiscal decentralization, once the central government reoriented economic resources and the administrative responsibility to the subnational governments, it had the time to react (in terms of Falleti) and retain legislative capacity and impose very strict rules on how

[1] https://resourcegovernance.org/sites/default/files/nrgi_sharing_Bolivia_case-study.pdf.

regional and local governments use the resources (Arellano Yanguas 2014: 217). Thus, in fact, one can conclude that decentralization has been much less profound in Peru.

"Both Geography and politics have contributed to make Colombia one of the least integrated countries in Latin America" (Falleti 2010: 122) "...in the mid 1980's, a political legitimacy crisis led to the formation of a mixed decentralization coalition of national and subnational actors, but in which subnational interest prevailed [...] this led to a political decentralization reform [...] which enhanced the power of mayors, that were now elected and not nominated by the central government" (Falletti: 123). The civic strikes that we mentioned in the previous chapter were a "...crucial antecedent to the popular election of mayors because this form of protest voiced the territorial interests of the underdeveloped regions of Colombia. Their demands were not nationwide in scope, they were specifically related to the problems of municipalities and regions where the protesters lived [...] they disappeared thanks to decentralization" (Falleti 2010: 133).

These strikes, led not only toward political affirmation of the local governments, but also toward fiscal decentralization, actually, the deepest such decentralization of the Andean countries, even profounder than the one of a federal country like Mexico. It was achieved in the 1991 constitution, promoted by the interests of the departmental and municipal levels. These changes led to an "...increased number and frequency of automatic transfers [...] and increased the revenue base upon which the transfers were calculated" (Falleti 2010: 140). "It is worth noting that while the fiscal situation was tied to specific responsibilities in the education and health sectors and no particular percentage was guaranteed by the Constitution, the municipal transfers were not linked to any particular line of expenditures, and the percentage by which they had to increase over time was established in the Constitution" (Falleti 2010: 141).

"...the mayors were able to write fixed percentages of transfers into the constitution and to achieve the constitutional guarantee that administrative decentralization would take place only if accompanied by the decentralization of fiscal resources" (Falleti 2010: 147). "As a result of decentralization, governors and mayors are politically autonomous from the national government and have the capacity to manage more resources and design innovative policies [...] when power is devolved, decentralization reforms can lead to higher levels of political accountability and improve public services" (Falleti 2010: 149).

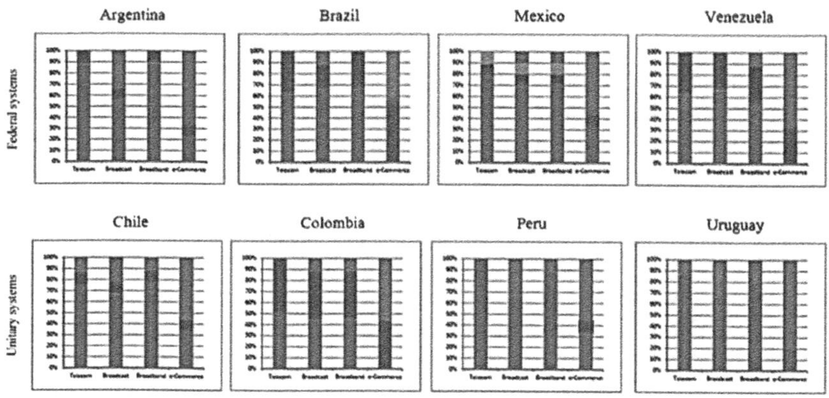

Fig. 7.1 Level of decentering (*Source* Aranha et al. 2014: 21)

The two following figures help us to define the relative level of decentering of some countries in Latin America. The first figure[2] illustrates how, although we are dealing with both federal and unitary countries, Brazil and Colombia share a high level of decentering, Argentina, Mexico, and Chile a medium level, while Peru has a very low level (Fig. 7.1).

If we now take into account the next figure, where the revenue of the subnational governments is outlined, we can see that Mexico is one of the most centralized countries, as 80% of the resources come from the central government, in equality with Peru; in addition in both of these countries transfers are conditioned/tagged by the federal government. Although Chile collects a very high percentage of resources at the subnational level, it is nonetheless a very centralized country, where the subnational governments spend only 14% of total State revenues (Rodríguez-Acosta 2015: 22). In comparison, Peru spends 34%, Bolivia 27%, Ecuador 22%, Colombia 33%, and Mexico 32%. More federal countries Argentina and Brazil, 50 and 55%, respectively (Ibid.) (Fig. 7.2).

[2]We have to take into consideration that this graph refers to the telecommunications industry, so it cannot be taken as a picture of what happens in all of the economic sectors. Nonetheless, it is an indicator of the question.

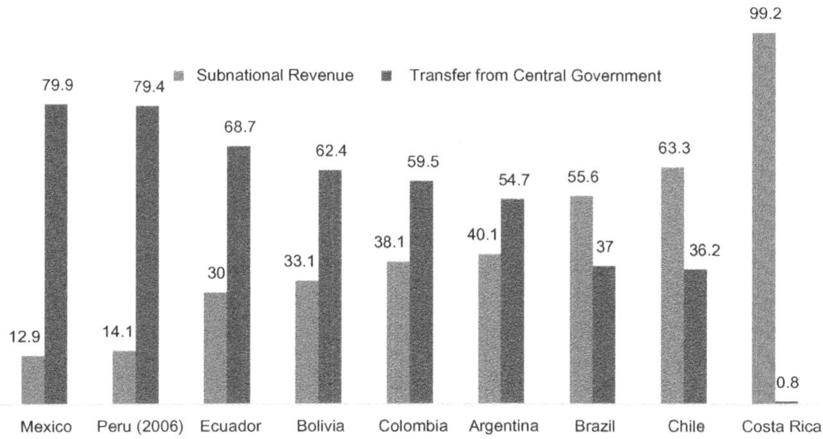

Fig. 7.2 Total revenue distribution of subnational governments, selected Latin American countries 2008 (% total) (*Source* Own elaboration, based on data from Gómez Sabatini and Jiménez 2012: 149)

Before we analyze the political system as such, we have to mention its capacity to decentralize or re-centralize. However, some authors consider that there is a unilateral link between decentralization and the political systems, meaning that a decentralizing process tends to inhibit the development of a national party system, because the political system "follows" decentralization. We have seen how Théret does not link both phenomena, but considers that the political system has the capacity to re-centralize or decentralize. The Mexican case is exemplary. During the rule of the PRI (an extremely centralized organization) federalism was practically canceled, as the party occupied the posts at both the national and the subnational levels. In the same manner, Théret (2015) describes the way the Peronist party and the labor unions exert a centripetal force on Argentinian federalism. In the case of Brazil, a strongly decentered federal system coincides with a very regionalized political system, with little discipline, that does not exert any pressure to centralize. Only during the military rule some centralization was achieved.

In the case of the Andean countries, the political hegemony of two party alliances in Chile probably has a very minor effect on a very centralized State structure. In Bolivia, although the MAS is a dominant organization, it is nevertheless a collection of regional social movements that are not centered. Finally, in the case of Peru, Colombia, and Ecuador, a disarticulated party system adds up to decentralization. As an example, in the case of Peru, the disarticulation of the existing system and decentralization gave birth to meso-level political organizations, called *movimientos regionales*, which in 2002 presented 62 candidates in 25 regions. "The Peruvian political system became a very fragmented one characterized by levels of government, each with its own political and electoral movement [...] in the last eight years an average of 80% of the regional governments has been in the hands of strictly meso-level organizations with almost no connections to the national level" (Vergara 2011: 77–78).

7.4 The Political Regimes

We are confronted with two different consequences of democratization and liberalization on the political system in the countries we are analyzing. In some countries, these two processes had the effect of deconstructing the political system, the parties that existed before democratization totally disappeared, the party system is deinstitutionalized, and politics is strongly personalized (Colombia, Peru, and Ecuador). In other countries, where social movements and organizations were especially strong and active, new parties or political coalitions emerged, like the Brazilian PT and the Bolivian MAS, and have been able to consolidate and to a certain degree re-institutionalize the political system. In others still, the political parties that existed before the coup, or before democratization, have reemerged in more or less the same form they had before the dictatorial period (Mexico, Chile, and Argentina), and the political system has restructured around them (Fig. 7.3).

In order to analyze these diverse situations, we have fashioned a typology of the different democratic political systems based on the three main characteristics of any party system: its degree of institutionalization, of representation, and the autonomy, density, and mobilization capacity of civil society. With these three variables, we construct seven ideal types of democracy. The particular countries are hybrids of these ideal types, thus they do not coincide with any one of them perfectly, although they may come close to one or the other. On the other hand, particular systems vary in time, moving inside the cube, approaching one or the other

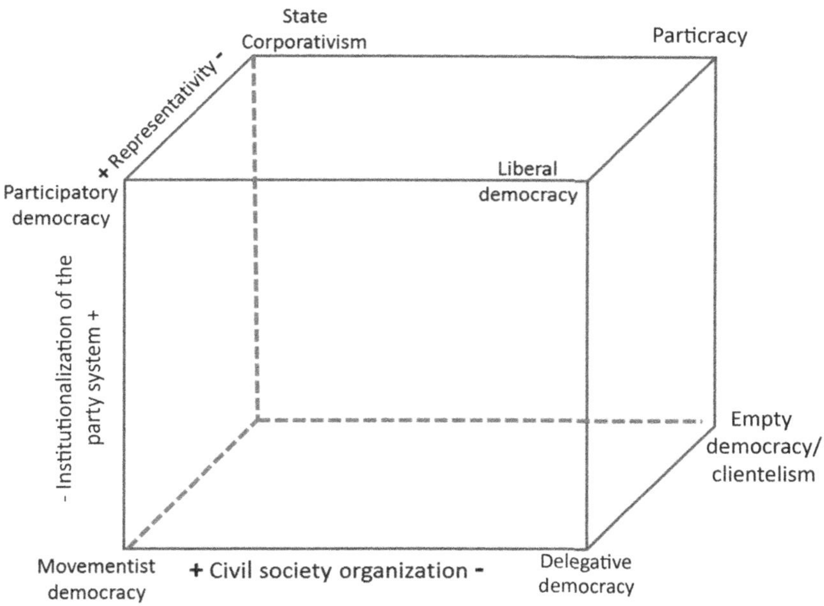

Fig. 7.3 Typology of democratic regimes (*Source* Own elaboration)

ideal type. It should also be clear that some types of political systems barely meet the minimum characteristics of democracy and may cross the sides of the cube to become authoritarian regimes. This is the case of Venezuela, for example, which during the presidency of Chavez was a delegative democracy, where social organizations were built from above, supported by the distribution of the financial resources that came from oil exports, through the *Misiones*. During his presidency, the government organized relatively free elections, something which is no longer the case in the government of Maduro.

In the first two front upper vertices of the cube, we have the **representative/liberal** democracy and the **socio-corporatist or participatory democracy**. While both coincide with respect to a high institutionalization of the party system and a high level of representation, in socio-corporatism civil society is organized autonomously and is mobilized and participates within a system that is rooted in it. We can also consider this type of political system as a participatory democracy, in contrast to the opposite type that is a system of representation that passes exclusively through political parties and its representatives in Congress; it is the ideal type of liberal representation.

There exist two regimes with a high level of institutionalization of the party system, which however lack representativity. We have, on the one hand, **State corporatism**, in which the parties corresponding to different social sectors are structured into corporations, which are either organized "from above" or, at the very least, recognized and/or co-opted by the State and subject to its power and its rules. The system has a low level of representation since the corporations represent interests defined or accepted by the State and have limited autonomy (Schmitter 1974). The different corporations in which society is structured are included within a party or parties, and although negotiations happen inside them, the last decision is in the hands of the head of the organization, which is in most cases also the head of the State. State corporatism is the opposite of socio-corporatism or participatory democracy. In both, civil society is organized and is capable of mobilization; nonetheless, the fundamental difference is that while in the first, civil society has been organized or co-opted by the State and is thus under its control, in socio-corporatism it is autonomous. Over time, this system may tend to become rigid and bureaucratic in such a way that progressively an ever larger part of the population is totally non-represented, and become authoritarian.

The other type of institutionalized regime that lacks representativity is **particracy**, in which well-instituted parties have managed to define the rules of a political system that limit the emergence of other parties or associations, and allows them to perpetuate in power. This is a system that has a weak rooting in civil society, and an self-referred party system that pursues its own interests, distanced from those of society. The closure of this system to other parties that may represent other currents and tendencies leads to an ever larger part of the population that does not feel represented.

In the lower base of the cube, we have the types of democratic political systems with un-institutionalized political parties. These are incoherent party systems, often personalistic, where usually candidates form a new party or coalition in order to present themselves to an election. One of these systems lacks representativity, the **clientelistic**, which is a system where individuals are related to government by intermediaries, "brokers," who rather than representing them, exchange services and goods for political loyalty. This political system is, to a certain degree, the zero degree of politics due to the fact that parties are not institutionalized, civil society is poorly organized, and the system is not representative. It is possible to build a political system on this basis, especially if the electoral system is very open to the creation of new parties, with very low limits for a party to reach Congress and with open electoral lists. This type of electoral system favors the personalization of electoral politics, which has been so significant in Latin American countries. It can be also called an empty democracy.

Delegative democracy is the mirror image of the clientelistic/empty democracy, and it may be a derivative of the latter as we have seen in the Ecuador of Correa, and in the Venezuela of Chavez, before its authoritarian turn. It is based on a very similar direct relationship between government and individuals, where government allocates resources linked to the person of the leader, in exchange of a *carte blanche* that the mobilized bases give to its leaders (O'Donnell 1996). Although the system is based on a patron–client relation, it is centralized on the leader, which may have a high degree of representativity. The political systems in Latin America have all a certain degree of this type of a system, as well as of clientelism.

It is possible, finally, that while the party system is destructured, civil society be very dense and mobilized, and that social organizations and movements closely represent the needs and projects of the population. In this case, the existing parties, or proto-parties, are to a large extent subordinated to social movements. We would be in the presence of a **movementist** democracy. In this case, political parties are weak in relation to the social organizations and are not very efficient as mediators. These mobilizing democracies are characterized by social organizations that have emerged "from below" and that are rooted in civil society.

7.5 Particracies: Chile and Mexico

Some examples of particracies are the *Pacto de Punto Fijo* of Venezuela, a pact between the two dominant parties to alternate in power (1958 until the mid-1990s), the *Frente nacional* between the liberal and conservative parties in Colombia (1958–1974), where the two main parties shared the governmental posts, and finally, the so-called *Democracia Pactada* between the three main parties in Bolivia (1985–2003), where in order to arrive to government they had to build coalitions between dissimilar and even contrary ideological parties.

Chile has a political system that is midway between a liberal democracy, rooted on the electoral sphere, and a particracy. Its tendency to particracy comes from the fact that the binominal electoral system[3] perpetuates the coalitions that emerged with democratization and that increasingly lack representativeness (from 1989 to 2017). On the other hand, although before the coup political parties were deeply rooted in social organizations, the present system is not. This is the consequence of the brutal repression of the authoritarian regime, of a very restrictive trade union law, and a transition that implied the demobilization of the organizations and social movements that emerged during the first half of the 1980s.

It is well known that Chile was one of the most institutionalized and stable democracies before the coup of 1973. In fact, many analysts still find behind the facade of the two alliances that emerged with the binomial system, the three political families that have existed in the Chilean political system since the nineteenth century, despite the will of Pinochet to destroy the old party system (Angell 2005). Until the last two elections, the political parties were concentrated in two coalitions: the right-wing one, constituted by two parties, one of them heir of the traditional right-wing parties before 1973 (National Renewal), and the Independent Democratic Union (UDI) that emerged during the dictatorship and was closely linked to it. The left on the other hand is represented by the Socialist Party, the Party for Democracy—created in 1987 to participate in the plebiscite as the dictatorship had banned left ideological parties—and the traditional center party, the Christian Democracy. The cleavage into two major alliances was favored by the binominal electoral system, conceived by the dictatorship to benefit the right-wing parties and which in fact promotes the creation of alliances of all kinds regardless of their ideological signs. Actually, Tironi and Aguero consider that since the return of democracy in 1989, a new cleavage was established, based on the basic conflict of the Chilean dictatorship. The cleavage that characterizes Chilean political society separates those who defended the dictatorship, though they distance themselves from its excesses, and those who denounce and reject it (Tironi and Aguero 1999: 68).

This system was conceived to benefit the two right-wing parties that buttressed the Pinochet government in the referendum (Huneeus 2005), and resisted for more than twenty five years, without being modified by the *Concertación* governments because it provided political stability, has served to preserve the economic model accepted by this coalition and,

[3] That existed until the most recent elections of 2017.

in addition, had favored its remaining in power. One of the main failures of this system is that until 2014 it left out completely any parties that did not form part of any coalition, regardless of their votes. In the 1992 elections, the Communist Party won 5% of the votes, in 1997 it was 6.9%, in 2001 it was 5.2%, and in 2005 it was 5.1%, in all cases without having achieved any representation (Joignant and López 2005: 66). Although in the last elections of 2017, the candidate of *Frente Amplio*, a coalition situated on the left of *Concertación* or its successor in 2013, *Nueva Mayoría*, was able to challenge the two coalitions that monopolized power in the last thirty years, obtaining 20% of the vote (Altman and Luna 2010).

This has led Garretón and Garretón (2010) and Altman and Luna (2010) to consider the Chilean political system critically. In the first place, it is the only democratic regime in which the Constitution adopted under the military regime is still in force (Garretón and Garretón 2010). Altman and Luna consider that although the Chilean political system seems to be highly institutionalized and the country enjoys a solid rule of law, the population is disenchanted of its politicians and its political system, because it generates little competition (Altman and Luna 2010: 273–274). The student demonstrations during the first Bachelet presidency and the ones during the first Piñera one, as well as the more recent ones of the pensioners, are the visible symptoms of a democracy that seems solid but that lacks representativity.

With respect to civil society, there is a consensus regarding the fact that because the transition took place exclusively at the electoral level, when the opposition parties accepted the rules of the plebiscite of Pinochet, one of the consequences was the demobilization of the civil society groups that had been very active in the mid-1980s. The Chilean transition was produced almost exclusively by the party system, in fact, "… the priority given to the formation of the political system will be the main characteristic of the Chilean democratization process. The identification between democracy and political system in this case receives its purest expression" (De la Maza, op. cit.: 225).

In fact, the political actors with the greatest political weight accepted the fundamentals of the economic model imposed by the dictatorship. On the one hand, this model had resulted in a sustained growth for more than 20 years, which translated into wage increases, greater purchasing power, and a significant reduction in poverty; although inequality also increased (De la Maza: 228). One can also consider that this evolution of the socioeconomic situation accentuated individualism and alienated Chileans from social organizations and activities.

As we have already discussed in the preceding chapter, most of the authors that analyze Chilean civil society mention a significant social demobilization. We have already analyzed how unionism was cut off from its traditional political roots and subjected to a very unfavorable legislation; something that has not been effectively modified with the most recent reform of the labor law in the presidency of Bachelet (Cerdas Sandi 2017). On the other hand, the democratic governments succeeded in recapturing the civil society organizations that emerged during the dictatorship, reorienting them towards the economic and social problems of the poor, that were at the center of the mobilizations of the 1980s in the marginalized neighborhoods of the cities.

The Mexican political system is also close to a particracy, as the institutional framework profits the three political parties that have played the principal role since the late 1980s, marginalizing all other parties that are obliged to ally with the three big ones to survive.[4] But due to the fact that these different parties have adopted the ways of the PRI, one can truly say that the Mexican political system is a hybrid between a corporatist system and a particracy.

The Mexican system has gone from a State corporatism to a particracy since the mid-1980s to the years 2000. Until the 1980s, it was a system where a dominant/State-controlled party held elections which it controlled. At present, it is built around three more or less national[5] parties. Facing different social challenges since the 1970s, the different governments of the PRI always succeeded in channeling democratization exclusively through the electoral scope, limiting the development of autonomous organizations of civil society. So much so that the PRI continues to control most of the unions, peasant, and popular organizations of the country. Even accepting that in recent years a large number of non-governmental organizations with different objectives have been created, unionism and autonomous peasant organizations remain small

[4] In the elections of 2017, the PRD has been substituted by Morena, and the former has had to integrate an alliance with the PAN.

[5] In fact while the PRI is in effect a national party, with presence in all States, the PAN is mainly a party of the center and north of Mexico, while the PRD is strong in Mexico city and the South.

compared to organizations linked to the PRI. The largest autonomous union organization, the National Union of Workers (UNT), has around 500,000 workers, barely about a tenth of the unionized workers in Mexico, and has not grown in the last decades. The autonomous peasant organizations are even fewer. On the other hand, it would also seem that the organizations that have left the PRI to ally with the PRD, and more recently with Morena, retain many of the vices of corporatism and clientelism (Combes 2004; Zermeño 2004).

However, the other dimension of democracy, the party system, seems quite institutionalized. For the last 25 years, three solidly constituted parties have dominated the electoral scene: the PRI, the PAN and the PRD; all three have been fairly stable, although they have internal problems. Two of them (the PRI and the PAN) are more than half a century old, almost 90 years for the first and 80 for the second. The PRD appeared in 1987, and because most of its militants have left the party to join the Movimiento de Regeneración Nacional (Morena) of López Obrador, this latter may be considered as a successor of the first rather than a totally new organization. The three largest parties concentrated 90% of the votes in the elections up to 2010 (Prud'homme 2010). The volatility of the vote is moderate: In the 2003 elections, the PRI won 30.6% of the parliamentary votes and 29% in 2006 in coalition with a small party, in 2009—again in coalition—44 and 38.2% in 2012. The Pan obtained 33.4% of the votes in 2003, 23.1% in 2006, 28% in 2009, and 25.4% in 2012. For the PRD, the percentages were 17.6% in 2003, 29% in 2006—in coalition—18% in 2009 and 31.6% in 2012. Coppedge (2010) estimates that the volatility of the vote in Mexico in 2006 was 17.6%, while in other Latin American countries, they are much higher. In Mexico, the effective number of parties, according to Sartori's definition, has been three: PRI, PAN, and PRD (now Morena). And it is these three that control most of the seats in both houses of Congress. On the other hand, the Mexican electorate has remained relatively stable until today: Each of the three parties has a rather stable hard vote, and the election results are decided by those who do not sympathize with any of them, as in the consolidated democracies. Finally, the electoral law imposes a threshold of votes of 2.5%, in order to achieve representation in Congress and keep the party registered, that has been able to avoid the fragmentation of the system. This has obliged the smaller parties to ally with one of the three large ones. This situation does not seem to have changed with the appearance of Morena, now the votes are concentrated in this party, the PAN (in alliance with the PRD) and the PRI.

The fragility of the Mexican political system lies, like in the Chilean case, in the supremacy of the main parties and their dissociation from civil society. In Mexico, the first issue worsened with the electoral reform of 2007 and again with that of 2013, which resulted in an increase in available resources, which favored large parties over small ones; advertising in the media was prohibited, but the financing of the parties was not reduced (Aziz 2010; Prud'homme 2010). On the other hand, starting in 2000, the parties gradually took control of the Federal Electoral Institute (IFE) and the Federal Electoral Tribunal (TRIFE), two central institutions in the process of democratization until that moment. It can be said that while in the 1990s the IFE and TRIFE were gaining autonomy from the State to become institutions that responded to the citizenship, in the beginning of the present century they fell prey to the control of the political parties; it is them who choose the members of these institutions. As a consequence, these institutions defend increasingly less the democratic principles of transparency and fairness and progressively more the interests of the parties that elected the functionaries (Alonso and Aziz 2009).

The roots of the distancing of the Mexican political system from civil society can be found in the trajectory followed by democratization. In contrast to democracy in Brazil that initiated within civil society, triggered by democratic unions declaring strikes against the military government, before attaining the political sphere; in Mexico the transition of the years 2000 was achieved without a rupture, being the result of two complementary processes: on the one hand, the slow but constant transfer of votes from the PRI to the opposition parties, towards the right-wing party—PAN—as well as the left party—PRD—and on the other, the strengthening of the regional and local oppositions, which managed to gradually win elections in municipalities, and from 1989 on, in some States previously governed by the hegemonic party.

The most important electoral reform that began this process was implemented by the government in 1977 as a response to the numerous union movements that demanded independence form the corporatist organizations controlled by the hegemonic party. This reform served to redirect the process of democratization towards the electoral sphere, and divert it from the social sphere, where it had been occuring since the beginning of that decade. This reform inhibited the attainement of their autonomy by the social organizations, which continued to be subject to the political parties with which they maintained clientelistic relations, especially with the PRI. Another opportunity which was lost for empowering civil society was the Zapatista rebellion of 1994. Numerous civil society organizations gathered round this movement and not only demanded that the government of Salinas (1988–1994) stop the war against the Indian movement, but began demanding a speedier democratization movement. The government was smart enough to impose the creation of an independent institution for the organization of the elections, a move that once again diverted the attention from the social to the political sphere. In synthesis, if one uses the famed formula of Stepan's (1985), stating that the process of democratization in Brazil resulted in the strengthening of both State and civil society, one could say that in Mexico the opposite happened, since only the political system was strengthened at the expense of the State and of civil society.

7.6 Movementist and Socio-Corporatist Democracies

The opposite of the situation we have described is one where civil society is strongly organized and mobilized, and there is a certain level of institutionalization of the political system. We have seen this situation where social organizations and movements played a significant role to set off democratization, as in Brazil, Argentina, and to a certain extent in Bolivia, although in this latter case it was not in an authoritarian or dictatorial context, but against a particracy. Social movements consolidated and either generated another party and another system (Brazil), or recuperated the main organization of the old system, and the old party system in itself (Argentina).

We will not repeat what we have already said about the importance of civil society in democratization, the constitutional process, and everyday life in Brazil, we will concentrate on the political system. And in this respect, although the corruption affairs of the *mensalao* and *Lava Jato* as well as the recent impeachment of President Dilma Roussef under dubious accusations have revealed grave disfunctions, one cannot ignore that the system was, until the impeachement of Dilma and the elction of Bolsonaro in 2018, in the process of institutionalizing, around three principal political parties: the PT, the PSD, and the PMDB. One has simply to remember that the Brazilian party system was considered the paradigm of a deinstitutionalized system. Nonetheless from the 1990s to the mid-2000, when the PT won the presidency, the system began to institutionalize (Meneguello 2002; Ribeiro 2013; Aziz 2015). Brazil transformed an incoherent political system, with an enormous lack of representativeness and rootedness in civil society, where generalized clientelism permeated, into a party system centered on three principal parties: the PMDB, an organization that united the opposition during the time of the dictatorship, a center-right, non-ideological, and pragmatic/clientelistic organization, that has usually supported either one of the other two larger parties in order to govern. The other two parties are the PSD, an organization created by Fernando Henrique Cardoso, a so-called social-democratic party, which is rather liberal, center-right, and the PT, based on the social movements that led the democratization process, especially the CUT. Truly, party volatility was greatly reduced: It decreased from a high 58.6% in 1990 to the "normal" levels in Latin America, 24.3% in 2014 (Melo 2015: 95), and the effective number of parties was reduced from 5.7 in 89–90 to 2.7 in 2010, although the number total of parties in Congress actually increased from 5 to 22 in the same period (Ribeiro 2013: 621). After the 2006 elections, Congress passed a reform intended to limit the number of parties in congress: It establishes a threshold of 5% to constitute a congressional group, get resources for electoral campaigns, and have the right to free publicity in the media (Guimaraes 2006).

What most analysts considered a factor of institutionalization was the tradition of building coalitions, established since the drafting of the 1988 Constitution and the first presidency of Cardoso. According to Meneguello, the process of consolidation of the Brazilian party system was an effect both of the relations that were established between the parties and civil society and of those between the parties and the State. The debate of the 1988 Constitution contributed to the definition of the ideological and programmatic profiles of the parties in congress, translating into more stable parties and alliances. On the other hand, Cardoso's presidency was based on a policy of more permanent coalitions with the PMDB, the PFL, and the PTB (Menguello 2002: 224). The presidency of Cardoso inaugurated a "virtuous circle" of the relationship between elections and the capacity to govern: The parties that arrived to power after 1995 showed an increasing governing competence that strengthened their electoral power (Cavarrozi and Casullo 2002: 18).

Other authors put the accent on the presence of a consolidated political actor: the *Partido dos Trabalhadores* (the PT), which in turn served to give consistency to the rest of the system (Meneguello 2002; Aziz 2015). The PT is a party based on the labor confederation, the CUT, and other social movements, although it progressively became a party like the others and distanced itself from the social movements, it continued to have a close relationship with the CUT, especially during the presidency of Lula (Carneiro and de Oliveira 2010). But the PT was not only the heir of one of the key actors in the transition, unionism, but also an actor that helped institutionalize the political system in two different ways: a) being the most coherent actor within an incoherent system: from the moment in which this party began to win governmental positions and to have possibilities of winning the presidential elections, it forced the other actors of the political system to become more coherent. The PT showed strong cohesion and internal discipline since the 1990s: The senators and deputies of the PT did not abandon the party once in Congress, like the other parties often did, and they showed a voting discipline that approached 100% (Raes 2001: 135). In fact, the PT expelled some of its deputies for casting a vote against its political line.

As we discussed in the previous chapter, the PT was strongly rooted in civil society, and its policies reflected this situation: The best known example is the participatory budget, a procedure that, although it has dwindled in the last years, resulted in the empowerment of the popular classes in the localities where it has been successfully implemented, to the detriment of the clientelistic relations that prevailed in the old political model. The PT adopted participatory budgeting in the cities it governed, initially only in Sao Paulo and Porto Alegre, but later in more than 200 other localities. The participation of the inhabitants of the poor neighborhoods in public policy decisions was considered as a way to empowering these populations in order to fight the clientelistic bases of Brazilian politics. In this way, participatory politics became not only a different way of relating to politics on the part of many inhabitants of poor neighborhoods, but it had an impact on the party system itself, since it became the mechanism by which the elected candidates of the PT singularize themselves from the legislators of other parties (Avritzer 2009; Goirand 2002). On the other hand, this organization has reinforced and stimulated the implementation of the different governance councils in the areas of health, education, and social services that were mandated by the constitution of 1988 (Houtzager and Gurza Lavalle 2010; Izunza Vera and Gurza Lavalle 2012).

During the 1990s, when the PT was rising from local power to the national, its legislators focused their activities in the districts and in close contact with the organized collectivities that supported them: associations, cooperatives, unions, local party structures, settler organizations, etc. Some observers saw in this process a tendency toward the Americanization of the Brazilian political life that implied the strengthening of the relations between the legislators and the local actors.

This helped the PT to move away from its more ideological (and radical) positions and to become more pragmatic (Nylen 2007).

However, although the Brazilian system was in effect structured around two poles (the PT and PSDB), which could be considered relatively modern parties, the PMDB is a conglomerate of regional powers and politicians without any attachment to their party that function as the old Brazilian parties have always done; in fact, it is called pejoratively a physiological party meaning that the elected officials make alliances with any other organization depending on their interests, which are usually monetary. The PMDB has allied with the PSDB under Cardoso, and with the PT under Lula and Dilma. The congressmen and congress women of the PMDB constitute the largest majority, and they sell themselves to the highest bidder, as most congressmen from the other small parties do.

This is what lead to the system of corruption discovered in 2005 during the government of Lula: the "*mensalao*," which consisted in monthly payments to the legislators of other parties that allied to the PT in order to ensure their support. Although this type of procedure has been commonplace under other governments, as in such a fragmented system all governments are coalition governments that depend on the votes of the representatives of the other parties[6], this affaire had disastrous effects on the supporters of the PT, especially because it was a party that had promised to behave ethically, in fact to introduce ethics into politics (Samuels 2006: 22). Following this scandal, many of his followers considered that the organization had become "a party like the others," a situation that is again confirmed in the present "*lava jato*" scandal.

That is why we consider Brazilian democracy to be a hybrid between a clientelistic and a participative, or socio-corporatist democracy. Bolivia, which we will analyze next, is what we have called a movementist democracy, where the party system is un-institutionalized, like in rest of the Andean countries, except Chile. Social organizations are very strong, and due to the fact that the MAS and especially Evo Morales has acquired a very high representativity, there is a tendency to adopt the characteristics of a delegative democracy.

[6]We should remember that although the number of effective parties is near 2, the nominal number of parties in 2010 was 22.

Unlike Peru and Venezuela, where the party system collapsed in the 1990s, the Bolivian political system was able to stabilize from 1985 until the mid-2000, in a type of particracy, especially owing to the establishment of ruling coalitions between the three main parties (Mayorga 2002, 2005). After the revolution of 1952, a multiparty system was established with a dominant party (MNR) that was closely linked to the State, based on its corporatist relationship with the Central Obrera Boliviana (the COB). After the fall of the military regime (1964–1982), between 1985 and 2003, Bolivia managed to live in a kind of "stable democratic pact," named *democracia pactada* (convened democracy), that contrasted with its history. According to Mayorga, the reasons this system materialized were: (1) the isolation of the parties of the traditional left and of the trade union movement that had been very radical in the 1950s; (2) a convergence to the center of broad sectors of society; (3) the economic policy of stabilization; (4) the pact between the political parties, based on a logic of arrangements and consensus between parties that replaced the traditional logic of conflict; and (5) the reduction of effective parties from 18 to five (Mayorga 2005: 3).

The most important aspect of the process was the emergence of a tripartite party structure (MNR, MIR, and ADN), on which the government and the coalitions of the congress were grounded. Between 1985 and 1997, these three parties obtained between 57 and 65% of the votes, and between 54% and 86% of the seats in the assembly. The rupture of the *democracia pactada* in 1989 did not lead to the return of an extreme multiparty configuration, but to a bipolarity where the MNR and AND alternated in alliance with the MIR (Mayorga 2005: 3).

The particratic features were clearly illustrated in the 1989 elections, which led to the break between the main partners of the *democracia pactada* and the entry of the MIR on the political scene. It should be considered that the Bolivian electoral law contains a rather curious measure for a presidential system, which stipulates that if none of the candidates running for the presidency obtain a simple majority of votes in the single round election, the system takes on the features of a parliamentary regime, that is, the president must be elected by Congress. This explains the need to establish alliances between the parties prior to the vote in order to obtain a majority in parliament (Lavaud 2007: 143). In this manner, in the 1989 elections, this system enabled the MIR candidate, Jaime Paz Zamora, to conquer the presidency although he arrived in third place in the elections, with only 19.6% of the votes, behind Sánchez de Lozada and the former dictator Hugo Banzer. Paz Zamora agreed on an alliance with Hugo Banzer: called the "Patriotic Agreement," in order to form a government. The symbolically most sensitive part of this alliance was not the low percentage of votes obtained by Paz Zamora, but that he allied with whom years before was his worst enemy,[7] as he had been one of the main opponents of the Banzer dictatorship. This purely pragmatic move was badly assimilated by the population; it contradicted the will of the voters, implied that the borders between parties had disappeared and that post-electoral agreements could lead to unpredictable results. According to most analysts, this profoundly undermined the legitimacy of the Bolivian system (Lavaud 2007: 143).

However, it took another ten years for the system to collapse. The presidential elections of 2002 produced a significant re-composition of the party system: One of the main parties of the *democracia pactada*, the ADN practically disappeared, as it obtained a mere 3.4% of the votes, compared to 22% in the previous ones. The descent to hell of the ADN was the beginning of the end of the existing system as the other two parties of the *democracia pactada* managed to stay in the game: the MNR with 22% and the MIR with 16%, although a new organization, the MAS of Evo Morales, made its entry with 21% of the votes. This situation forced the two remaining parties to create a coalition with another small party, a solution too weak to govern effectively (Mayorga 2005: 5).

The collapse of the system and the increase of the power of the MAS cannot be simply explained by the characteristics of the existing party system and the advent of a charismatic leader who managed to unify the sentiment of rejection that had arisen in various sectors of the population. A more accurate explanation is the intensification of social mobilization on several fronts. Two movements occupied the social scenario: the MAS, which regrouped several social organizations around the project to re-found the Bolivian State based on the identity, values, and conceptions of the original nations and the end of neoliberalism, granting the rightful place to indigenous regions. On the other, the Indigenous

[7] In fact, the present alliance between the two most opposing parties in the Mexican political scenario, the leftist PAN and the rightist PRD in order to faire barrage to both the PRI and Morena echoes of this situation.

Movement Pachakuti (MIP),[8] based on the peasant-indigenous movement that fought for the end of the political and cultural discrimination of the indigenous people (the end of the "two Bolivias"), for the adoption of participatory democracy, and the preservation of the culture of the coca leaf (Torrico Terán 2006: 89–90).

Beginning with the Banzer government (1997–2001), both the economy and politics began to deteriorate. It should also be considered that, since the 1997 elections, four of the leaders of the social movements had already arrived to congress, among them Evo Morales. The event that increased Morales's popularity enormously was his exclusion from parliament after the violent clashes between the coca leaf producers, the *cocaleros*, and the armed forces in the Chaparé. This strengthened the movement against the traditional parties and in favor of the idea of convening a constituent assembly to transform the structure of the State and the political system, in short, to "re-found the country" (Torrico Terán 2006: 89–90). In 2002, Evo Morales and the MAS won the elections of 2002 with more than half of the votes, making him the first president of the post-transition that was directly elected. In addition, for the first time in Bolivian history, peasants and indigenous people had an important presence in the political life of the country.

The movement that led Evo Morales to the presidency is not totally subordinated to his leadership. The MAS is an assemblage of autonomous social actors that emerged "from below," that translated into a political actor, and have managed, to a certain degree, to preserve its autonomy. The relationship between the government and the social movements, both those integrated to the MAS itself, as well as those that were independent or have moved away from it, is flexible, they respond to the government when their interests coincide, and they exert pressure in order to obtain certain demands or to oppose the government. "In 2006, the MAS engaged in extensive consultation with grassroots organizations to determine their priorities and then, when the land reform was stalled in the senate, called on them to take to the streets to exert

[8]The MAS candidate triumphed over the Bolivian ethnic movement, the Pachakutik Indigenous Movement (IPM), led by Felipe Quispe, which proposed the end of the postcolonial Bolivian State and the re-indianization of Bolivia, the end of the Westernization of this country. For Evo Morales and the MAS, the priority is not the ethnic issue but equality and justice, vindicating the State as the basic instrument to achieve that goal. (Rouquié 2010: 256, 256–257).

the pressure necessary to get the law approved" (Farthing and Kohl 2014: 156). Nevertheless, they protested in 2010 against the attempt to reduce gas subsidies and the construction of the TIPNIS highway; both of which were abandoned by the government (Mayorga 2005: 139). In addition, as of the 2009 constitution, political parties subordinate themselves to indigenous organizations in terms of the selection of candidates in indigenous constituencies (Mayorga 2011: 23).

The 2009 Bolivian Constitution defines its political system as an intercultural democracy that is not limited to the exercise of universal and individual voting (Mayorga 2011: 133). That is why Mayorga considers this regime as a hybrid between a representative and communal democracy, with elements of participatory and direct democracy: referendum, citizen legislative initiative, revocation of mandate, recognition of the assembly, the *cabildo*, and prior consultation (Mayorga 2011: 133–134). Except in the case of the peasant unions that are the permanent social base of the MAS, all the other organizations and social movements are linked to government in obedience to their own interests and projects in a social corporatist relationship, rather than a State corporatist one as the PRI imposed on its organizations, or Perón on the unions. This, added to the frequent mobilizations of these organizations and the lack of unity of the MAS, characterizes the Bolivian regime as a "movementist" democracy.

Still, the political system of Bolivia also suffers from a tendency to delegative democracy, to a concentration of power in the hands of the leadership (basically president Evo Morales) that the population accepts, because it feels represented. After two successive elections, since 2009, Evo began considering staying in power for a decade or more. "Preservation of power, critics would say, became more important than the process of change as the circle around Evo Morales and Alvaro [Linera] isolated themselves from the grass roots" (Farthing and Kohl 2014: 156). On the one hand, Evo and the MAS have concentrated power, both due to the charisma of the leader and the electoral supremacy of the MAS, and on the other hand, the fact that in common with other charismatic leaders, his government has not been keen in building political institutions, favoring an increased personalization of the regime. This tendency has been rejected by certain organizations of civil society, with the exception of his more faithful bases, the *cocaleros* of the Chaparé. This situation is very unstable, as it depends on the dynamics of the social organizations and on their relationship to the leadership, they can either tend toward a delegative democracy if too much power is concentrated, or toward a socio-corporatist democracy if the social movement achieves institutionalizing its organizations and eventually a political party that represents it.

Finally, Argentina can be considered a hybrid between the Brazilian and the Bolivian democracies, the movementist and the socio-corporatist or participative democracies. The social movements, in this case the Peronist unions, were linked to the leadership of a charismatic figure that helped organize or co-opted them: Juan Domingo Perón. Nonetheless, they preserved a certain autonomy, which grew in time. First, unions had a certain autonomy since their existence preceded that of the Peronist movement. Second, there were long periods in which the movement was in opposition: the period in which Peronism was banished from 1955 to 1973, after the overthrow that deposed Perón in 1955, and again during the military dictatorship from 1976 to 1983. This had the lasting effect of maintaining Peronism more as a social and political movement than a political organization, contrary to what happened in Mexico, where State corporatism became a regime. In reality, Peronism was not only characterized by the circumstance that the party was subordinated and was deeply identified with the leader, but also by the fact that charismatic leadership called for its plebiscitary ratification through permanent mobilization (Mustapic 2002: 144); that is precisely its movementist character. On the other hand, this relation between the Peronist movement and the *Justicialista* Party has been described as socio-corporatist (Etchemendy and Collier 2007). In synthesis, it has fluctuated between a movementist and a socio-corporatist system, depending on whether opposition or Peronism governed.

A fundamental characteristic of the Argentine system was its stability until the late 1990s. During the entire second half of the twentieth century, it was dominated by two main parties: the Radical Civic Union (UCR) and the *Justicialista* Party (PJ-Peronist). However, behind the appearances, stability did not mean institutionalization, but quite the opposite, as Juan Carlos Portantiero wrote at the beginning of the 1980s. Argentina was a fragmented society in a plurality of de facto power centers that constituted a dense political system that was incapable of translating into institutional pluralism. Facing these centers of power, there existed a system of weak parties that did not have the capacity to serve as integrators of the interests of pressure groups and, therefore, as intermediaries between them, in order to activate a negotiation process. For this reason, the political parties provoked crises (as they still do nowadays) every time they reached the presidency (Portantiero 1982: 23–29). More specifically, traditionally, Argentine political parties have had a marginal role in terms of representation and channeling the interests of large landowners and urban workers, which are the two most consolidated sectors in Argentina. The large landowners of the Pampa have never had stable relations with any of the parties capable of winning free elections. Between 1880 and 1909, there existed a conservative party (the National Autonomist Party) that represented their interests, but unlike what happened in the Chilean case, where the parties were transformed to integrate different sectors of the electorate, the Argentine conservative party did not manage to survive the political inclusion of the middle classes and the workers, which were incorporated by the UCR and the Peronist party. The landowners of the Pampa constituted a small social sector, and unlike Chile, there was no large sector of stable rural population that could be co-opted or forced to vote for the parties dominated by the landlords. On the other hand, when the Argentine landowning sector lost its influence to the Radical Party, it moved away from the party system and used its powerful class organizations to exert political influence (McGuire 1995: 199–202).

An additional paradox of the Argentine political system is that even if the *Justicialista* Party is considered to be the representative of the interests of the workers, the relations between this organization and the unions have never been institutionalized as has been the case, for example, of the European social-democratic parties. From its creation, in the mid-1940s, Peronism was a movement of collective identity that revolved around the charismatic figure of Juan Domingo Perón and his particular style of exercising his role as leader. Perón forged a direct and affective relationship between him and his supporters, which undermined the bases of the organization of his party, led to an anti-party sentiment and, in short, hindered its institutionalization (McGuire 1995: 201–202). The relationship between the Justicialist Party and the unions was never institutionalized, even if there was an evident relationship between the two, Perón rejected all attempts to do so. The place of unionism within the PJ was never formally defined, even though the unions participated in the corporate process of selection of the candidates known as the "system of thirds," by which a third of the seats was assigned to the worker's, another to the political sector and the last one reserved to a gender quota (Levitsky 2001: 42).

In this way, the central actors of Argentine society had no formal political representation, nor an institutionalized relationship with the party system; they thus had to rely on their capacity to exert pressure. The agro-exporting oligarchy employed the *Sociedad Rural Argentina* (SRA) to influence government and public opinion or to withdraw its production from the market. The General Confederation of Workers (CGT) organized strikes and demonstrations and occupied factories. In synthesis, social actors in Argentina have acted more like social movements and lobby groups than as intermediates of the political system (McGuire 1995: 202). This is what led Portantiero (1982) to say, shortly before the departure of the military from power, that Argentina had always been subject to "cesarism," a situation that periodically headed the country to opt for authoritarian solutions to its crises.

Since the political transition, but especially from the presidency of Menem on, the relationship between unionism and the Peronist party changed significantly. In the 1990s, the trade union bases of Peronism were severely weakened and were gradually replaced by an underemployed, impoverished, and disorganized population (Sidicaro 2003–2004: 45). During the 1990s, the economic policy applied by Menem had increased unemployment to unprecedented rates: Unemployment had multiplied by two since 1993, reaching 18% of the active urban population by May 1995. This situation affected the mode of insertion in the labor market on which Peronism was based: a job with stable salary, articulated with health services, unemployment insurance, pension, etc. At the mid of the 1990s, only one in six workers had such labor conditions (Palomino 2000: 122).

For its part, the UCR also underwent major changes. One was derived from a very controversial decision by Raúl Alfonsín, who in December 1993 signed an agreement with Carlos Menem (the Pact of the *Olivos*) that led to the constitutional reform that allowed for the immediate re-election of the president, a reform that benefited Menem. As a result of this pact, the Radical Party divided, giving birth to three different forces: the *Unión del Centro Democrático* (UCD) of Alvaro Alzogaray, the Intransigent Party, center-left, and what was left of the UCR. In the 1995 elections, this latter had one of its worst votes in history: 16.4%. In this same election, a center-right coalition formed by Peronists and dissidents of the UCR—the UCD and another group called the Frepaso (*Frente País Solidario*)—got 28.2% of the votes (Sigal 2003–2004: 10).

All these transformations incurred by the two main Argentine parties during the 1990s eventually led, in the years 2000, to the emergence of a multitude of new parties, and to the division of the *Justicialista* Party. In fact, in the elections that led Kirchner to power in 2003, three Peronist candidates, governors from three different States, contended. This was the result of a process of "territorialization" of the organization that had begun in 1983, when the party, despite having lost the presidency, managed to retain 12 provinces and hundreds of local mayors. This led to the replacement of the political resources of the unions by those of the State governments that then began to build clientelist networks based on their local power. It is these networks that formed the organizational base of the group of "the renovators," Menem among them, who arrived to power a few years later (Levitsky 2001: 43). In this manner, the Peronist party became an electoral instrument controlled by the local authorities, mainly the governors (Sidicaro 2003–2004: 51).

Although, after the economic and political crisis that shook Argentina in 2001–2002, the conditions seemed ripe for the country to follow the path of the political systems of Peru, Venezuela, and Bolivia that disaggregated, Peronism took over. The crisis of representation seemed to have been overcome with the return of one of the most traditional parties in Argentina. It is, in effect true that after the economic and political chaos of 2001, when the convertibility system collapsed dragging the rest of the economy, the circumstance of an almost normal election and the victory of the Peronist party with a majority in Congress seemed to point to a certain consolidation of the political system. As a matter of fact, the presidency that preceded (Menem 1989–1999) and succeeded (Néstor Kirchner 2003–2007), the government of De La Rua that ended in a crisis, had concluded and yielded power to elected civil governments, something that had occurred only rarely in the twentieth century, where between 1928 and 1989 only one president-elect (Juan Domingo Perón) had finished his mandate (Levitsky and Cameron 2003: 26). Finally, while in the elections of 2015 in which Mauricio Macri was elected numerous parties were contending, behind the two main fronts, the one of Macri, *Cambiemos*, and that of Scioli, *Frente para la Victoria*, we can recognize the traditional parties, the UCR and the *Justicialista* Party as the main partners.

Thus, on the one hand, the system seems quite solid and the traditional parties are still strongly anchored, although they are not solidly institutionalized due to the character of the two parties we have been describing, and due to the increased atomization of the party system. On the other hand, the Argentinian political system continues to be very open and subject to social movements, showing a tendency to movementism; something that may be changing with the offensive of Macri against the social bases of peronism.

7.7 Empty Democracies: Clientelism and Delegation

We call empty democracies those systems that lack both an institutionalized party system and an organized and autonomous civil society organization, such as they exist in Ecuador, Peru, and Colombia. In our schema, they either tend toward clientelistic or delegative democracies. The political systems of many of the countries in Latin America were destructured by the military regimes that ruled them in the 1960s and 1970s, to the particracy that followed some of the democratization processes and the implementation of the neoliberal agenda. In addition, in Peru and in Colombia, both civil society and the political system were destructured by the war against guerilla and drug cartels. In some of these countries, the governments in place, without parties and civil society organizations, have been defined as "pure" technocratic governments, impervious to popular interests (Tanaka and Vera 2010). In some countries, this situation pervades, Peru and Colombia, and in others, it gave way to a reaction of civil society that imposed a political system led by social movements: Bolivia and Ecuador.

The first indication of the crisis of the party system in Peru was the election of a radio personality, Ricardo Belmont, as mayor of Lima in 1989. A year later, Alberto Fujimori, an outsider, an anti-political candidate, won in the second round the presidency of the Republic with a spectacular media campaign, against another better known candidate but also not belonging to the traditional parties: the writer Mario Vargas Llosa. Alberto Fujimori climbed from little more than 1% of the voting intentions in February 1990 to the presidency in June, inaugurating a decade in which he accumulated unprecedented power in Peru in company of his advisor Vladimiro Montesinos (Degregori 2003: 243).

In the case of Perú, the context that allowed for the arrival of Fujimori to power was the same that had favored the other anti-system leaders, like Chavez and Morales: the weakness of the party system. During the 1980s, the Peruvian parties had undergone very profound changes: The last barriers to universal suffrage were eliminated, and there was a strong rural migration to the cities and the informal sector expanded to more than 50% of the active population; all these factors weakened class organizations, eroded collective and partisan identities, and produced a considerable number of unaffiliated voters (Levitsky and Cameron 2003: 6). In addition, the more traditional center-left party, the APRA, was facing an economic crisis characterized by hyperinflation and the incongruous economic policy of its president Alan García, and the increased activity of the Maoist guerrilla *Sendero Luminoso*.

In this same decade, the left parties were gaining force, had won the government of Peru's capital, Lima, in 1983, but were profoundly affected by their position regarding *Sendero Luminoso*. According to Tanaka, the left *Izquierda Unida* had become the second largest party in Peru, with real possibilities of accessing power through elections. It had achieved to unite social movements and political parties of the left and attain the sympathy of the middle classes. However, it divided and almost ceased to exist basically due to internal divisions, between a left that focused on a radical confrontational strategy and a more reformist left. The rift was decided in its first Congress, facing the elections of 1990, which resulted in two different left parties that contended against the FREDEMO of Vargas Llosa and against Fujimori: the moderate left, with Barrantes the best known candidate, the ancient mayor of Lima, and a new party *Izquierda Socialista*, with the social movement base, but an unknown candidate (Tanaka 2004–2005: 66). The fact that the left had lost part of its base due to the socioeconomic transformations of liberalism and was divided between those that formally rejected the violent path of the Maoist guerrilla and those that did not define a clear position or that actually supported it aggravated the crisis of the system.

The election of Fujimori ended up destroying the Peruvian party system. He was a political amateur, without a program, without a party, and without a government team. Alan García, who had sustained him against the candidates of his own organization, quickly left. He also faced opposition from very influential sectors of the political, economic, and religious establishment. On the other hand, his followers had less than a fifth of the seats in the congress. All these factors were decisive for Fujimori's adoption of an authoritarian political strategy, conceived by his security adviser, Vladimiro Montesinos (Levitsky and Cameron 2003: 7).

Between August 1990 and March 1992, the traditional political parties collaborated with Fujimori, as a survival strategy. In fact, both the APRA and the left in Congress faintly reacted to his neoliberal measures.

However, the question that opened the gap between the two powers and led to the *auto-golpe* was built around the strategy against the Maoist guerrillas, which was becoming increasingly military. The Congress modified a bill sent by the executive at the end of 1991, regarding its anti-subversive strategy against Shining Path, intending more political actions implicating the government and civil organizations. But a more decisive element to define Fujimori's self-coup d'Etat was the congressional vote on a law that limited the president's powers in early 1992. On April 5, Fujimori suspended congress and placed regional governments, the judiciary, the electoral tribunal, and the constitutional court under presidential control. The regime became an emergency government of national reconstruction (Degregori 2003: 246–247).

This explicitly authoritarian turn constitutes one of the important differences between the Fujimori government and the other anti-party, personalistic, delegative governments that have recently appeared in Latin America. Another fundamental distinction is that the Fujimori government did not invest any efforts in the institutionalization of his organization or in allying organically with civil society. His party of origin, *Cambio 90*, had no program, no national structure nor activists. Fujimori could have used the popularity he gained due to his government's control of inflation, the defeat of the guerrilla, and his clientelistic social policy, that enabled him to win a constitutional referendum and two elections, to consolidate his party. Yet, he did everything possible to avoid it and govern in an increasingly authoritarian manner: He replaced it with State agencies and continued using the media to address the masses directly.

This situation had profound and enduring effects on the Peruvian political system. The party system ended up totally destructured, the dominant political form being the independent political movements, without national structure, with minimum support in civil society, based on certain personalities and their privileged relationship with the media (Levitsky and Cameron 2003: 10–12). A political system that has been described by Tanaka as a democracy without parties and without social organizations. It is characterized by weak and purely pragmatic parties, with no clear ideology, in a context where anti-political rhetoric is predominant. On the other hand, by frequent, weak, disconnected, and non-articulated social protests that are incapable of expressing themselves nationally (Tanaka and Vera 2010). In such a situation, the State, without intermediation with instituted political parties and organized social actors, is totally dominated by a technocracy. If we now return to the terms of our typology, while Fujimori's Peru was clearly a case of delegative democracy controlled by a strong political leader, delegation has since then been transferred to a purely technocratic leadership. Kuschinsky was a perfect example: an economist that worked in the World Bank and occupied several economic posts in the Peruvian government before becoming president of Peru.

Although the case of Colombia has many differences with the Peruvian, it also has many similarities that allow us to consider it as a an empty democracy. There is, on the one hand, the destruction of the party system: its atomization, pragmatism, ideological undefinition, and anti-political tendencies. During the pact of the *Frente Nacional*, the system was defined by the allotment of all posts at the three levels of government between the two main parties, the liberal and the conservative, and the alternation at the presidency. The constitution of 1991 set up new rules intended to facilitate the creation of new parties that would break the particracy created by the long domination of the traditional parties. The result was an extreme fragmentation: In 2002, there were 72 legally recognized parties of which 42 were represented in Congress. A modification of the electoral law has since reduced the number of parties to 22, 10 of which are represented in Congress (Bejarano et al. 2010: 111–112).

This atomization reflects the fact that many of these parties are actually closely dependent on personalities, like in Peru, Ecuador, as well as in the Brazil of the 1990s. The example of Alvaro Uribe, who governed from 2002 to 2010, is instructive as he created his own organization, *Partido Social de Unidad Nacional*, also called *Partido de la U* (for unity, but also for Uribe). This personage fomented an anti-political discourse all along his presidency and after twice serving as president, he tried to modify the constitution in order to reelect himself for a third time. This latter intent, harmful to the stabilization of the party system, was finally blocked by the Supreme court (Bejarano et al. 2010: 114). But the consequences were that 30% of citizens consider themselves independent and the abstention rate in elections reached a high of 55% (Losada 2013: 193).[9]

[9] At the end of the 1980s, after the assassination of Luis Carlos Galán, the favored candidate to the presidential election of 1990, together with the deaths of Bernardo Jaramillo Ossa of the Patriotica Union and Carlos Pizarro of the M19, the electoral abstention reached 70% (Falleti 2010: 135).

These characteristics of the political system of Colombia, but also of that of Perú and Ecuador, do not mean the demobilization of society, but rather its incapacity to construct a national movement, which in the case of Ecuador did exist with the CONAIE. In the case of Colombia, there were two very significant and massive social movements: the civic ones in the 1970s and the student movement in the 1980s. The civic movement concretized as civic strikes, carried out at the territorial level. There were more than 200 such strikes between 1971 and 1985 that addressed local issues such as electricity, water, sewage, road infrastructure, education, ecological problems, all, in reality, a consequence of the unequal distribution of financial resources, which were concentrated in the large cities (Falleti 2010: 132–133). These "*paros cívicos*" had as their outcome a first moment of political decentralization that resulted in the direct election of the local authorities, both governors and mayors, which were previously nominated by the presidency (Falleti 2010). This reform was accompanied by a recrudescence of repression against other such actions as well as other social movements that resulted in a dramatic decrease of these kinds of movements. "The civic strikes did not contain neoliberalism; instead, they strengthened those who called for repressive treatment against trade union organizations and leaders of the left, a task that was increased during the government of the liberal Turbay Ayala (1978–1982)" (Restrepo Botero 2015: 286). Demobilization and repression were facilitated by the institutional vacuum. Although the *paros cívicos* represented "…an act of power in which forms of political expression distinct of those offered by the market society, such as political clientelism, trade union tradition and the vanguards of the radical left, are exalted and promoted" (Restrepo Botero 2015: 293), these movements have not endured due to the institutional and organizational vacuum in which they unfold, they are "…without stable and hierarchical representation, without the construction of a permanent intermediation, struggle platforms that were not aligned with the great currents of the international left…" (Restrepo Botero 2015: 293). Similarly, the student movement that emerged in reaction to the flagrant violence of the eighties, that had claimed the lives of three presidential candidates in the 1990 elections. This movement achieved to unite a far reaching front consisting of the unions, the entrepreneurs, the political parties, and a majority of the population. It managed to collect 30,000 signatures to demand the inclusion of a question in the referendum of 1990, regarding a clause of the new constitution. The mouvement disolved although, it gathered more than a million votes, and ensued in the Constitutional Assembly in 1991 (Falleti 2010: 136).

In the case of Colombia, the expression of social movements was hindered by both the institutional and organizational vacuum, as well as by the polarization that existed during Uribe's presidency, where any effort of association and protest was considered a support to "terrorists" or guerilla; thus, calling for the retaliation of the private paramilitary groups (Bejarano et al. 2010: 126). It is well known that Colombia is one of the countries where more trade unionists, journalists and other social leaders are assassinated.

Finally, the case of Ecuador could have evolved toward a political system such as the one that exists in Bolivia, if the CONAIE would have not been involved in the coup d'Etat of Gutierrez, first, and then in his government. The fact that this organization was deeply weakened at the time that Correa won his first elections in 2006 had a significant impact on the future of the Ecuadorian political system. That is what makes this case more similar to the Venezuela of Chavez (obviously without its terrifying present situation), than to that of Bolivia. "Like Chavez's, Correa's rapid ascent took place in the political vacuum created by Ecuador's crumbling party system" (Conaghan 2011: 261). In fact, the party system collapsed after ten years of political crises expressed by the fleeing, removal of office by congress, and resignation, of four successive presidents (Alberto Dahik, Abdalá Bucaram, Jamil Mahuad, and Lucio Gutierrez). Nonetheless, the circumstance that all these political crises were not merely the demise of the party system due to corruption, inefficiency, economic crises, and the stalemate between Congress and the presidency (Basabe Serrano et al. 2010: 170), but as we analyzed in Chapter 6, that they were accompanied by massive manifestations by the CONAIE, the labor movement, and the population, the so-called pueblazos (Conaghan 2011: 262–263), makes the difference between this situation and that of Peru and Colombia.

On the other hand, although we agree with De la Torre in considering that Correa did not promote social organizations and that he tried to rule as if society was an "...empty space where [he] could design totally new institutions and practices" (De la Torre 2015: 177), the circumstance that the nineties saw massive popular eruptions led by the indigenous and labor organizations forced Correa to implement economic and social policies that were a response to the popular anti-liberal demands of the 1980s and 1990s. Notwithstanding, with regard to the political dimension, and because the social movement did not fill the void created by the collapse of the political system as in Bolivia, it was Correa himself that did so, inaugurating a ten-year rule where he combined a concentration of power in the hands of the presidency and a redistributive type of capitalism.

In this manner, Correa instituted a political system based on the high legitimacy resulting from the social policies of his government and used the "...popular sector mobilization that helped elect him into a source of support against obstructionist traditional socioeconomic elites defending their privileges" (Silva 2009: 194). Thus, in reference to the name he gave his movement, the citizen's revolution, we could say that while in socioeconomic terms Correa in effect intended to implement a "citizen's reform," in the political one, he implemented a "leadership revolution" rather than a revolución ciudadana. His rule was characterized by extensive use of decrees, criticism against the press and groups that did not agree with his points of view. In addition, his majority included in the constitution of 2008, in addition to the right of nature, the good life (Buen Vivir), the popular legislative initiatives, popular referenda, revocation of mandate, all conducive to participative democracy, and numerous articles that buttress the presidency versus the legislative and the judiciary (Basabe Serrano et al. 2010); a situation that situates Ecuador closer to a delegative than to an empty democracy.

7.8 Final Note

In these two last chapters, we have been discussing first the capacity of civil society to organize and become an actor of social, cultural, economic, and political transformations, and then the openess and capacity of the State structures and of the political system to receive and transmit social demands and projects to the State. This discussion is synthesized in Schema 2, where we can see figuratively, how some State structures are more open, because they are federal and decentralized, while others are more closed, because centered and centralized. And how more responsive political systems are those where political systems are institutionalized and civil society is organized, while particracies, clientelistic, and delegative democracies are less responsive to social demands. Where we find a more decentralized, more responsive political system and an active civil society, we also find a more active role of the State, that popular interests that are part of the social coalition, and in consequence a higher probability of State/wage-led economy with redistribution. Where a less decentralized structure coincides with a less responsive political system and a less active civil society, we also have less State intervention, popular interests excluded from the social coalition, and in consequence a higher probability of a market/profit-led economy without redistribution. Figure 7.4 illustrates the diversity of capitalisms according to the dimensions we have been discussing in this chapter.

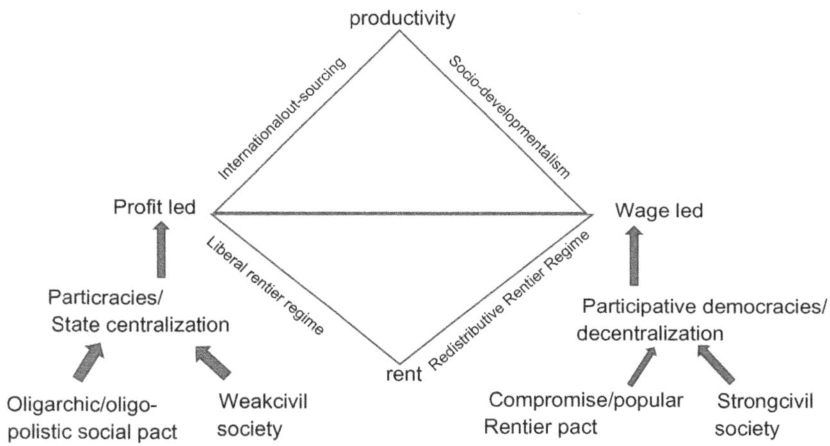

Fig. 7.4 Dominant social coalition and type of political regime (*Source* Own elaboration)

References

Altman, D., & Luna, J. P. (2010). Chile: ¿institucionalización con pies de barro? In M. A. Cameron & J. P. Luna (Eds.), *Democracia en la Región Andina* (pp. 273–314). Lima: Instituto de Estudios Peruanos/Plural editores.

Angell, A. (2005). Party change in Chile in comparative perspective. *A Contracorriente, 2*(2), 34–65.

Aranha, M. I., Cruz, J. M., & Pinheiro, A. A. (2014). Latin American federative variables for ICT and development research: A comparison between Argentina, Brazil, Chile, Colombia, Mexico, Peru, Uruguay, and Venezuela.

Revista Redes.com, revista de estudios para el desarrollo social de la Comunicación, 9, 211–231.

Arellano Yanguas, J. (2014). *¿Mineria sin fronteras? Conflicto y desarrollo en regiones ineras del Perú*. Lima: IEP.

Avritzer, L. (2009). Associativismo e participação na saúde: uma análise da questão na região Nordeste do Brasil. In S. Fleury & L. de Vasconcelos Costa Lobato (Eds.), *Participação, Democracia e Saúde* (pp. 151–174). Rio de Janeiro: Cebes.

Aziz, A. (2010). Una polémica reforma electroral. In I. Bizberg (Ed.), *México en el espejo latinoamericano. ¿Democracia o crisis?* (pp. 361–386). Mexico: El Colegio de México.

Aziz, A. (2015). ¿Democracias diferentes?: México, Brasil y Argentina. In I. Bizberg (Ed.), *Variedades de Capitalismo en América Latina: los casos de México, Brasil, Argentina y Chile* (pp. 283–380). México: El Colegio de México.

Aziz, A., & Alonso, J. (2009). Tres instituciones de la democracia Mexicana: IFE, TRIFE e IFAI. In I. Bizberg & L. Meyer (Eds.), *Una Historia Contemporánea de México, Tomo 3. Instituciones*. México: Océano.

Basabe Serrano, S., Pachano, S., & Mejía Acosta, A. (2010). In M. A. Cameron & J. P. Luna (Eds.), *Democracia en la Región Andina* (pp. 165–195). Lima: Instituto de Estudios Peruanos/Plural editores.

Bejarano, A. M., Alviar, H., Botero, F., Hoskin, G., & Pachón, M. (2010). Colombia: Democracia Amenazada. In M. A. Cameron & J. P. Luna (Eds.), *Democracia en la Región Andina* (pp. 101–164). Lima: Instituto de Estudios Peruanos/Plural Editores.

Brosio, G., & Jiménez, J. P. (Eds.). (2012). *Decentralization and reform in Latin America: Improving intergovernmental relations*. Cheltenham, UK and Northampton, MA, USA: ECLAC/Edward Elgar.

Carneiro, Â. M., & Veras de Oliveira, R. (2010). O sindicalismo na era Lula: entre paradoxos e novas perspectivas. Paper presented at the VI Congresso da Associação Latinoamericana de Sociologia do Trabalho, Mexico, April 16–22, p. 24.

Cavarrozi, M., & Casullo, E. (2002). Los partidos en América Latina hoy: ¿Consolidación o crisis? In M. Cavarozzi & J. A. Medina (Eds.), *El asedio a la política. Los partidos latinoamericanos en la era neoliberal*. Rosario: Homo Sapiens.

Cerdas Sandí, D. (2017). *La Disputa por el Poder de Asociación de los Trabajadores: Veto Empresarial y Democracia Restringida en América Latina*. Tesis doctoral del Programa de Doctorado en Investigación en Ciencias Sociales, con mención en Ciencia Política. México: Facultad Latinoamérica de Ciencia Sociales.

Combes, H. (2004). Élections internes et transitions démocratiques: le cas du Parti de la révolution démocratique au Mexique. *Problèmes d'Amérique latine, 54*, 53–74.

Conaghan, C. M. (2011). Ecuador: Rafael Correa and the citizen's revolution. In S. Levitsky & K. M. Roberts (Eds.), *The resurgence of the Latin American left* (pp. 260–282). Baltimore: The Johns Hopkins University Press.

Degregori, C. I. (2003). Perú: el desvanecimiento de un régimen y el desafío de la reconstrucción democrática. In J. I. Domínguez & M. Shifter (Eds.), *Construcción de gobernabilidad democrática en América Latina*. México: Fondo de Cultura Económica.

De la Torre, C. (2015). El liderazgo populista de Rafael Correa y la desinstitucionalización de la política. In S. Gómez Tagle (Ed.), *Alternativas para la democracia en América Latina* (pp. 151–185), México: El Colegio de México.

Etchemendy, S., & Collier, R. B. (2007). Down but not out: Union resurgence and segmented neocorporatism in Argentina (2003–2007). *Politics & Society, 7*(3), 363–401.

Faguet, J. P. (2012). *Decentralization and popular democracy: Governance from below in Bolivia*. Ann Arbor: University of Michigan Press.

Falleti, T. G. (2010). *Decentralization and subnational politics in Latin America*. New York: Cambridge University Press.

Farthing, L. C., & Kohl, B. H. (2014). *Evo's Bolivia: Continuity and change*. Austin: University of Texas Press.

Garretón, M. A., & Garretón, R. (2010). La democracia incompleta en Chile: La realidad tras los rankings internacionales. *Revista de Ciencia Política, 30*(1), 115–148.

Goirand, C. (2002). La démocratie participative au Brésil: les expériences de budgets municipaux participatifs. *Cahiers du Gela-IS*, (2), 125–136. Paris: L'Harmattan.

Goméz Sabaini, J. C., & Jiménez, J. P. (2012). The financing of subnational governments. In G. Brosio & J. P. Jiménez (Eds.), *Descentralization and reform in Latin America* (pp. 140–171). Cheltenham, UK and Northampton, MA: United Nations and Edward Elgar.

Guimaraes, L. (2006). *Excluídos pela clásula de barreira partidos vão à Justiça e estudam fusões*. http://eleicoes.uol.com.br/2006/reportagens/clausula.jhtm. Accessed 15 May 2018.

Houtzager, P. P., & Gurza Lavalle, A. (2010). Civil society's claims to political representation in Brazil. *Studies in Comparative International Development, 45*, 1–29.

Huneeus, C. (2005). Chile: A system Frozen by Elite interests. In A. Reynolds, B. Reilly, & A. Ellis (Eds.), *Electoral system design: The new international IDEA handbook*. Stockholm: IDEA.

Inostroza Lara, J., & Fuenzalida Aguirre, J. (2015). Promises and risks: Challenges to the decentralization agenda in chile. In *30 years of reform: Decentralization, subnational governments and development in Latin America* (pp. 42–46). *Hemisphere, 24*(1). Available at: http://digitalcommons.fiu.edu/lacc_hemisphere/vol24/iss1/1.

Izunza Vera, E., & Gurza Lavalle, A. (2012). Arquitetura da participacao e controles democráticos no Brasil e no México. *Novos Estudos, 92,* 105–121.

Joignant, A., & López, M. A. (2005). Le comportement électoral au Chili: paradoxes et présomptions sur la continuité ou la rupture de l'orientation du vote. *Problèmes d'Amérique Latine,* #56. Paris: Choiseul Éditions.

Lavaud, J.-P. (2007). Bolivia: ¿un futuro político hipotecado?. *Nueva Sociedad,* (209), 142–159.

Letelier, S., & Neyra, A. (2013). The political economy of regional grants in Peru. *CEPAL Review, 109,* 147–161.

Levitsky, S. (2001). Organization and labor-based party adaptation: The transformation of Argentine Peronism in comparative perspective. *World Politics, 54*(1), 27–56.

Levitsky, S., & Cameron, M. A. (2003). Democracy without parties? Political parties and regime change in Fujimori's Peru. *Latin American Politics and Society, 45*(3), 1–33.

Losada, R. (2013). La alternativa colombiana en años recientes. In S. Gómez Tagle (Ed.), *Alternativas para la democracia en América Latina* (pp. 187–224). México: El Colegio de México.

Mayorga, F. (2011). *Dilemas. Ensayos sobre democracia intercultural y Estado* plurinacional. La Paz: Centro de Estudios Superiores Universitarios, Universidad Mayor de San Simon and Plural Editores.

Mayorga, R. A. (2002). Sistema de partidos y neopopulismo en Bolivia. In M. Cavarozzi & J. A. Medina (Eds.), *El asedio a la política. Los partidos latinoamericanos en la era neoliberal.* Rosario: Homo Sapiens.

Mayorga, R. A. (2005). La crisis del sistema de Partidos Políticos y el experimento del Gobierno sin partidos en Bolivia. *Revista Futuros, 3*(9).

McGuire, J. W. (1995). Political parties and democracy in Argentina. In S. Mainwaring & T. R. Scully (Eds.), *Building democratic institutions; Party systems in Latin America* (pp. 200–246). Stanford, CA: Stanford University Press.

Melo, C. R. (2015). The 2014 Elections and the Brazilian Party System. *Brazilian Political Science Review, 9*(1), 93–114.

Meneguello, R. (2002). El Impacto de la democratización del Estado en el desarrollo de los partidos brasileños (1985–1998). In M. Cavarozzi & J. A. Medina (Eds.), *El asedio a la política los partidos latinoamericanos en la era neoliberal.* Rosario: Homo Sapiens.

Mustapic, A. M. (2002). Del partido peronista al justicialista: las transformaciones de un partido carismático. In M. Cavarozzi & J. A. Medina (Comps.), *El asedio a la política. Los partidos latinoamericanos en la era neoliberal.* Rosario: Homo Sapiens.

Nylen, W. R. (2007). Participatory Legislative "Home Styles" and Party Renewal in the Workers Party (PT) in Brazil. Paper presented at the Congress of the Latin American Studies Association (LASA), Montréal, Canada.

O'Donnell, G. (1996). Ilusiones sobre la Consolidación. *Nueva Sociedad, 144*, 70–89. http://nuso.org/revista/144/nueva-representacion-vieja-politica/.

Oxhorn, P. (2001). *La construcción del Estado por la sociedad civil: la Ley de Participación Popular de Bolivia y el desafío de la democracia local. Documentos de Trabajo del INDES.* Washington, DC: BID.

Palomino, H. (2000). Los sindicatos en la Argentina contemporánea. *Nueva Sociedad, 169,* 121–134.

Portantiero, J. C. (1982). *Transición a la democracia en Argentina.* México: Facultad Latinoamericana de Ciencias Sociales.

Posner, P. W. (2005). Local democracy and the transformation of popular participation in Chile. *Latin American Politics and Society, 46*(3), 55–81.

Prud'homme, J.-F. (2010). El sistema de partidos. In S. Loaeza & J.-F. Prud'homme (Eds.), *Los grandes problemas de México, t. 14: Instituciones y procesos políticos* (pp. 121–158). México: El Colegio de México.

Raes, F. (2001). Consolidation démocratique et médiation politique au Brésil. *Cahiers du GELA-IS,* (1), 129–162. Paris: L'Harmattan.

Restrepo Botero, D. (2015). *Procesos de descentralización en Bolivia y Colombia, 1980–2005.*

Ribeiro, P. F. (2013). El modelo de partido cartel y el sistema de partidos de Brasil. *Revista de ciencia política (Santiago), 33*(3), 607–629.

Rodríguez-Acosta, C. A. (2015). Decentralization in Latin America: History and future prospects. In *30 years of reform: Decentralization, subnational governments and development in Latin America* (pp. 19–23). *Hemisphere, 24*(1). Available at: http://digitalcommons.fiu.edu/lacc_hemisphere/vol24/iss1/1.

Rouquié, A. (2010). *À l'ombre des dictatures. La démocratie en Amérique Latine* (p. 377). Paris: Albin Michel.

Samuels, D. J. (2006). Sources of mass partisanship in Brazil. *Latin American Politics and Society, 48*(2), 1–27.

Samuels, D. J., & Mainwaring, S. (2004). Strong Federalism, constraints on the central government, and economic reform in Brazil. In E. L. Gibson (Ed.), *Federalism and democracy in Latin America* (pp. 85–130). Baltimore: The Johns Hopkins University Press.

Schmitter, P. C. (1974). Still the century of corporatism? *The Review of Politics, 36*(1), 85–131.

Sidicaro, R. (2003–2004). Les Transformations du Péronisme. *Problèmes d'Amérique Latine, 51,* 37–56.

Sigal, S. (2003–2004). Argentine 2003: La Sortie de l'Abîme? *Problèmes d'Amérique Latine, 51,* 9–36.

Silva, E. (2009). *Challenging neoliberalism in Latin America.* Cambridge: Cambridge University Press.

Stepan, A. (1985). State power in the Southern Cone of Latin America. In P. B. Evans, D. Rueschemeyer, & T. Skocpol (Eds.), *Bringing the state back in.* Cambridge: Cambridge University Press.

Tanaka, M. (2004–2005). Révolutionnaires, réformistes ou 'hommes politiques traditionnels'. Montée en puissance et effondrement de la gauche au Pérou. *Problèmes d'Amérique Latine, 55*, 65–88. http://eska-publishing.com/fr/1328-problemes-d-amerique-latine.

Tanaka, M., & Vera, S. (2010). In M. A. Cameron & J. P. Luna (Eds.), *Democracia en la Región Andina* (pp. 197–243). Lima: Instituto de Estudios Peruanos/Plural editores.

Théret, B. (2015). La diversidad de los federalismos en América Latina: Argentina, Brasil y México. In I. Bizberg (Coord.), *Las variedades del capitalismo en América Latina: los casos de México, Brasil, Argentina y Chile* (pp. 147–282). Mexico: El Colegio de México.

Tironi E., & Agüero, F. (1999). Chili: quel avenir pour le nouveau paysage politique? *Problèmes d'Amérique Latine, 35*, 65–77.

Torrico Terán, M. (2006). ¿Qué Ocurrió Realmente en Bolivia? *Perfiles Latinoamericanos, 28*, 231–261.

Vergara, A. (2011). United by discord, divided by consensus: national and sub-national articulation in Bolivia and Peru, 2000–2010. *Journal of Politics in Latin America, 3*(3), 65–93.

Zermeño, S. (2004). La participación ciudadana bajo los gobiernos perredistas del Distrito federal (1997–2003). In A. Ziccardi (Ed.), *Participación ciudadana y políticas sociales en el ámbito local* (pp. 145–166). México: IIS-UNAM.

CHAPTER 8

The Social Contract: The Wage Relation

We are going to use the concept of social contract in the sense of a social arrangement, a less totalizing conception than that of Rousseau, yet large enough to englobe economy, society, and politics. While Rousseau conceived the social contract as the foundation of any society in its relationship with the State, we refer to what the French regulation school calls "*compromis social*," which is more than a mere short-term arrangement, but less than Rousseau's foundational contract. *Compromis social* is an agreement that conveys an epoch, a social pact that expresses a type of capitalism, that includes how a certain society organizes production and distributes the wealth it produces. The social compromise emerges from a certain relation between the social sectors, the State, and what we have called the dominant social coalition. It therefore depends on the position that the State, the popular sectors and capital occupy in it. In addition, the State structure and the political system make it more or less difficult for the sectors that are not included in the coalition to exert pressure, defend their interests in order to be eventually included or break the existing coalition in order to create another one that benefits them more. Federalist and decentralized State structures, as well as the participative, socio-corporatist and movementist democracies, facilitate this possibility, while on the contrary more centralized State structures and closed political systems, such as empty democracies, particracies and State corporatisms are more impervious to social pressures.

I. Bizberg, *Diversity of Capitalisms in Latin America*,
https://doi.org/10.1007/978-3-319-95537-7_8

Fordism was a social contract that founded a type of capitalism that lasted since the end of the Second World War to the mid-1970s, and was based on the allocation of the gains of economic growth to the working population through collective negotiations and redistribution by the State. This pact was established between the workers, represented by trade unions, the employers, and the State, and included redistribution through direct wage increases and different social security benefits, pensions, health, paid vacations, etc. that, in many cases, the State was charged to distribute what we have called, following the regulation school, a wage relation.

The wage relation does not concern exclusively wages, as it includes "...the totality of the juridical and institutional conditions that determine the use of labor as well as the existence of the workers" (Boyer 2015). It thus comprises also indirect forms such as the regulations of the labor market and the social security system (health, pensions, unemployment benefits, etc.), and the conditions in which labor is negotiated in the labor market. The specificities of the wage relation are either negotiated directly between the unions and the employers or set by the intervention of the State. It is thus closely dependent on the strength and capacity of action of the labor movement and of the employer's organizations, and their cooperative or confrontational relation. On the other hand, in most Latin American countries the minimum salaries are fixed by the State or by a commission where the government has a strong role. The State is also responsible or co-responsive of the regulation of the labor market, and of the social security system.

The wage relation defines the characteristics of the mode of consumption that we discussed in Chapter 2, where we distinguished between two modes, a profit-led mode of consumption, that has as its result the decline of the proportion of the participation of wages in GDP, and a wage-led mode of consumption that results in an increase of the proportion of wages in GDP. Fordism was a wage-led mode of consumption based on the idea that increased demand would lead to an expansion of offer, through investment, productivity hikes, and innovation. Fordism was concretized through an increase of wages and the expansion of social security that allowed workers to save less for their future and be able to consume more in the present. This mode of consumption resulted in a significant incentive to increase the offer of the different agro-industrial and manufacturing products, as well as of all sorts of commercial and social services. Since the crisis of Fordism in the mid-1970s, under the pressure of national and international business and financial interests, and the advice of the main international organizations (FMI, WB, OECD), governments have been trying to impose a profit-led growth in most countries (Streeck 2014).

Because the Fordist mode of capitalism depended fundamentally on the scope of "salarization," i.e., the formalization of the workers, and as in Latin America this process never included the majority of the working population because the informal sector was, then as now, very large, Fordism in this continent was at best incomplete. While most countries in the continent attempted to implement a wage-led growth during the ISI period, and some of them, again during the commodities super cycle, other countries gave up the implementation of a redistributive social contract after the crisis of the 1980s. The crisis of the 1980s, the "lost decade," terminated the social pact implicit in the import substitution model that existed in many countries, between the State, the popular classes and the entrepreneurs. This pact, sometimes referred to as partial or limited Fordism, because it was limited to a sector of the country's population: the workers of the formal sector and the government functionaries, the national entrepreneurs and the State, was abandoned in Mexico, Chile, Colombia, and Peru. In other countries of the continent, the military regimes had already broken the pact before the 1980s: in Brazil since 1964, in Chile in 1973 and in Argentina in 1975. The democratization that ensued in most Latin American countries in the 1980s gave rise to different social compromises that depended on the force of the social organizations and their influence on the democratization process. The strength of these organizations in Brazil, Argentina (after the end of convertibility in 2000), Bolivia, and Ecuador defined an intent to reedit such a pact. The implementation or not of a wage-led model of consumption during the first decade of the years 2000, based on a redistributive social pact, depends, as we have seen in the last two chapters, on the force and organizing capacity of civil society and on the responsiveness of the political system, which depends on the openness of the party system and the decentering of the State.

Each social pact translates into a specific wage relation. In this chapter, we will analyze the contents of the redistributive social pact which some countries had contracted until the economic ad political reversal of the years 2013–14, leading to a wage-led growth on the basis of increasing wages and the expansion of the coverage of social protection, with decreasing rates of inequality and poverty. We will also analyze the liberal social contract which other countries have adopted, which has led to a profit-led growth, entailing lower salaries, the transition from a universal social security system to a focalized, assistance-oriented system, and to a stagnation of the rates of inequality and poverty.

We will now discuss how two different social contracts translate into distinct wage relations as determined by the institutions defined in Table 8.1.

8.1 Wages

Minimum wages are one of the principal components of the wage relation. It is a close indicator of the character of this relation because it has a direct impact on both active workers and pensioners. In Fig. 8.1, we can clearly see how, while in the liberal rentier type (Peru, Colombia, and Chile), minimum salaries have grown moderately, in the outsourcing type (Mexico), they have stagnated; in this latter country, the State represses salaries as they constitute the principal competitive advantage of the model; that is the reason why, as we will see below, the minimum salary is the lowest among the group of countries we are considering. In contrast, in both the socio-developmentalist (Brazil, Uruguay, and Argentina) and in the redistributive rentier types (Bolivia and Ecuador), minimum salaries have grown strongly.

The absolute data of minimum wages are also very instructive. In Fig. 8.2, we can see how, even in the midst of a crisis, Argentina, Uruguay, and Brazil have the highest minimum salaries. Ecuador and Bolivia have high minimum wages if we consider that they are much poorer countries than the other three, although one also has to take into consideration the existence of a very great proportion of informal workers that do not get paid that amount. Three countries stand out, the ones we have considered as liberal, Peru, Colombia and especially Mexico, with half the minimum salary of the first two. The high level of Chile is due to the fact that although it has been applying a liberal economic policy, the almost continuous economic growth in the last thirty years of this relatively small country dependent on mineral and agricultural exports, has allowed the more recent left-leaning governments to ease the pressure on salaries, just as it has done with the implementation of more generous social policies, as we will see below.

In order to better understand the wage relation, it is crucial to analyze the relation between minimum salaries and average salaries. If we look at Fig. 8.3 regarding this relationship, we can see that while in Argentina average salaries increased significantly, they did so less rapidly than minimum wages. In Uruguay, Brazil, and Bolivia average remunerations remained

Table 8.1 Wage relation

	International outsourcing	*Socio-developmentalist*	*Rentier/liberal*	*Rentier/redistributive*
Wage policy	Wage repression	Strong increase of minimum salaries	Increase in salaries according to productivity	Strong increase in minimum salaries
Labor market policy	Non-formalization	Strong formalization	Non-formalization (except Chile)	Some Formalization
Union density/civil society	Low	Neo-corporatism	Low	Strong social movements
Pensions	Low coverage of contributory and of social pensions	Increasing coverage of contributory and social pensions	Low coverage of contributory (except Chile) and of social pensions	Low coverage, increasing social pensions
Health system	Social security/public/private; strong segmentation/non coverage	Public/private (Brazil); plus social security (Uruguay, Argentina); high coverage	Social security/public/private; strong segmentation low (Peru) and high (Colombia and Chile) coverage	Low social security, high public, low coverage
Character of the social protection regime	Assistance	Uncertain tendency to universalization	Assistance	Tension between universalization and assistance
Inequality	No reduction	Strong reduction	Moderate reduction	Strong reduction
Poverty	Growth	Strong reduction	Moderate reduction	Strong reduction

Source Own elaboration

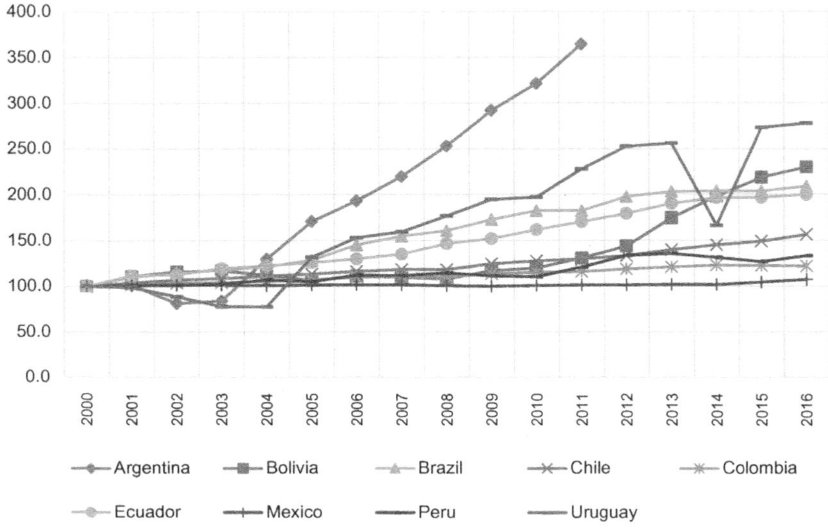

Fig. 8.1 Minimum wage index (*Source* Own elaboration based on CEPALSTAT)

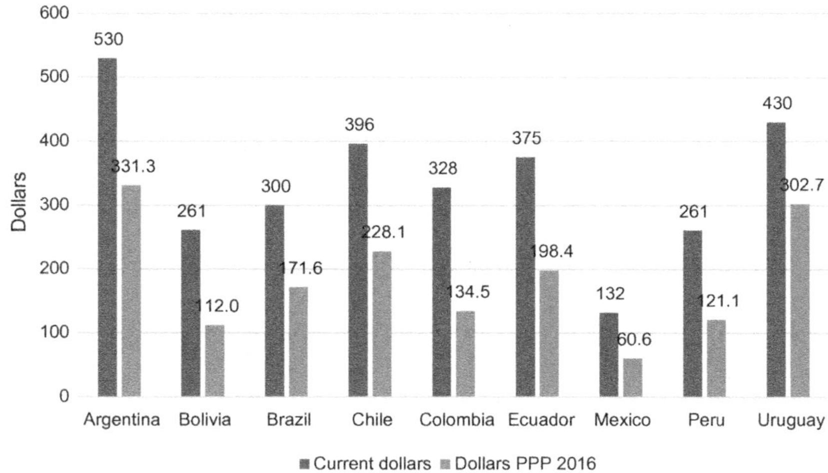

Fig. 8.2 Absolute minimum wages in Latin America, 2017 (*Source* Own elaboration based on CEPALSTAT)

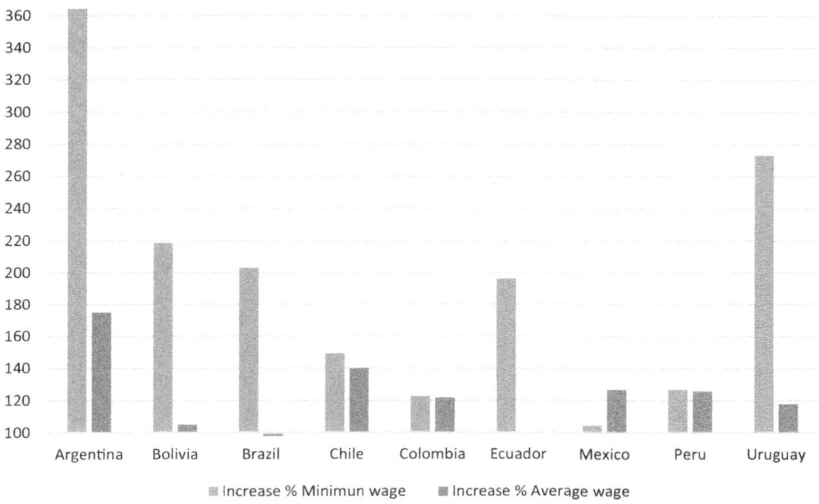

Fig. 8.3 Minimum and average salaries (2000–2015) (increase in percentage) (*Source* Own elaboration based on CEPALSTAT. Year 2000=100. Data of Argentina until the year 2010)

practically stagnant, while minimum wages increased considerably. As these latter fundamentally depend on a governmental decision in Latin America, one can infer that this situation is closely related to a deliberate governmental policy to reduce the gap between minimum and medium wages.

In the more liberal countries, the increase in average wages is very similar to that of minimum wages, a situation that is related to the fact that they both increase in relation to market forces. Finally, the case of Mexico is very telling, as average wages increase much faster than minimum wages, which is related to the fact that the first increase according to the pressure of the highest paying sectors, while minimum wages are kept depressed as a deliberate policy of the government to try keep the general wage relation of the economy at low levels.

8.2 Social Protection Systems

The social protection regimes are very complex systems that originate from multiple interrelations between the dimensions of familiar, economic, social and political life (Théret 2011). The regimes that exist in Latin America have evolved throughout most of the twentieth century and what has elapsed of the present one, and they may thus not correspond directly to the type of capitalism that exists in a specific country, although their tendency does have a relation with it. The specificities of the social protection system modify familiar life, as they involve not only financial resources but also care services for small children, the sick, the old; all of which have a significant impact on family life, as they determine whether all these are matters correspond to the individual families or if they are social/public responsibility. They define, in sum, a more or less familiaristic or public/social protection scheme.

In the second place, social protection systems are a fundamental means to assure social cohesion. While economic dynamics creates winners and losers, generates inequality, and tensions between different social sectors, social protection systems are a way to reduce these tensions, as Polanyi (1944) has taught us. The more extended, more universal, more generous, a social security system is, the more efficiently it assures social cohesion. Nonetheless, as Esping Andersen has written, how much is spent or even how extended a social security system, is part, but not the whole of the story. While a social security system may be very extended and cover the majority or all of the population, it may nevertheless divide society in very different social protection systems, reproduces inequality, like the corporatist systems of Germany and France. A system that is universal, but allocates a minimum to all the population, like the British one, although it reduces social tensions, it does not reduce inequality nor assures social cohesion. Finally, a system that only takes care of the poor, because it supposes that all the others can take care of themselves, like the one of the United States, and where, in addition, the poor have to accept their failure and have to admit (and actually prove) they are poor and accept aid as charity, does not fulfill the mission of easing social tensions, in fact it probably increases them (Esping-Andersen 1990).

The most fundamental meaning of social protection systems is, as Théret (1995) has written, the debt the State and society itself has toward its citizens, by having been born where they did; this debt implies that the risks they incur in (accidents, unemployment, disease, old age) have to be socialized and should not depend solely on the individual. Esping-Andersen's main principle is decommodification; according to this concept, none of the systems we have mentioned above de-commodify the life of the individual, because they continue to make him depend on his position in the labor market. The only system that does so is a universal, unified, generous and most probably totally public system. Some systems come close to this ideal type, others are very far from it.

The more universal and generous social security systems are both more decommodifying, in the sense of Esping-Andersen, and more fitting a conception of the social rights of citizens to be protected from the adversities of accidents, unemployment, health problems, and old age in the sense of Théret's life debt.

In addition, the social security system also serves a political function, that of legitimizing the State, a political regime, or even a specific political party. It may be used to favor one sector or the other in order to gain its allegiance. Legitimization may be both oriented toward a limited sector of the population, the most strategic in economic or political terms, as it was at the genesis of most (if not all) of the systems; for example the army, the police, the State functionaries, then the workers, in a typical corporatist scheme. It can be, as it is nowadays in most of Latin America, the poor, the majority of the population, something that has implied the dismantling of the previous corporatist scheme and addressing this majority in an assistance design, like the more liberal governments have done. Or, it may point to a more universalistic plan, intended to address the population in its totality, as the more redistributive governments have attempted, although they did not achieve this goal because they lacked the resources.

Finally, social policies have a direct and an indirect economic effect: spending in education, health, pensions, directly increases internal demand because people have to spend less in these services, need to save less for old age or health problems, and thus have more resources to spend. The extension of pensions, their increase, also allows people to spend more. When the government implements a more universal and more efficient health system, whether it be public, or a mixture of public and private, people need to save or spend less in case of a disease; health risks, as well as unemployment risks, are socialized (when unemployment insurance exists) and can thus commit more resources to consumption. The same can be said of governmental spending in education and housing. On the other hand, social spending (although not all of it) has a medium and long-term effect; social policy adds to human capital, especially when it concerns investment in health and education. In fact, one of the most significant differences between the way in which the countries in Latin America and those in Asia have tried to develop is the priority given to investment in health and education in the latter. Thus, social protection policies can have short-term impacts on demand through pensions, unemployment compensations, health investment and expenditure, and as has been shown by the example of the Asian countries, a medium and long-term impact on the economy, and on the possibility of a country to develop, through upgrading, technological change, and productivity growth.

During the "Fordist" epoch in Latin America, import substitution industrialization, the expansion of social protection oriented to the growing population that was being integrated to salaried work legitimized a fundamentally corporatist State. At the present time, assistance-oriented social policies, focalized on the poor, have been a way to legitimize governments that administer this population, by assigning them a minimum to survive in a system that generates ever-growing inequalities, informalization, and poverty (Lautier 2004). In this section, we will discuss how during the commodity boom, the States that we have characterized as socio-developmentalist, signaled themselves by attempting to unify the different subsystems of the social security system into a more coherent whole. These States were actively searching to formalize workers, increase minimum wages (even over the mean wages), boost social security expenditure to reach a more universal scheme, through the expansion of contributory or through non-contributory (social) pensions, or both. Finally, they tried to extend the extent of the health system, either by universalization or focalization. On the contrary, the more liberal States (both outsourcing and rentier), did not actively seek formalization, but rather accepted the existence of informality and poverty, implementing assistance policies (basically conditional monetary transfers) in order to reduce social pressures.

Figure 8.4 clearly shows that the proportion of public resources dedicated to social policies and health is very significant in the three countries (Argentina, Brazil, and Uruguay) we have catalogued as socio-developmentalist. The rest of the countries have all lagged well behind, even the rentier redistributive ones. The case of Argentina and Brazil are interesting because of the very significant growth of social expenditure in both. The cases of Peru and Mexico are, in contrast, two countries where this expenditure has progressed the least.

Unsurprisingly, public expenditure in the social protection system determines the proportion of the population that is protected by social security. A first approximation to this issue is the percentage of formal workers, who in principle are protected. In Fig. 8.5, we have the percentage of informal workers in each of our countries. We can see that there is a coincidence between public social expenditure and the countries that

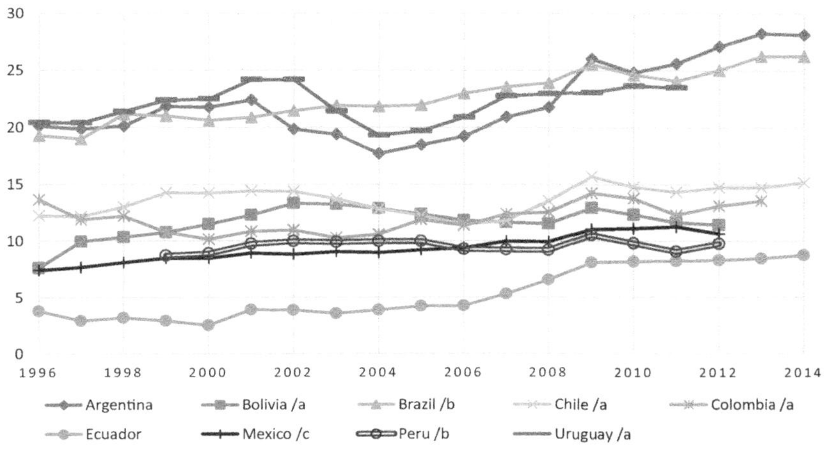

Fig. 8.4 Public social expenditure (1996–2014) (% GDP)

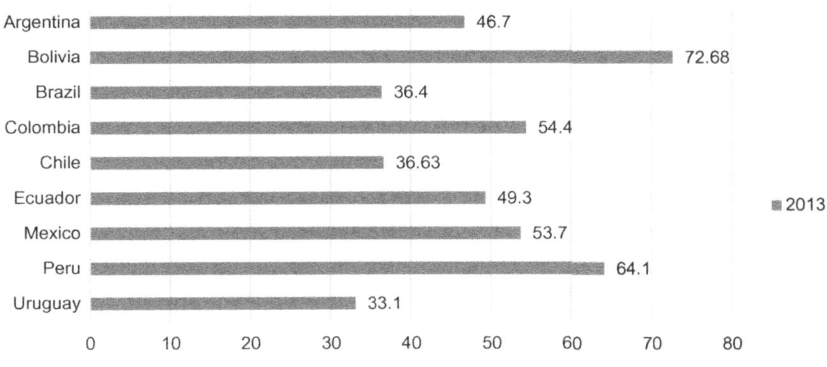

Fig. 8.5 Non-agricultural informal employment-2013 (population over 15 years) 2013 (percentages) (*Source* OIT [2014b: 33])

have the lowest level of informality; in the case of Brazil and Uruguay this relation is conclusive, while in the case of Argentina it is less so. The case of Chile stands out as the percentage of the informal population is lower than in the rest (except Brazil and Uruguay), however social expenditure is low. We can explain this by the fact that, although the leftist

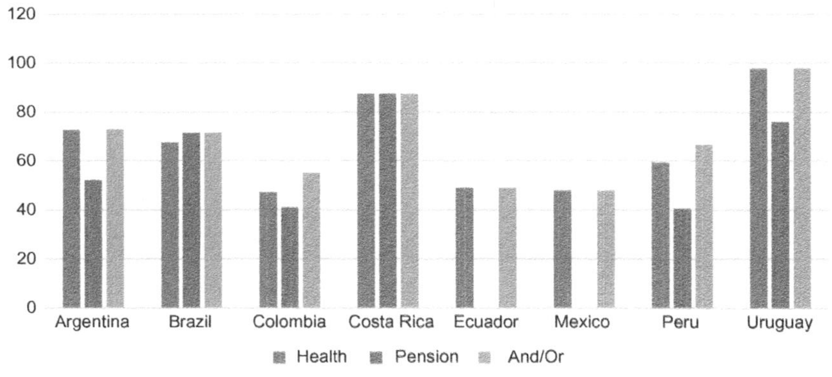

Fig. 8.6 Proportion of the population covered by health and/or pension system (2013) (*Source* Own elaboration on the basis of OIT [2014a])

governments of the *Concertation* (during the first decade of the years 2000) did not modify the liberal character of the economic model they inherited from the dictatorship, they have nonetheless tried to eliminate the more unjust aspects of it. A different explanation for this disparity between expenditure and coverage in the case of this country is that the requirements and benefits of coverage are more expanded, but actually lower than those in the rest of the countries (Bensusán 2016).

In fact, according to Maurizio (2014: 7), governmental policy aimed at the formalization of workers has been very successful in Argentina and Brazil, where it was reduced by around 10%, and to a lesser extent in Ecuador and Peru, where it was reduced by about 7%, between 2000 and 2009. In the case of Mexico, informality increased by about 2%. What in Argentina and Brazil had such an impact were tax incentives and stricter work inspection (Maurizio 2014; Berg 2011), as well as actions empowering labor unions.

A more direct indicator of the effect of social public expenditure is health and pension coverage. We see practically the same relation. Uruguay, Brazil, and Argentina have the highest level of protection (excepting Costa Rica, which is not being discussed in this book), while Colombia, Mexico, and Peru, all liberal countries, have a much lower scope, together with Ecuador (Fig. 8.6).[1]

[1] Unfortunately, the ILO publication does not have this kind of data for Bolivia.

8.3 Pensions

We will now analyze more in detail the different dimensions of the social protection system. For this purpose, it is helpful to remember, as Esping-Andersen (1990) has written, that the amount a country spends on welfare is not enough to understand its characteristics, it is necessary to know *how* these resources are used. Nor is it, in fact, sufficient to describe the level of coverage, it is crucial to analyze the type and characteristics of the benefits each system allots. Not all pension systems are the same, and coverage does not describe well the conditions of the individuals.

One of the main subsystems of the social protection system is pensions. If one looks at pension extension (Fig. 8.7), the countries with the highest proportion of their population receiving retirement benefits are Brazil, Argentina, and Uruguay, together with a liberal country, Chile. This latter case is interesting: it was one of the countries that had the most widespread protection before the military regime, before the "pay as you go system" was privatized and converted into a purely individual capitalization scheme, a system that drastically reduced benefits. So much

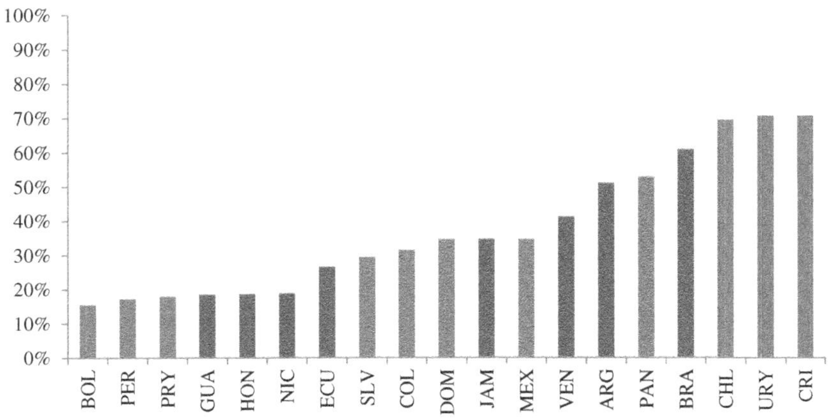

Fig. 8.7 Contributors or affiliates as a percentage of total workers (ages 15–64), around 2010 (*Source* Bosch, M., Melguizo, A., & Pagés, C. [2013]. *Better pensions, better jobs: Towards universal coverage in Latin America and the Caribbean.* Inter-American Development Bank, Washington, DC. Pensions at a Glance Latin American and the Carribean 2014—© OECD, 01-01-2014)

Table 8.2 Net pension replacement rates by earning

	Individual earnings, multiple of mean salaries for men (women, where different)			
	0.5	*1.0*	*2.0*	*3.0*
Argentina	104.6 (96.1)	90.6 (82.1)	89.6 (81.4)	83.3 (76.1)
Bolivia	36.4	41.7	36.0	33.9
Brazil	661.1 (55.7)	64.1 (58.4)	72.8 (66.4)	64.3 (58.7)
Chile	69.2 (58.3)	50.5 (39.6)	46.3 (31)	47.3 (31)
Colombia	102.7	73.8 (66.8)	75.3 (68.2)	75.8 (68.6)
Costa Rica	90.3	84.5	86.0	87.4
Ecuador	102.8	103.3	103.6	105.3
Mexico	58.0	31.2 (30.3)	32.1 (29.2)	32.4 (29.4)
Peru	88.3	81.1	40.6	28.5
Uruguay	67.7	65.9	75.2	86.2
LAC26	76.4 (74.9)	66.2 (64.4)	60.9 (58.6)	57.3 (55)

Source OCDE, BID, and WB (2015: 59). Modified by the author

so that the Lagos government (2000–2006) instituted a minimum salary pension for workers that did not arrive at this modicum level of replacement with capitalization. Thus, in this country there is a high coverage but a low replacement rate, especially for higher salaries, as we can notice in Table 8.2.

We have been able to see different ways in which the Latin American countries have tried to expand the scope of the pension system. In some countries, we have seen an intent to formalize a larger part of the population, even domestic employees (Brazil, Argentina, and Uruguay). In other countries, the trend has been to allocate an allowance to the entire population that is over a certain age, irrespective of whether they contributed to a pension scheme or not (Argentina with *Asignación Universal por Hijo*, Chile, Costa Rica, Bolivia, Mexico) (Cecchini et al. 2014: 34). Others have implemented focalized measures for certain strata of the population. For example, Brazil gives a pension to agricultural workers and the disabled.

The case of Mexico is basically the same as the one we have discussed regarding salaries. In terms of pensions, we can see that Mexico, although not in the lowest level in Latin America with respect to coverage, is much lower than the larger countries of the continent, and even some of the smallest ones, as Costa Rica and Panama. This is basically due to the large number of informal workers in this country. And it has to do with the fact that the economic model, international outsourcing, in such a large country as Mexico, that competes in the international economy based on low salaries and low labor costs, generates informality and poverty. The Mexican State tries to alleviate the social costs of informality and poverty through an ample assistance-oriented policy, through conditional cash transfers and a health system directly linked to it, that shields the minimum needs as we will see ahead, but that does not protect all the population.

The social protection system in Mexico was closely linked to the needs of the authoritarian PRI; it was the way in which the State exchanged benefits for control by the social organizations, in a corporatist scheme. Since the 1980s, this system is being dismantled, in part because the unions have been considerably weakened, and it has been evolving toward a more individualistic system for formal workers, on the one hand, and a more assistance-oriented system for the poor, on the other. One of the central pieces of this transformation was the "privatization" of the pension system. The transformation of this system into a copy of the Chilean one dates from 1995. The new system, based exclusively on individual capitalization, was initially applied to the private sector workers affiliated to the IMSS (about 80% of the total), and then extended to government employees (ISSSTE), as well as to workers in other sectors such as oil and electricity, the army, the navy and IMSS's own employees, in 2007, just as the problems of private pensions began to become evident in Chile. In this case, there is a small non-contributive, or social pension program, that includes 63% of the population aged 65 or more, that is geographically focalized to the poorer regions. This program has a very low impact on income, it represents a mere 5% per capita (Table 8.3), and, in addition, it leaves many poor urban inhabitants exposed (except in Mexico City, which has universal coverage) (OCDE, BID, and WB 2015: 33).

The contrast with the socio-developmentalist model is manifest. The Brazilian pension programs, including the non-contributory ones, as well as the universal health system, which in spite of its many faults and loopholes, are all still unique in Latin America; with the exception of Costa Rica and Uruguay. This country did almost no modifications to its pension system.[2]

[2] Although we do have to mention the fact that at time of writing this book, the government of Temer is trying to introduce important modifications to the pension system.

Brazil has the most universal pension system if one takes into consideration both the high percentage of formal workers with pension coverage (between 60 and 70%) and the expansion of non-contributive pensions that include rural workers (17.2%) and the disabled (33%), both of which contribute to reduce the percentage of older people in poverty (OCDE, BID, and WB 2015: 29). In this country, in 2007, 12.8 million rural workers got a minimum salary, and 2.7 million old or incapacitated individuals over 65 years obtain the BPC (*Benefício de Prestação Continuada*) (Lautier 2007: 60–62). In this manner, Brazil covers almost 100% of its population over 65 years, with a per capita benefit of 17% for Providencia Rural and 33%, for BPC; this latter benefit is the highest in the continent (Table 8.3).

In Argentina, major changes in the SNPS were undertaken during the presidency of Menem (1989–1999). In 1993, this government created a mixed pension system with two components: one for individual capitalization and another for intergenerational distribution (Papadoupulos 1999: 121). In 2008, the Fernandez de Kirchner government renationalized the pension funds, eliminating the segment of capitalization administered by the *Administradoras de Fondos de Jubilaciones* (AFJP), and re-unified the system under a State-controlled solidary regime (CEPAL 2010: 8–9). This measure was only partly a response to the

Table 8.3 Social/non-contributive pensions

Country	*Name*	*Age*	*Coverage pop over 65 (%)*	*Per capita income (%)*	*GDP per capita (%)*
Argentina	Pensiones asistenciales	70	1.8	25.0	1.7
Bolivia	Renta dignidad	60	91.0	12.6	2.4
Brazil	Previdencia Rural	65/55	86.0	17.2	5.0
	Benefício de prestação continuada	65	12.0	33.0	–
Chile	Pensión Básica Solidaria de Vejez	65	83.0	12.0	2.1
Colombia	PPSAM	57/52	44.0	4.3	1.0
Ecuador	Pensión para Adultos Mayores	65	56.0	7.7	1.8
Mexico	65 y más	65	63.0	5.0	0.6
Peru	Pensión 65	65	41.0	8.6	1.3
Uruguay	Pensiones no contributivas	70	7.0	22.0	3.3

Source Own elaboration on the basis of the data of Fig. 1.5, OCDE, BID, and WB (2015: 33)

global economic crisis, since it had been preceded by a 2005 reform that allowed early retirement (with reduced benefits) for the unemployed who could attest 30 years of service. In 2007, a new reform allowed all workers at retirement age to have a pension even if they had not defrayed the required 30 years of contributions. With these two reforms, the coverage of the population of aged people which had declined to around 10% in the previous decade, returned to 77% in 2007 (Huber and Stephens 2012: 187), which situates this country in the fifth place in terms of coverage of retirement benefits. In contrast, social pensions shield a very low proportion of the population. Finally, Uruguay, together with Costa Rica, has the highest level of affiliates in a pension system, around 70%, and correspondingly have a very low level of social pensions.

The contrast between the liberal rentier countries, such as Peru, Colombia, on the one hand, and Bolivia, a redistributive economy, is basically the proportion of the population protected by social pensions. Bolivia has a system that was implemented in 1996, that is based on capitalization and administered by private institutions (AFP) like Chile and Mexico. On the other hand, it has a huge informal worker population (70%) and thus a very low percentage of population shielded by formal pensions (15%). But it has a universal non-contributory pension, *Renta Dignidad*, that substituted Bonosol. While Bonosol allocated around 247 dollars annually to the population over 65 years old that did not have a pension, *Renta Dignidad* is universal and allocates approximately double that amount to the same population, and around 20% less to those that have a pension (Monterrey Arce 2013: 17). Although this amount may not seem much, one has to take into consideration that it nevertheless represents 1.9% of GDP of Bolivia, a much higher amount that most of the conditional cash transfers (CCT) of larger countries like *Prospera* in México, *Bolsa Familia* in Brazil, and even the CCT's existing in Bolivia like the *Bono Juancito Pinto* (0.3% of GDP), that are allocated to poor families in order to help them maintain children in school, or Bono Juana Azurduy, given to pregnant women to induce them to regular medical check-ups (0.2% of GDP) (Klein 2015: 373). *Renta Dignidad* is practically a universal pension as it covers 91% of the population over 65 years; it allocates a comparatively high 12.6% of the per capita income of this sector of the population (OCDE, BID, and WB 2015: 33). This is the reason why this country (together with Brazil, Uruguay, Chile, and Peru) has the highest divergence between the proportion of poor in the general population, and the proportion of old poor, meaning that they have a much lower old population in poverty (OCDE, BID, and WB 2015: 28).

Colombia has near 30% of its working population under a pension system, and Peru, like Bolivia, has the lowest proportion of protected workers, around 15%. In the case of non-contributive pensions, Colombia covers 44% of its old-aged population, while Peru shields 41%. In both Colombia and Peru, these pensions are focalized geographically, to the poorest regions of the country, and the benefit is a mere 4.3 and 8.6% per capita income, respectively; that is why the difference between the general poor and the old poor is much smaller than that existing in Brazil and Uruguay, and somewhat smaller than the one existing in Bolivia and Chile, where the aged are protected either by contributive or by social pensions (OCDE, BID, and WB 2015: 28).

In Chile, where the coverage of the social security system was the continent's most extensive until the coup d'état of Pinochet, a fierce dictatorship imposed the purest model of liberal orthodoxy. The reform of Chile's pension system (from a system of intergenerational solidarity managed by the State to a pure capitalization scheme managed by private banks) took place in 1981. With this transformation, the extension of the pension system was considerably reduced and sentenced many workers to a minimum income.

Nonetheless, this country has had three social-democratic presidents in the last 17 years, that while they have not abandoned the liberal character of the model, have tried to limit its most pernicious consequences. The Lagos government (2000–2006) instituted a minimum salary pension for workers whose pensions did not reach this level through capitalization. In 2008, there was another significant pension reform, realized by the *Concertación* government, that modified the system considerably. It implemented a triple pillar system: the compulsory individual capitalization, the Voluntary Pension Saving pillar and the solidarity pillar PBS. "In the first place, the reform introduced changes to the individual capitalization system, the Disability and Survivorship Insurance ceased to be the responsibility of the employee and became the responsibility of the employer. It also introduced the obligation to contribute for independent workers who declare income from remunerated activities as of 2015. In both scenarios, the contributors gain access to a set of health benefits—whether in the public system, the Fund National Health Service (FONASA) or through the *Instituciones de Salud Previsional* (ISAPRE). In the third and last place, the Solidarity

Pension System (PBS) replaces the old non-contributory pension programs, the Welfare Pension Program (PASIS) and the State Guarantee of Minimum Pension (GEPM), and increases the amounts delivered in pensions. It created the Basic Solidarity Pension (PBS) for people 65 and over with some disability that do not have another pension. Since July 2009, the amount of the pension is equivalent to 159.7 dollars per month and is adjusted based on the annual inflation rate, which guarantees income above the poverty threshold. In the beginning, this benefit was oriented to the poorest 40% of the population, but later it was expanded to 50% and projects to include 60% of the same group in July 2012. On the other hand, the reform also includes the Solidarity Pension Contribution (APS) for elderly people and for those with disabilities whose contributions are insufficient to reach the predetermined level known as Maximum Pension with Solidarity Contribution (PMAS). The State complements the pension until it reaches the value of the PMAS. In July 2009 the value of the PMAS was set at $255.5 per month and is expected to increase to $543, both amounts higher than the Basic Solidarity Pension." (Robles Farías 2013: 21–23). The *Pensión Básica Solidaria* (PBS) is a direct monthly transfer that shields 83% of the aged, those who, for various reasons,[3] have not been able to save enough in their capitalization scheme. This social pension benefits them with 12% of per capita income, which is considerable compared to other countries (OCDE, BID, and WB 2015: 33). Nonetheless, although this country has reached a high coverage as a result of these reforms, it has is a low replacement rate for higher salaries as can be seen in Table 8.2.

8.4 Health

To begin with, in Fig. 8.8 we can see how it is again the same countries, Argentina, Brazil, Uruguay, Chile, and Costa Rica that have the largest extension of health services. Nonetheless, in third place we have a new entrant, Colombia, which includes around 90% of the population. We will analyze this case below. In fact, this is an example of the intent of most (if not all) of the countries in the continent to expand health insurance in order to achieve universal coverage, in one way or another.

[3] Because they did not work enough years, had many years of not contributing because of unemployment, or had many years of low salaries, among others.

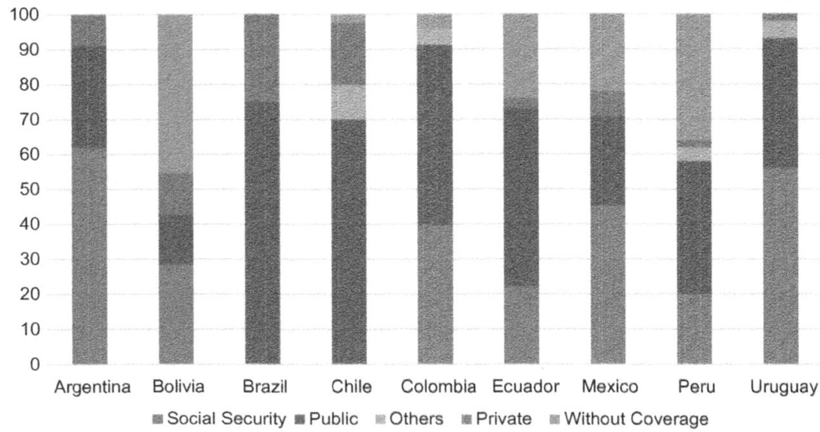

Fig. 8.8 Health coverage by subsystem (%) (*Source* Various country studies, *Salud Pública de México*, vol. 53, 2011. In the case of Colombia, the public sector is in reality a compulsory, subsidized, contributory system)

That is why it is essential to analyze ***how*** the different countries have achieved expanding health services and whether they have effectively accomplished their intention of actually and not just formally reaching universality.

And, in this respect, we find a number of crucial differences. Some countries have implemented a universal health system with the intention not only of including all the population, but of homogenizing access to it and comprising the totality of diseases and conditions, like the SUS in Brazil. An example of this fact is the free and general treatment for all patients of AIDS, which have extended their lives considerably. This has required a combination of negotiating prices with the pharmaceutical companies, as well as the increase of local production of the medications, which has resulted in a significant reduction of costs (Bernal and Barbosa 2015). Notwithstanding, while the Brazilian public system is universal and has had significant accomplishments, it does not assure efficient health services. This has resulted in the continuous growth of the proportion of the private sector, as we can see in Fig. 8.9.

After the reforms of the Chilean health system imposed by the Pinochet regime, where the private system was prioritized and the public one left

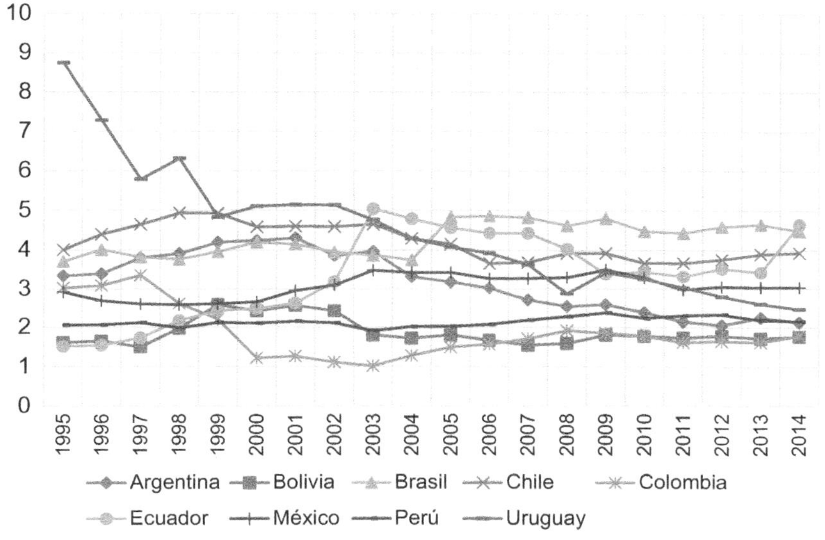

Fig. 8.9 Private health expenditure (% of GDP) (*Source* Own elaboration based on CEPALSTAT)

aside, the democratic governments, especially the socialist ones since the years 2000 (Lagos and Bachelet), have extended the public health sector and the government has compelled the private insurance health system to equate its guaranteed basket of basic illnesses with that of the public system; although the latter does not include all treatments (Becerril-Montekio 2011b; Cecchini et al. 2014). Thus, although in terms of the coverage and proportion of public and private health, the systems of Brazil and Chile have converged, the Brazilian SUS in principle covers all illnesses and medical acts. Both systems are characterized by a dual public/private health system, which insures almost the entire population (Fig. 8.10).

Other countries, like Uruguay and Argentina, where the majority of those that are insured are in a social security system, which is neither public nor private, but as in the case of Argentina administered by the unions, the *Obras Sociales*, have adopted procedures to extend health protection to the family members of the population that contributes to the social security subsystem and by expanding and improving the public service (Cecchini et al. 2014: 35). In this case, the health system is

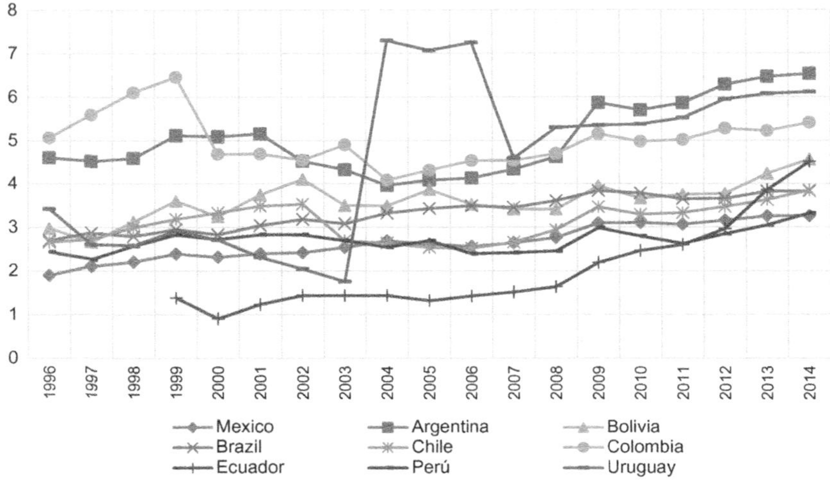

Fig. 8.10 Public health expenditure (% of GDP) (*Source* Own elaboration based on World Bank database)

segmented basically into a social security sector and a public one, the private one being much less significant.

Finally, all the other systems, both of the liberal as well as the rentier redistributive countries have simply extended the focalized policies they apply to administer poverty, in order to offer the non-shielded population minimum health services. In general, although this model has the intention of protecting all those who do not have health insurance, in reality (for different reasons, one of them that enrollment is not mandatory) it has left a great number of people without protection, as we can see in Fig. 8.8, for the cases of Perú, Bolivia, Ecuador, and Mexico. The only exception is Colombia, which has reached almost total inclusion with such a model. The main explanation is that it has made the incorporation to the social or to the contributory system compulsory, and that the government subsidizes the fees to be paid to enter the latter. In contrast, in Mexico, where incorporation to the *Seguro Popular* is voluntary and where individuals whose income is over the third decile have to pay a fee, the coverage is around 70%. Although the rentier redistributive countries (Bolivia and Ecuador) have intended to universalize health services, they have not achieved it, due to the enormous costs that it entails.

The universality of the Brazilian Health was inscribed in the 1988 Constitution, that resulted from a process of democratization that involved the unions and a very intense mobilization of civil society organizations and movements. The Constitution created a Unified Health System (*Sistema Único de Saúde*—SUS) that includes 75% of the population (Becerril-Montekio 2011a), that comprises all diseases (does not define a basket of them like the Mexican or the Chilean), in the model of the British NHS. The SUS rapidly expanded the access of health services for the general population: in 2003, 57% of all medical procedures were funded by the State through the SUS, 26% were funded by private insurance and 15% directly by the patient. In terms of hospitalization, SUS funded 68% of cases, while private plans did so for 24% (Lautier 2007: 56–57). It is worth noting that although the per capita amount of expenditure increased considerably in this country, as it did in Argentina and Chile, what increased most was not the public expenditure, but the private one, that reached 25% of the total. The reason for the expansion of the latter is related to the problems of the SUS, in terms of both quality and waiting time (Becerril-Montekio 2011a).

The growth of the proportion of the private health services led some authors, already during the 1990s, to consider that the system was in a process of "americanization," meaning the system that exists in the USA. Workers with stable purchasing power and the middle classes abandoned the SUS to buy private insurance, either individually (for the middle classes) or collectively, through collective contract negotiations between unions and companies in the largest enterprises (Vianna1997: 264–265). The new middle classes that developed with the process of redistribution during the commodity boom have also sided toward private health. A process that has, in turn, accelerated the deterioration of the quality of public health services and undermined its credibility, as the population that has the best salaries abandons it (ibid.: 265; Draibe 1997: 225–226).

Paradoxically, the other health system that reposes on public and private pillars is the Chilean, a country that had a totally contrasting social policy until the years 2000. The military government of Chile implemented radical changes to a health system that until the coup was a unitary system, the *Sistema Nacional de Salud*. On the one hand, the military decentralized health to the level of the municipalities, while on the other, it allowed for and, in fact, stimulated the creation of private insurance health schemes, which mainly cover the middle and upper classes (Draibe 1997: 224); the ISAPRES protect 17.5% of the population (Becerril-Montekio 2011b). Both of the systems receive allocations from the FONASA, a fund that collects the contributions of formal workers of both the private and the public sectors, as well as those that contribute independently.

Although the democratic governments embraced the economic model imposed by the dictatorship in order to ensure a smooth transition to democracy, since the arrival of a socialist president (Ricardo Lagos, 2000–2004) under the coalition that governed that country until 2010, the government has tried to eliminate the most blatant injustices of the social protection system; as we have already seen in the case of the pensions. The government of Lagos and the first one of Bachelet, have extended the coverage of the public health system and imposed on the ISAPRES the inclusion of several of the most common diseases (Mesa-Lago 2009: 13). In 2008, the Bachelet government implemented mandatory membership for all workers in a health system by 2016. It also imposed the Universal Access Plan for Explicit Guarantees (AUGE, in Spanish) that delineates definite guaranties concerning, both private and public health systems: (1) Both FONASA and the ISAPREs are obliged to treat a number of diseases and health conditions, starting with 40 in 2008 and increasing gradually to reach 80 at the end of 2017; (2) the health providers must be duly accredited by the Superintendence of Health and grant benefits according to predefined service protocols; (3) a guarantee defining the maximum term for granting the provision by a supplier accredited or registered by FONASA or an ISAPRE; (4) The amount paid by the affiliate must not exceed 20% of the total (Robles Farías 2013: 28).

Nonetheless, the system continues to be deeply segmented, 73% of the population is affiliated to the public FONASA and are attended by the public *Sistema Nacional de Servicios de Salud* (SNSS); they do not have the right to be attended at the private sector. On the other hand, while 16% have private insurance with the ISAPRES and go to private hospitals and clinics, another 10% have another type of insurance (the military, the police) (Robles Farías 2013: 30–31). Although these two subsystems shield the great majority of Chileans, there are significant disparities between them, in addition to the differences between regions due to the decentralization of the system. In fact, although the Lagos and Bachelet governments reformed the system, private firms provide health services to people who have the resources to pay for a private insurance, of working age, with good health and employed in risk-free sectors, while the rest is protected by the public scheme. In this manner, FONASA provides health services to the poorest, or to private sector "migrants" that lose their job or are so sick that they cannot afford the co-payments of the private sector, as well as those working in high-risk sectors (Gutierrez Arriola 2002: 65). If one divides affiliation by income, one can see that while in the poorest first and second quintile only 1.5 and 3.2% of the population is incorporated to the ISAPRES, in the fourth and fifth quintile the proportion is 16.7 and 44.2%, respectively (Robles Farías 2013: 31). An age disparity also exists, although it has been dimishing in the last years, 71% (in 2010 it was 85%) of those insured by private ISAPREs are aged between 15 and 59, and only 8% (3%) exceed 60 years. While in Fonasa, 63% (54%) of the insured are between 20 and 60 years old, and 17% (18%) are over 60 (Comisión Presidencial ISAPRES 2014: 55). In this way, the State is subsidiary of the private health sector, as the individuals who are not, or no longer are, profitable for the private insurers, either stay or migrate to the public health services.

So, although it is true that, up to a certain degree, one could equate the Brazilian system with the Chilean, due to the fact that in both the health system is divided between a public and a private pillar, there is practically no social security sector, the proportion of people sheltered by the public system and the private is similar, the public sector system is financed by taxes and contributions, and finally both encounter somewhat the same problems, that of the existence of a system for the "rich" and another for the "poor," with different levels of efficiency and quality, there are still very significant differences. The principal one deals with the philosophy of both systems, the Brazilian is universal, while the Chilean centers on the private initiative. The first trickles its population toward the private sector, in the second the public pillar is a residual one, although in the case of Chile it actually deals with the majority of the population. On the other hand, while the SUS incorporates all diseases and medical acts, the Chilean one is limited to a list, which at present considers 80 (Becerril-Montekio 2011a). Another crucial difference is that while the SUS does not charge co-payments and may send the patients to private hospitals or clinics, this is not the case for the Chilean public system, where patients have to pay between 10 and 20% in co-payments (excluding the poor and those over 60 years old) and can only receive treatment in public institutions. Finally, the SUS is a system under the surveillance of 5000 municipal health councils, where more than 100,000 citizens participate (ibid.). Although not all of them function as they should, many do so, assuring that services and decisions are overseen by civil society, something that neither the Mexican nor the Chilean system assures.

The main characteristic of the Uruguayan and Argentinean health systems is that in both the majoritarian scheme is the social security one, and that the private is much more limited. As can be seen from Fig. 8.9, while coverage is virtually universal in both countries, in contrast to Brazil and Chile, the majority (56% in Uruguay and 62% in Argentina) usually attend a very segmented contributory health service. On the other hand, the Uruguayan system is the only one in Latin America that could be considered equivalent to a social-democratic European, or Canadian one, because the State is the single payer and protects 95% of the population (Aran and Laca 2011). In fact, the Uruguayan FONASA is the single payer that concentrates both State taxes, employers and employees contributions. They are allotted both to the health services administered directly by the State (*Administración de Servicios de Salud del Estado*—ASSE), that takes care of 37% of the poorer population, and the *Instituciones de Asistencia Médica Colectiva* (IAMC) that are private non-profit organizations that offer an integral health attention to 56% of Uruguayans (Aran and Laca 2011: 269). The existence of a single payer that includes most of the health services mitigates the segmentation of the system, and results in the homogenization of the conditions of these services; something that is neither the case in more segmented systems, such as the Brazilian and the Argentinian, and of course the Chilean and the Mexican. We can see from the different Figures that Uruguay is in the first place of per capita health expenditure, that the part of the public health services is continuously increasing, and that both the private participation and out-of-pocket expenditure are decreasing. All of this is proof of a highly efficient, public/private (non-profit) health system, at least for Latin American standards (Figs. 8.11 and 8.12).

The Argentinian health system is more segmented than the Uruguayan, and can thus be considered as most similar to the corporatist European systems. The *Obras Sociales* are the social security health system administered by the different unions, financed with the contributions of the workers and the employers (8% of their wage), in

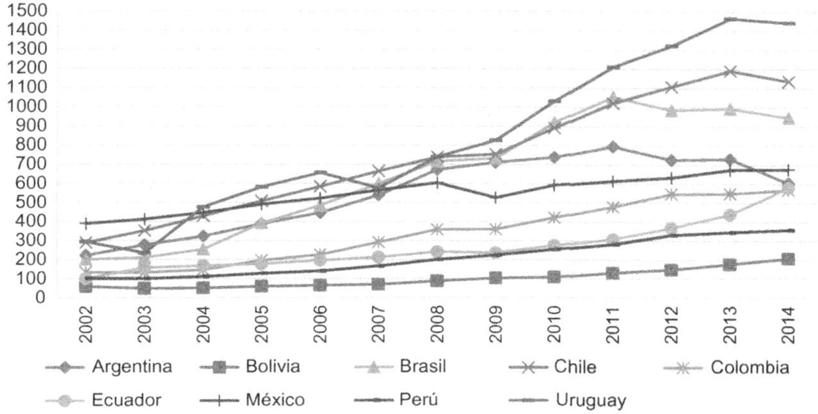

Fig. 8.11 Per capita health expenditure (present US dollars) (*Source* Own elaboration based on CEPALSTAT)

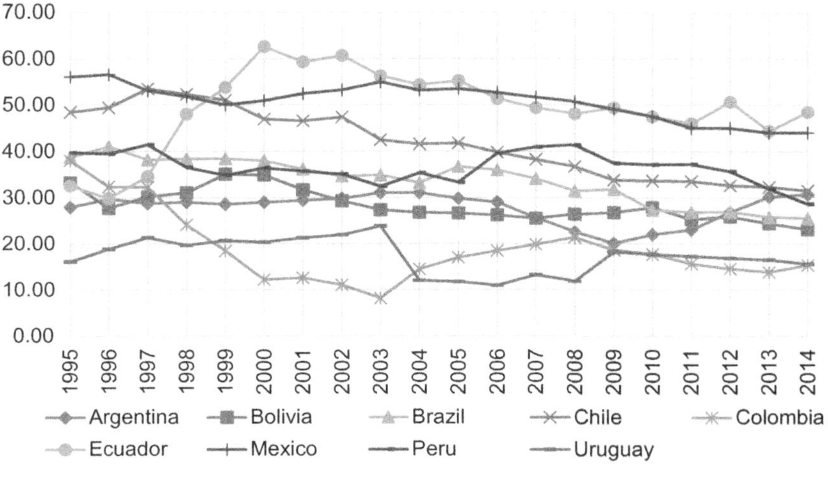

Fig. 8.12 Out-of-pocket health expenditure (% of total expenditure on health) (*Source* Own elaboration, based on CEPALSTAT)

total autonomy from the State; they account for 46% of the total. One should add the national contributory system (8%) and the provincial *Obras Sociales* (14%); which add up to 62% (Repetto and Potenza Dal Masetto 2011). The rest, 38%, is protected by the public hospitals or private insurance (Belló and Becerril-Montekio 2011). Argentina has a high level of per capita expenditure, although much lower than that of Uruguay and Chile. This probably reflects the fact that while the *Obras Sociales* are known to grant satisfactory health services (although there are signficant differences between them), the public sector is much less efficient. Another characteristic of this system is that it is basically public (both social security, that is the *Obras Sociales*, and the State). Private expenditure is one of the lowest in Latin America and although out of pocket expenditure has had ups and downs, it has stayed at around 30%.

The third manner of universalizing health care is through the expansion of the focalized health programs, as has been intended in Mexico, Peru, and Colombia. The model is the Mexican *Seguro Popular*, implemented by Julio Frenk, a well-known social health specialist who was health minister of president Fox (2000–2006). In this case, the model was not the Chilean, as privatization could not be conceivable in the Mexican case due to the low percentage of people who were protected by the social security system. The system tried to alleviate two of the most important problems of the Mexican health system, its low coverage (around 50% of the population) and the impressive out-of-pocket expenses, more than 50% of total health expenditure.

The Mexican government decentralized health services in 1995 and allowed the voluntary incorporation of uninsured workers and families, upon payment of a fee that varied on income, to the national social security/contributory system of the private sector workers: the IMSS. Because voluntary adhesion was unsuccessful, the Fox government launched the *Seguro Popular* program in 2003, another equally voluntary program based on a limited package of medical services offered by the public hospitals. Those who earn less than three minimum wages would be affiliated for free, while those who earn more would be charged a relatively small fee. Although in principle, the insured could go to any health center, even to a private one, in practice they only have access to the hospitals and clinics of the federated states health ministries.

While this program aimed to extend health coverage universally and the government declares that it has done so, it has not accomplished to attract the totality of the informal workers who would have to contribute to join; in fact according to the OECD, the *Seguro Popular* has increased health shielding to around 80% of the population. Nonetheless, public spending and infrastructure have not grown in the same proportion as we can see in Figs. 8.9, 8.10 and 8.11 (and in Bizberg and Martin

2012). On the other hand, the percentage of health expenditure that has to be paid by the patients themselves has been marginally reduced; it is still the highest in the group of countries we are dealing with, except Ecuador; in contrast, in Brazil out of pocket expenditure has fallen to around 26% (See Fig. 8.12 and Becerril-Montekio 2011a).

The health expansion of Peru and Colombia responds to the same logic, with similar results in the case of Peru, where 36% of the population does not achieve in getting protection, while we will see that Colombia is a "success story" of this type of strategy. The reason why a high percentage of Peruvians have no protection is that the subsidiary system of affiliation to what is called the *Sistema Integral de Salud* is voluntary, just as in Mexico. On the other hand, although in principle all Peruvians have the right to be attended in the public health services offered by the Ministry of Health (MINSA), the fact that this services are offered in exchange of a recovery fee that "…is variable, liable to the discretionality of the organizations…" in a great impediment (Alcalde-Rabanal et al. 2011: 274). Finally, low public health expenditure means that public services are totally insufficient; as witnessed by the low per capita expenditure and high out-of-pocket expenditure. In these conditions, people prefer to go to a private clinic or doctor, rather than wait and lose a day's work. In most countries in Latin America, there exist pharmacies where there is a doctor allowed to prescribe a medicament or a treatment, most of the times consulting very cheaply or freely, when the drugs are bought in the same dispensary.

The only country that has effectively reached universality with a third health pillar, oriented to the poor, most of whom are already incorporated to an assistance program, is Colombia. It did so through a public subsystem that is identical to the Mexican *Seguro Popular*, but that owns its success to two measures: that it has made incorporation compulsory; the 1990 *Sistema General de la Seguridad Social en Salud*, called law 100, established the universal compulsory affiliation to the *Entidades Promotoras de Salud* (EPS) that administer the contributions and offer a *Plan Obligatorio de Salud* (POS) through the *Instituciones prestadores de Servicios de Salud* (IPS). In order to implement this obligation, government allocates subsidies that complement to the contributions of that individuals that have to pay due to their level of income. In this manner, almost 100% of the Colombians are shielded through 968 public and 4565 private health institutes (Bernal and Barbosa 2015: 434). In this manner, the scheme has been converted into a sole payer system.

The State concentrates the contributions of the individuals, the enterprises, and the State (12.5% of the income of the workers) in the *Fondo de Solidaridad y Garantía*; 42.8% of the total corresponding to the contributive regime (*Régimen Contributivo*) and 48.5% to the Subsidized Regime (*Régimen Subsidiado*) (Guerrero et al. 2011: 150); they exclude 4.9% of the population which has its own special services: the teachers, the army, the police, the public universities and the petrol workers. From 1993 to 2008, these contributions gave the right to a Compulsory Health Plan that excluded some services, which differed according on whether they belonged to the subsidized or to the contributory regime (the latter was ampler). Since 2008 the law was modified to homogenize both services and disallow the different EPS of each system to deny health assistance to anybody in the system. Nonetheless, there are still health acts that are excluded and the system charges co-payments and moderator tickets from patients (Bernal and Barbosa 2015: 435). More importantly, the EPS of the subsidiary regime and those of the contributory one, are channelled to different health centers and hospitals, the first ones are public and send their patients to public health providers, while the second ones send their patients to private providers; this, although the law obliges the private EPS to seek at least 60% of public providers. There are also significant differences between what each EPS includes, although there is a minimum defined by the *Plan Obligatorio de Salud* (Bernal and Barbosa 2015; Guerrero et al. 2011). Nonetheless, although Colombia has a segmented system and per capita expenditure is at the average, one has to highlight that it has reached universalization and a public expenditure that is near to the highest, that of Argentina and Uruguay, and its private health expenditure and the out-of-pocket expenditure are among the lowest.

Bolivia and Ecuador have both pretended to universalize health care by way of a public sector, destined to become a sole system like the Brazilian SUS or the Costa Rican system that has been in place since the 1970s (Huber and Stephens 2012: 233), although their actual systems are very similar to the ones of Mexico and Peru. In both Bolivia and Ecuador, there exists a social security system which concentrates the best paid workers and a small private sector which shields the middle and higher classes Even though in these two countries the public sector has tried to incorporate all who lack health coverage, they have not succeed for lack of resources.

The case of Bolivia is interesting because the country's Constitution mandates to include all of the Bolivian population by way of the Ministry of Health and Sports, and that it has had, since 2003, a redistributive social policy that has expanded its public system considerably; the public expenditure has been increasing continuously. In fact, it has been growing since the mid-1990s and has surpassed, in proportion to GDP, the expenditure of Peru, Mexico, Chile, and even Brazil. Social security consists of eight health and two mixed funds, that include formal workers and their families (Ledo and Soria 2011: 112). There also exists a voluntary social security system to which independent workers may affiliate but, like in the case of Mexico or Peru, and as we will see also in Ecuador, voluntary affiliation leaves many outside. The present public health insurance originated in the expansion of the *Seguro Universal Materno Infantil* (SUMI) implemented in 2003, destined to include all children under 5 years of age and all women in reproductive age; around 41% of the population (Ledo and Soria 2011: 112). It includes 547 services, but excludes some of the most expensive ones. Nonetheless, the available data for 2009 assert that 45% of Bolivians do not have health insurance and depend on traditional medicine; moreover being the poorest country of our sample, the per capita expenditure and the private expenditure are the lowest. On the other hand, the government of Evo Morales has focused on awarding universal social pensions, something that benefits all Bolivians and is quite costly, around 1.9 of GDP (Klein 2015: 373), a program that is easier to achieve, as well as electorally more efficient.

Finally, Ecuador's is not too different from the case of Bolivia. It was also governed by a left party for 10 years, although, as we saw in Chapter 6, the political system has a much weaker connection with civil society. Since the reform of the Constitution of 1998, health is considered a constitutional right. In 2006, a universal health program, the *Programa de Aseguramiento Universal en Salud*, was created. Nevertheless, universality was not achieved, although the Ecuadorian State has been more successful than the Bolivian in including a larger percentage of its citizens in the public health system, as it covers around half of the population. Nonetheless, it still leaves out at least[4] 24% of the Ecuadorians without protection. This although the Ecuadorian government pledged universal coverage and although funding for social programs increased significantly since 2007 after Correa increased taxes on foreign oil companies. (Conaghan 2008: 209, cited by Kennemore and Weeks 2011) it spends

[4]We say at least, because although in all these countries formal coverage may be high, real coverage, that is access to prompt, efficient, and comprehensive services may not be available.

per capita as much as Chile and Mexico, overpassing Peru and Bolivia. In fact, what has increased most in this country is private health expenditure, and especially out-of-pocket spending. In any case, like in all the other countries of the continent, there exists a social security service that offers much better services, as it has access to the resources of the contributions of the formal workers; in Ecuador, social security protects around 22% of the population.

If we lastly analyze how the health system looks in terms of number of doctors, nurses, beds, etc., we can see the way in which Argentina and Brazil, the two socio-developmentalist countries, and Ecuador have seen the greatest advancements. Although we have observed significant improvements of the Chilean health system, with respect to doctors and beds, it has lagged behind the countries it resembles more such as Argentina, Uruguay, and even Brazil (Table 8.4).

8.5 Assistance

As we have already discussed, according to Esping-Andersen and Théret, universal measures, defined on the basis of citizenship, can be considered as a way of decommodification of the life of the people and a debt that the State is obliged to pay its citizens; they are thus less a concession of the State than a citizen right. From these perspectives, conditional cash transfers, as well as any other focalized assistance, are the zero degree of social protection, a residual concession of the State, allocated under the obligation of proving that the individual is really poor, sick, unemployed, etc. In fact, these kinds of systems are the opposite of a debt of the State versus its citizens, they are the modern derivative of the oppressive poor laws implemented during the liberal epoch in England and other countries that considered being poor as a crime or an individual liability, rather than as a fault of society versus its members (Polanyi 1944).

In Latin America, all countries have adopted focalized assistance protection, monetary transfers. Nonetheless, while in some these are promoted as an absolute substitute to any other kind of social security, and become the center around which all other measures depend, in some of them, they are conceived as complementary to a universal type of social security system. Mexico is a paradigm of the first tendency, that the liberal rentier countries follow, while Brazil, and Uruguay have been paradigms of the second one. In Mexico, since the mid-1990s the social protection system has decidedly shifted from a system that reposes on the

Table 8.4 Doctors (D) per 1000 inhabitants and Beds (B) per 10,000 inhabitants

Country	*Argentina*		*Bolivia*		*Brazil*		*Chile*		*Colombia*		*Ecuador*		*Mexico*		*Peru*		*Uruguay*	
	D	B	D	B	D	B	D	B	D	B	D	B	D	B	D	B	D	B
1990	2.6	n.d.	n.d.	n.d.	1.1	n.d.	1.0	n.d.	1.0	n.d.	1.0	n.d.	n.d.	n.d.	n.d.	n.d.	n.d.	n.d.
1995	3.0	n.d.	n.d.	n.d.	1.2	n.d.	n.d.	n.d.	1.2	n.d.	1.3	n.d.	n.d.	n.d.	n.d.	n.d.	n.d.	n.d.
2000	3.2	41	1.2	n.d.	1.1	n.d.	0.9	n.d.	1.4	n.d.	1.5	n.d.	1.9	n.d.	1.2	n.d.	3.7	n.d.
2005	3.2	n.d.	0.3	n.d.	1.7	24	1.0	n.d.	1.5	n.d.	n.d.	15	n.d.	16	n.d.	n.d.	n.d.	n.d.
2010	3.8	45	0.4	11	1.8	24	1.0	20	1.6	14	2.1	16	2.1	17	1.1	15	3.9	30
2014	n.d.	50	n.d.	11	n.d.	22	n.d.	22	n.d.	15	n.d.	15	n.d.	16	n.d.	16	n.d.	28

Source Own elaboration based on CEPALSTAT

right to social protection to an assistance model of last resort, where the State is only responsible for those who fail to integrate the labor market. The main Mexican social program *Prospera* focalizes on the poor, and while this system is expanding, for example by creating a health insurance *Seguro Popular* as its complement, the existing contributory health and pension subsystems have either been privatized or are threatened. While income-based programs played only a marginal role in the ISI period because assistance to the poor was residual, as exclusion was seen as a temporary phenomenon that economic growth would solve, nowadays with the growth of the poor they have become a sector to be administered and taken advantage of as a political support through clientelism (Lautier 2004).

In the Mexican case, Prospera is a program based on direct cash transfers to a selection of households living in extreme poverty. The stated goal is to help the poor overcome some of their present deprivations and to avoid the reproduction of poverty in the medium term by increasing human capital of their descendants (Valencia Lomelí 2008). Assistance is received directly by the mother, who has the obligation to regularly take her children to school and to the health centers. It is perfectly clear that these programs cannot be considered as a right, but that they are part of a government policy based on a sophisticated focalization mechanism (ibid.) Compared to resources oriented toward the corporatist sectors, around 5% of GDP, assistance-oriented resources are very low, less than 1%. Yet, they have a huge impact as they impact more than 6 million families, around 25 million people, 20% of the total population (Valencia Lomelí et al. 2013). Notwithstanding, a significant part of the poor population is excluded: single men, families without children and who live in places where there are no schools or health centers (Lautier 2007: 65).

Chile was, until the Lagos presidency at the beginning of the years 2000, also a good example of the shift toward assistance. On the one hand, the privatization of the pension funds and the creation of the ISAPRES were two central actions to dismantle the previous contributory and right based scheme. Although it is clear that Chile has maintained its liberal character, in which economic rationality prevails over the social, which justifies Cecchini et al. (2014) to consider its social protection system as a productivist type, nevertheless it has certainly corrected some of the most unfair elements of the social reforms of the dictatorship (Riesco 2009). The democratic governments have extended protection to sectors of society beyond those in extreme poverty: such as poor women, the young, indigenous population, the elderly and the disabled (Papadopoulus 1999: 115–116). They also created the *Fondo de Solidaridad e Inversión Social*, which fights poverty through the active and direct participation of beneficiaries and is not only with focused monetary resources. In the 2008, the reform of the Bachelet government created a non-contributory universal pension for the poor and for the elderly (Mesa-Lago 2009). It has also flexibilized the access of the old to contributory pensions (Mesa-Lago 2009: 15–16). In addition, the government extended unemployment insurance to include those workers without a permanent contract. It also implemented an exceptional measure, even for the more advanced economies, fiscal exemptions for companies that maintain and qualify their workers (CEPAL 2010: 17).

In contrast, although assistance programs in Brazil are important, especially *Bolsa Familia*, they are not central, but rather complementary to the more universal ones. In fact, although Brazil has adopted assistance programs similar to those applied in other Latin American countries, it has not followed the paradigm of substitution of contributory or public social policy by assistantship (Draibe 1997: 229–234). Brazil spends three times as much money in social pensions as in *Bolsa Familia*, a program that favors basically children (OCDE, BID, and WB 2015: 29). On the other hand, Bolsa Familia is not a conditional transfer, as it does not depend on the families having children or not (as is the case of Prospera in Mexico, and all the other similar systems in the continent), but it is a universal allocation for the poor (Cecchini et al. 2014: 35).

From the time the PT arrived at power in 2003, there was a significant increase of the income of the poorest categories protected by these programs: a doubling of pensions for rural workers, the creation of scholarships for children and the program "zero hunger." These programs are in general more universal and unconditional than those in other countries: funds are not allocated according to poverty rates as elsewhere and are not tied to requirements, a way of excluding many poor people (Valladares 1999: 62–67). During Lula's second term, all assistance programs were brought together in Bolsa Familia, which expanded inclusion and resources, reaching nearly 50 million people in 2009 (Dowbor 2009: 194). In addition, pensions for rural workers have been expanded since 1991; now 12.8 million people receive a minimum wage without having contributed previously.

In Argentina, there is a before and an after the 2001–2002 crisis, a moment that marks a 180-degree turn in virtually every aspect of the country's social and economic policies (Bensusán 2010; Palomino and Trajtemberg 2006; Alonso and Di Costa 2011).[5] Néstor Kirchner's government espoused the principles of the *Trabajar* program, that was created in the mid-1990s in response to the *piquetero* movement that demanded employment, the right to work, and not just assistance. His government adopted the "Labor Emergency Program" that consisted in temporary jobs focused on community work such as the construction or the repair of roads, clinics, schools, etc., instead of just being a program of monetary distribution without financial or labor contributions (Weitz-Shapiro 2006). The program *Jefes y Jefas de Hogar Desocupados* also had as its main idea a fight against poverty through temporary jobs. In exchange for an allowance, the beneficiaries had the obligation to participate either in community tasks, such as the construction or maintenance of the infrastructure, social services (defined by NGOs, religious organizations, or by local governments), their requalification or continuation of their formal studies, or finally the launching of microenterprises (Kostzer 2008). The big difference between assistance and these programs is the sense of dignity that they provide the beneficiaries and the prevention of the degradation of human capital from long-term unemployment by insertion into work (Kostzer 2008). Many of these programs were gradually placed under direct control of the *piquetero* movements, which in part meant their use as a means of clientelist control (Franceschelli and Ronconi 2005: 15).

In this manner, the case of Brazil and Argentina (after 2003 and until 2013), contrasts sharply with the two liberal ones. In the first place, Brazil was the only country that did not see a decline in health and education spending during the crisis of the 1980s (Lautier 2007: 53). On the other hand, this country did not abandon the "pay as you go" pension system or even implement a hybrid model. Not only did civil society play a major role in the drafting of the 1988 Constitution, which established a universal system of social protection as a right, but the PT in opposition resisted all intents to modify the system, and once in government intended to implement a more universal system through its public actions. On the other hand, unlike other Latin American countries, where former officials of institutions linked to the SNPS in place were driven out, in Brazil they remained in the social ministries. This

[5] The present Macri government is again giving a 180-degree turn in the other direction.

group of experts had strong support from the main trade union organization (CUT) and the Workers Party (PT) (De Melo 1997: 295–296). Although some studies on the evolution of the Brazilian social protection system speak of a "deconstruction" of the main objectives of the 1988 Constitution (De Melo 1997: 295–296), there has been some unmistakable progress toward universalization. Nonetheless, the situation has radically changed since the impeachment of Dilma in Brazil and the arrival of Macri to the presidency of Argentina. It is even more threatened by the arrival of Bolsonaro to the presidency of Brazil. We might be seeing, in the near future, in both countries, a total reversal of the situation we have been describing regarding social policies, and in the case of Brazil even in other aspects of the economic, social, political, and even cultural life. This menace may be stopped by the remobilization of civil society, as has been the case in the past in these countries.

References

Alcalde-Rabanal, J., Lazo-González, O., & Nigenda, G. (2011). Sistema de salud de Perú. *Revista Salud Pública de México, 53*(2), 243–254.

Alonso, G., & Di Costa, V. (2011). Cambios y continuidades en la política social argentina, 2003–2010. In M. Uribe Gómez (Coord.), *Los vaivenes de las políticas sociales en Argentina, Colombia, Chile, México y Uruguay*. México: Miguel Ángel Porrúa.

Aran, D., & Laca, H. (2011). Sistema de salud de Uruguay. *Revista Salud Pública de México, 53*(2), 265–274.

Becerril-Montekio, V. (2011a). Sistema de salud de Brasil. *Salud Pública de México, 53*(2), 120–131.

Becerril-Montekio, V. (2011b). Sistema de salud de Chile. *Revista Salud Pública de México, 53*(2), 132–143.

Belló, M., & Becerril-Montekio, V. (2011). Sistema de Salud de Argentina. *Revista Salud Pública de México, 53*(2), 96–108.

Bensusán, G. (2010, July 2). Políticas laborales en América Latina: orientaciones, alcances y resultados. *Ponencia presentada en CEISAL*, Toulouse.

Bensusán, G. (2016). Organizing workers in Argentina, Brazil, Chile and Mexico: The authoritarian-corporatist legacy and old institutional designs in a new context. *Theoretical Inquiries in Law, 17*(1), 131–161.

Berg, J. (2011). Laws or luck? Understanding rising formality in Brazil in the 2000s. In S. Lee & D. McCann (Eds.), *Regulating for decent work: New directions in labour market regulations*. Geneva and Basingstoke: ILO and Palgrave Macmillan.

Bernal, O., & Barbosa, S. (2015). La nueva reforma a la salud en Colombia: el derecho, el aseguramiento y el sistema de salud. *Revista Salud Pública de México, 57*(5), 433–440.

Bizberg, I., & Martin, S. (2012). *El Estado de Bienestar ante la Globalización, el caso de Norteamérica*. México: El Colegio de México.

Boyer, R. (2015). *Économie politique des capitalismes.Théorie de la régulation et des crises*. Paris: La Découverte.

Cecchini, S., Filgueira, F., & Robles, C. (2014). *Sistemas de protección social en América Latina y el Caribe. Una perspectiva comparada*. Santiago de Chile: CEPAL.

CEPAL. (2010). *La reacción de los gobiernos de las Américas frente a la crisis internacional: una presentación sintética de las medidas de política anunciadas hasta el 31 de diciembre de 2009*. United Nations: Santiago de Chile.

Comisión Presidencial ISAPRES. (2014). *Informe Final*. Santiago de Chile: Comisión Asesora Presidencial para el Estudio y Propuesta de un Nuevo Régimen Jurídico para el Sistema de Salud Privado.

Conaghan, C. M. (2008). Ecuador: Correa's plebiscitary presidency. In L. Diamond, M. F. Platner, & D. A. Brun (Eds.), *Latin America's struggle for democracy* (pp. 199–213). Baltimore: The John Hopkins University Press.

De Melo, M. A. (1997). As reformas constitucionais e a previdência social 1993–1996. In E. Diniz & S. de Azevedo (Eds.), *Reforma do estado e democracia no Brasil*. Brasília: Editora Universidade de Brasília.

Dowbor, L. (2009). La crisis no es solo económica. Reflexiones globales y algunos apuntes sobre Brasil. *Nueva Sociedad, 224*, 179–200.

Draibe, S. M. (1997). A política social na américa latina: o que ensinam as experiências recentes de reformas? In E. Diniz & S. de Azevedo (Eds.), *Reforma do Estado e Democracia no Brasil*. Brasilia: UnBenap.

Esping-Andersen, G. (1990). *The three worlds of welfare capitalism*. Princeton, NJ: Princeton University Press.

Franceschelli, I., & Ronconi, L. (2005). *Clientelism, workfare and the emergence of the piqueteros in Argentina*. LACEA Conference. http://depot.gdnet.org/gdnshare/pdf2/gdn_library/annual_conferences/seventh_annual_conference/Franceschelli_Parallel_1_4.pdf. Accessed 15 May 2018.

Guerrero, R., Gallegos, A. I., Becerril-Montekio, V., & Vásquez, J. (2011). Sistema de Salud de Colombia. *Revista Salud Pública de México, 53*(2), 144–155.

Gutierrez Arriola, A. (2002). *México dentro de las refromas a los sistemas de salud y seguridad social en América latina*. México: Siglo XXI.

Huber, E., & Stephens, J. D. (2012). *Democracy and the left*. Chicago and London: The University of Chicago Press.

Kennemore, A., & Weeks, G. (2011). Twenty-first century socialism? The elusive search for a post-neoliberal development model in Bolivia and Ecuador. *Bulletin of Latin American Research, 30*(3), 267–281.

Klein, H. S. (2015). *Historia Mínima de Bolivia*. México: El Colegio de México.

Kostzer, D. (2008). *Argentina: A case study on the plan Jefes y Jefas de Hogar Desocupados, or the employment road to economic recovery* (Working Paper No. 534). Annandale-on-Hudson, NY: The Levy Economics Institute of Bard College.

Lautier, B. (2004). Las políticas sociales en México y Brasil: seguridad social, asistencia, ausencia. In C. Alba & I. Bizberg (Eds.), *Democracia y Globalización en México y Brasil*. México: Colegio de México.

Lautier, B. (2007). Les politiques sociales au Brésil durant le goouvernment de Lula: aumône d'Etat ou droits sociaux? *Problèmes d'Amérique latine, 63*, 51–76.

Ledo, C., & Soria, R. (2011). Sistema de Salud de Bolivia. *Revista Salud Pública de México, 53*(2), 109–119.

Maurizio, R. (2014). *Labour formalization and declining inequality in Argentina and Brazil in the 2000s: A dynamic approach* (ILO Research Paper No. 9). Geneva: ILO.

Mesa-Lago, C. (2009). *Efectos de la crisis global sobre la seguridad social de salud y pensiones en América Latina y el Caribe y recomendaciones de políticas. Serie Políticas Sociales*. Santiago de Chile: CEPAL.

Monterrey Arce, J. (2013). *Sistemas de protección social en América Latina y el Caribe: Estado Plurinacional de Bolivia*. Santiago: CEPAL.

OCDE, BID, & World Bank. (2015). *Panorama de las pensiones: América latina y el Caribe*. Washington, DC: Banco Interamericano de Desarrollo.

OIT. (2014a). *Panorama laboral 2014*. Lima: OIT/Oficina Regional para América Latina y el Caribe.

OIT. (2014b). *Panorama Laboral Temático: Transición a la formalidad en América Latina y el Caribe*. Lima: OIT/Oficina Regional para América Latina y el Caribe.

Palomino, H., & Trajtemberg, D. (2006). Una nueva dinámica de las relaciones laborales y la negociación colectiva en la Argentina. *Revista de Trabajo, 2*(3), 47–68.

Papadoupulos, J. (1999). Igualdad, democracia y políticas sociales. In M. Schteingart (Ed.), *Políticas sociales para los pobres en América Latina*. México: Miguel Ángel Porrúa.

Polanyi, K. (1944). *The great transformation*. New York: Farrar & Rinehart.

Repetto, F., & Potenza Dal Masetto, F. (2011). Protección social en la Argentina. *Serie Políticas Sociales*, (174), 68. Santiago de Chile: CEPAL.

Riesco, M. (2009). El modelo social chileno comienza a cambiar. *Revista Internacional del Trabajo, 128*(3), 311–330.

Robles Farías, C. (2013). *Sistemas de protección social en América Latina y el Caribe: Chile*. Santiago: CEPAL.

Streeck, W. (2014). *Buying time: The delayed crisis of democratic capitalism*. London: Verso.

Théret, B. (1995). *L'État, la finance et le social. Souveraineté nationale et construction européenne*. Paris: La Découverte.

Théret, B. (2011). The place of national systems of social protection and political representation in socio-economic regulation: A morphogenetic structuralist view on institutional change in comparative perspective with special references to Japan and France. *Evolutionary Institutional Economic Review, 7*(2), 177–208.

Valencia Lomelí, E. (2008). Las transferencias monetarias condicionadas como política social en América latina. Un balance: Aportes, límites y debates. *Annual Review of Sociology, 34*, 499–524.

Valencia Lomelí, E., Foust Rodríguez, D., & Tetreault Weber, D. (2013). *Sistemas de Protección Social en América Latina y el Caribe*. Santiago de Chile, MX: CEPAL.

Valladares, L. (1999). Programas sociales para los pobres en Brasil. Los casos de Río de Janeiro y Belo Horizonte. In M. Schteingart (Coord.), *Políticas sociales para los pobres en América Latina*. México: Miguel Ángel Porrúa.

Vianna, M. L. T. W. (1997). Benefícios Privados, Vícios Públicos: Dilemas Atuais da Seguridade Social No Brasil. In E. Diniz & S. de Azevedo (Eds.), *Reforma do estado e democracia no Brasil* (pp. 295–348). Brasília: Editora Universidade de Brasília.

Weitz-Shapiro, R. (2006). Partisanship and protest: The politics of workfare distribution in Argentina. *Latin American Research Review, 41*(3), 122–147.

CHAPTER 9

Conclusions: Performance and Frailties of the Latin American Capitalisms

Rather than reviewing what we have already discussed in the previous chapters, in these conclusions we want to discuss the performance, but especially the limits of the four types of capitalism that we have analyzed all along this book. We will first review the socioeconomic performance of each type of capitalism.

9.1 Performance

We have already analyzed the impact of the different types of capitalism in terms of the social compromise that defines a wage relation that is more or less favorable to the socioeconomic situation of the popular classes. While the outsourcing and liberal rentier types of capitalism are profit led, the socio-developmentalist and rentier redistributive types are wage led (Lechevalier 2011; Valencia 2018). This has an effect on the wage relation while the profit-led type tends to less substantial salary hikes and less generous, more focalized assistance-oriented social protection systems, both the socio-developmentalist and the rentier redistributive types are wage-led types, allowing for more generous salary increases, a social protection system with a universalistic tendency, and assistance programs that are complementary rather than at the heart of the social protection systems.

Redistribution results in a reduction of extreme and moderate poverty and in the expansion of the middle class, as well as in decreasing inequality. Between the year 2000–2013, Brazil cut extreme poverty by

I. Bizberg, *Diversity of Capitalisms in Latin America*,
https://doi.org/10.1007/978-3-319-95537-7_9

17%, increased the middle class by 16%, and cut inequality by 9 points. Argentina succeeded in diminishing extreme poverty by 11% and moderate poverty by 9%, increased middle classes by 21%, while reducing inequality by 7 points. This is also the case of a redistributive rentier economy such as Bolivia, where the extremely poor fell by 23%, the middle classes grew by 16%, and inequality was reduced by 10 points. Extreme poverty in Ecuador also fell by more than 27% and the middle classes grew by 17%.

The outsourcing model, typified by Mexico, is exemplary by its incapacity to diminish poverty, to increase the middle classes and reduce inequality. In fact, in this case poverty continues to represent around 50% of the population, middle classes have barely grown, and inequality has scarcely decreased. Some of the countries that can be counted as the liberal rentier type/profit-led growth have also shown a positive performance in reducing extreme and moderate poverty, and increasing the middle classes, though they have been less successful in reducing inequality. Colombia, for example, was very successful in diminishing extreme poverty (−22%), increasing the middle-class sector (15%), but not so much in reducing inequality (only 3 points). Chile is also such a case, as it expanded middle classes by 12%, reduced poverty, but almost did not diminish inequality, that went down by only 4 points. Among the liberal rentier countries, Peru is an exception, as it has not only been able to reduce poverty, increase the middle classes, but also diminish inequality from 54 to 44 Gini index. While the origin of the transformations in the case of the redistributive capitalisms is wage increases, formalization, and expansion of social security expenditure, in the liberal rentier cases it is a "mechanical" result of the growth of the economy. This is what explains that inequality is not reduced, because when the economy grows with a bias toward profits, it concentrates the benefits of growth in such unequal societies as the Latin American ones (Cortés Cáceres 2010). A reduction of inequality requires a deliberate policy of the State, be it through redistribution, or more sustainably by way of the imposition of a progressive tax structure (Lo Vuolo 2015).

We should also mention that what we have called the growth of the middle classes is accompanied by the growth of another sector of the population that the CEPAL has called the vulnerable. It is a segment of the population that has risen from poverty, but that is vulnerable to any shock the economy suffers; they may easily fall again into poverty with an economic turnabout. This is, in fact, because what we are calling the middle class is not really one, if we take into consideration that being middle class means having the capacity to withstand an economic crisis by having a capital (patrimonial or human) that enables an individual to endure a relatively long time without a job and having an educational level or a skill that can allow him to rapidly obtain a job once the economy starts growing (Cortés Cáceres 2013; Solís 2016, Neubert 2016) (Figs. 9.1, and 9.2).

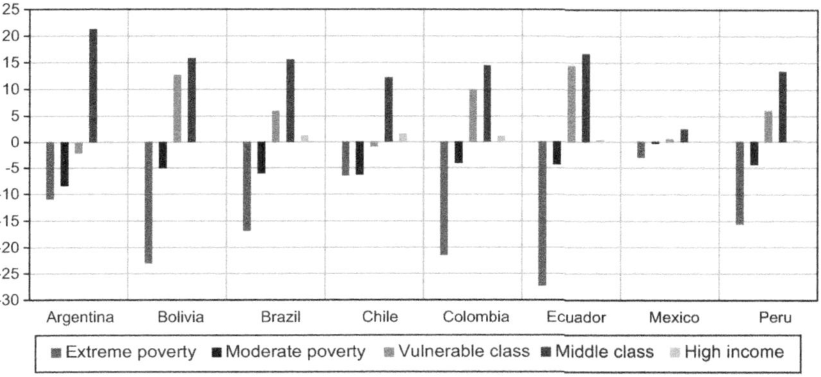

Fig. 9.1 Social stratification in Latin America, % variation 2000–2013 (*Source* Stampini et al. 2015, Figure 1, p. 10)

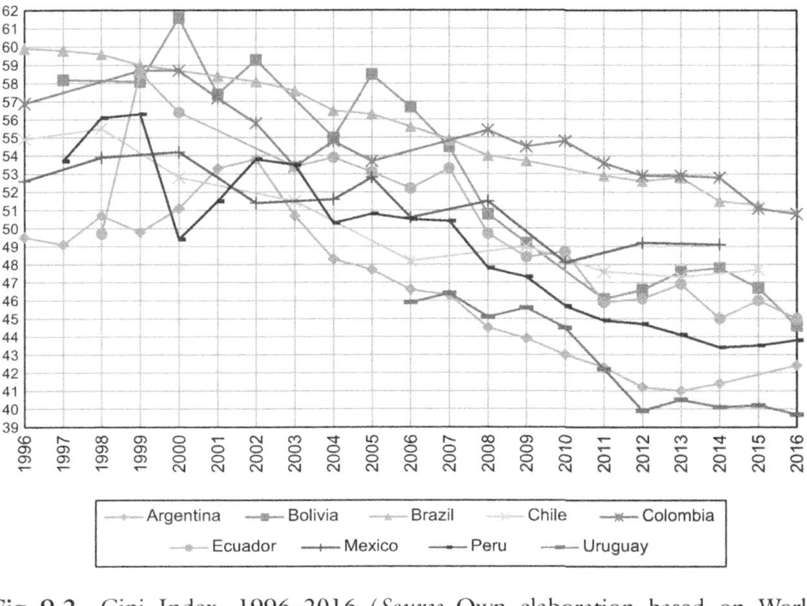

Fig. 9.2 Gini Index, 1996–2016 (*Source* Own elaboration based on World Bank database. *Mexico data based on Cepalstat)

9.2 The Frailties of the Diverse Types of Capitalism

Once we have very briefly discussed the diverse performances of the types of capitalism, we want to explain the origins of the open crisis in which the country which represented the most advanced of the types of capitalism, socio-developmentalism, has stumbled. Does this crisis mean that socio-developmentalism is inviable for the Latin American countries? That development accompanied by redistribution is impossible? Why has Brazil fallen into such a deep crisis while the other countries that seem even weaker, like Bolivia and Ecuador, because they are almost purely rentier, haven't?

In the first place, we have to remember that, as we discussed in the introduction, our four ideal types of capitalism do not coincide with any particular country as they are formalizations/stylizations of the trajectory of one or a group of countries. When we have made references to a particular country, we have done so with the intention of stressing a specific characteristic of a type of capitalism. All real countries are, to a greater or lesser extent, hybrids of these ideal types. In this manner, when we analyze particular countries, we are able to stress not only some of the strengths but also the weaknesses of the ideal types. This is even more the case in this last concluding chapter as the frailties of each model do not result in a crisis in each of the particular countries, and the crisis of the each of the countries is diverse. In this manner, as we have done in the rest of the book, we will discuss the frailties of each of the types and refer to the particular cases as concrete examples.

The 1929 crisis and the Second World War gave rise to the Fordist economic model in Europe and in the USA, and the import substitution model in many of the countries of Latin America. Ensuing the crisis of the mid-1970s, countries that had different institutional conformations but had developed a similar economic model (Fordism) began diverging (Aglietta 1979; Boyer 2005); the crisis of ISI that hit the Latin American countries in the 1980s also triggered a process of divergence (Pereira and Théret 2004). In the 1970s, both Mexico and Brazil tried to implement the third phase of import substitution, but while Brazil was successful, Mexico was less so, basically because of internal political and external financial conditions. Argentina and Chile abandoned the import substitution model in order to embrace an export-led growth that was successful in a small country such as Chile, but led Argentina to de-industrialization and to a disarticulated economy (Boyer 2017b). Once again, facing the 2008 global crisis, the differences between the economic models followed by the diverse countries of Latin America appeared more clearly (Bizberg 2011). Similarly, although we are at present facing a situation characterized by the decline of the enormous quantity of financial resources available due to the policies of the FED to counter the global crisis and the reduction of the demand of commodities (mainly from China), seems to homogenize the condition of the countries of the continent and erase the differences we have emphasized in this book. However, we consider that these differences will not disappear, but even risk to strengthen. The main idea of these conclusions is that this is so, because each type of capitalism has specific frailties and strengths that may lead up to a different open crisis.

We will describe these general characteristics and then delve deeper into the examples of Brazil and Mexico. In the case of Brazil, we will describe the trajectory of the profound crisis that the closest representative of the socio-developmentalist type is undergoing, as it clearly displays the way the different dimensions that lead to a crisis in a redistributive type of capitalism interact. We will discuss the situation of the Mexican economy because it characterizes the way in which the liberal types of capitalism undergo external shocks. The analysis of these two cases will be also useful to exemplify the fact that while the weaknesses to adapt to external shocks may be similar in each type of capitalism, the interrelation of the political, social and economic dimensions differ from one country to the other.

The main weakness of both the liberal and the redistributive rentier types of economies is evident: their dependence on the demand and on the price of the products they extract and export, as well as on their capacity to attract foreign investment. Both of these are extremely volatile and subject to external economic conditions that are totally out of control of these countries. On the other hand, as the State in the liberal rentier capitalism has abandoned nearly all its mechanisms to intervene in the economy, it has great difficulty or is unable to implement Keynesian measures in order to stimulate economic growth and counter the fundamental shortcomings of this type of capitalism: low salaries, inequality, and informality. In addition, the socioeconomic weaknesses of these capitalisms are aggravated by the fact that their social security systems are very narrow.

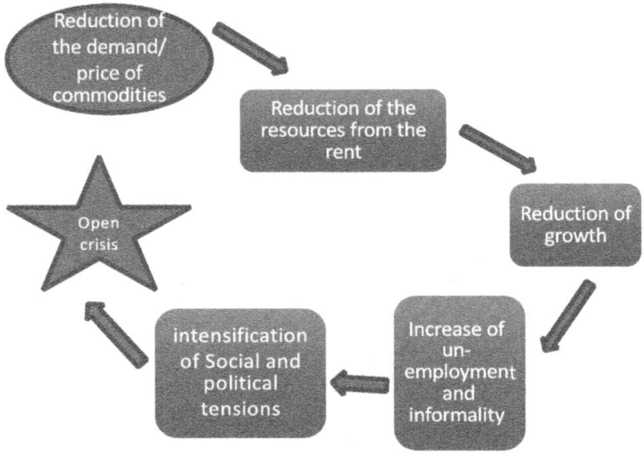

Fig. 9.3 Crisis scenario: liberal rentier capitalism (*Source* Own elaboration)

Nonetheless, because civil society is weak and unorganized, as the dominant coalition that leads this profit-led type of capitalism does not include the popular classes, and finally as the political system is either an empty democracy, a political system led by technocrats, or a particracy, social dissatisfaction and unrest are incapable of attaining the political system in order to try to modify the state of social forces and the general orientation of the economy. It is a situation where social and redistributive demands accumulate and the political system and the State does not have the capacity of satisfying them. In this manner, although the economic shocks do not lead to an open social and political crisis until the situation becomes totally untenable, as it did in the Argentinean crisis of 2001–2002, or the Ecuadorian crisis of 1999, social unrest expresses itself in anomic ways, through increasing criminality, sporadic local manifestations, etc. (Fig. 9.3). The political solution (perceived, though totally incapable of doing so) to such an anomic crisis may be the choice of a charismatic leader that promises to solve the situation through heightened violence and exclusion.

In fact, the liberal State not only lacks a national redistributive policy, but also a regional one. Peru is a very significant example as the manner in which it distributes the resources it gets from extractive activities reinforces inequality. The main tax that is allocated to the localities (the canon), which represents 50% of the income tax that the State recollects from the mining concerns, goes to the local governments where the mines are situated. Although the amount that the localities have received in the last years has considerably increased, the type of decentralization implemented in Peru does not give them the autonomy to decide on its use, as political decentralization did not follow the fiscal one. On the other hand, not only have these resources increased regional inequality, as they are allocated to the regions where mineral investments flow (in a sense as a compensation or as a way of convincing the local population to cope with the damages this type of production entails), but rather than diminishing social conflict, they have increased it. Conflicts arise in order to extract more resources from the mining companies and from the federal State, to speed up the allocation of these taxes, or it appears between different localities in order to obtain jurisdiction of the territories where the mines are situated (Arellano Yanguas 2014: 46, 266–267). Thus, at least in the case of Peru, in addition to the environmental damages that we have not addressed in this book and that are surely very significant, the extractivist model of the rentier economies coupled with liberalism not only does not address, but accentuates the national and territorial inequality that generates social conflicts.

In addition, in the case of the particular countries we have named rentier liberal, as they depend almost exclusively on private investment and the State limits itself to set the conditions in order to lure capital, it does not impose conditions and does not orient investments where they are needed. In addition, as civil society is weak, it does not have the force to deter these investments and control their more negative social and environmental consequences, and as a result, these investments are purely extractive. No project to achieve a vertical integration of the extractive sector to other branches of the economy, or an effort to increase added value to the products extracted, or the upgrading in the production chain can be undertaken without either the pressure of social actors, or a State-led project.

In fact, one of the most significant differences that Fornillo (2018) finds between extractive investments in a country where there is no social opposition to these types of investments (in this case Argentina), and another where there is a compromise between national and regional interests and capital investment (Bolivia), is the existence of social movements. Analyzing the case of lithium reserves in both countries, this author considers (as we have done in this book) that the character of the State and the economy is closely linked to the density and action capacity of civil society. Although one cannot be sure about the real possibilities of Bolivia to achieve its plans to develop the vertical integration of the lithium industry, going from extraction to the production of batteries, in this country the State has the ownership of the reserves and has conceived a project with Chinese collaboration. On the contrary, in Argentina, a country with a much higher scientific capacity, the government of Macri has no vertical integration project and has even reduced royalties and taxes to the minimum in order to attract investments. His conclusion is that Bolivia's "...strategic project is inseparable from the historicity of the extraction of lithium [...] and the leading role that the original communities have had in it" (ibid.: 198).

Paradoxically, redistributive rentier capitalism may be both more unstable, but also more resilient. Because redistribution is the effect of the pressure of organized civil society and the fact that the popular classes are represented in the dominant coalition in a State-led compromise, and as the State structure and the political system are both more open, it allows for a stronger social and political reaction against the decline of redistribution due to the fall of the resources that derive from exports of commodities. In fact, in these cases, the external shocks can lead to an increased pressure from both the popular and the entrepreneurial classes, the situation may then be resolved through social pressure or through institutional means, elections to change the government. Another possibility is that redistributive rentier capitalism totally avert a crisis coming from an external shock or fall into an open crisis. The decline of the resources of the rent leads to the incapacity of the State to continue redistributing, imperiling the social compromise and its political legitimacy. The government is obliged to apply austerity measures and risk alienating its social supports, a situation which may be exploited by social actors that are against the economic model. The outcome depends on the legitimacy of the governing elites, as well as on the force of the opposing sectors. In the case of Venezuela, a purely rentier redistributive system, with no compromise with the economic elites, resulted in an economic war and the collapse of the economy. In the case of Bolivia, the government of Evo Morales, sustained by the popular organizations and social movements unified in the MAS, has found a modus vivendi with the agro-exporters. The legitimacy of the government and its more cautious economic administration have averted a crisis (Fig. 9.4).

In fact, in both Bolivia and Ecuador, the pressures and resistances may arise from within the dominant coalition, from the social organizations that support the government. The indigenous movements that fought

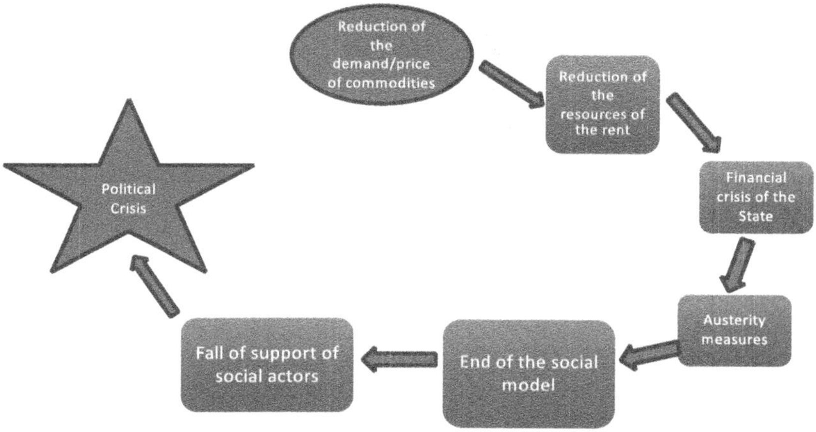

Fig. 9.4 Crisis scenario: rentier-redistributive (*Source* Own elaboration)

against the neoliberal policies of the 1990s went beyond a pure reaction against them, pointing toward more fundamental questions concerning development itself, from a perspective defined by the relation of humanity to nature. They were the bearers of a less exploitative rapport to nature that considers it as a partner rather than a mere resource-at-hand to be used by humans. This is very clear when one considers that two of the most significant and successful social movements in Bolivia and Ecuador were called the "March for Life" and the "Mobilization for Life," respectively (Silva 2009). Such encompassing revindications pointing beyond mere socioeconomic demands, to an appeal to cultural and ecological transformations, empowered the resistance of these movements to neoliberalism, due to the fact that they called for a different manner of seeing the world. They represented more than a change of governmental policy and were instrumental for the arrival of a leadership that began to deconstruct neoliberalism, especially in the case of Bolivia.

The pressure of the indigenous movements led to the inclusion, in both Bolivia and Ecuador, of the concept of "good life" (el buen vivir) in the constitutions of both countries. Although it is still a non-fulfilled promise, it is a continuous reference for social movements, like the Brazilian Constitution of 1988 for the social movements of this country.

Although Maristella Svampa (2010) considers that the governments of Evo Morales and Rafael Correa have betrayed this promise by excluding the forces that were defending this sustainable project inside their governments in order to embrace an extractivist/developmentalist one, a more balanced stance considers that, at least in the case of Bolivia, the government has had to arbitrate "... between demands to protect the environment and the rights of indigenous people on one side, and the need to grow the economy through resource extraction" (Farthing and Kohl 2014: 158). It is clear that in contrast to other extractivist/rentier economies where civil society is less active and organized, as those of Peru, Colombia, and Chile, in both Bolivia and Ecuador, the existence of strong social movements, the MAS in the first and the CONAIE in the second, part of the resources extracted from mining, gas and oil exploitation has been redistributed. Although in both economies extractivism is present, a significant difference is that in redistributive rentier economies the gains of the rent profit the most needed population to a greater extent that in the liberal ones.

This is one of the main differences between the liberal rentier and the rentier redistributive types. Another distinction is the paradox of being both more fragile and more resilient to external shocks. The existence of a strongly organized civil society, the fact that the popular interests are represented in the dominant social coalition, the existence of a decentralized State structure and a political system that is responsive to social movements may signify a faster transmission of the crisis to the political system. It may, on the contrary, have greater capacity to endure the crisis due to its heightened legitimacy. Like the small countries of northern Europe, where a socio-corporatist social compromise allows them to better withstand external shocks, a more legitimate government where the popular classes are represented may be able to go through the shock, as Bolivia has done in the last few years, while a situation like the Brazilian where the government entertains a compromise between the interests of the rentiers and financiers and the popular classes is more fragile, as we will immediately discuss.

Although the socio-developmentalist model seemed to allow Brazil to upgrade and advance toward the level of development of the central countries, it is paradoxically the only country with an open crisis; its intent failed, ensued premature de-industrialization, and culminated in a profound economic and political crisis (Salama 2012). This does not prove that the socio-developmentalist model is unsustainable, but rather that a hybrid between a socio-developmentalist and a rentier model such as the one adopted by Brazil is fragile.

This was partly due to the fact that Brazil shared many of the characteristics of the rentier model: increasing exports of commodities, overvaluation of the national currency due to the entry of foreign currency resulting from increasing exports and foreign investments (Bresser-Pereira 2012, 2015). Brazil's mode of capitalism depends heavily on its external market, basically on the exports of commodities, a dependency that has been increasing. Up to 60% of Brazilian exports are primary or manufactured goods based on commodities (data for 2008 from CEPAL). Many authors (Salama, Bresser-Pereira, Marques Pereira) have remarked that the country became more and more dependent on the export of commodities as a way to maintain its commercial surplus, the capacity of its State to redistribute the profits through wage increases and expansion of its social policy, and embark upon a wage-led growth. The State tried to arbitrate between a dependency on the external market, where it had an advantage by way of the exports of commodities, with the internal market which was boosted by an increased demand led by an expansive wage and social policy.

The political economy of the rentier character of the Brazilian economy resulted from the compromise of the State with the commodities exporters and the financial interests that invested in State bonds that allocated extremely high interest rates. As we have analyzed above, the dominant social compromise in Brazil was set up between the financial and commodities exporters, on one side, and the popular sectors, the poor and the vulnerable, on the other. This forced the preservation of economic conditions favorable to financial and agri-business interests that were implemented during the 1990s (Aguila and Lo Vuolo 2016). On the other hand, the link of the PT government with the popular classes exerted pressure on the State to redistribute productivity gains and commodity rents. In addition, the State required abundant resources through taxes and debt in order to implement its redistributive policies; something that in return profited the interests of the financial sector, as the State crowded out the capital market and the central bank raised the interest rates; the SELIC is one of the highest central bank's interest rates in the world (Marques Pereira and Bruno 2015).

The stable or overvalued real was favorable for increasing the buying capacity of the Brazilians who came out of poverty and of the new middle classes created through the hiking of the minimum salaries, the formalization of jobs, and the expansion of social security. In addition, there was an intensive program of housing for the poor, financed wholly or partly by the State as well as an increased access to loans by the popular sectors; which permitted them to acquire durable consumer products. All these factors resulted in a significant growth of the internal demand which was set at the center of the new model of development, a wage-led growth model (Stockhammer 2011). Nonetheless, while this model was assumed to lead, together with active industrial policies, to the deepening of industrialization, the fact that it was accompanied by the overvaluation of the real, an ineffective industrial policy, high interest rates, and the orientation of loans from the BNDS basically to the big companies rather than small and middle sized ones, all worked against it (Hochstetler and Montero 2012).

The compromise with the financial and commodity-exporting interests led to a situation where the protectionist measures and the stimulus to the industrialists were not able to compensate the high interest rates, the openness of the capital market, the impulse of agri-business; all of which led to the "Dutch disease." This served to counteract everything the government did in order to stimulate internal production: the revaluation of the real made internal production costlier and imports cheaper and the stimulus to the financial sector caused investments in the rentier sectors to be more attractive than those in industry (ibid.). A process that the government was not able to counteract with investment in infrastructure, the protection of the internal market, and industrial policies favoring the middle and small enterprises. The decline of poverty and the expansion of the middle classes that had resulted in a significant growth of the internal demand, which was at the center of the socio-developmentalist model, that was assumed to achieve (with the guidance of active industrial policies) the deepening of industrialization, resulted in its contrary. As this process was accompanied by the overvaluation of the national currency due to the entry of foreign currency resulting from the increased exports of commodities and foreign investments (the "Dutch disease"), the premature expansion of the internal demand before the productive structure was ready to meet the demand, the much faster growth of the internal demand in relation to the internal offer, and a multiplier effect benefiting the external market (ibid.), ensued in an increase of imports and de-industrialization (Bresser-Pereira 2012, 2015; Aguila and Lo Vuolo 2016).

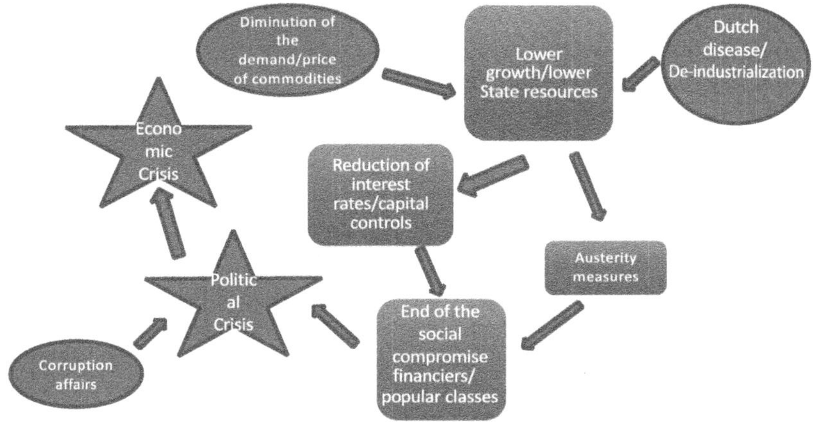

Fig. 9.5 Crisis scenario: socio-developmentalism (*Source* Own elaboration)

The "dual" compromise with the financial and commodity-exporting interests that eventually led to the "Dutch disease" made internal production costlier and imports cheaper and defeated all the industrial policies that the government had undertaken (Bresser-Pereira 2012, 2015). The "Dutch disease" resulted from an increased export of commodities, the influx of foreign exchange, both as a result of these exports, as well as in the form of foreign capital in different activities, especially in State bonds. This influx of foreign exchange overvalued the real, while the increase of spending by the Brazilian government maintained the interest rate at very high levels; both resulted in the fact that investment in governmental bonds were very lucrative for both foreigners and nationals. This situation had as its consequence a tendency rise in favor of rentier investments, in both government bonds and commodities, rather than more productive ones in industry or knowledge technology (Bresser-Pereira 2012, 2015; Marques Pereira and Bruno 2015; Salama 2012) (Fig. 9.5).

This situation alone would have probably not led to an open crisis, as we can see from the examples of the rentier redistributive countries such as Bolivia and Ecuador, if it had not been coupled with the explosion of corruption cases and political maneuvers around the trials and denunciations of the Lava Jato affair, that broke down the presidential coalition and that eventually led to the impeachment of Dilma Roussef at the end of 2016. The economic-political crisis that Brazil is suffering since 2014 was the result of the way in which economic difficulties interacted with the political crisis. This latter crisis was partly the result of the impossibility of preserving the compromise that the PT governments had reached with both the popular sectors and the financial and commodity-exporting interests; the reduction of resources of the government on the one part and the need to implement economic policies to reduce the overvaluation of the real and of the interest rates in order to boost the internal economy in view of the external economic restrictions, led both to the gradual decline of the backing of the PT government by the popular classes, and to the reaction of the rentier–financier sectors, that profited from this situation to dislocate the government of Dilma.

The Lula government had established a compromise between orthodox/liberal and heterodox policies to boost the domestic market through the increase of minimum wages and the expansion of social policies. This commitment was unstable as it was based on the financial resources flowing into the country, due the high interest rates of government bonds and the revaluation of the real, on the one hand, and of the rise of the demand and of the prices of commodities, on the other. It was also unstable because it depended on political support in Congress for both Lula's and Dilma's government: from the representatives linked to the financial and business sectors, as well as of those of the workers and social movements, in a coalition that collapsed first with the decline of the commodity prices and of the flow of capital from the emerging to the central countries, then by the austerity measures forced by this situation.

It was the Brazilian government under the rule of the Workers Party that imposed the socio-developmentalist model (Bresser-Pereira 2015, Prates et al. 2017), an organization linked to the main Brazilian trade union, the CUT, and the social organizations that emerged during the last years of the dictatorship, that eventually displaced the military, forced elections and the writing of a new Constitution (in 1988) which gave significant social rights to the Brazilian population. Its origins forced the PT to implement an ample social redistribution program. Nevertheless, the logic of redistribution was not exclusively attributable to the social pact between the State and civil society, but converged with an economic rationale. A continental and highly populated country had the possibility (and the need) of an economy turned toward the internal market. That was the basis of the import substitution industrialization strategy of the "golden thirties," and of the wage-led growth mode implemented by the PT governments (Bresser-Pereira 2015, Prates et al. 2017). The efforts to increase the buying power of the popular classes, reduce poverty and expand the middle class, as well as State investment in infrastructure and economic policies in favor of specific sectors of the economy were all crucial to reorient part of the profits generated by the export of commodities to develop the country on the basis of the internal market. (Bizberg 2011, 2014).

However, this model of development was very dependent on the financial expansion and low-interest policies of the USA, together with the spectacular growth of China, that raised both the demand and the price of commodities (Boyer 2017b). Once these two conditions waned, the Brazilian economy began to suffer from strong external pressures: first the credit crunch, due to the global crisis, that led to the retreat of foreign capital from the emerging countries and the reduction of foreign investment, then the increase of interest rates in the USA, and finally the deceleration of the Chinese economy (Boyer 2014). Facing this situation, the government of Dilma Roussef implemented a mix of orthodox and heterodox policies (Prates et al. 2017) which had the consequence of alienating both the social bases of the PT and the agro-exporting and financial sector, and weakened its political position.

On the one hand, the second government of Dilma finally tried to counter the Dutch disease and de-industrialization by reducing the interest rates of the government bonds and imposing capital controls (Prates et al. 2017). Although these measures were intended to favor industrialization and effectively devalued the real, they did not achieve their goals as the industrialists had also become rentier-financier and saw their interests affected more than stimulated (Boschi and Santos Pinho 2018). On the other hand, as the government had less resources to redistribute, it began cutting its expenses, and applying a more orthodox monetary and fiscal policy, which alienated its social base. A social base that began to protest since 2013, first in Rio de Janeiro against the hikes of prices, especially of public transport, and the displacement of inhabitants from the places where the stadiums were to be constructed, as a result of the organization of both the World Cup and the Olympic Games. This situation was aggravated by the fact that the poor were not able to attend the football matches as the prices of the tickets were out of their reach. The manifestations soon expanded toward other urban centers, demanding better transports and health services, and in general more efficient public services (Zibechi 2013). The economic growth and redistribution that had allowed a significant sector of the population to rise out of poverty and have for the first time in their lives access to these services (education, health, housing, credit) was now addressing demands concerning their quality.

As these manifestations of the poor and the new middle classes subsided, the traditional urban middle classes took over. This occurred in the context of the "Lava Jato" investigation, led by judge Moro of Curitiba, on the corruption of numerous functionaries of all parties by the construction company Odebrecht, that had already led to the imprisonment of numerous entrepreneurs and politicians. In massive manifestations in Rio and Sao Paulo, these sectors began protesting basically against the PT, although the investigation had involved all the parties and even if corruption is not new in Brazil, it has been a very common characteristic of the political life of the country. Some authors (Costa 2018) consider that these manifestations also derived from the resentment of these sectors of society against the consequences of the social policies of the PT, especially the fact that had created a new middle class that was "invading" the places and social positions that had been until then reserved for the traditional middle class.

The consequences of these investigations were far-reaching. In the first place, investments by Petrobras were significantly reduced, and some of the most important entrepreneurs were imprisioned; for example the owner of Odebrecht. Concurrently, the crisis became political, when the political establishment began to be affected, as ever higher placed politicians started being prosecuted. When it reached the speaker of Congress, Eduardo Cunha (PMDB), who was the pivot of the congressional coalition that allowed Dilma to govern, the scenario was set for a standout between the PMDB and the PT. When the president and the PT refused to block the accusations against Cunha and allowed the trial to rid him of immunity to progress, Cunha began the impeachment procedure against Dilma that eventually sealed her fate, based upon very questionable accusations.

The Brazilian political system is a coalition presidential regime (Aziz 2015), as a myriad political parties are present in Congress. As coalitions are the only way to necessary to govern and Congress is atomized in so many parties, corruption is very frequent, not only in order to fund the campaigns of the different political parties, but to maintain a majority once in government. The coalition that supported Dilma began weakening when she alienated her own party deputies, as the government began imposing austerity measures. The PMDB, an organization known for its corrupt and clientelistic foundations (known as a physiological party) broke with Dilma when the accusations hit its highest figures. This led to a final break with Dilma and to her destitution, which did not solve the political, nor the economic crisis, but in fact aggravated both.

The measures taken by Dilma to try to palliate the economic crisis that had affected the financial interests, the forsaking of the popular classes due to the implementation of orthodox measures at the beginning the first year of Dilma's second mandate, the manifestations of the traditional middle classes against corruption and the politics of the PT, and the investigations of "Lava Jato," all converged to weaken the position of Dilma and permit her ousting and the arrival of her vice president to the head of the State. A situation that only aggravated the economic crisis due to the austerity measures undertaken by the government of Temer. These events also deepened the political crisis and eventually led to the results of the election of October 2018, that have meant the demolition of the principal parties of Brazil that were in the process of consolidating, and the election of Bolsonaro, a representative of an insignificant political party, who had very low voting intentions a few months before the election; a situation that reminds us of what occurred in Peru at the beginning of the 90's with the election of Fujimori.

We have also considered the case of Argentina as a socio-developmentalist economy, after the radical crisis that began with the end of convertibility, with the arrival of Néstor Kirchner to the presidency in 2003. The crisis, and especially the 2001 devaluation generated a change in the relative prices of the Argentinean manufacturing industry, which together with the increased external demand for commodities, eased the external foreign currency restrictions this country has traditionally faced. This gave way to a process of reindustrialization and job creation. "First, the period from mid-2002 to 2007 was characterized by an incipient and significant job creation. Second, the period from 2007 to mid-2011 was crossed by the international crisis and the fall and subsequent recovery of local economy. Finally, since the middle of 2011, the economy and specially the manufacturing sector stagnated, as external imbalances reappeared again" (Santarcángelo et al. 2017: 23).

Since 2003, the Kirchner and Fernandez governments effectively reoriented the social and labor policies both in response to increased social pressure and to their own ideological convictions. This translated into important salary increases and an integrated social and wage policy coherent with socio-developmentalism (Palomino and Trajtemberg 2006: 50). Nonetheless, in a similar manner as Brazil, this did not substantially modify the Argentinean investment and productive structure, which is increasingly based on natural resources. (Boyer 2017a; Fernandez Bugna and Porta 2008, 223).

In fact, Argentina can be characterized as an economy that oscillates diachronically, between a dependency on foreign markets, like the Mexican, and a structuralist development like the Brazilian. Argentina was one of the richest countries of the world in the late nineteenth and beginning of the twentieth century, based on the exports of meat and grains to Great Britain, and imports of manufactured products. Although there was an incipient manufacturing production stimulated by this external led growth, after the crisis of the late 1920s and early 1930s, and then the Second World War, the country embarked in a process of import substitution industrialization like the rest of Latin America, first "automatically", due to the modification of the international context, then willingly based on a social coalition built around Perón and Peronism, that pushed for import substitution of durable consumer goods. Nonetheless, this process of industrialization of Argentina has been always questioned with regard to the export-oriented period that represented the wealthiest period of the economic history of this country. Thus, in a sense, this country has always oscillated between two opposing projects, one oriented to exports, traditionally agro-exporting but more and more financialized, and another one oriented toward the internal market. This oscillation has happened without any possible conciliation, it's either one or the other. While the very favorable external situation lasted, the governments of Kirchner and Fernández were able to reconcile the export and financial interests with the popular and internal market ones, in a similar manner as we described for Brazil. Nonetheless, once the external situation changed, again as in Brazil, the new government elected, that of Macri, shifted the pendulum toward the external market and in favor of the rentier–financier interests. This oscillation between two contrasting and irreconcilable projects is the principal weakness of the country.

Finally, although the Mexican economy is specialized in manufacturing products rather than commodities, it is equally very dependent on the external market, on direct foreign investment as well as portfolio, in order to equilibrate its current account balance due to its structural commercial deficit. It is thus a good example of a dependent liberal economy which shares many of the frailties of the liberal rentier types. The fragility of the international outsourcing model is this dependence. In the second place, and more importantly, its disarticulation; the fact that the economy is not articulated internally with the rest of the Mexican productive structure, but externally with the US productive structure. This disconnection means that the growth of the transnational platform does not stimulate the internal productive structure. On the other hand, in the exporting enclave salaries and labor conditions are much higher and better than those of the rest of the economy. Nonetheless, the low salaries, poor working conditions, as well as the large informal sector of the rest of the economy, function as an anchor to maintain the conditions in the exporting enclave competitive, that is lower than in the more advanced economies and even in some of the other underdeveloped ones.

The Mexican economy is a platform that integrates labor at the final stages of the productive chain, where aggregate value is lowest. The international competitivity of Mexico depends on low labor costs (both wages and social security costs), high flexibility of the labor market, low taxes, and low environmental regulations. Low salaries result in low internal demand, which together with reduced productivity gains, leads to low growth and job creation, and the incapacity to integrate productive chains that incorporate more added value. Although there are sectors of the economy that have high salaries, the dominant economic mode requires low salaries that attract foreign investments on industrial processes with high aggregate of labor. The repression of the internal market makes it as dependent on the external market as the rentier types.

The Mexican economy is basically a "maquiladora" industry, although some other industries (mainly automotive) integrate a larger proportion of spare parts produced internally, mainly by foreign providers. This explains why Mexico has become one of the largest manufacturing exporting countries in the world and the largest in Latin America. Nonetheless, the impact of this boom has been very low on the internal productive structure and internal market because of its low aggregate value. In fact, the "maquiladoras" proper, that still constitute around 60% of total exports, are exclusively assembling enterprises that incorporate a minimum part of nationally produced products (around 5%). Other export industries, such as the automobile, integrate between 30 and 40%, also on the more labor-intensive stages of the productive process. The international (basically with the USA) articulation of the productive basis of the Mexican economy requires a labor policy that exerts a restrictive control on salaries, and a social policy defined purely as a safety net, allocated by the government, that does not add extra costs to the investors.

As the Mexican economy is totally intertwined and synchronized with the US economy, when the latter slows down exports fall and the strains on its economy increase considerably. The present mercantilist pressures on the part of the Trump administration, that blame the low salaries for the commercial deficit of the USA with Mexico, puts its economy at risk. The only possibility of escaping this situation would be promoting a shift to the growth of the internal market, an increase of salaries and incentives for vertical integration of the industry by way of the incorporation of national providers to the export industry; something that the Mexican governments of the last 30 years have considered that the market would take care spontaneously. The difficulty of such a strategy is that once the productive chains are broken, it is very difficult to reconstruct them. This is especially true as the treaty with the USA and Canada does not give the Mexican government much leeway in terms of a protection from imports, subsidies to Mexican producers, and in general the application of industrial policy. On the other hand, one of the main mechanisms of industrial policy, devaluation of the national currency, does not have a significant impact on Mexican exports, as most of them have a very high import content. This is also the reason why the multiplier of exports is so low; it collapsed from 3.6 to 1.6 from 1987 to 2007 (Ibarra 2008; Palma 2005).

Wages could rise as a result of social pressure, even against the will of the government. Nonetheless, wage and labor policies are decentralized at the enterprise level and tend to be easily contained by the government, as it has a strong capacity of control by way of the Ministry of Labor. But more importantly, Mexican worker's organizations are weak and there is no coordination between them, they are thus incapable of exerting this kind of pressure.

The fact that the dominant social coalition is very narrow, consisting of the multinational companies and the large national groups, that the State structure is very centralized and, finally, that the political system is

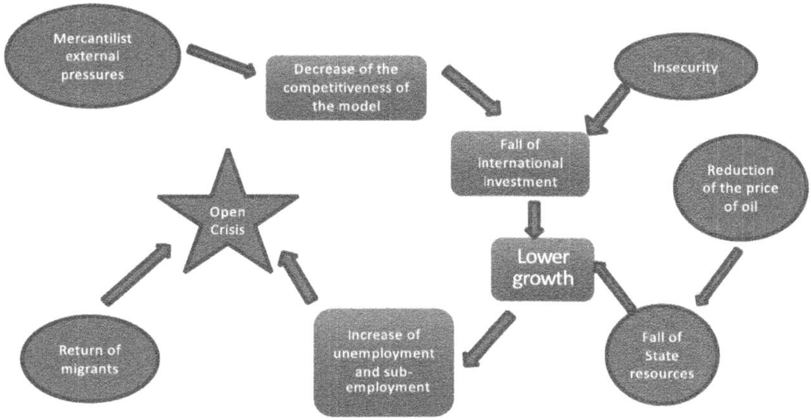

Fig. 9.6 Crisis scenario: international outsourcing (*Source* Own elaboration)

a particracy, makes it very difficult for social revendications to attain the political system and the State. This situation leads to the accumulation of unsolved demands for better salaries, more jobs, more equality, that generate a type of permanent or rampant crisis,[1] that drives the population to all sorts of illegal, and even criminal activities. If the mercantilist pressures coming from the main economic partner of Mexico continue, added to the closure of the escape valve of migration to the USA and the return of migrants resulting from harshest migratory policies, the rampant crisis may become an open one (Fig. 9.6).

Nonetheless, the fact that Andres Manuel Lopez Obrador, from the leftist political party Morena, won the most recent presidential elections on the 1st of July, marks the possibility of the re-activation of workers' organizations and social movements that may modify the dominant social alliance, allow room for popular interests that would push for better salaries and job formalization, that may eventually lead to an alternative economic policy. Nonetheless, the structural and sociopolitical restrictions we mentioned above would seem to give very narrow margin of maneuver to the future government.

[1]A situation well described by Laclau in his major work *La razón populista*.

The frailties of each of the types of capitalism we have described may, but do not necessarily, lead to an open crisis, as this depends on the manner in which the different dimensions we have been discussing in this book articulate with each other: an accumulation regime, a social pact/wage relation, a dominant social coalition, and a political system. In this manner, if one of the dimensions undergoes a strong internal or external pressure, the other dimensions may resist in order to preserve the specific country from plunging into an open crisis. For example, although Argentina (2003–2014) has been described as having implemented an economic mode similar to the one followed by Brazil, while this latter country is enduring a deep economic and political crisis, Argentina is undergoing an economic but not a political crisis. And although the rentier countries have been suffering from the downturn of the demand and the price of commodities, only Venezuela has fallen prey to an open crisis, while the others have resisted. Thus, our discussion regarding the weaknesses of each of the types of Latin American capitalism does not imply that all the countries that can be described as close to one particular type will undergo the same destiny. While we can describe the frailties of each type of capitalism and the trajectory that may lead it to a crisis, we cannot predict a crisis in any particular country.

References

Aglietta, M. (1979). *Régulation et crises du capitalisme*. Paris: Calmann-Lévy.

Águila, N., & Lo Vuolo, R. (2016). *Argentina y Brasil: los límites de los regímenes de crecimiento liderados por el empleo y los salarios*. Paper presented in the Symposium: "Las diversidades del capitalismo en América Latina. Un estudio sobre la complementariedad entre las distintas conformaciones socio-políticas y las políticas económicas", 8° Congress, Consejo Europeo de Investigaciones Sociales en América Latina, Instituto de Iberoamérica, University of Salamanca.

Arellano Yanguas, J. (2014). *¿Mineria sin fronteras? Conflicto y desarrollo en regiones ineras del Perú*. Lima: IEP.

Aziz, A. (2015). ¿Democracias diferentes?: México, Brasil y Argentina. In I. Bizberg (Ed.), *Variedades de Capitalismo en América Latina: los casos de México, Brasil, Argentina y Chile* (pp. 283–380). México: El Colegio de México.

Bizberg, I. (2011). The global economic crisis as disclosure of different types of capitalism. *Swiss Journal of Sociology/World Society Studies, 37*(2), 321–329.

Bizberg, I. (2014). Types of capitalism in Latin America. *Interventions économiques/Papers in Political Economy (Online)*, (49), p. 31. Canada: Université de Québec á Montréal.

Boschi, R. R., & Santos Pinho, C. E. (2018). Desarrollo capitalista, austeridad fiscal y democracia en Brasil. In A. Aziz & I. Bizberg (Eds.), *La Diversidad de Capitalismos en Crisis*, in preparation.

Boyer, R. (2017a). Formas de capitalismo, América Latina y el sistema internacional después de la gran crisis. In C. Alba Vega & I. Bizberg (Eds.), *Dimensiones sociopolíticas y económicas de la crisis global y su impacto en los países emergentes*. México: El Colegio de México.

Boyer, R. (2017b). *What does the growing communality of contemporary capitalisms mean for economic theory?* (Unpublished manuscript prepared for the International Conference on Economic Theory and Policy). Tokyo: Meiji University.

Boyer, R. (2005). How and why capitalisms differ. *Economy and Society, 34*(4), 509–557.

Boyer, R. (2014). *Is more equality possible in Latin America? A challenge in a world of contrasted but interdependent inequality regimes* (DesiguALdades.net, Working Paper Series 67). Berlin: Freie Universität Berlin.

Bresser-Pereira, L. C. (2012). Os trés ciclos da sociedade e do estado. *Perspectivas, 41*, 13–51.

Bresser-Pereira, L. C. (2015). *Reflecting on new developmentalism and classical developmentalism* (Working Paper 395). São Paulo: FGV.

Cortés, F. (2010). Pobreza, desigualdad en la distribución del ingreso y crecimiento económico, 1992–2006. In F. Cortés & O. de Oliveira (Eds.), *Los Grandes Problemas de México: Desigualdad social*. Mexico: El Colegio de México.

Cortés Cáceres, F. (2013). Sobre las clases medias en México. *Mexico Social, Internet Journal*. http://www.mexicosocial.org/index.php/2017-05-22-14-12-20/alianzas/pued-en-ms/item/190-sobre-las-clases-medias-en-m%C3%A9xico.

Costa, S. (2018). *Persistent Inequalities, Mutable Classes? Social Structure and Political Crisis in Brazil*. Paper presented at the XIX ISA World Conference, Toronto, July 15–21.

Farthing, L. C., & Kohl, B. H. (2014). *Evo's Bolivia: Continuity and change*. Austin: University of Texas Press.

Fernandez Bugna, C., & Porta, F. (2008). El crecimiento reciente de la industria Argentina: Nuevo Régimen sin cambio estructural. In M. R. Soares de Lima (Ed.), *Desempenho de Governos Progressistas no Cone Sul: Agendas alternativas ao Neoliberalismo*. Rio de Janeiro: Edições IUPERJ.

Fornillo, B. (2018). La energía del litio en Argentina y Bolivia: comunidad, extractivismo y posdesarrollo. *Colombia Internacional, 93*, 179–201.

Hochstetler, K., & Montero, A. (2012, May 23–26). Inertial statism and the new developmentalist state in Brazil. In XXX *International Congress of the Latin American Studies Association*, San Francisco.

Ibarra, C. (2008). La paradoja del crecimiento lento de México. *Revista de la CEPAL, 95*, 83–102.

Lechevalier, S. (2011). *La grande transformation du capitalisme japonais*. Paris: Presses de Sciences Po.

Lo Vuolo, R. (2015). The limits of redistributive policies in Latin America: Complementarities between economic and social protection systems. In B. Fritz & L. Lavinas (Eds.), *A moment of equality for Latin America? Challenges for redistribution* (pp. 31–52), Surrey and Burlington: Ashgate.

Pereira, Marques, & Théret, B. (2004). Mediaciones institucionales de regulación social y dinámicas macroeconómicas: los casos de Brasil y México. In Carlos Alba & Ilán Bizberg (Eds.), *Democracia y Globalización en México y Brasil*. El Colegio de México: México.

Marques Pereira, J., & Bruno, M. (2015). *Path dependence blocking the emergence of a new type of capitalism favoring redistribution in brazil: A new view on the possibility of a developmental coalition* (Unpublished manuscript). Université d'amiens, France.

Neubert, D. (2016). *The simplified assumptions of the global middle class narrative: Global middle groups in Kenya* (Unpublished paper presented at the conference middle class in world society). World Sociaty Foundation and ISEC, Bangalore, India.

Palma, J. G. (2005). The seven main 'stylized facts' of the Mexican economy since trade liberalization and NAFTA. *Industrial and Corporate Change, 14*(6), 941–991.

Palomino, H., & Trajtemberg, D. (2006). Una nueva dinámica de las relaciones laborales y la negociación colectiva en la Argentina. *Revista de Trabajo, 2*(3), 47–68.

Prates, D., Fritz, B., de Paula, L. F. (2017). *Brazil at crossroads: A Critical assessment of developmentalist policies* (manuscript). Berlin: Freie University of Berlin.

Salama, P. (2012). China-Brasil: industrialización y 'desindustrialización temprana'. *Cuadernos de Economía, 31*(56), 223–252.

Santarcángelo, J. E., Schteingart, D., & Porta, F. (2017). Industrial policy in Argentina, Brazil, Chile and Mexico: A Comparative Approach. *Revue Interventions économiques*, 59. http://journals.openedition.org/interventioneconomiques/3852. Accessed 13 June 2018.

Silva, E. (2009). *Challenging neoliberalism in Latin America*. Cambridge: Cambridge University Press.

Solís, P. (2016). *Clases sociales, carencias sociales, pobreza y distribución del ingreso en México* (Unpublished power point). Permanente Seminar on inequality in Mexico, Mexico: Instituto Belisario Domínguez, Senado de la República.

Stampini, M., Robre, M., Sáenz, M., Ibarrarán, P., & Medellín, N. (2015). *Pobreza, vulnerabilidad y la clase media en América Latina* (Working Paper No. 591). Washington, DC: IDB.

Stockhammer, E. (2011). Crecimiento basado en los salarios: introducción. *Boletín Internacional de Investigación Sindical, 3*(2), 183–208.

Svampa, M. (2010). *Movimientos Sociales, matrices socio-políticos y nuevos escenarios en América Latina* (One world Perspectives Working Papers No. 1).

Valencia Lomelí, E. (2018). *¿Hacia nuevos compromisos sociales en las trayectorias de los regímenes de bienestar? Los casos de Brasil, Corea del Sur y México* (Unpublished article). Universidad de Guadalajara.

Zibechi, R. (2013). Brasil. Debajo y detrás de las grandes movilizaciones. *Camminardomandando* (revista electrónica). https://camminardomandando.wordpress.com/in-lingua-originale/movimientos/raul-zibechi-brasil-debajo-y-detras-de-las-grandes-movilizaciones/.

References

Acemoglu, D., & Robinson, J. (2012). *Why nations fail, the origins of power, prosperity and poverty*. New York: Crown Business.

Acemoglu, D., Johnson, S., & Robinson, J. A. (2002). Reversal of fortune: Geography and institutions in the making of the modern world income distribution. *The Quarterly Journal of Economics, 117*(4), 1231–1294.

Actis, E. (2011). La estrategia "híbrida" de desarrollo del gobierno de Lula: neodesarrollismo Heterodoxo. *Temas y Debates, 22*, 115–135.

African Development Bank Secretariat. (2009). What can the G20 do on trade that can benefit Africa? In R. Baldwin & S. Evenett (Eds.), *The collapse of global trade, murky protectionism, and the crisis: Recommendations for the G20*. London: VoxEU.org Publication/Centre for Economic Policy Research (CEPR).

Aglietta, M. (1979). *Régulation et crises du capitalisme*. Paris: Calmann-Lévy.

Aglietta, M., & Bai, G. (2012). *La Voie Chinoise. Capitalisme et Empire*. Paris: Odile Jacob.

Águila, N., & Lo Vuolo, R. (2016). *Argentina y Brasil: los límites de los regímenes de crecimiento liderados por el empleo y los salarios*. Paper presented in the Symposium: "Las diversidades del capitalismo en América Latina. Un estudio sobre la complementariedad entre las distintas conformaciones socio-políticas y las políticas económicas". *8º Congress, Consejo Europeo de Investigaciones Sociales en América Latina, Instituto de Iberoamérica*, University of Salamanca.

Aidt, T., & Tzannatos, Z. (2002). *Unions and collective bargaining: Economic effects in a global environment*. Washington, DC: World Bank.

Alarco Tosoni, G. (2014). Participación salarial y crecimiento económico en América Latina, 1950–2011. *Revista CEPAL*, (113), 43–60.

I. Bizberg, *Diversity of Capitalisms in Latin America*,
https://doi.org/10.1007/978-3-319-95537-7

Alarcon Tosoni, G. (2015). Estado y mercado en el Perú contemporáneo. In I. Mendoza (Ed.), *Perú Hoy: Hacia otro desarrollo* (pp. 19–46). Lima, Perú: Desco.

Alba, C. (2004). Los dirigentes económicos de Brasil y México en el cambio económico y la transición política. Notas para una comparación. In C. Alba Vega & I. Bizberg (Coords.), *Democracia y globalización en México y Brasil.* Mexico: El Colegio de México.

Alba, C. (2005). Relaciones entre los empresarios y el Estado. In I. Bizberg & L. Meyer (Coords.), *Una Historia Contemporánea de México, Tomo 2. Actores.* México: Océano.

Albó, J. (2008). *Movimientos y poder indígena en Bolivia, Ecuador y Perú.* La Paz: CIPCA.

Alcalde-Rabanal, J., Lazo-González, O., & Nigenda, G. (2011). Sistema de salud de Perú. *Revista Salud Pública de México, 53*(2), 243–254.

Alonso, G., & Di Costa, V. (2011). Cambios y continuidades en la política social argentina, 2003–2010. In M. Uribe Gómez (Coord.), *Los vaivenes de las políticas sociales en Argentina, Colombia, Chile, México y Uruguay.* México: Miguel Ángel Porrúa.

Altman, D., & Luna, J. P. (2010). Chile: ¿institucionalización con pies de barro? In M. A. Cameron & J. P. Luna (Eds.), *Democracia en la Región Andina* (pp. 273–314). Lima: Instituto de Estudios Peruanos/Plural Editores.

Amable, B. (2005). *Les cinq capitalismes.* Paris: Editions du Seuil.

Amitrano, R. C. (2017). Income distribution, productive structure and growth in South America. *Panoeconomicus, 64*(2), 139–168.

Amsden, A. H. (2001). *The rise of "the rest": Challenges to the west from late-industrializing economies.* New York: Oxford University Press.

Angell, A. (2005). Party change in Chile in comparative perspective. *A Contracorriente, 2*(2), 34–65.

Anria, S., Cameron, M. A., Goenaga, A., Torranzo Roca, C., & Zuazo, M. (2010). Bolivia: democracia en construcción. In M. A. Cameron & J. P. Luna (Eds.), *Democracia en la Región Andina* (pp. 243–272). Lima: Instituto de Estudios Peruanos/Plural Editores.

Aran, D., & Laca, H. (2011). Sistema de salud de Uruguay. *Revista Salud Pública de México, 53*(2), 265–274.

Aranha, M. I., Cruz, J. M., & Pinheiro, A. A. (2014). Latin American federative variables for ICT and development research: A comparison between Argentina, Brazil, Chile, Colombia, Mexico, Peru, Uruguay, and Venezuela. *Revista Redes. com, revista de estudios para el desarrollo social de la Comunicación, 9,* 211–231.

Araníbar Quiroga, E. (2015). *Del péndulo al cubo: la configuración del mercado nacional en una era transnacional.* Bolivia: Editorial 3600.

Arato, A. (2000). *Civil society, constitution, and legitimacy.* Lanham, MD: Rowman and Littlefield.

Arce Catacora, L. A. (2015). *El modelo económico social comunitario productivo Boliviano*. La Paz: SOIPA Ltda.

Arellano Yanguas, J. (2014). *¿Mineria sin fronteras? Conflicto y desarrollo en regiones ineras del Perú*. Lima: IEP.

Auboin M. (2009). Restoring trade finance: What the G20 can do. In R. Baldwin & S. Evenett (Eds.), *The collapse of global trade, murky protectionism, and the crisis: Recommendations for the G20*. London: VoxEU.org Publication/Centre for Economic Policy Research (CEPR).

Avritzer, L. (2009). Associativismo e participação na saúde: uma análise da questão na região Nordeste do Brasil. In S. Fleury & L. de Vasconcelos Costa Lobato (Eds.), *Participação, Democracia e Saúde* (pp. 151–174). Rio de Janeiro: Cebes.

Aziz, A. (2010). Una polémica reforma electroral. In I. Bizberg (Ed.), *México en el espejo latinoamericano. ¿Democracia o crisis?* (pp. 361–386). Mexico: El Colegio de México.

Aziz, A. (2015). ¿Democracias diferentes?: México, Brasil y Argentina. In I. Bizberg (Ed.), *Variedades de Capitalismo en América Latina: los casos de México, Brasil, Argentina y Chile* (pp. 283–380). México: El Colegio de México.

Aziz, A. (2018). *Democracias en crisis. México y Brazil* (Unpublished manuscript). México: CIESAS.

Aziz, A., & Alonso, J. (2009). Tres instituciones de la democracia Mexicana: IFE, TRIFE e IFAI. In I. Bizberg & L. Meyer (Eds.), *Una Historia Contemporánea de México, Tomo 3. Instituciones*. México: Océano.

Bachiller, J. V. (2012). *El BNDES y las estrategias de desarrollo económico en Brasil. Banca pública de desarrollo, instituciones gubernamentales y trayectorias de intervención estatal (1952–2010)*. Tesis doctoral del Programa de Doctorado Procesos Políticos Contemporáneos, Universidad de Salamanca.

Baldi-Delatte, A. L. (2004). La stabilité monétaire après les crises argentine et brésilienne. *Rapport d'étude pour la Caisse des Dépôts et Consignations*, Manuscrit, avril.

Baldwin, R., & Evenett, S. (Eds.). (2009). *The collapse of global trade, murky protectionism, and the crisis: Recommendations for the G20*. London: VoxEU.org Publication/Centre for Economic Policy Research (CEPR).

Barba Solano, C. (2007). Claroscuros de la reforma social en México y América Latina. *Espiral (Guadalajara)*, *13*(39), 35–76.

Barba Solano, C., & Valencia Lomelí, E. (2013). La transición del régimen de bienestar mexicano: entre el dualismo y las reformas liberales. *Revista Uruguaya de Ciencia Política*, *22*(2), 28–54.

Barbosa, Fernando de Holanda, & Barbosa Filho, Fernando de Holanda. (2014). O Brasil pode repetir o milagre econômico? *Brazilian Journal of Political Economy*, *34*(4), 608–627.

Barrera, M. (1994). Política de ajuste y proceso de democratización en Chile: sus efectos sobre los trabajadores. *Revista Mexicana de Sociología*, *56*(1), 105–129.

Barros de Castro, L. (2005). Esperança, Frustração e Aprendizado: A Historia da Nova República. In Giambiagi et al. (Eds.), *Economía Brasileira Contemporânea (1945–2004)* (pp. 116–140). Rio de Janeiro: Elsevier.

Basabe Serrano, S., Pachano, S., & Mejía Acosta, A. (2010). In M. A. Cameron & J. P. Luna (Eds.), *Democracia en la Región Andina* (pp. 165–195). Lima: Instituto de Estudios Peruanos/Plural editores.

Becerril-Montekio, V. (2011a). Sistema de salud de Brasil. *Salud Pública de México, 53*(2), 120–131.

Becerril-Montekio, V. (2011b). Sistema de salud de Chile. *Revista Salud Pública de México, 53*(2), 132–143.

Beck, U. (2002). *Poder y Contrapoder en la Era Global, La nueva economía política global.* México: Paidos.

Becker, U. (2011, June). *Comparing institutional change in the BRICs and Central European political economies. Theoretical considerations and first empirical results.* Paper presented at the SASE Annual Meeting, Madrid.

Bejarano, A. M., Alviar, H., Botero, F., Hoskin, G., & Pachón, M. (2010). Colombia: Democracia Amenazada. In M. A. Cameron & J. P. Luna (Eds.), *Democracia en la Región Andina* (pp. 101–164). Lima: Instituto de Estudios Peruanos/Plural Editores.

Bekerman, M., & Dalmasso, G. (2014). Políticas productivas y competitividad industrial. El caso de Argentina y Brasil. *Brazilian Journal of Political Economy, 34*(1), 158–180.

Belló, M., & Becerril-Montekio, V. (2011). Sistema de Salud de Argentina. *Revista Salud Pública de México, 53*(2), 96–108.

Benetti, G., & Iglesias, E. (2015). Partidos, sindicatos y movimientos sociales en Argentina y Brasil (2003–2011): la compleja relación con gobiernos afines. *Temas y Debates, 30*, 59–84.

Bensusán, G. (2008). Regulaciones laborales, calidad de los empleos, modelos de inspección: México en el contexto latinoamericano. *Cuaderno de la CEPAL.* México: CEPAL.

Bensusán, G. (2010, July 2). Políticas laborales en América Latina: orientaciones, alcances y resultados. *Ponencia presentada en CEISAL.* Toulouse.

Bensusán, G. (2016). Organizing workers in Argentina, Brazil, Chile and Mexico: The authoritarian-corporatist legacy and old institutional designs in a new context. *Theoretical Inquiries in Law, 17*(1), 131–161.

Bensusán, G., & Middlebrook, K. (2013). *Sindicatos y Política en México. Cambios, continuidades y contradicciones.* México: UAM, Flacso y Clacso.

Bensusán, G., & Moreno-Brid, J. C. (2012). *El desempeño de las política macroeconómicas y laborales y las respuestas a la crisis internacional (1990–2010).* In M. Puchet Anyul, M. Rojas, R. Salazar, G. Valenti, & F. Valdés Ugarte (Eds.), *América Latina en los albores del Siglo XXI: 2. Aspectos sociopolíticos.* México: Flacso.

Berg, J. (2009). Brasil. El Salario mínimo como respuesta a la crisis. *OIT Notas sobre la crisis*. Santiago de Chile: OIT.

Berg, J. (2011). Laws or luck? Understanding rising formality in Brazil in the 2000s. In S. Lee & D. McCann (Eds.), *Regulating for decent work: New directions in labour market regulations*. Geneva and Basingstoke: ILO and Palgrave Macmillan.

Bergquist, C. (1986). *Labor in Latin America. Comparative Essays on Chile, Argentina, Venezuela, and Colombia*. Stanford, CA: Stanford University Press.

Berins Collier, R. (1999). *Paths toward democracy: The working class and elites in Western Europe and South America*. New York: Cambridge University Press.

Bernal, O., & Barbosa, S. (2015). La nueva reforma a la salud en Colombia: el derecho, el aseguramiento y el sistema de salud. *Revista Salud Pública de México, 57*(5), 433–440.

Bielschowsky, R. (2015). Structuralist reflections on current Latin American development. In B. Fritz & L. Lavinas (Eds.), *A moment of equality for Latin America? Challenges for redistribution* (pp. 129–143), Surrey and Burlington: Ashgate.

Bizberg, I. (1999). Le Syndicalisme Mexicain face à la mondialisation et à la recomposition du régime politique. *La Revue de L'IRES, 29*, 131–164.

Bizberg, I. (2004a). Trayectorias políticas e institucionales de México y Brasil: el caso de las relaciones entre el Estado y el sindicalismo. In C. Alba Vega & I. Bizberg (Coords.), *Democracia y globalización en México y Brasil*. Mexico: El Colegio de México.

Bizberg, I. (2004b). Auge y decadencia del corporativismo mexicano. In I. Bizberg & L. Meyer (Eds.), *Una Historia Contemporánea de México, Tomo 1. Transformaciones y permanencias*. México: Océano.

Bizberg, I. (2010). La democracia vacía. In I. Bizberg & F. Zapata (Eds.), *Los Grandes Problemas de México. Los movimientos sociales*. México: El Colegio de México.

Bizberg, I. (2011). The global economic crisis as disclosure of different types of capitalism. *Swiss Journal of Sociology/World Society Studies, 37*(2), 321–329.

Bizberg, I. (2014a). Los nuevos movimientos sociales en México: el movimiento por la paz con justicia y dignidad y #YoSoy132. *Foro Internacional 55*(217): 262–301.

Bizberg, I. (2014b). Types of capitalism in Latin America. *Interventions économiques/Papers in Political Economy (Online)*, (49), p. 31. Canada: Université de Québec á Montréal.

Bizberg, I. (Coord.) (2015). *Las variedades del capitalismo en América Latina: los casos de México, Brasil, Argentina y Chile*. Mexico: El Colegio de México.

Bizberg, I., & Martin, S. (2012). *El Estado de Bienestar ante la Globalización, el caso de Norteamérica*. México: El Colegio de México.

Bizberg, I., & Théret, B. (2012). La diversité des capitalismes latino-américains: les cas de l'Argentine, du Brésil et du Mexique. *La Revue de la Régulation*, Paris, No. 11.

Bizberg, I., & Théret, B. (2015). Las coaliciones sociopolíticas y las trayectorias de los capitalismos latinoamericanos. In I. Bizberg (Coord.), *Las variedades del capitalismo en América Latina: los casos de México, Brasil, Argentina y Chile* (pp. 95–146). Mexico: El Colegio de México.

Blecker, R., & Esquivel, G. (2010). *NAFTA, trade and development.* University of San Diego, 41.

Bojanic, A. N. (2015). Crowding out private investment in Bolivia: Evidence for the 1988–2010 period. *Latin American Research Review, 50*(3), 225–244.

Borri, C. (2016). El movimiento estudiantil en Chile 2001–2014 La renovación de la educación como aliciente para el cambio político-social. *Otras Modernidades, 4,* 141–160.

Boschi, R., & Gaitán, F. (2017). El Estado desarrollista en Brasil: Crisis, continuidad, incertidumbres. In C. Alba Vega & I. Bizberg (Eds.), *Dimensiones sociopolíticas y económicas de la crisis global y su impacto en los países emergentes.* México: El Colegio de México.

Boschi, R. R., & Santos Pinho, C. E. (2018). Desarrollo capitalista, austeridad fiscal y democracia en Brasil. In A. Aziz & I. Bizberg (Eds.), *La Diversidad de Capitalismos en Crisis,* in preparation.

Bouët, A., & Laborde, D. (2009). The potential cost of a failed Doha round. *SSRN Electronic Journal.* Available at SSRN: https://doi.org/10.2139/ssrn.1396335.

Boulding, C., & Nelson-Núñez, J. (2014). Civil society and support for the political system in times of crisis. *Latin American Research Review, 49*(1), 128–154.

Bourdieu, P. (2013). *La nobleza de Estado.* Buenos Aires: Siglo XXI.

Boyer, R. (2002). Varieté du Capitalisme et Théorie de la Regulation. In Association recherche et régulation, *L'année de la Régulation, n° 6 (2002–2003): Économie, institutions, pouvoirs* (pp. 125–194). Paris: Presses de Sciences Po (P.F.N.S.P.).

Boyer, R. (2005). How and why capitalisms differ. *Economy and Society, 34*(4), 509–557.

Boyer, R. (2012). The Chinese growth regime and the world economy. In R. Boyer, H. Uemura, & A. Isogai (Eds.), *Diversity and transformations of Asian capitalisms* (pp. 184–208). London and New York: Routledge.

Boyer, R. (2013). Brazil as the pioneer in Latin American inclusive growth. *Plataforma Politica Social,* 1–12. Available at: https://plataformapoliticasocial.com.br/cadernos-tematicos/.

Boyer, R. (2014). *Is more equality possible in Latin America? A challenge in a world of contrasted but interdependent inequality regimes* (DesiguALdades.net, Working Paper Series 67). Berlin: Freie Universität Berlin.

Boyer, R. (2015). *Économie politique des capitalismes, Théorie de la régulation et des crises.* Paris: La Découverte.

Boyer, R. (2017a). Formas de capitalismo, América Latina y el sistema internacional después de la gran crisis. In C. Alba Vega & I. Bizberg (Eds.),

Dimensiones sociopolíticas y económicas de la crisis global y su impacto en los países emergentes. México: El Colegio de México.

Boyer, R. (2017b). Orthodoxie, hétérodoxies et capitalismes contemporains. *Revue de la régulation*. http://journals.openedition.org/regulation/12626.

Boyer, R. (2017c). *What does the growing communality of contemporary capitalisms mean for economic theory?* (Unpublished manuscript prepared for the International Conference on Economic Theory and Policy). Tokyo: Meiji University.

Boyer, R., Uemura, H., & Isogai, A. (2012). *Diversity and transformations of Asian Capitalisms*. London and New York: Routledge.

Bresser-Pereira, L. C. (2012). Os trés ciclos da sociedade e do estado. *Perspectivas, 41*, 13–51.

Bresser-Pereira, L. C. (2015). *Reflecting on new developmentalism and classical developmentalism* (Working Paper No. 395). São Paulo: FGV.

Bresser-Pereira, L. C. (2017). The two forms of capitalism: developmentalism and economic liberalism. *Brazilian Journal of Political Economy, 37*(4), 680–703.

Bresser-Pereira, L. C. (2018). *Rentier-financier capitalism* (Unpublished manuscript to be published in the *Revue de la Régulation*).

Bresser-Pereira, L. C., & Gala, P. (2012). Macroeconomía estructuralista del desarrollo: ¿un segundo momento del estructuralismo latinoamericano? In J. L. Calva (Coord.), *Análisis Estratégico para el Desarrollo, Vol. 4* (pp. 245–272). México: Juan Pablos Editor.

Bringel, B., & Falero, A. (2016). Movimientos sociales, gobiernos progresistas y estado en América Latina: transiciones, conflictos y mediaciones. *Caderno CRH, 29*(spe3), 27–45.

Brosio, G., & Jiménez, J. P. (Eds.). (2012). *Decentralization and reform in Latin America: Improving intergovernmental relations*. Cheltenham, UK and Northampton, MA, USA: ECLAC/Edward Elgar.

Brown, C. P. (2009). Protectionism is on the rise: Antidumping investigations. In R. Baldwin & S. Evenett (Eds.), *The collapse of global trade, murky protectionism, and the crisis: Recommendations for the G20*. London: VoxEU.org Publication/Centre for Economic Policy Research (CEPR).

Cabalín-Quijada, C. (2014). Online and mobilized students: The use of Facebook in the Chilean student protests. *Comunicar, 22*(43), 25–33.

Cadestin, C., Gourdon, J., & Kowalski, P. (2016). *Participation in global value chains in Latin America: Implications for trade and trade-related policy* (OECD Trade Policy Papers, No. 192). Paris: OECD Publishing.

Calderón Hoffmann, A., & Stumpo, G. (2016). La evolución económica y social del Ecuador: las restricciones de la estructura productiva. *Los desafíos del Ecuador para el cambio estructural con inclusión social* (pp. 11–58). Santiago: CEPAL, LC/L. 4281.

Cameron, M. (2010). The State of democracy in the Andes: Ontroduction to a thematic issue of Revista de Ciencia Política. *Revista de Ciencia Política, 30*(1), 5–20.

Canelo, P. (2009). La política contra la economía: los elencos militares frente al plan económico de Martinez Hoz durante el Proceso de Reorganización Nacional (1976–1981). In A. Pucciarelli (Ed.), *Empresarios, tecnócratas y militares. La trama corporativa de la última Dictadura*. Buenos Aires: Siglo XXI.

Cardoso, A., & Gindin, J. (2009a). Industrial relations and collective bargaining Argentina, Brazil and Mexico compared. *Dialogue* No. 5, 1–108.

Cardoso, A., & Gindin, J. (2009b). *Industrial relations and collective bargaining: Argentina, Brazil and Mexico compared* (Working Paper No. 5). Geneva: Industrial and Employment Relations Department, International Labour Office.

Cardoso, F. H. & Faletto, E. (1969). *Dependencia y Desarrollo en América Latina*. México: Siglo XXI.

Carneiro, Â. M., & Veras de Oliveira, R. (2010). O sindicalismo na era Lula: entre paradoxos e novas perspectivas. Paper presented at the VI Congresso da Associação Latinoamericana de Sociologia do Trabalho, Mexico, April 16–22, p. 24.

Castells, M., & Calderon, F. (2015). *Economic faultlines*. Berkeley: Review of Latin American Studies.

Castillo Torres, M. (2005). Evolución, perspectivas y diseño de politicas sobre la banca de desarrollo en el Perú. *Serie financiamiento del desarrollo (174)*. Santiago de Chile: CEPAL.

Cavarrozi, M., & Casullo, E. (2002). Los partidos en América Latina hoy: ¿Consolidación o crisis? In M. Cavarozzi & J. A. Medina (Eds.), *El asedio a la política. Los partidos latinoamericanos en la era neoliberal*. Rosario: Homo Sapiens.

Cecchini, S., Filgueira, F., & Robles, C. (2014). *Sistemas de protección social en América Latina y el Caribe. Una perspectiva comparada*. Santiago de Chile: CEPAL.

Centellas, M. (2015). Cycles of reform: Placing Evo Morales's Bolivia in context. *Latin America Research Review, 50*(1), 229–241.

CEPAL. (2010). *La reacción de los gobiernos de las Américas frente a la crisis internacional: una presentación sintética de las medidas de política anunciadas hasta el 31 de diciembre de 2009*. Santiago de Chile: United Nations.

Cerdas Sandí, D. (2017). *La Disputa por el Poder de Asociación de los Trabajadores: Veto Empresarial y Democracia Restringida en América Latina*. Tesis doctoral del Programa de Doctorado en Investigación en Ciencias Sociales, con mención en Ciencia Política. México: Facultad Latinoamérica de Ciencia Sociales.

Chamon, M., & Garcia, M. (2016). Capital controls in Brazil: Effective? *Journal of International Money and Finance*, (61), 163–187.

Chaves Teixeira, A. C., Dagnino, E., & Almeida Silva, C. (2002). La constitución de la sociedad civil en Brasil. In E. Dagnino (Coord.), *Sociedad civil, esfera pública y democratización en América Latina: Brasil* (pp. 21–76). México: Unicamp-Fondo de Cultura Económico.

Chen, J. (2013). *A middle class without democracy: Economic growth and the prospects for democratization in China*. Oxford: Oxford University Press.

Cheresky, I. (2004). Argentina. Cambio de rumbo y recomposición política. *Nueva Sociedad, 193,* 4–16.

Cheresky, I. (2015). La segunda presidencia de Cristina Kirchner en sus inicios. Las elecciones de 2011 y la evolución del giro "Cristinista". In S. Gómez Tagle (Ed.), *Alternativas para la democracia en América Latina* (pp. 249–289), México: El Colegio de México.

Chiarini, T. (2016). A inercia estructural da base productiva brasileira: O IDE e a transferencia internacional de tecnologia. *Revista de Economia Política, 36*(2), 286–308.

Chomsky, A. (2016). Social impacts of resource extraction. *Latin American Research Review, 51*(1), 243–254. Latin American Studies Association.

Coelho, V. S. P., Pozzoni, B., & Cifuentes, M. (2006). Participation and public policies in Brazil. In J. Gastil & P. Levine (Eds.), *The deliberative democracy handbook.* San Francisco: Jossey-Bass.

Collier, R. B. (1999). *Paths toward democracy: The working class and elites in Western Europe and South America.* New York: Cambridge University Press.

Combes, H. (2004). Élections internes et transitions démocratiques: le cas du Parti de la révolution démocratique au Mexique. *Problèmes d'Amérique latine, 54,* 53–74.

Comisión Presidencial ISAPRES. (2014). *Informe Final.* Santiago de Chile: Comisión Asesora Presidencial para el Estudio y Propuesta de un Nuevo Régimen Jurídico para el Sistema de Salud Privado.

Conaghan, C. M. (2008a). Ecuador: Correa's plebiscitary presidency. In L. Diamond, M. F. Platner, & D. A. Brun (Eds.), *Latin America's struggle for democracy* (pp. 199–213). Baltimore: The John Hopkins University Press.

Conaghan, C. M. (2008b). Ecuador: Correa's plebiscitary presidency. *Journal of Democracy, 19*(2), 46–60.

Conaghan, C. M. (2011). Ecuador: Rafael Correa and the citizen's revolution. In S. Levitsky & K. M. Roberts (Eds.), *The resurgence of the Latin American left* (pp. 260–282), Baltimore: The Johs Hopkins University Press.

Contreras, C., & Zuloaga, M. (2014). *Historia mínima de Perú.* México: El Colegio de México.

Cook, M. L. (2007). *The politics of labor reform in Latin America: Between flexibility and rights.* Pennsylvania: The Pennsylvania State University Press.

Coppedge, M. (2010). Continuidad y cambio en los sistemas de partidos en América latina. In I. Bizberg (Ed.), *Mexico en el espejo latinoamericano.* México: El Colegio de México/KAS.

Cortés Conde, R. (2007). *La economía política de la Argentina en el siglo XX.* Buenos Aires: Edhasa.

Cortés Cáceres, F. (2013). Sobre las clases medias en México. *Mexico Social, Internet Journal.* http://www.mexicosocial.org/index.php/2017-05-22-14-12-20/alianzas/pued-en-ms/item/190-sobre-las-clases-medias-en-m%C3%A9xico.

Cortés, F. (2010). Pobreza, desigualdad en la distribución del ingreso y crecimiento económico, 1992–2006. In F. Cortés & O. de Oliveira (Eds.), *Los Grandes Problemas de México: Desigualdad social*. Mexico: El Colegio de México.

Costa, S. (2018). *Persistent Inequalities, Mutable Classes? Social Structure and Political Crisis in Brazil*. Paper presented at the XIX ISA World Conference, Toronto, July 15–21.

Crouch, C. (1993). *Industrial relations and European State traditions*. Oxford: Oxford University Press.

Dagnino, E. (2003). Citizenship in Latin America. *Latin American Perspectives, 30*(2), 211–225.

Dawyd, D. M. M. (2013). Oposiciones sociales a las dictaduras del cono sur. El nuevo sindicalismo argentino y brasileño en los años 70, entre la oposición sindical y la revolución. *Historia Caribe, 23*(8), 117–147.

De la Torre, A., Ize, A., & Schmukler, S. L. (2012). *Financial development in Latin America and the Caribbean. The Road Ahead*. IBRD, World Bank: Washington, DC.

De la Torre, C. (2015). El liderazgo populista de Rafael Correa y la desinstitucionalización de la política. In S. Gómez Tagle (Ed.), *Alternativas para la democracia en América Latina* (pp. 151–185), México: El Colegio de México.

De Melo, M. A. (1997). As reformas constitucionais e a previdência social 1993–1996. In E. Diniz & S. de Azevedo (Eds.), *Reforma do estado e democracia no Brasil*. Brasília: Editora Universidade de Brasília.

De Olloqui, F., & Palma, C. (2013). Panorama y evolución reciente de los bancos públicos de desarrollo. In F. De Olloqui, M. D. Chrisney, J. J. Gomes Lorenzo, A. Maffioli, R. Monge-González, M. Netto, F. Nieder, C. Palma Arancibia, & C. M. Rodríguez (Eds.), *Bancos públicos de desarrollo: ¿hacia un nuevo paradigma?* (pp. 1–19). Washington, DC: BID.

De Soto, H. (2005). *Le mystère du capital : Pourquoi le capitalisme triomphe en Occident et échoue partout ailleurs*. Paris: Flammarion.

De Souza Keller, W. (1994). Neocorporativismo y relações de trabalho: elementos para um debate sobre a experiência brasileira recente. *Boletim de Conjuntura: Política social, 14*, 31–40.

Degregori, C. I. (2003). Perú: el desvanecimiento de un régimen y el desafío de la reconstrucción democrática. In J. I. Domínguez & M. Shifter (Eds.), *Construcción de gobernabilidad democrática en América Latina*. México: Fondo de Cultura Económica.

Delamata, G. (2013a). Actualizando el derecho al ambiente: Movilización social, activismo legal y derecho constitucional al ambiente de sustentabilidad fuerte en el sector extractivista megaminero, *Entramados y perspectivas, 3*(3), 55–90.

Delamata, G. (2013b). Movimientos sociales, activismo constitucional y narrativa democrática en la Argentina contemporánea. *Sociologias, Porto Alegre, 32*(15), 148–180. DOSSIE.

Diario La Información. (2012, April 16). Empresas estatalizadas o nacionalizadas en Argentina. *Diario La Información*. https://www.lainformacion.com/politica/nacionalizacion/empresas-estatalizadas-o-nacionalizadas-en-argentina_FnN4HbzqLRMe9znUxHddp1/. Accessed 16 October 2017.

Doran, M. C. (2000). La Palabra Soberana: Los pobladores Chilenos frente a la Política. *Versión, 10*, 287–329.

Dowbor, L. (2009). La crisis no es solo económica. Reflexiones globales y algunos apuntes sobre Brasil. *Nueva Sociedad, 224*, 179–200.

Drahokoupil, J., & Myant, M. (2015). Putting comparative capitalism research in its place: Varieties of capitalism in transition economies. In M. Ebenau, I. Bruff, & Christian May (Eds.), *New directions in critical comparative capitalisms research*. London: Palgrave Macmillan.

Draibe, S. M. (1997). A política social na américa latina: o que ensinam as experiências recentes de reformas? In E. Diniz & S. de Azevedo (Eds.), *Reforma do Estado e Democracia no Brasil*. Brasilia: UnBenap.

Duhalde, S. (2013). Organización y acción en el sindicalismo de base en Argentina: un abordaje Conceptual. *Revista de Sociología e Politica, 21*(48), 161–177.

Dussel Peters, E. (2006). Hacia una política de competitividad en México. *ECONOMÍA unam, 3*(9), 65–81.

EFE Agency. (2017, January 6). Colombia improves the free zones regime to increase its competitiveness. *El Heraldo Newspaper*. https://www.elheraldo.co/colombia/colombia-mejora-regimen-de-zonas-francas-para-aumentar-su-competitividad-317458. Accessed 19 October 2017.

EFE Economía. (2012, September 4). Brasil anuncia la subida de aranceles para proteger la industria. *El País*. https://elpais.com/economia/2012/09/05/agencias/1346798596_101945.html. Accessed 16 October 2017.

Eibenschutz, C., Saco, A., Tamez, Silvia, Zafra, X., & Ramírez, R. M. (2014). Reflexiones sobre el proceso de reforma sanitaria (1993–2013) y participación social en Perú. *Saúde Debate, 38*(103), 872–885.

Engerman, S., & Sokoloff, K. (1997). Factor endowments, institutions, and differential paths of growth among new world economies. A view from economic historians of the United States. In S. Haber (Ed.), *How Latin America fell behind. Essays on the economic histories of Brazil and Mexico* (pp. 261–304). Stanford: Stanford University Press.

Engerman, S., & Sokoloff, K. (2000). History lessons. Institutions, factor endowments, and paths of development in the new world. *Journal of Economic Perspectives, 14*(3), 217–232.

Eslava, M., Meléndez, M., & Perry, G. (2014). *Notas sobre Política de Desarrollo Productivo en Colombia*. Bogotá: Centro de Estudios sobre Desarrollo Económico, Universidad de los Andes.

Esping-Andersen, G. (1990). *The three worlds of welfare capitalism*. Princeton, NJ: Princeton University Press.

Espinosa, M., & Chible, M. (2016). La huelga pacífica en la negociación colectiva y el proyecto de reforma laboral: un análisis crítico. *Revista Chilena de Derecho del Trabajo y de la Seguridad Social, 6*(12), 56–80.

Esquivel, G. (2010). De la inestabilidad macroeconómica al estancamiento estabilizador: el papel del diseño y la conducción de la política económica. In N. Lustig (Ed.), *Los grandes problemas de México. IX Crecimiento Económico y Equidad*. México: El Colegio de México.

Etchemendy, S., & Collier, R. B. (2007). Down but not out: Union resurgence and segmented neocorporatism in Argentina (2003–2007). *Politics & Society, 7*(3), 363–401.

Evans, P. (1995). *Embedded autonomy. States and industrial transformation*. Princeton, NJ: Princeton University Press.

Fagnani, E. (2015). Social policy, inequality, and development: Notes on Brazil in the first decade of the 21st century. In B. Fritz & L. Lavinas (Eds.), *A moment of equality for Latin America? Challenges for redistribution* (pp. 217–234), Surrey and Burlington: Ashgate.

Faguet, J. P. (2012). *Decentralization and popular democracy. Governance from below in Bolivia*. Ann Arbor: University of Michigan Press.

Falleti, T. G. (2010). *Decentralization and subnational politics in Latin America*. New York: Cambridge University Press.

Farthing, L. C., & Kohl, B. H. (2014). *Evo's Bolivia: Continuity and change*. Texas: University of Texas Press.

Fernandez Bugna, C., & Porta, F. (2008). El crecimiento reciente de la industria Argentina: Nuevo Régimen sin cambio estructural. In M. R. Soares de Lima (Ed.), *Desempenho de Governos Progressistas no Cone Sul: Agendas alternativas ao Neoliberalismo*. Rio de Janeiro: Edições IUPERJ.

Ffrench-Davis, R. (2008). *Chile entre el neoliberalismo y el crecimiento con equidad. Reformas y políticas económicas desde 1973*, Santiago: J. C. Sáez Editor.

Fornillo, B. (2018). La energía del litio en Argentina y Bolivia: comunidad, extractivismo y posdesarrollo. *Colombia Internacional, 93*, 179–201.

Franceschelli, I., & Ronconi, L. (2005). *Clientelism, workfare and the emergence of the piqueteros in Argentina*. LACEA Conference. http://depot.gdnet.org/gdnshare/pdf2/gdn_library/annual_conferences/seventh_annual_conference/Franceschelli_Parallel_1_4.pdf. Accessed 15 May 2018.

Fritz, B. (2017). *Conceptos Actuales del desarrollo económico y social: Opciones para Ecuador*. Cámara de Comercio de Guayaquil, Ecuador: Power Point.

Fritz, B., & Lavinas, L. (Eds.). (2015). *A moment of equality for Latin America? Challenges for redistribution*. Surrey and Burlington: Ashgate.

Gajardo, S. V. (2011). El resplandor de las mayorías y la dilatación de un doble conflicto: El movimiento estudiantil en Chile el 2011. *Anuario del conflicto social, 1*(1), 286–309.

Galhardi, R. (2009a). México. Programa para la preservación del empleo. *OIT Notas sobre la crisis*. Santiago de Chile: OIT.

Galhardi, R. (2009b). Programa de empleo temporal ampliado (PETA). *OIT Notas sobre la crisis*. Santiago de Chile: OIT.

Gallagher, K. P. (2011). Trading away financial stability in Colombia: Capital controls and the US-Colombia trade agreement. *SerieBrief*, (66), Latin American Trade Network. http://www.ase.tufts.edu/gdae/Pubs/rp/Brief66_TradingAway_Gallagher.pdf. Accessed 15 May 2018.

Gallo, A. (2012). Trade policy and protectionism in Argentina. *Economic Affairs, 32*, 55–59.

Gamberoni, E., & Newfarmer, R. (2009). Trade protection: Incipient but worrisome trends. In R. Baldwin & E. Simon (Eds.), *The collapse of global trade, murky protectionism, and the crisis: Recommendations for the G20*. London: VoxEU.org Publication/Centre for Economic Policy Research (CEPR).

Garretón, M. A. (1991). La redemocratización política en Chile. Transición, inauguración y evolución. *Estudios Públicos, 4*(1), 101–133.

Garretón, M. A., & Garretón, R. (2010). La democracia incompleta en Chile: La realidad tras los rankings internacionales. *Revista de Ciencia Política, 30*(1), 115–148.

Gellner, E. (1983). *Nations and nationalisms*. Paris: Payot.

Ghosh, A. R., & Qureshi, M. S. (2016). *What's In a Name? That Which We Call Capital Controls IMF*. Working Paper 16/25. Available at: https://www.imf.org/external/pubs/ft/wp/2016/wp1625.pdf. Accessed 15 May 2018.

Gibson, E. L. (Ed.). (2004). Federalism and democracy. Theoretical connections and cautionary insights. In E. L. Gibson (Ed.), *Federalism and democracy in Latin America* (pp. 1–28). Baltimore: Johns Hopkins University Press.

Gil, R., & Grampone, A. (2014). Sindicalismo y política en el Perú: una breve aproximación en perspectiva comparada. *Documento de Trabajo N°2. Serie de Documentos de Trabajo*. Lima: Asociación Civil Politai.

Goirand, C. (2002). La démocratie participative au Brésil: les expériences de budgets municipaux participatifs. *Cahiers du Gela-IS*, (2), 125–136. Paris: L'Harmattan.

Goldfrank, B. (2011). The left and participatory democracy. In S. Levitsky & K. M. Roberts (Eds.), *The resurgence of the Latin American left* (pp. 162–183). Baltimore: The Johs Hopkins University Press.

Goldstein, A., & Lemoine, F. (2013). *L'économie des BRIC: Brésil, Russie, Inde, Chine*. Paris: La Découverte Editions.

Golonbek, C. (2008). Banca de desarrollo en Argentina: breve historia y agenda para el debate. *Documento de Trabajo N° 21*. Buenos Aires: CEFID-AR.

Gómez Dantés, O., Sesma, S., Becerril, V., Knaul, F., Arreola, H., & Frenk, J. (2011). Sistema de salud de México. *Salud Pública de México, 53*(2), S220–S232.

Goméz Sabaini, J. C., & Jiménez, J. P. (2012). The financing of subnational governments. In G. Brosio & J. P. Jiménez (Eds.), *Descentralization and Reform in Latin America* (pp. 140–171). Cheltenham, UK and Northampton, MA: United Nations and Edward Elgar.

Gonçalves Couto, C. (2015). Cambios y continuiddades em la política brasileira reciente. In S. Gómez Tagle (Ed.), *Alternativas para la democracia en América Latina* (pp. 291–335). México: El Colegio de México.

González, L. (2012). The redistributive effects of centralization and decentralization across subnational units. *Latin American Research Review, 47*(3), 109–133.

Goya, D. (2014). *Industrial policy: What is it, why it is necessary, and its past, present and future in Chile* (MPRA Paper No. 64881). Munich: Munich Personal RePEc Archive.

Graña, J. M., & Kennedy, D. (2008). *Distribución funcional del ingreso, salario real y productividad en Argentina en perspectiva latinoamericana. Desde mediados de los setenta hasta la actualidad*. Buenos Aires: CEPED, Universidad de Buenos Aires. Available at: http://209.177.156.169/libreria_cm/archivos/pdf_981.pdf.

Guerrero, R., Gallegos, A. I., Becerril-Montekio, V., & Vásquez, J. (2011). Sistema de Salud de Colombia. *Revista Salud Pública de México, 53*(2), 144–155.

Guillen Romo, H. (2012). México: del desarrollo "hacia adentro" al desarrollo "hacia fuera". In J. L. Calva (Coord.), *Análisis Estratégico para el Desarrollo* (Vol. 3, pp. 245–283). México: Juan Pablos Editor.

Guimaraes, L. (2006). *Excluídos pela clásula de barreira partidos vão à Justiça e estudam fusões*. http://eleicoes.uol.com.br/2006/reportagens/clausula.jhtm. *Accessed 15 May 2018*.

Gustafsson, M. T. (2016). Private conflict regulation and the influence of peasant communities over natural resources. *Latin American Research Review, 51*(2), 86–106.

Gutierrez Arriola, A. (2002). *México dentro de las refromas a los sistemas de salud y seguridad social en América latina*. México: Siglo XXI.

Haber, S. (1991). Industrial concentration and the capital markets: A comparative study of Brazil, Mexico and the United States, 1830–1930. *Journal of Economic History, 51*(3), 559–580.

Haber, S. (Ed.). (1997). *How Latin America fell behind. Essays on the economic history of Brazil and Mexico*. Stanford: Stanford University Press.

Haggard, S. (1990). *Pathways from the Periphery. The Politics of Growth in the Newly Industrializing Countries*. New York: Cornell University Press.

Haggard, S., & Kaufman, R. (2008). *Development, democracy, and welfare states: Latin America, East Asia, and Eastern Europe*. Princeton: Princeton University Press.

Hall, P. A., & Soskice, D. (Eds.). (2001). *Varieties of capitalism: The institutional foundations of comparative advantage*. Oxford: Oxford University Press.

Harada, Y., & Tohyama, H. (2011). Asian capitalisms: Institutional configurations and firm heterogeneity. In R. Boyer, H. Uemura, & A. Isogai (Eds.),

Diversity and transformations of Asian capitalisms (pp. 243–263). London and New York: Routledge.

Hausmann, R., & Rigobon, R. (2003). An alternative interpretation of the 'resource curse': Theory and policy implications. In J. M. Davis, R. Ossowski, & A. Fedelino (Eds.), *Fiscal policy formulation and implementation in oil-producing countries*. Washington, DC: IMF.

Hayter, S., & Stoevska, V. (2011). *Social dialogue indicators. International statistical inquiry 2008–09. Technical Brief.* Geneve: ILO.

Hermann, J. (2005a). Reformas, endividamento externo e o 'milagre' econômico. In F. Giambiagi, A. Villela, L. Barros de Castro, & J. Hermann (Eds.), *Economia brasileira contemporânea (1945–2004)* (pp. 69–92). Rio de Janeiro: Elsevier.

Hermann, J. (2005b). Auge e Declínio do Modelo de Crescimento com Endividamento: O II PND e a Crise da Dívida Externa (1974–1984). In F. Giambiagi, A. Villela, L. Barros de Castro, & J. Hermann (Eds.), *Economia brasileira contemporânea (1945–2004)* (pp. 93–115). Rio de Janeiro: Elsevier.

Hiratuka, C., & Sarti, F. (2017). Transformações na estrutura produtiva global, desindustrialização e desenvolvimento industrial no Brasil. *Brazilian Journal of Political Economy, 37*(1), 189–207.

Hochstetler, K., & Montero, A. (2012, May 23–26). Inertial statism and the new developmentalist state in Brazil. In XXX *International Congress of the Latin American Studies Association*, San Francisco.

Hoshino, T. (2015). Conference at El Colegio de México.

Hoshino, T. (2018). *Red de proveeduría de la industria automotriz en México. ¿Es posible la incorporación de las empresas mexicanas?* Guadalajara: Universidad de Guadalajara.

Houtzager, P. P., & Gurza Lavalle, A. (2010). Civil society's claims to political representation in Brazil. *Studies in Comparative International Development, 45*, 1–29.

Huber, E. (1983). The Peruvian military government, labor mobilization, and the political strength of the left. *Latin American Research Review, 18*(2), 57–93.

Huber, E., & Stephens, J. D. (2012). *Democracy and the left.* Chicago and London: The University of Chicago Press.

Huber, E., Pribble, J., & Stephens, J. D. (2010). The Chilean left in power: Achievements, failures and omissions. In K. Weyland, R. L. Madrid, & W. Hunter (Eds.). *Leftist governments in Latin America*. Cambridge: Cambridge University Press.

Huneeus, C. (2005). Chile: A system Frozen by Elite interests. In A. Reynolds, B. Reilly, & A. Ellis (Eds.), *Electoral system design: The new international idea handbook*. Stockholm: IDEA.

Ibarra, C. (2008). La paradoja del crecimiento lento de México. *Revista de la CEPAL, 95*, 83–102.

Ibarra, C. (2011). México: la maquila, el desajuste monetario y el crecimiento impulsado por las exportaciones. *Revista CEPAL, 104,* 199–215.

Inostroza Lara, J., & Fuenzalida Aguirre, J. (2015). Promises and risks: Challenges to the decentralization agenda in chile. In *30 years of reform: Decentralization, subnational governments and development in Latin America* (pp. 42–46). Hemisphere, 24(1). Available at: http://digitalcommons.fiu.edu/lacc_hemisphere/vol24/iss1/1.

Invernizzi, N. (2006). Disciplining the workforce: Controlling workers in the restructuring of production. *Latin American Perspectives, 33*(3), 89–110.

Izunza Vera, E., & Gurza Lavalle, A. (2012). Arquitetura da participacao e controles democráticos no Brasil e no México. *Novos Estudos, 92,* 105–121.

Jeanneau, S., Tovar, C. E., & Moreno, R. (2007). Introduction. In S. Jeanneau, & C. E. Tovar (Eds.). *Evolving banking systems in Latin America and the Caribbean: Challenges and implications for monetary policy and financial stability* (BIS Papers No. 33) (pp. 1–2). Basel, Switzerland: Monetary and Economic Department, Bank for International Settlements.

Jeria, J. F. (2010). El difícil parto de otra democracia: La Asamblea Constituyente de Bolivia. *Latin American Research Review, 45*(4), 5–26. Latin American Studies Association.

Joignant, A., & López, M. A. (2005). Le comportement électoral au Chili: paradoxes et présomptions sur la continuité ou la rupture de l'orientation du vote. *Problèmes d'Amérique Latine,* #56. Paris: Choiseul Éditions.

Kandogan, Y., & Johnson, S. D. (2016). Role of economic and political freedom in the emergence of global middle class. *International Business Review, 25,* 711–725.

Karl, T. L. (1997). *The paradox of plenty: Oil booms and Petro-States.* Berkeley and Los Angeles, CA: University of California Press.

Katzenstein, P. J. (1985). *Small states in world markets industrial policy in Europe.* Ithaca and London: Cornell University Press.

Kay, C. (2002). Why East Asia overtook Latin America: Agrarian reform, industrialization and development. *Third World Quarterly, 23*(6), 1073–1102.

Kennemore, A., & Weeks, G. (2011). Twenty-first century socialism? The elusive search for a post-neoliberal development model in Bolivia and Ecuador. *Bulletin of Latin American Research, 30*(3), 267–281.

Kingstone, P. R. & A. F. Ponce. (2010). From Cardoso to Lula. The Triumph of pragmatism in Brazil. In K. Weyland, R. L. Madrid, & W. Hunter (Eds.), *Leftist governments in Latin America* (pp. 98–123). Cambridge: Cambridge University Press.

Klein, H. S. (2015). *Historia Mínima de Bolivia.* México: El Colegio de México.

Kosacoff, B. (2003). The Argentine Industry: A Thwarted restructuring process. In Banco BICE/Universidad Nacional de Quilmes, *Producción y trabajo en la Argentina. Memoria fotográfica 1860–1960*. Buenos Aires: Banco BICE/ UNQ.

Kostzer, D. (2008). *Argentina: A case study on the plan Jefes y Jefas de Hogar Desocupados, or the employment road to economic recovery* (Working Paper No. 534). Annandale-on-Hudson, NY: The Levy Economics Institute of Bard College.

Kupfer, D. (2012). *Case studies of successful and unsuccessful industrial policies: The case of Brazil*. New Thinking on Industrial Policy International Economic Association (IEA)-World Bank Roundtable, Washington, DC, May 22–23.

Laclau, E. (2006). *La razón populista*. Mexico: FCE.

Laserna, R. (2010). Mire, la democracia boliviana, en los hechos. *Latin American Research Review, 45*(4), 27–58. Latin American Studies Association.

Lautier, B. (2004). Las políticas sociales en México y Brasil: seguridad social, asistencia, ausencia. In C. Alba & I. Bizberg (Eds.), *Democracia y Globalización en México y Brasil*. México: Colegio de México.

Lautier, B. (2007). Les politiques sociales au Brésil durant le goouvernment de Lula: aumône d'Etat ou droits sociaux? *Problèmes d'Amérique latine, 63*, 51–76.

Lautier, B. (2009). Gouvernement moral des pauvres et dépolitisation des politiques publiques en Amérique Latine. In N. Borgeaud-Garciandía, B. Lautier, R. Peñafiel, & A. Tizziani (Eds.), *Penser le politique en Amérique Latine* (pp. 19–36). Paris: Karthala.

Lavarello, P., & Sarabia, M. (2015). *La política industrial en la Argentina en la década de los 2000. Serie Estudios y Perspectivas de la CEPAL*. Buenos Aires: CEPAL.

Lavaud, J.-P. (2007). Bolivia: ¿un futuro político hipotecado? *Nueva Sociedad*, (209), 142–159.

Lavigne, M. (2013). *Sistemas de protección social en América Latina y el Caribe Perú*. Santiago de Chile: CEPAL.

Le Bot, Y. (2009). *La Grande révolte indienne*. Paris: Robert Laffont.

Lechevalier, S. (2011). *La grande transformation du capitalisme japonais*. Paris: Presses de Sciences Po.

Ledo, C., & Soria, R. (2011). Sistema de Salud de Bolivia. *Revista Salud Pública de México, 53*(2), 109–119.

Leiva, S., & Campos, A. (2013). Movimiento social de trabajadores subcontratados en la minería privada del cobre en Chile. *Psicoperspectivas, 12*(2), 51–61.

Letelier, S., & Neyra, A. (2013). The political economy of regional grants in Peru. *CEPAL Review, 109*, 147–161.

Levitsky, S. (2001). Organization and labor-based party adaptation: The transformation of Argentine Peronism in comparative perspective. *World Politics, 54*(1), 27–56.

Levitsky, S., & Cameron, M. A. (2003). Democracy without parties? Political parties and regime change in Fujimori's Peru. *Latin American Politics and Society, 45*(3), 1–33.

Levitsky, S., & Roberts, K. M. (2011). *The resurgence of the Latin American left*. Baltimore: The Johs Hopkins University Press.

López Pacheco, J. A., & Hincapié Jiménez, S. (2015). De la movilización tradicional a las redes de presión transnacional: violencia antisindical y derechos humanos en Colombia. *Foro internacional, 55*(4), 1082–1114.

Losada, R. (2013). La alternativa colombiana en años recientes. In S. Gómez Tagle (Ed.), *Alternativas para la democracia en América Latina* (pp. 187–224). México: El Colegio de México.

Lo Vuolo, R. (2015). The limits of redistributive policies in Latin America: Complementarities between economic and social protection systems. In B. Fritz & L. Lavinas (Eds.), *A moment of equality for Latin America? Challenges for redistribution* (pp. 31–52). Surrey and Burlington: Ashgate.

Luna, J. P. (2010). ¿Participación versus representación? Partidos políticos y democracia en la región andina. In M. A. Cameron & J. P. Luna (Eds.), *Democracia en la Región Andina* (pp. 373–420). Lima: Instituto de Estudios Peruanos/Plural Editores.

Machado, R. (2014). La economía informal en el Perú: magnitud y determinantes (1980–2011). *Apuntes. Revista de Ciencias Sociales, 41*(74), 197–233.

Magud, N. E., Reinhart, C. M., & Rogoff, K. S. (2005). *Capital controls: Myth and reality—A portfolio balance approach* (Working Paper). Oregon: Economics Department, University of Oregon.

Manrique, C. (2007). Banca de desarrollo en México: un futuro necesario. In J. L. Calva (Ed.), *Agenda para el Desarrollo, Vol. 6: Financiamiento del crecimiento económico* (pp. 100–116). México: Porrúa-UNAM.

Maradona, S. (2012, May 4). Seis años de nacionalizaciones forzosas en América Latina. *Sección 5 Días, Diario El País*. https://cincodias.elpais.com/cincodias/2012/05/04/empresas/1336298336_850215.html. Accessed 16 October 2017.

Maravall, J. M. (1997). *Regimes, politics and markets: Democratization and economic change in Southern and Eastern Europe*. Oxford: Oxford University Press.

Marichal, C. (2003). La deuda externa. In I. Bizberg & L. Meyer (Eds.), *Una historia contemporánea de México, Tomo 1. Transformaciones y permanencias* (pp. 451–491). México: Océano.

Marques, R. M. (2015). Le protection sociale publique sous les gouvernements Lula et Dilma: entre avancée et recul des droits sociaux. *Chronique internationale de l'IRES, 150*, 30–38.

Marques Pereira, J., & Bruno, M. (2015). *Path dependence blocking the emergence of a new type of capitalism favoring redistribution in Brazil: A new view on the possibility of a developmental coalition* (Unpublished manuscript). Université d'amiens, France.

Marques Pereira, J., & Murillo, V. S. (2015). El problema del tipo de cambio y la posibilidad de revertir la desindustrialización. Una comparación entre Argentina, Brasil y México a la luz de una concepción alternativa de la moneda como institución social. In I. Bizberg (Coord.), *Las variedades del capitalismo en América Latina: los casos de México, Brasil, Argentina y Chile* (pp. 381–472). México: El Colegio de México.

Marques Pereira, J., & Théret, B. (2004). Mediaciones institucionales de regulación social y dinámicas macroeconómicas: los casos de Brasil y México. In C. Alba & I. Bizberg (Eds.), *Democracia y Globalización en México y Brasil*. El Colegio de México: México.

Martina, M. (2017, August 24). Exclusive: In China, the party's push for influence inside foreign firms stirs fears. *Reuters*. https://www.reuters.com/article/us-china-congress-companies/exclusive-in-china-the-partys-push-for-influence-inside-foreign-firms-stirs-fears-idUSKCN1B40JU. Accessed 15 May 2018.

Maurer, N., & Haber, S. (2004). *Related lending and economic performance* (Manuscript). Instituto Tecnológico Autónomo de Monterrey & Stanford University, Monterrey.

Maurizio, R. (2014). *Labour formalization and declining inequality in Argentina and Brazil in the 2000s: A dynamic approach* (ILO Research Paper No. 9). Geneva: ILO.

Mayorga, F. (2011). *Dilemas. Ensayos sobre democracia intercultural y Estado plurinacional*. La Paz: Centro de Estudios Superiores Universitarios, Universidad Mayor de San Simon and Plural Editores.

Mayorga, F. (2015). El segudo gobierno de Evo Morales: dilemas del proyecto estatal del MAS. In S. Gómez Tagle (Ed.), *Alternativas para la democracia en América Latina* (pp. 117–149), México: El Colegio de México.

Mayorga, R. A. (2002). Sistema de partidos y neopopulismo en Bolivia. In M. Cavarozzi & J. A. Medina (Eds.), *El asedio a la política. Los partidos latinoamericanos en la era neoliberal*. Rosario: Homo Sapiens.

Mayorga, R. A. (2005). La crisis del sistema de Partidos Políticos y el experimento del Gobierno sin partidos en Bolivia. *Revista Futuros, 3*(9).

McGuire, J. W. (1995). Political parties and democracy in Argentina. In S. Mainwaring & T. R. Scully (Eds.), *Building democratic institutions; party systems in Latin America* (pp. 200–246). Stanford, CA: Stanford University Press.

Medina, A., Manuel, J., & Julieta Suárez, C. (2002). La competencia partidaria en Argentina: sus implicancias sobre el régimen democrático. In M. Cavarozzi & J. M. Abal Medina (Eds.), *El asedio a la política: los partidos latinoamericanos en la era neoliberal*. Rosario: Homo Sapiens—Konrad Adenauer Stiftung.

Melo, C. R. (2015). The 2014 Elections and the Brazilian Party System. *Brazilian Political Science Review, 9*(1), 93–114.

Melo, J. O. (2017). *Historia minima de Colombia*. México: El Colegio México.

Mendoza Cota, J. E. (2011). La crisis de la industria automotriz en México en el marco de la integración económica con Estados Unidos. *Economía UNAM, 8*(22), 55–73.

Meneguello, R. (2002). El Impacto de la democratización del Estado en el desarrollo de los partidos brasileños (1985–1998). In M. Cavarozzi & J. A. Medina (Eds.), *El asedio a la política los partidos latinoamericanos en la era neoliberal*. Rosario: Homo Sapiens.

Merlano-Porras, C., & Gorbanev, I. (2013). Sistema de salud en Colombia: una revisión sistemática de literatura. *Gerencia y Políticas De Salud, 12*(24), 74–86.

Mesa-Lago, C. (1994). *Changing social security in Latin America. Towards alleviating the social costs of economic reform*. Boulder and London: Lynne Rienner Publishers.

Mesa-Lago, C. (2009). *Efectos de la crisis global sobre la seguridad social de salud y pensiones en América Latina y el Caribe y recomendaciones de políticas. Serie Políticas Sociales*. Santiago de Chile: CEPAL.

Milanovic, B., & Yitzhaki, S. (2002). Decomposing world income distribution: Does the world have a middle class? *Review of income and wealth, 48*(2), 155–178.

Moguillansky, G., Ramírez, E., & Furnaro, A. (2013). *Las políticas de desarrollo productivo en Chile, 1990–2012*. Programa de Cohesión Territorial para el Desarrollo Rural-RIMISP.

Molina, F. (2015). *El modelo económico de Bolivia y su inevitable fracaso*. Libros Nómadas.

Mollo, M. L. R., & Moreira Amado, A. (2015). O debate desenvolvimentista no Brasil: tomando partido. *Economia e Sociedade, 24*(1), 1–28.

Montes Cató, J., & Dobrusin, B. (2016). El sindicalismo Latinoamericano ante una nueva encrucijada: De la centralidad del Estado al de las empresas multinacionales. *Trabajo y sociedad, 27*, 7–22.

Monterrey Arce, J. (2013). *Sistemas de protección social en América Latina y el Caribe: Estado Plurinacional de Bolivia*. Santiago: CEPAL.

Montinola, G., Qian, Y., & Weingast, B. R. (1996). Federalism, Chinese style: The political basis for economic success in China. *World Politics, 48*(1), 50–81.

Moore, B. (1969). *Social origins of dictatorship and democracy lord and peasant in the making of the modern world*. London: Penguin Books.

Morales, A. (2013). *La política económica boliviana 1982–2010*. La Paz: Plural Editores.

Mouthón, L. (2017, May 2). Colombia, the country with the most free zones in Latin America. *El Heraldo Newspaper*. https://www.elheraldo.co/economia/colombia-el-pais-con-mas-zonas-francas-en-america-latina-355483. Accessed 19 October 2017.

Mújica, J. 2014. *Interview by Jordi Évole*. https://www.youtube.com/watch?v=ZlE-9ohXgDI. Accessed 19 October 2017.

Munck, R. (2004). Introduction. *Latin American Perspectives, 31*(4), 3–20.

Muniesa, F., & Callon, M. (2013). 8. La performativité des sciences économiques. In P. Steiner & F. Vatin (Eds.), *Traité de sociologie économique* (pp. 281–316). France: Presses Universitaires de France.

Murillo, M. V. (2000). From populism to neoliberalism: Labor unions and market reforms in Latin America. *World Politics, 52*(2), 135–174.

Mustapic, A. M. (2002). Del partido peronista al justicialista: las transformaciones de un partido carismático. In M. Cavarozzi & J. A. Medina (Comps.), *El asedio a la política. Los partidos latinoamericanos en la era neoliberal.* Rosario: Homo Sapiens.

Nassif, A., & Feijó, C. (2013). Liberal versus neo-developmental convention to growth: Why has Brazil shown a poor performance since the 1980s? *Brazilian Journal of Political Economy, 33*(4), 555–576.

Nassif, A., Feijó, C., & Araújo, E. (2015a). Structural change and economic development: Is Brazil catching up or falling behind? *Cambridge Journal of Economics, 39*(5), 1307–1332.

Nassif, A., Feijo, C., & Araújo, E. (2015b, October 22–24). The BRICS's long-term economic performance: A comparative analysis. In *19th Conference of the Research Network Macroeconomics and Macroeconomic Policies (FMM): The Spectre of Stagnation, Europe in the World Economy*, Berlin.

Neri, M. C. (2008). *A nova classe média*. Rio de Janeiro: FGV/IBRE.

Neri, M. C. (2011). *A nova classe média: o lado brilhante da base da pirâmide.* São Paulo: Editora Saraiva.

Neto, O. A., & Coelho, C. F. (2008). Brasil en el 2007: el desencuentro entre la economía y la política. *Revista de ciencia política (Santiago), 28*(1), 81–102.

Neubert, D. (2016). *The simplified assumptions of the global middle class narrative: Global middle groups in Kenya* (Unpublished paper presented at the Conference Middle Class in World Society). World Sociaty Foundation and ISEC, Bangalore, India.

Niemetz, K. (2009). La nacionalización de los fondos de jubilación privados en Argentina. *Economic Affairs, 29*(1), 49–53.

Ninomiya, Y. (2015). Industrial policy and the post-new Brazil. In R. Konta (Ed.), *The post-new Brazil.* Chiba: IDE-JETRO.

Nölke, A., & Vliegenthart, A. (2009). Enlarging the varieties of capitalism: The emergence of dependent market economies in East Central Europe. *World Politics, 61*(4), 670–702.

North, D. C., & Weingast, B. R. (1989). Constitutions and commitment: The evolution of institutional governing public choice in seventeenth century England. *Journal of Economic History, 49*(4), 803–832.

North, D. C., Summerhill, W., & Weingast, B. R. (2002). Orden y desorden y cambio económico: Latinoamérica vs Norte América. *Revista Instituciones y Desarrollo, 12–13*, 9–59.

Novick, M., Lengyel, M., & Sarabia, M. (2009). De la protección laboral a la vulnerabilidad social. Reformas neoliberales en la Argentina. *Revista Internacional del Trabajo, 128*(3), 257–275.

Nylen, W. R. (2007). Participatory Legislative "Home Styles" and Party Renewal in the Workers Party (PT) in Brazil. Paper presented at the Congress of the Latin American Studies Association (LASA), Montréal, Canada.

OCDE. (2016). *Fomentando un Crecimiento Inclusivo de la Productividad en América Latina. Serie Mejores Políticas.* Paris: OECD Publishing. Available at: https://www.oecd.org/latin-america/fomentando-un-crecimiento-inclusivo-de-la-productividad-en-america-latina.pdf.

OCDE, BID, & World Bank. (2015). *Panorama de las pensiones: América latina y el Caribe.* Washington, DC: Banco Interamericano de Desarrollo.

O'Donnell, G. (1996). Ilusiones sobre la Consolidación. *Nueva Sociedad* (144), 70–89. http://nuso.org/revista/144/nueva-representacion-vieja-politica/.

OECD, WTO, & WB. (2014). *Global value chains: Challenges, opportunities, and implications for policy.* Report prepared for submission to the G20 Trade Ministers Meeting Sydney, Australia.

OIT. (2011a). *Panorama laboral 2011.* Lima: OIT/Oficina Regional para América Latina y el Caribe.

OIT. (2011b). Hacia una recuperación sostenible: por una política de crecimiento basada en los salarios. *Boletín Internacional de Investigación Sindical, 3*(2). Ginebra: Oficina Internacional del Trabajo.

OIT. (2014a). *Panorama laboral 2014.* Lima: OIT/Oficina Regional para América Latina y el Caribe.

OIT. (2014b). *Panorama Laboral Temático: Transición a la formalidad en América Latina y el Caribe.* Lima: OIT/Oficina Regional para América Latina y el Caribe.

OIT. (2015). *Panorama laboral 2015.* Lima: OIT/Oficina Regional para América Latina y el Caribe.

Ortiz Crespo, S., & Mayorga, F. (2012). Introduction to the dossier: Movimientos sociales, Estado y democracia en Bolivia y Ecuador en el tránsito del neoliberalismo al postneoliberalismo. *ÍCONOS, Revista de Ciencias Sociales, 44,* 11–17.

Ortiz, H. C. (2014). Política y crecimiento económico en Colombia, 1906–2009. *Revista De Economía Institucional, 16*(31), 195–222.

Oxhorn, P. (1994). Where did all the protesters go? Popular mobilization and the transition to democracy in Chile. *Latin American Perspectives, 21*(3), 49–69.

Oxhorn, P. (2001). *La construcción del Estado por la sociedad civil: la Ley de Participación Popular de Bolivia y el desafío de la democracia local. Documentos de Trabajo del INDES.* Washington, DC: BID.

Oxhorn, P. (2011). *Sustaining civil society.* University Park: Penn State University Press.

Ozturk, A. (2016). Examining the economic growth and the middle-income trap from the perspective of the middle class. *International Business Review, 25,* 726–738.

Palma, J. G. (2005). The seven main 'stylized facts' of the Mexican economy since trade liberalization and NAFTA. *Industrial and Corporate Change, 14*(6), 941–991.

Palomino, H. (2000). Los sindicatos en la Argentina contemporánea. *Nueva Sociedad, 169,* 121–134.

Palomino, H., & Trajtemberg, D. (2006). Una nueva dinámica de las relaciones laborales y la negociación colectiva en la Argentina. *Revista de Trabajo, 2*(3), 47–68.

Papadoupulos, J. (1999). Igualdad, democracia y políticas sociales. In M. Schteingart (Ed.), *Políticas sociales para los pobres en América Latina.* México: Miguel Ángel Porrúa.

Parikh, S., & Weingast, B. R. (1997). A comparative theory of federalism: India. *Virginia Law Review, 83*(7), 1593–1615.

Pebe, C., Radas, N., & Torres, J. (2017). Canon minero y ciclo político presupuestal en las municipalidades distritales del Perú, 2002–2011. *Revista CEPAL, 123,* 181–200.

Perreault, T., & Valdivia, G. (2010). *Hydrocarbons, popular protest and national imaginaries: Ecuador and Bolivia in comparative context.* https://doi.org/10.1016/j.geoforum.2010.04.004.

Pineda Duque, J. (2015). Colombia: el sesgo antilaboral del modelo de desarrollo y las políticas de formalización. *Cuadernos del CENDES, 32*(89).

Polanyi, K. (1944). *The great transformation.* New York: Farrar & Rinehart.

Ponce-Lara, C. (2013). La socialización política en el aula: Comparación entre las movilizaciones de Francia y Chile. *Revista Latinoamericana de Ciencias Sociales, Niñez y Juventud, 11*(2), 603–615.

Ponce López, J. I. (2016). Oportunidad, conflicto y reconocimiento: El movimiento de trabajadores subcontratados de CODELCO y el Gobierno de Michelle Bachelet, 2006–2007. *Izquierdas, 29,* 106–132.

Porta, F. (2006). Especialización productiva e inserción internacional: Evidencias y reflexiones sobre el caso argentino. In G. Lugones & F. Porta (Comp.): *Enfoques y metodologías alternativas para la medición de las capacidades innovativas, ANPCYT-REDES, Buenos Aires Postero, Nancy, The struggle to créate a radical democracy in Bolivia.* San Diego: University of California.

Portantiero, J. C. (1982). *Transición a la democracia en Argentina.* México: Facultad Latinoamericana de Ciencias Sociales.

Posner, P. W. (2005). Local democracy and the transformation of popular participation in Chile. *Latin American Politics and Society, 46*(3), 55–81.

Pousadela, I. M. (2013). Protest and proposal, participation and representation: The Chilean student movement, 2011–12. *Development in Practice, 23*(5–06), 685–700. https://doi.org/10.1080/09614524.2013.800837.

Prates, D., Fritz, B., & de Paula, L. F. (2017). *Brazil at crossroads: A critical assessment of developmentalist policies* (Manuscript). Berlin: Freie University of Berlin.

Pribble, J., & Huber, E. (2011). Social policy and redistribution. Chile and Uruguay. In S. Levitsky & K. M. Roberts (Eds.), *The resurgence of the Latin American left* (pp. 117–138). Baltimore: The Johs Hopkins University Press.

Progrebinschi, T., & Samuels, D. (2014). The impact of participatory democracy. *Comparative Politics, 46*(3), 313–332.

Prud'homme, J.-F. (2010). El sistema de partidos. In S. Loaeza & J.-F. Prud'homme (Eds.), *Los grandes problemas de México*, t. 14: *Instituciones y procesos políticos* (pp. 121–158). México: El Colegio de México.

Puyana, A. (2008). El manejo del petróleo mexicano: ¿política o economía? *Perfiles latinoamericanos, 16*(32), 67–102.

Puyana, A., & Romero Tellaeche, J. (2009). *México. De la crisis de la deuda al estancamiento económico.* México: El Colegio de México.

Quenan, C., & Velut, S. (Eds.). (2011). *Les enjeux du développement en Amérique latine. Dynamiques socioéconomiques et politiques publiques.* Paris: Institut des Amériques-Agence Française de Développement.

Quispe, M. U. (2017). La desigual capacidad del Estado en América Latina. *Política y gobierno, 24*(2), 435–457.

Raes, F. (2001). Consolidation démocratique et médiation politique au Brésil. *Cahiers du GELA-IS,* (1), 129–162. Paris: L'Harmattan.

Rapoport, M., & Collaborators. (2005). *Historia económica, política y social de la Argentina.* Córdoba: Ediciones Macchi.

Repetto, F., & Potenza Dal Masetto, F. (2011). Protección social en la Argentina. *Serie Políticas Sociales,* (174), 68. Santiago de Chile: CEPAL.

Restrepo Botero, D. (2015). *Procesos de descentralización en Bolivia y Colombia, 1980–2005: Una propuesta de economía espacial comparada.* Bogotá: Universidad Nacional de Colombia.

Rezende, R., & Goldestein, A. (2016). Brasil: fin de los gobiernos del PT, presente, de crisis y resistencias. *Revista política Latinoamericana, 2,* 1–16.

Ribeiro, P. F. (2013). El modelo de partido cartel y el sistema de partidos de Brasil. *Revista de ciencia política (Santiago), 33*(3), 607–629.

Riesco, M. (2009). El modelo social chileno comienza a cambiar. *Revista Internacional del Trabajo, 128*(3), 311–330.

Riethof, M. (2004). Changing strategies of Brazilian labor movement, from opposition to participation. *Latin American Perspectives, 31*(6), 31–47.

Roberts, K. M. (2011). Chile. The left after neoliberalism. In S. Levitsky & K. M. Roberts (Eds.), *The resurgence of the Latin American left* (pp. 323–347). Baltimore: The Johns Hopkins University Press.

Robles Farías, C. (2013). *Sistemas de protección social en América Latina y el Caribe: Chile.* Santiago: CEPAL.

Rodrigues, I. J. (2015). Trabalhadores e sindicalismo no Brasil: para onde foram os sindicatos? *Caderno CRH, 28*(75), 479–491.

Rodríguez-Acosta, C. A. (2015). Decentralization in Latin America: History and future prospects. In *30 years of reform: Decentralization, subnational governments and development in Latin America* (pp. 19–23). *Hemisphere, 24*(1). Available at: http://digitalcommons.fiu.edu/lacc_hemisphere/vol24/iss1/1.

Rodriguez Salazar, O. (2015). Prologo. In D. Restrepo Botero (Ed.), *Procesos de descentralización en Bolivia y Colombia, 1980–2005. Una propuesta de economía política comparada* (pp. 11–22). Bogotá, Colombia

Rodríguez, E., & Barbosa, B. R. (2010). Los movimientos populares y el Estatuto de la Ciudad. In C. Carvalho & A. Rossbach (Org). *O Estatuto da Cidade*. São Paulo: Ministério das Cidades, Aliança das Cidades.

Rodrik, D. (2001). ¿Por qué hay tanta inseguridad económica en América Latina? *Revista de la CEPAL,* (73), 7–31. https://repositorio.cepal.org/bitstream/handle/11362/37886/RVE73_es.pdf?sequence=1&isAllowed=y.

Rodrik, D. (2007). *One economics, many recipes. Globalization, institutions and economic growth*. Princeton and Oxford: Princeton University Press.

Rodrik, D. (2010, April 12). The return of industrial policy. *Project Syndicate*. http://www.project-syndicate.org/commentary/rodrik42/English. Accessed 15 May 2018.

Romero Tellaeche, J. (2003). Crecimiento y comercio. In I. Bizberg & L. Meyer (Eds.), *Una historia contemporánea de México, Tomo 1. Transformaciones y permanencias* (pp. 155–221). México: Océano.

Romero Tellaeche, J. (2014). *Grandes Problemas. Los límites al crecimiento económico de México*. El Colegio de México-UNAM.

Rouquié, A. (2010). *À l'ombre des dictatures. La démocratie en Amérique Latine* (p. 377). Paris: Albin Michel.

Saboia, J. (2015). Macroeconomics, the job market, and income distribution i Brazil over the recent past: Progress, regression, and challenges. In B. Fritz & L. Lavinas (Eds.), *A moment of equality for Latin America? Challenges for redistribution* (pp. 145–178). Surrey and Burlington: Ashgate.

Salama, P. (2012). China-Brasil: industrialización y 'desindustrialización temprana'. *Cuadernos de Economía, 31*(56), 223–252.

Salama, P. (2014). *Les classes moyennes peuvent-elles dynamiser la croissance du PIB dans les économies émergentes?* (Working Paper No. 61). Paris: FMSH.

Salama, P. (2015). Se redujo la desigualdad en América Latina? Notas sobre una ilusión. *Nueva Sociedad, 257,* 1–8.

Sallum, B., Jr. (1996). *Labirintos. Dos generáis à nova república*. São Paulo: Universidade de São Paulo-Editora Hucitec.

Sallum, B., Jr. (2010). El Brasil en la 'pos-transición': la institucionalización de una nueva forma de Estado. In I. Bizberg (Ed.), *México en el espejo latinoamericano. Crisis o Democracia*. México: El Colegio de México-Fundación Konrad Adenauer.

Samuels, D. J. (2006). Sources of mass partisanship in Brazil. *Latin American Politics and Society, 48*(2), 1–27.

Samuels, D. J., & Mainwaring, S. (2004). Strong federalism, constraints on the central government, and economic reform in Brazil. In E. L. Gibson (Ed.), *Federalism and democracy in Latin America* (pp. 85–130). Baltimore: The Johns Hopkins University Press.

Santana, C. H. V. (2011). Conjuntura crítica, legados institucionais e comunidades epistêmicas: limites e possibilidades de uma agenda de desenvolvimento no Brasil. In R. Boschi (Ed.), *Variedades de Capitalismo, Política e desenvolvimento na América Latina*. Belo Horizonte, MG: Editora UFMG.

Santarcángelo, J. E., Schteingart, D., & Porta, F. (2017). Industrial policy in Argentina, Brazil, Chile and Mexico: A comparative approach. *Revue Interventions économiques, 59*. http://journals.openedition.org/interventionseconomiques/3852. Accessed 13 June 2018.

Scalon, C., & Salata, A. (2012). Uma Nova Classe Média no Brasil sa última década? O debate a partir da perspectiva sociológica. *Revista Sociedade e Estado, 27*(2), 387–407.

Schmitter, P. C. (1974). Still the century of corporatism? *The Review of Politics, 36*(1), 85–131.

Schneider, B. R. (2004). *Business politics and the state in twentieth-century Latin America*. Cambridge: Cambridge University Press.

Schneider, B. S. (2005). *Business politics and policy making in contemporary Latin America*. Available at: http://www.oecd.org/dev/devcom/35496225.pdf.

Schneider, B. R. (2013). *Hierarchical capitalism in Latin America: business, labor, and the challenges of equitable development*. New York: Cambridge University Press.

Schneider, B. R., & Soskice, D. (2009). Inequality in developed countries and Latin America: Coordinated, liberal and hierarchical systems. *Economy and Society, 38*(1), 17–52.

Sidicaro, R. (2003–2004). Les Transformations du Péronisme. *Problèmes d'Amérique Latine, 51*, 37–56.

Sigal, S. (2003–2004). Argentine 2003: La Sortie de l'Abîme? *Problèmes d'Amérique Latine, 51*, 9–36.

Sikkink, K. A. (1988). *Developmentalism and democracy: Ideas, institutions and economic policy making in Brazil and Argentina 1954–1962*. PhD dissertation, Columbia University, New York.

Silva, E. (2007). The import substitution model: Chile in comparative perspective. *Latin American Perspectives, 34*(3), 67–90.

Silva, E. (2009). *Challenging neoliberalism in Latin America*. Cambridge: Cambridge University Press.

Silva, C., Kronmüller, C., Cruz, M., & Riffo, I. (2015). Empoderamiento en el movimiento estudiantil durante 2011 y 2012 en Chile. *Universitas Psychologica, 14*(4), 1299–1309.

Solís, P. (2016). *Clases sociales, carencias sociales, pobreza y distribución del ingreso en México* (Unpublished power point). Permanente Seminar on inequality in Mexico, Mexico: Instituto Belisario Domínguez, Senado de la República.

Skockpol, T. (1984). *Los Estados y las revoluciones sociales.* México: Fondo de Cultura Económica.

Stampini, M., Robre, M., Sáenz, M., Ibarrarán, P., & Medellín, N. (2015). *Pobreza, vulnerabilidad y la clase media en América Latina* (Working Paper No. 591). Washington, DC: IDB.

Steinmo, S. (2010). *The evolution of modern states: Sweden, Japan, and the United States.* New York: Cambridge University Press.

Stepan, A. (1985). State power in the Southern Cone of Latin America. In P. B., Evans, D. Rueschemeyer, & T. Skocpol (Eds.), *Bringing the state back in.* Cambridge: Cambridge University Press.

Stockhammer, E. (2011). Crecimiento basado en los salarios: introducción. *Boletín Internacional de Investigación Sindical, 3*(2), 183–208.

Streeck, W. (2014). *Buying time: The delayed crisis of democratic capitalism.* London: Verso.

Svampa, M. (2010). *Movimientos Sociales, matrices socio-políticos y nuevos escenarios en América Latina* (One World Perspectives Working Papers No. 1).

Svampa, M. (2011). Extractivismo neodesarrollista y movimientos sociales: ¿ Un giro ecoterritorial hacia nuevas alternativas. *Más allá del desarrollo, 1,* 185–218.

Svampa, M., & Pereyra, S. (2004). La política de los movimientos piqueteros. *Revista da Sociedade Brasileira de Economía Política,* (15).

Svampa, M., & Pereyra, S. (2005). La experiencia piquetera. *Medio Ambiente y Urbanización, 61*(1), 97–112.

Svampa, M., & Pereyra, S. (2009). *Entre la ruta y el barrio: la experiencia de las organizaciones piqueteras.* Buenos Aires: Biblos.

Szwarcberg, M. L. (2007, September 5–8). Strategies of electoral mobilization in comparative perspective: Lessons from the Argentine case. In C. Hale (Ed.), *After the Washington Consensus: Collaborative Scholarship for a new América.* Canada, Montréal: Congress of Latin American Studies Association.

Tanaka, M. (2004–2005). Révolutionnaires, réformistes ou 'hommes politiques traditionnels'. Montée en puissance et effondrement de la gauche au Pérou. *Problèmes d'Amérique Latine* (55), 65–88. http://eska-publishing.com/fr/1328-problemes-d-amerique-latine.

Tanaka, M. (2005). *Democracia sin partidos. Perú 2000–2005: los problemas de representación y las propuestas de reforma política.* Lima: Instituto de Estudios Peruanos.

Tanaka, M. (2010). La dinámica 'neodualista' de una democracia sin sistema de partidos. In M. A. Cameron & J. P. Luna (Eds.), *Democracia en la Región Andina* (pp. 197–242). Lima: Instituto de Estudios Peruanos/Plural Editores.

Tanaka, M., & Vera, S. (2010). In M. A. Cameron & J. P. Luna (Eds.), *Democracia en la Región Andina* (pp. 197–243). Lima: Instituto de Estudios Peruanos/Plural editores.

Taylor, M. (2004). Labor reform and the contradictions of 'Growth with Equity' in Post dictatorship Chile. *Latin American Perspectives, 31*(4), 76–93.

Thelen, K. (2014). *Varieties of liberalization and the new politics of social solidarity*. New Yok: Cambridge University Press.

Therborn, G. (2015). Moments of equality—Today's Latin America in a global historical context. In B. Fritz & L. Lavinas (Eds.), *A moment of equality for Latin America? Challenges for redistribution* (pp. 13–30). Surrey and Burlington: Ashgate.

Théret, B. (1995). *L'État, la finance et le social. Souveraineté nationale et construction européenne*. Paris: La Découverte.

Théret, B. (2002). *Protection Sociale et Fédéralisme. L'Europe dans le miroir de l'Amérique du Nord*. Montréal: Presse de l'Université de Montréal – Peter Lang.

Théret, B. (2004). Del principio federal a una tipología de las federaciones: algunas propuestas. *Foro Internacional, 44*(1), 29–65.

Théret, B. (2011). The place of national systems of social protection and political representation in socio-economic regulation: A morphogenetic structuralist view on institutional change in comparative perspective with special references to Japan and France. *Evolutionary Institutional Economic Review, 7*(2), 177–208.

Théret, B. (2015). La diversidad de los federalismos en América Latina: Argentina, Brasil y México. In I. Bizberg (Coord.), *Las variedades del capitalismo en América Latina: los casos de México, Brasil, Argentina y Chile* (pp. 147–282). Mexico: El Colegio de México.

Tironi, E., & Agüero, F. (1999). Chili: quel avenir pour le nouveau paysage politique? *Problèmes d'Amérique Latine, 35*, 65–77.

Tolentino Silva, M. (2009). Sistema único de salud: la experiencia brasileña en la universalización del acceso a la salud. *Revista Peruana de Medicina Experimental y Salud Pública, 26*(2), 251–257.

Torres Gutiérrez, C. (2014). *La privatización parcial y su efecto en el crecimiento de las ventas y el activo de Pemex: evidencia en Petrobras y Ecopetrol*. Tesis de Doctorado. Nuevo León: Universidad Autónoma de Nuevo León Facultad de Contaduría Pública y Administración.

Torrico, M. (2014). Bolivia: nuevo sistema electoral presidencial y coordinación política de los partidos. *Perfiles Latinoamericanos, 22*(43), 77–102.

Torrico Terán, M. (2006). ¿Qué Ocurrió Realmente en Bolivia? *Perfiles Latinoamericanos, 28*, 231–261.

Tupac Panigo, D., & Chena, P. I. (2012). Regulationist macro-models for developing countries. An application to the Argentine new development pattern. *Revue de la régulation. Capitalisme, institutions, pouvoirs* (Online journal), (11). Available at: http://journals.openedition.org/regulation/9705.

UNCTAD. (2013). *World investment report, global value chains: Investment and trade for development*. New York and Geneva: United Nations Publication.

Valencia Lomelí, E. (2008). Las transferencias monetarias condicionadas como política social en América latina. Un balance: Aportes, límites y debates. *Annual Review of Sociology, 34*, 499–524.

Valencia Lomelí, E. (2018). *¿Hacia nuevos compromisos sociales en las trayectorias de los regímenes de bienestar? Los casos de Brasil, Corea del Sur y México* (Unpublished article). Universidad de Guadalajara.

Valencia Lomelí, E., Foust Rodríguez, D., & Tetreault Weber, D. (2013). *Sistemas de Protección Social en América Latina y el Caribe*. Santiago de Chile, MX: CEPAL.

Valenzuela, A. (1995). Chile: Origins and consolidation of a Latin American Democracy. In L. Diamond et al., (Eds.), *Politics in Developing Countries: Comparing experiences with democracy*. Boulder: Lynne Rienner.

Valladares, L. (1999). Programas sociales para los pobres en Brasil. Los casos de Río de Janeiro y Belo Horizonte. In M. Schteingart (Coord.), *Políticas sociales para los pobres en América Latina*. México: Miguel Ángel Porrúa.

Varela, P. (2013). Los sindicatos en la Argentina Kirchenerista: entre la herencia de los 90 y la emergencia de un nuevo sindicalismo de base. *Archivos de Historia del movimiento obrero y la izquierda, 2*, 77–100.

Vejar, J., & Alfonso, D. (2016). Identidades y re-significados del actor sindical. Diez Núcleos de tensión del sindicalismo en Chile. *Andamios, 13*(30), 171–194.

Vera, S. (2011). Cronología del conflicto: El movimiento estudiantil en Chile, 2011. *Anuario del Conflicto Social, 1*(1), 247–251.

Verduzco Igartúa, G. (2005). Las organizaciones solidarias en México. In I. Bizberg & L. Meyer (Coords.), *Una historia contemporánea de México, tomo 2, actores* (pp. 367–402). México: Océano.

Vergara, A. (2011). United by discord, divided by consensus: national and sub-national articulation in Bolivia and Peru, 2000–2010. *Journal of Politics in Latin America, 3*(3), 65–93.

Vianna, M. L. T. W. (1997). Benefícios Privados, Vícios Públicos: Dilemas Atuais da Seguridade Social No Brasil. In E. Diniz & S. de Azevedo (Eds.), *Reforma do estado e democracia no Brasil* (pp. 295–348). Brasília: Editora Universidade de Brasília.

Vidal Bermúdez, Á., Cuadros Luque, F., & Sánchez Reyes, C. (2012). *Flexibilización laboral en el Perú y reformas de la protección social asociadas: Un balances tras 20 años. Serie de Política Sociales N° 175*. Santiago de Chile: CEPAL.

Vommaro, G. (2004). Comment sortir de la crise? Organisation partisane et volonté politique sous le gouvernement Kirchner. *Cahiers des Amériques latines, 46*, 33–47.

Weingast, B. (1995). The economic role of political institutions: Market-preserving federalism and economic development. *The Journal of Law, Economics, and Organisations, 11*(1), 1–31.

Weisbrot, M., Ray, R., & Johnston, J. (2009). *Bolivia: The economy during the Morales administration* (No. 2009–47). Washington, DC: Center for Economic and Policy Research (CEPR).

Weitz-Shapiro, R. (2006). Partisanship and protest: The politics of workfare distribution in Argentina. *Latin American Research Review, 41*(3), 122–147.

Welch, J. H. (1991). *Hyperinflation and internal debt repudiation in Argentina and Brazil: from expectations management to the "Bonex" and "Collor" plans* (Research Paper No. 9107). Dallas: Federal Reserve Bank of Dallas.

Werneck, V., & Texeira, M. L. (1997). In E. Diniz & S. de Azevedo (Eds.), *Reforma do estado e democracia no Brasil* (pp. 295–348). Brasília: Editora Universidade de Brasília.

Weyland, K. (2007, September 5–8). Politics and policies of Latin America's two lefts: The role of party systems vs. resource Bonanzas. *XXVII International Congress of the Latin American Studies Association*, Montreál.

Weyland, K., Madrid, R. L., & Hunter, W. (2010). *Leftist governments in Latin America*. Cambridge: Cambridge University Press.

World Bank. (2018). *Doing business 2018. Reforming to create jobs*. Washington, DC: World Bank Publications.

Wylde, C. (2010). *Argentina, Kirchnerismo, and Neodesarollismo: Argentine Political Economy under the Administration of Nestor Kirchner 2003–2007. Documento de Trabajo n°44*. Buenos Aires: Área de Relaciones Internacionales, Flacso-Argentina.

Zapata, F. (1992). Transición democrática y sindicalismo en Chile. *Foro Internacional, 32*(5), 703–721.

Zermeño, S. (2004). La participación ciudadana bajo los gobiernos perredistas del Distrito federal (1997–2003). In A. Ziccardi (Ed.), *Participación ciudadana y políticas sociales en el ámbito local* (pp. 145–166). México: IIS-UNAM.

Zibechi, R. (2013). Brasil. Debajo y detrás de las grandes movilizaciones. *Camminardomandando* (revista electrónica). https://camminardomandando.wordpress.com/in-lingua-originale/movimientos/raul-zibechi-brasil-debajo-y-detras-de-las-grandes-movilizaciones/.

Zimmerer, K. S. (2011). "Conservation Booms" with agricultural growth? Sustainability and shifting environmental governance in Latin America, 1985–2008 (Mexico, Costa Rica, Brazil, Peru, Bolivia). *Latin American Research Review, 46*, 82–114.

Websites

Discurso ante la OIT, http://staging.ilo.org/public/libdoc/ilo/2009/109B09_327_span.pdf.

Discurso completo del presidente Uribe durante instalación del Congreso, 20 de julio de 2008, https://www.elespectador.com/noticias/politica/articulo-discurso-completo-del-presidente-uribe-durante-instalacion-del-congreso.

Plan de Desarrollo Bolivia digna, soberana, productiva y democrática para vivir bien, p. 3, https://extranet.who.int/nutrition/gina/sites/default/files/BOL%202006%20-%20Plan%20Nacional%20de%20Desarrollo.pdf.

World Bank. Data base. https://data.worldbank.org/.
http://anterior.gacetaoficialdebolivia.gob.bo/normas/verGratis_gob2/154210.
http://atlas.cid.harvard.edu.
http://www.2006-2012.economia.gob.mx/comunidad-negocios/industria-y-comercio/instrumentos-de-comercio-exterior/fomento-a-la-produccion-y-las-exportaciones.
http://www.eleconomista.es/materias-primas/noticias/8856549/01/18/Bolivia-quiere-ser-la-Arabia-Saudi-del-Litio-y-avisa-Vamos-a-poner-el-precio-para-a-todo-el-mundo.html.
http://www.eltiempo.com/archivo/documento/MAM-1339914.
http://www.eluniversal.com.mx/articulo/cartera/economia/2017/01/18/trasnacionales-concentran-un-tercio-de-exportaciones.
http://www.lanacion.com.ar/1394530-con-nuevo-plan-brasil-protege-su-industria.
http://www.lanacion.com.ar/498849-el-texto-completo-del-discurso-presidencial.
http://www.milenio.com/node/372874.
http://www.pac.gov.br/noticia/68777baf.
http://www.redlat.net/site/wp-content/uploads/2016/06/peru-trabajo_decente.pdf.
http://www.sinembargo.mx/09-07-2012/291704.
http://www.urosario.edu.co/urosario_files/76/7692c2f4-e5dd-46bd-aafa-2f505d6dcff2.pdf.
http://www.vanguardia.com/historico/69584-lea-discurso-completo-de-alvaro-uribe-velez-en-instalacion-del-congreso.
http://www4.congreso.gob.pe/museo/mensajes/Mensaje-2001-2.asp.
http://www4.congreso.gob.pe/museo/mensajes/Mensaje-2010-1.asp.
http://www4.congreso.gob.pe/museo/mensajes/Mensaje-2011-1a.asp.
https://exame.abril.com.br/brasil/as-propostas-de-dilma-para-a-economia.
https://resourcegovernance.org/sites/default/files/nrgi_sharing_Bolivia_case-study.pdf.
https://www.20minutos.com.mx/noticia/100682/0/inversion-extranjera-permitira-crecer-mas-aceleradamente-videgaray/.
https://www.camara.cl/camara/media/docs/discursos/21mayo_2009.pdf.
https://www.camara.cl/camara/media/docs/discursos/21mayo_2010.pdf.
https://www.forbes.com.mx/el-tabu-de-la-politica-industrial/.
https://www.gob.mx/presidencia/prensa/palabras-del-presidente-licenciado-enrique-pena-nieto-durante-el-evento-4-anos-transformando-a-mexico-encuentro-con-servidores-publicos?idiom=es.
https://www.gob.mx/presidencia/prensa/reafirma-el-presidente-enrique-pena-nieto-su-total-compromiso-con-la-transformacion-de-mexico.
https://www.terra.com.br/noticias/brasil/lula-volta-defender-maior-presenca-do-estado-na-economia-e-na-promocao-social,d03b4999eed4b310VgnCLD200000bbcceb0aRCRD.html.

Index

I. Bizberg, *Diversity of Capitalisms in Latin America*,
https://doi.org/10.1007/978-3-319-95537-7

The manufacturer's authorised representative in the EU is Springer Nature Customer Service Centre GmbH, Europaplatz 3, 69115 Heidelberg, Germany. If you have any concerns regarding our products, please contact ProductSafety@springernature.com

Printed and bound by CPI Group (UK) Ltd, Croydon, CR0 4YY

22/09/2026

02220984-0005